In the Realm of the Circuit

Computers, Art, and Culture

Charles H. Traub
Jonathan Lipkin

PEARSON

Prentice
Hall

Upper Saddle River, New Jersey 07458

Library of Congress Cataloging-in-Publication Data

Traub, Charles H.
    In the realm of the circuit : computers, art, and culture / Charles H. Traub, Jonathan Lipkin.
        p.   cm.
    Includes bibliographical references and index.
    ISBN 0-13-093674-X
    1. Computers and civilization.   2. Computer art.   I. Lipkin, Jonathan.   II. Title.

QA76.9.C66 T72 2003
303.48'33–dc21

2002035465

Editor-in-Chief: Stephen Helba
Director of Production and Manufacturing:
    Bruce Johnson
Executive Editor: Elizabeth Sugg
Managing Editor–Editorial: Judy Casillo
Editorial Assistant: Cyrenne Bolt de Freitas
Managing Editor–Production: Mary Carnis
Manufacturing Buyer: Cathleen Petersen
Production Liaison: Denise Brown
Interior Design: Ellen Whitney

Full Service Production: Fred Dahl, Inkwell Publishing
Director, Image Resource Center: Melinda Reo
Manager, Rights and Permissions: Zina Arabia
Interior Image Specialist: Karen Sanatar
Image Permission Specialist: Charles Morris
Design Director: Cheryl Asherman
Senior Design Coordinator: Miguel Ortiz
Cover Design: Paul Lombardi/Miguel Ortiz
Cover Printer: Phoenix Color
Printer/Binder: Von Hoffman Press, Inc.

Cover Images: *Background Image*–NASA/GSFC/METI/ERSDAC/JAROS and U.S./Japan ASTER Science Team. *Piano*–Steinway & Sons, Model D Concert Grand. *Chip*–Courtesy Intel Corporation. *Remainder of images* from the authors' collections.

Pearson Education LTD.
Pearson Education Singapore, Pte. Ltd
Pearson Education, Canada, Ltd
Pearson Education–Japan
Pearson Education Australia PTY, Limited
Pearson Education North Asia Ltd
Pearson Educaçion de Mexico, S.A. de C.V.
Pearson Education Malaysia, Pte. Ltd

10 9 8 7 6 5 4 3 2 1

ISBN 0-13-093674-X

For Jean Traub (1909–2002) and Sophia Lipkin (b. 2000),
past and future.

Contents

Preface

In the Realm of the Circuit begins with the premise that digital technology has value only as it reinforces the needs of our communities. This text was written as a response to colleagues and students who were often unable to position their interests in the arts and humanities within the new context provided by the digital network and its technical stigma. These people were often skeptical or uninformed or uninterested in the role of digital applications in furthering human discourse. Others, particularly students, dive into the new tides of the dataset, surfing mindlessly through the proliferation of opportunities, without discernment of that which is meaningful. We can find meaning and purpose in the ongoing flow of our history and the evolution of ideas and relationships in the deep reservoir of possibilities enabled by new technology.

At the millennium juncture, we are no longer anticipating a technological revolution: It has already taken place. This book outlines the dramatic implications that affect those who aspire to be creative during an age in which creativity is no longer limited by physical constraints. Much of the world has only limited access to what lies within the realm of the circuit; nevertheless we envision that the basic digital tools offer hope, democracy, and potential, which can help to level the disparities in our communities. Digital tools have simultaneously lowered the price and raised the level of creative exploration to the point that many more people now have access to these powerful means of expression. Because of the ease and seductiveness of these new programs, it is easy to think that one can master these new means of expression. But mastery lies not with the tool, but with what one does with the tool. Learning how to type does not make someone a writer any more than learning how to use Photoshop® makes one a photographer.

This is neither a typical primer, nor a typical textbook or guide. It is a montage of cultural histories, creative ideas, and factual information that will serve as a starter, a handbook for those who seek to understand the interconnectedness in the constellation of artistic creativity, scientific thought, invention, and our basic human needs. This is a book to be explored, to prospect for new relationships between seemingly disparate fields of interest. Like the Web itself, this book opens windows on broad subjects. Images do not merely illustrate text (or vice versa). Each are of equal value in stimulating our associations between ideas. We hope to encourage readers to further investigate the content that most interests them. The bibliography, glossary, chronologies, and our last chapter are designed to suggest that much exists beyond the frame of our window.

Are we culturally prepared for an engagement with the computer, whereby each of us should have a voice in the greater realm of the circuit, where creativity is no longer the stuff of the elite? The dialog of a community nurtures creativity, and allows for an individual talent to find a space and reception where expression is given meaning. How to use the multitude of information stimuli we receive depends on how we filter it and glean from it new understandings that serve our personal aspirations and our society. Being mimetic, merely cutting and pasting without reason, does not serve the greater cultural aspiration. Everything needs to be placed in a context, and understanding history is a means to that end. All too often we are caught in the overspecialization of our fields of interest, unable to break out of the box imposed by them in order to see the broader relationships. We are suggesting that certain fundamental elements of creativity are empowered by the dataset and are relatively the same whether one functions as a researcher or an artist. To accumulate a complete knowledge of anything is impossible, but by contributing knowledge to the "world brain," and sharing with others, we can all explore vast fields of thought imaginatively, selecting from them purposefully. The desire to communicate must be placed in an historical perspective. As creative practice has moved into the digital realm, it is subject to an evolving set of rules and becomes something entirely different from expression wrought in older media. The product today is more than just an evolution from previous forms; it is a quantum leap.

The audience for this book is those who aspire to create and who need to be connected to the thousands of years of cultural practice that have informed and humanized those who came before us. They need to be aware of three important points that demonstrate how our creative tools have changed: First, facilitation of distribution creates a more universal audience. Second, production tools are now easier to manage, less expensive, and more readily available, democratizing what was once the domain of the corporation or institution. Third, reduction of all creativity to a digital file allows its inclusion in an accessible "world brain" created and archived by the computer, as described in Chapter One.

Imaginative expression continues to be the process of conveying meaning through metaphor, explored in Chapter Two. Until now, this expression has been contained in physical forms, such as the book or painting. Once creativity is digital, it can be transmitted instantly through the networks that have historically built our culture, through the modern museum or library, which may be no larger than our laptop computers. The basic human needs for communication and expression, outlined in Chapter Three, result in creative acts that share certain common constituent elements, explored in Chapter Four. Lasting value is not a result of undisciplined practice, but of engaged craft. We address in Chapter Four the organizing principles that creative individuals have always needed to utilize, and which need to be reexamined for the digital age.

To understand the full implications of the creative act and their relationship to our society, we can foster innovative learning that crosses diverse fields and emphasizes the commonality of procedures and goals within them. We hope to stimulate that learning. The educator or facilitator is, in a sense, a new artist—a "systems humanist," Ted Nelson's notion of a new creative individual, and ideally should be a product of an enlightened engagement, fostered by the new resources available to us through the circuit. We use the term *creative interlocutor* in Chapter Five to define a person (or collective) who facilitates the exchange of ideas and information in a digital arena. This facilitator is the producer, director, and organizer, as well as curator, editor, collector, concierge, guide, sensor, and quality controller. He or she or they help us form not only the message, but also the package and the means of delivering it in an effective way. Through innovative programming, directorial expertise, or editorial overview, creative interlocutors assist other individuals in their exploration of the promise of the digital revolution.

In the past, society saw the artist as a solitary genius. Today's collective involvement, through the new networks and channels, can foster a synergistic genius, an amalgam of many individuals each contributing to a culture of creativity. Contemporary heroes are those persons or collectives who challenge and facilitate others to use their imaginative resources in cultural dialog. For this reason, humanists need not be estranged from the world of technology.

The realm of the circuit mandates a new approach to the creative process. Whether in artistic or scientific practice, creativity can no longer be just the product of isolated, idiosyncratic behavior, but rather it is the coming together of multiple intuitions. Technology of all sorts allows for many forms of interrelationships, intermingling, new associations, new coefficients, and new paths that are unexpected and were previously not navigable. The questions are where do we want to go, and how do we get there?

Acknowledgments

The authors are indebted to many people who aided us in the conception, editing, and production of this book. An endeavor such as this would not have been possible without the computer and modern networks such as the Internet, whose qualities of collection, management and production have allowed us to research, write, design, and collaborate. Our ideas have taken shape in ways that never would have been possible before. This book was produced on an Apple Macintosh Powerbook®.

We are particularly grateful to Deborah Hussey, whose astute editing helped guide this project from start to finish. Mark Stafford helped us find our voice, and Thryza Nichols Goodeve provided us with a critical model. Denise Brown, Judy Casillo, and Elizabeth Sugg at Prentice Hall had the vision to recognize our book proposal, and to guide it through publication. The design sample was prepared by Charlene Rule. The book was meticulously and imaginatively designed through countless hours by Ellen Whitney, to whom we are indebted. Image production was led by Ross Schwartman, with assistance from Kevin Googin, at scanners provided by Here Is New York. We thank all those who lent us images from their collections.

Institutional support, including facilities and staff, was provided by the School of Visual Arts. We thank David Rhodes, the president, Alice Beck-Odette, and the staff of MFA Photography and Related Media, Adrienne Deppe in particular. We are also thankful for the assistance of SVA graduate students, in particular Kari Grimsby, Kristin Costello, Johanna Evans, and Steve Endicott. Ramapo College of New Jersey provided a Separately Budgeted Research Grant and use of the college's library.

Peer reviewers were: Joseph Ciaglia (University of New Mexico), Brian Lonsway (Rensselear Polytech), Patricia Maurides (Carnegie-Mellon), and Bob Peterson (Westwood College). Our picture researchers, Margaret Eliot-Sheri and Suellen Parker worked many hours to collect the remarkable images in this book. The following people provided content research: Adam Bell, Charles Peirce, Keith Reinert, and Ted Szczepanski. Finally, we are grateful to our students, friends, families, and loved ones for their patience and support.

About the Authors

Charles Traub is Chair of the Graduate MFA Program in Photography and Related Media, School of Visual Arts in New York City, the largest independent college of art in the United States. Mr. Traub has authored and edited many books including *Beach, Italy Observed,* and *Anglers Album,* and his work has been published in *Connoisseur, Fortune, Newsweek, U.S. News and World Report, American Photographer, Popular Photography, Aperture,* and *Afterimage.* He is also principal of Charles H. Traub Photography, a consulting photographic firm, and was formerly the director of The Light Gallery. He is President of Tecota (Technology Conservatory of America), a nonprofit organization for the support of humanities and technology, and President of the Aaron Siskind Foundation for the support of creative photography. He is a cofounder of the organization and exhibition Here Is New York. He has had numerous one-person exhibitions, including those at Marcus Pfeifer Gallery, Van Straaten Gallery, Art Directors Guild of New York, Chicago Center for Contemporary Photography, the Art Institute of Chicago, and the Hudson River Museum. He has received awards from the New York State Council on the Arts, Hendrecks Foundation, Illinois Art Council, Manda Foundation, and Olympics Arts Organization Committee.

Jonathan Lipkin is associate professor of digital media at Ramapo College, New Jersey's public liberal arts college, and is on the graduate faculty of the School of Visual Arts' Computer Art and Photography and Related Media programs. His photographic work has appeared in many newspapers and magazines, from the *New York Times* to *Hip Hop Connection,* and has been exhibited across the country in public spaces like the Port Authority of New York and in exhibitions such as Imaging/Aging. His writing has appeared in many academic journals, and he has been a columnist for electronic publications such as the *ASCI* newsletter. His book, *Digital Art and Design: Photography,* is due from Harry N. Abrams in Spring 2003. As a designer, he created the first web art exhibited by New York's prestigious PS1 Museum. He has lectured across the country and internationally on issues of digital media.

CHAPTER ONE
FOUNDATIONS

circuit ▭ dataset ▭ multimedia ▭ world brain

The realm of the circuit is a domain of limitless territory. Electronic digital technologies give us newfound freedom to form and shape the creative acts that produce culture. Interactive and multimedia virtual worlds contain and transform our accumulated accomplishments and heighten our continuing aspirations for knowledge. The dataset—the digital file that holds creative endeavor—is the foundation for this new network. The democratizing effects of this new condition are available to a wide audience who aspire to be creative. The network is both the superstructure and the foundation for a global economy of creativity.

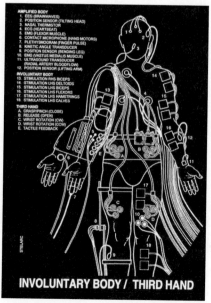

Stelarc, *Involuntary Body*

This chapter describes the new ways in which digital technologies allow us to be creative. In a sense, these methodologies are not new: They have been a part of human endeavor since the dawn of civilization. The circuit is the superstructure not only of digital technologies but also of culture itself. Through the realm of the circuit we can create and transmit datasets, those digital files that hold creative endeavor. These endeavors can be combined and manipulated in the computer as multimedia (we discuss the new creative fomulations of the computer in Chapter Two). The computer's vast storage capacity allows for the creation of a networked repository that we have called the World Brain. Interactivity is also a hallmark of digital creativity; we have chosen to explore it throughout the book, as it is essential to every aspect of human endeavor. Interactivity as a means of building culture is discussed extensively in Chapter Four. While these technologies exist, it remains for the creative interlocutor (described in Chapter Five) to use them to their full potential, to engage in the dialog described in Chapter Three.

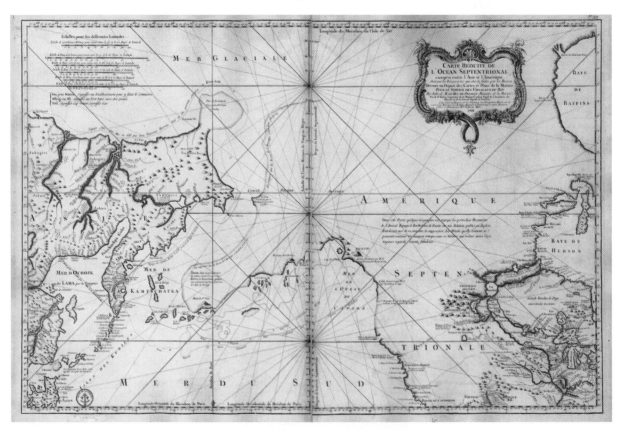

Carte Reduite de l'Ocean Sepetentrional, 1766

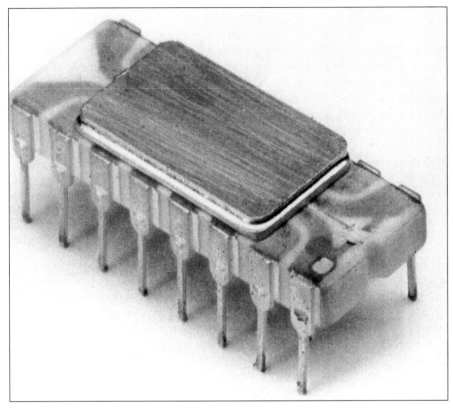

Intel's 4004 microprocessor, 1971

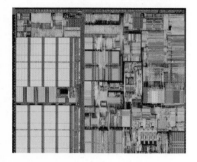

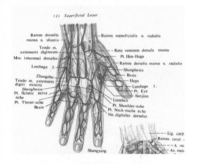

Top: Close-up of Intel's Celeron processor, 1999

Middle: The acupuncture points of the human hand

Bottom: Calcutta, India, as seen from space

When we think of the word circuit today, we think of the electrical wiring that composes the heart of modern electronic devices. But the term has a longer and richer history. It once meant a line that contained the limits of an area: the circumference or boundary. It also denoted a journey, the action of circumambulation, of going around and around. It is to these older meanings that we refer when we discuss the realm of the circuit: digital culture as the physical realm in which we live, as well as the processes and procedures enabled by the digital tools—the things we do in the realm. The realm of the circuit is formed by the digital networks, the electronic digital tools we use, and the people connected by it. The circuit is, ultimately, the superstructure of our culture, and civilization is the reflection of communities formed by our need to share physical, emotional, and intellectual resources.

The realm is composed of interlocking networks. A network is defined as the linkage of nodes (components) into a system, or a web of connections. A node can be anything that is connected: a computer, a person, or a town. Networks of communication draw connections between people, whereas networks of pathways and roads link villages and cities. The earliest networks were the routes early man used to travel from shelter to food. As people met at the watering hole, the exchange of goods gave way to the exchange of information. It is through such interaction and exchange that culture is formed.

A network is not valuable for what it is, but for what it does: Facilitates the distribution, exchange, and assemblage of information and goods, and allows human beings to move between communities. Networks also serve multiple functions. For instance, the road built to move an army also moves commerce. Networks are not always creative; they can be destructive as well. Furthermore, networks connect and enhance one another: Telegraph lines put down along a road connect to a train depot where a telephone will allow a person to call a relative thousands of miles away.

While networks have always been a part of our civilization, the advent of digital technologies has greatly furthered our ability to connect to others, to weave the very fabric of human society in more complex and provocative ways. A teenager can gather friends from anywhere through a text message on a cell phone or an Internet-based instant message. A dating service can use sophisticated algorithms to match members from its **database**. The material of the digital network is what we call "metafora." We have resurrected the term to describe the media and material of artistic production and expression in the digital age. Metafora is discussed at length in Chapter Two.

Understanding the network of the human mind is one of our greatest quests. Throughout history the mind has been described by metaphors drawn from the dominant technology of the day. The Greeks compared the mind to a catapult; seventeenth-century philosopher, scientist, and mathematician René Descartes interpreted the mind as a clock; and in the eighteenth century, the **Deists** saw the entire universe as a machine set in motion by God. In the mid-twentieth century, computer pioneers such as John von Neumann were influenced by metaphors of biology, especially the brain, and later in the twentieth century cognitive neuroscientists were heavily influenced by metaphors from the computer. Scientists today understand the mind primarily as "the brain," described in the language of a complex and dynamic system of interconnected neurons, or a neural network. Each of the 100 billion neurons in the brain is connected to thousands of other neurons by synapses: Connections through which information is passed. As the neural networks of the brain are stimulated by input neurons, they produce a certain set of outputs, depending on the configuration of the network. For example, the stimulation of certain nerves will cause a specific muscle to contract. As the system becomes stimulated repeatedly, certain synaptic pathways become reinforced, and this produces memory.

The redundancy of the neural network allows the brain to function even after parts of it have become damaged. (A redundant network is one in which there are multiple pathways from one node to another.) The designers of the Internet, especially Paul Baran, who came up with the notion of **packet switching**, were influenced by this fact. When they considered ways of improving network reliability, they chose to model it after the brain: distributed rather than central control, with many redundant pathways. Recently, computer scientists have adapted the model of the neural network to design computers themselves. The program performs tasks and eventually begins to "learn" on its own, by reinforcing connections between events. Modern computing systems model neural networks and are used to recognize fingerprints or to predict weather. Even though these computers cannot replicate the complexity of the human brain, they can vastly outperform traditional computers. American computer scientist Danny Hillis' 1985 Connection Machine, one of the earliest of these computers, had 16,000 processors, a miniscule number when compared with the billions of neurons in the human brain, yet a huge number when compared with other computers of the day, which had only one processor.

Networks, those of both communication and distribution, changed little from their earliest incarnations until recent times. Early networks used human and/or animal power (with the notable exception of wind-powered ships) to transport goods or information (in the form of either written messages or messages stored in memory). Networks grew in complexity as the world's population grew and spread across the globe, heightening the needs to communicate and to trade. In the nineteenth century, mechanical means of transportation from the steamship to the railroad vastly increased the speed at which goods and people could travel. During the same century, the telegraph allowed the transmission of information at the speed of light.

Ironically, as with many inventions, improvements resulted in constraints. The faster rail network centralized distribution and was tied to the schedule of the trains and the location of the train depot. Previously, one could ride a horse at any chosen time and the rider did not have to follow a series of predetermined trails. But horses were slow: Even the Pony Express, which delivered mail through a relay system by which it was handed from rider to rider, took ten days to carry a letter from St. Joseph, Missouri, to Sacramento, California. It was not until the development of the horseless carriage (the automobile) and the network of the interstate highway system that this would change.

In 1839, Rowland Hill proposed a standard rate for sending mail through the British Post: one penny for each half ounce. This made the network more efficient and so more affordable.

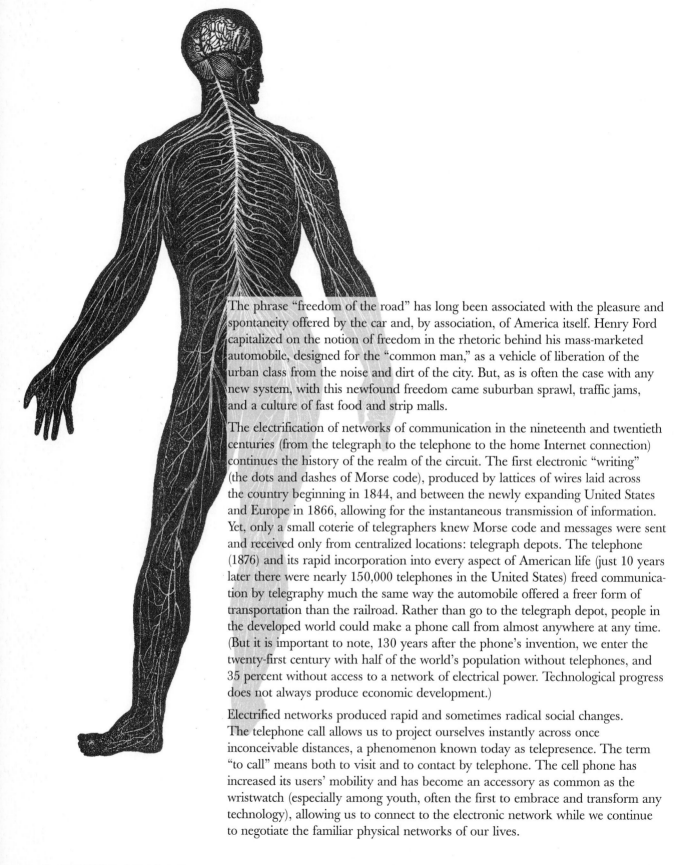

The phrase "freedom of the road" has long been associated with the pleasure and spontaneity offered by the car and, by association, of America itself. Henry Ford capitalized on the notion of freedom in the rhetoric behind his mass-marketed automobile, designed for the "common man," as a vehicle of liberation of the urban class from the noise and dirt of the city. But, as is often the case with any new system, with this newfound freedom came suburban sprawl, traffic jams, and a culture of fast food and strip malls.

The electrification of networks of communication in the nineteenth and twentieth centuries (from the telegraph to the telephone to the home Internet connection) continues the history of the realm of the circuit. The first electronic "writing" (the dots and dashes of Morse code), produced by lattices of wires laid across the country beginning in 1844, and between the newly expanding United States and Europe in 1866, allowing for the instantaneous transmission of information. Yet, only a small coterie of telegraphers knew Morse code and messages were sent and received only from centralized locations: telegraph depots. The telephone (1876) and its rapid incorporation into every aspect of American life (just 10 years later there were nearly 150,000 telephones in the United States) freed communication by telegraphy much the same way the automobile offered a freer form of transportation than the railroad. Rather than go to the telegraph depot, people in the developed world could make a phone call from almost anywhere at any time. (But it is important to note, 130 years after the phone's invention, we enter the twenty-first century with half of the world's population without telephones, and 35 percent without access to a network of electrical power. Technological progress does not always produce economic development.)

Electrified networks produced rapid and sometimes radical social changes. The telephone call allows us to project ourselves instantly across once inconceivable distances, a phenomenon known today as telepresence. The term "to call" means both to visit and to contact by telephone. The cell phone has increased its users' mobility and has become an accessory as common as the wristwatch (especially among youth, often the first to embrace and transform any technology), allowing us to connect to the electronic network while we continue to negotiate the familiar physical networks of our lives.

We can see an example of new social structures emerging in what writer Howard Rheingold calls "smart mobs," groups of people who can coordinate their actions through technology even though they may be physically separated.[1] These "thumb tribes" (so-called because messages are often entered into the miniature keyboards of cell phones and pagers with the thumbs) can converge on cafés or clubs, or even in political demonstrations, such as those that toppled the government of Manila in 2001. The wireless electronic tools serve to reinforce the ties that bind members together.

The circuit is home to people and hardware, and the networks that link them together. Increased demand in a free-market society creates pressures that result in increasingly inexpensive and better quality products through competition. Although the rapid obsolescence of such things as home computers, whereby a product bought today might feel out of date within six months, may mean we buy more computers in a lifetime than we actually need, nonetheless it is possible for anyone with access to the technology to create broadcast-quality video, or CD-quality audio on a desktop computer, for a fraction of what it would have cost only a decade ago. When these creative acts are cast into the realm of the circuit, they can reach a global audience, bypassing mainstream production channels (i.e., corporations whose primary concern is profit, not creativity or the greater social good).

This ease of production has generated a sense of optimism that borders on utopianism: Anyone can create his or her own record label. A similar optimism greeted the advent of cable access television (CATV), heralded as a medium that would allow anyone to create video and to broadcast it across the new electronic network. Through the public access gained by connecting to CATV, a new era of creativity—grassroots in nature—would flourish. Unfortunately, the impact of early experiments in cable-access television faded as the pressures of commercialization reduced cable television to what it is now: a mostly one-way medium for corporate-based content (call-in shows are an exception). The Internet holds a similar promise, although one whose utopian possibilities are just as threatened by corporatization, government surveillance, government control, and our own lack of creative will.

The history of technology, like human history itself, is defined by the struggle between those in power and those who are ruled and exploited by it. From the ancient trade routes to robber barons' monopoly over railroads and oil in the nineteenth century, to Microsoft's domination over personal computer software, the struggle for power has always been between monopoly and free enterprise. Discontent with the dominance of a particular political, social, or economic system has often produced new inventions and new networks. The Underground

Programs such as Napster will inevitably change the very essence of intellectual property rights. Ownership of intellectual property—a music CD, for instance—was once based in the metaphors of owning real property: scarcity and possession. If I have a CD, you cannot have it. But in the twenty-first century, music can be shared over the networks that distribute and duplicate resources. Culture will need to develop new metaphors for ownership, ones that acknowledge the nature of the circuit, while assuring that artists can prosper by creating intellectual property.

Internet pioneer Paul Baran's sketches of a:

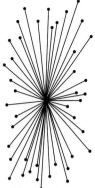
Centralized network.

Decentralized network.

Distributed network. A distributed network offers more redundancy and so is more robust.

Circuit board of Intel's 4004 chip

When Iran got the telegraph in the early 1900's it helped trigger the first constitutional revolution against the despotic Qajar regime. When telephones and tape cassettes spread around Iran in the 1970's, they became tools through which Ayatollah Khomeini spread his revolution against the Shah. Today the Internet and satellite TV have come to Iran, bringing with them new appetites and aspirations for Iran's Third Generation.

Thomas L. Friedman[2]

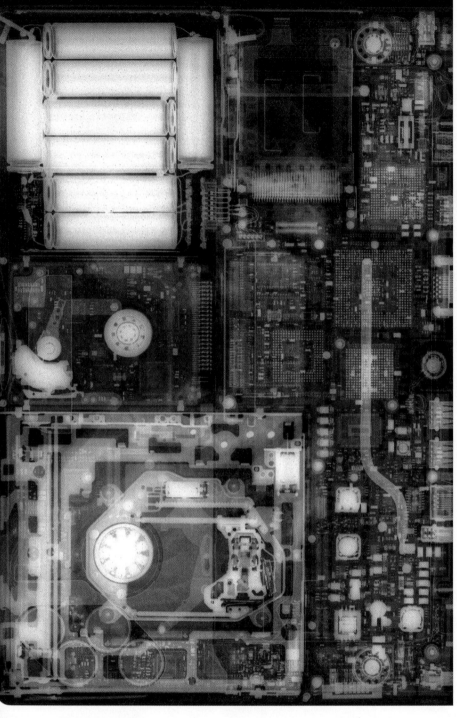

X-ray of Apple Powerbook G4

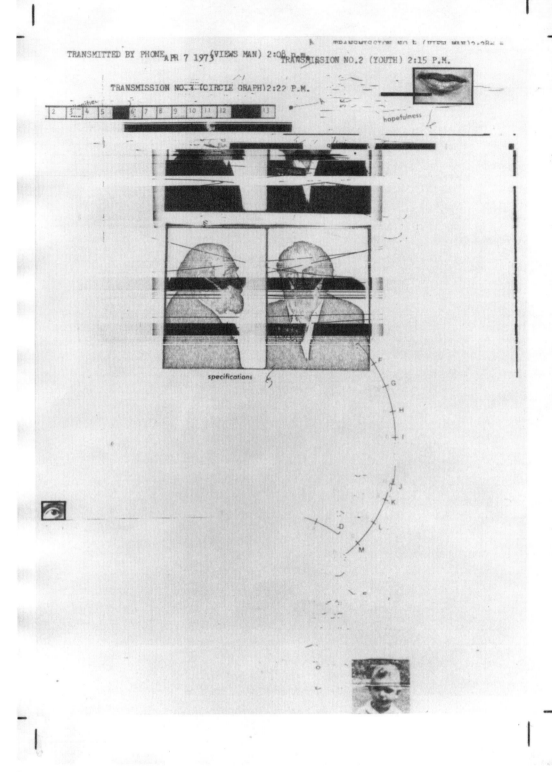

Facsimile transmission by William Larson, April 7, 1973

Railroad in the United States attempted to circumvent the horrors of slavery. Networks serve to destabilize authority and established order, usually through the dissemination of information critical of the dominant culture. This can be done by connecting people to create an opposition movement or by disseminating information to the outside world in an attempt to sway global public opinion. An example of the first is the French resistance to the German occupation during World War II, which relied heavily on the use of personal radios to communicate with the Allies. The second is illustrated through Indonesia's occupation of East Timor. In 1996, East Timor civil rights activists registered the .tp top level domain and used web sites to publicize their struggle. The Irish Internet service provider that hosts the .tp domain has repeatedly accused the Indonesian government of trying to break into its systems to remove the web sites.

The modern electronic network is part of a revolutionary form of communication. As human endeavor is translated into dataset, it can be transmitted, broadcast, or distributed across new networks of electronic interaction. As with all social engagements, those within dataspace are subject to rules, regulations, and controls. It is clear that the guidelines that dominated older pathways of communications and distribution systems are not applicable in cyberspace.

Networks serve to link us together by allowing the sharing of resources, of the elements that build culture. Virtual venues, instantly and permanently linked together, no longer require physical proximity for collaborative projects. We can assemble our personal creativity in collections, then link them together with those of a potentially unlimited number of collaborators, allowing us to amplify our creative endeavors by combining them with those of others.

The steamship *Great Eastern*, which laid a cable from Valentia, Ireland, to Heart's Content, Canada, in 1865

Jack Kerouac wrote the original manuscript for his novel *On the Road* in a three-week, drug-fueled frenzy in 1957. Kerouac fed sheets of paper taped together into his typewriter, so he could write without having to stop. He believed this was a new form of writing and described the manuscript as looking like a road when unrolled. The book describes Kerouac's travels across the country: He saw the road as a metaphor for life, change, the American way.

*With latest connections, works, the
inter-transportation of the world,*

*Steam-power, the great express lines,
gas, petroleum,*

*These triumphs of our time,
the Atlantic's delicate cable,*

*The Pacific railroad, the Suez canal,
the Mont Cenis and Gothard and
Hoosac tunnels, the Brooklyn Bridge,*

*This earth all spann'd with iron rails,
with lines of steamships threading in every sea,*

Our own rondure, the current globe I bring.

Walt Whitman, *Leaves of Grass*

The Brooklyn Bridge as seen
from lower Manhattan, c. 1896

circuit

Istanbul, Turkey, as "seen"
by NASA's ASTER (Advanced
Spaceborne Thermal Emission and
Reflection Radiometer). This is a
"false color" image—the picture's
colors do not represent colors as the
human eye would see, but thermal
and infrared data collected by the
instrument. In the water, for
instance, the darker and lighter
areas of color indicate data
that show colder and warmer
temperatures measured by the
satellite. The colors have been
chosen for their ability to convey
information, not to represent the
way the scene "looks."

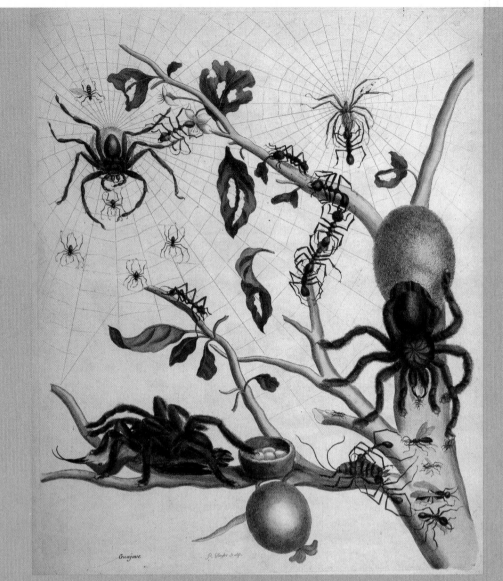

Maria Sibilla Merian, *Tarantula and Army Ants on Calabash Tree*, 1705

The web of our life is of a mingled yarn, good and ill together.

William Shakespeare, *All's Well That Ends Well*

Peruvian witching veil, used to wrap mummies, c. 400. The
pattern does not repeat and is thought to have magical powers.

Byte traffic into the ANS/NSFNET T3 backbone (Dec. '94)

0   1 trillion

Copyright 1996 Donna Cox and Robert Patterson

Data map of the NSFNET, part of the Internet backbone, 1994

circuit

Railroad hub, early twentieth century

Highway

Several decades before he became the thirty-fourth president of the United States in 1953, General Dwight D. Eisenhower traveled as an observer on the U.S. Army's first intercontinental truck convoy as part of the government's research of truck and rail travel. It took 62 days to move 81 vehicles the 3,000 miles from the East Coast to the West Coast. Although slower than trains, the convoy demonstrated the feasibility of the truck as a means to transport large numbers of troops and amounts of matériel from one location to another. Transport of goods by truck heralded the breakup of the monopolies owned by the great railroad barons as the proliferation of the truck gave rise to a kind of commercial individualism, which allowed commerce to deliver its goods when and where it wanted to, without a centralized network such as the railroad.

Influenced by the German autobahn and the efficiency of its unhindered four-lane byway, in 1956 Eisenhower initiated the largest public works project ever undertaken, spending $50 billion to construct 40,000 miles of road known as the National System of Interstate and Defense Highways. This remarkable network is the lifeblood of modern intercourse, a defining characteristic of contemporary American culture. In 1957, Eisenhower funded the Advanced Research Projects Agency, which would lay the groundwork for the Internet.

Together, the united forces of our communication and transportation systems are dynamic elements in the very name we bear—United States. Without them, we would be a mere alliance of many separate parts.

President Dwight D. Eisenhower

I think that cars today are almost the exact equivalent of the great Gothic cathedrals: I mean the supreme creation of an era, conceived with passion by unknown artists, and consumed in image if not in usage by a whole population which appropriates them as a purely magical object.

Roland Barthes,
Mythologies

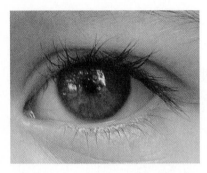

001010101010101010101010
010101010101011010101010
101010101010101010101101
010101100110010110011 0
110100010110101110010 0
111101010101010010101 0
101001010001101001010 1
001110010101010100110011

Digital photographs such as the one
above are composed of nothing
more than zeros and ones.

The raw material of the realm of the circuit is the dataset. Every digital file, every trace of human creativity placed into the memory of the computer, is composed of a string of zeros and ones. They are the realm's *lingua franca*, literally the "medium of communication between peoples of different languages." The computer (the keeper of zeros and ones), when combined with the optical scanner, the music sampler, or a myriad of other computer input devices, enables us to place our creative acts in a digital file—a dataset. When we have digitized sound or photographs or film, or created a digital image or music file on the computer, each can coexist in the memory of the computer precisely because each is a dataset. In other words, each digital product is nothing more than a sequence of zeros and ones before it is anything else. When creativity is dataset, it can be worked on in the computer and distributed through the circuit.

Working with digital files is profoundly different from working with physical objects. The first, and perhaps most salient, difference is the malleability and adaptability of digital media. When a traditional sculptor chips a piece of marble from a large block, the block and piece are forever detached from each other. Changes to digital files are nowhere so permanent. Second, working with digital information requires expenditures of intellectual capital rather than material goods. Working in marble requires a piece of rock, chisels, and a place to work. Working in 3-D computer animation requires an initial expenditure for a fast computer and appropriate software. But, after that, the digital sculptor need purchase little more than electricity. Third, a digital sculpture or animation can be saved in dozens of versions, at a cost of no more than disk space and the creator's time. This infinite mutability allows the digital sculptor to review his or her working process at any stage, experimenting in ways a traditional sculptor simply could not. A crack in the marble is not repairable. The sketchbook is the traditional sculptor's way of experimenting with variation. A digital sculptor, on the other hand, has an unlimited "sketchbook" already built into the very tool he or she is working with.

It is clear that, in the realm of the circuit, the nature of the creative act has fundamentally changed. The creator has the ability to show the audience as much or as little of the creative process as he or she desires and can even invite them to participate through the network. Today, the creative act may be the process of production itself, an exchange of culture that produces dialog rather than the end result of the process, an unchanging artifact like a painting. In this sense virtual creativity has similarities to conceptual art (minus the element of critique, which some would say is the sole drive behind conceptual art). In other words, the experience of digital creativity is inherently more abstract, less tangible than traditional film, sculpture, or painting: those defined as a physical product. The notion of process as the goal of creativity predates the computer: Tibetan

Electric technology fosters and encourages unification and involvement.

Marshall McLuhan, *The Medium Is the Massage*

Buddhist practice includes the construction of elaborate **mandalas** made of colored sand. Monks painstakingly construct these elaborate circular figures over a period of days, only to destroy them. It is not the end result that is important, but the spiritual energy brought to and expended in the construction.

The dataset in its most basic form—as a series of zeros and ones—can be described like the latent image on a roll of undeveloped film. In order for it to be perceived, it must be translated into a physical manifestation, such as an image on a computer screen, a digital print, or sound waves traveling through the air. The dataset is the image on the screen and at the same time nothing more than the description of the image in code. The computer screen, on which most digital images are seen, is a device to decode the contents of the dataset. It is an interface, a means of interacting with the contents of the digital file. Conceivably, one could edit digital images by manually rearranging the zeros and ones that compose their digital files, but it is infinitely easier to use an image-editing program to do this. The screen is the boundary between the virtual and the real, the potential and the actual.

As an example of how a dataset becomes an image, we could take the numbers 010010010 and map them onto a grid like this:

0	1	0
0	1	0
0	1	0

When this grid is fed into an output device such as a printer, the zeros will be interpreted as black pixels and the ones as white pixels. The result: a white line on a black field.

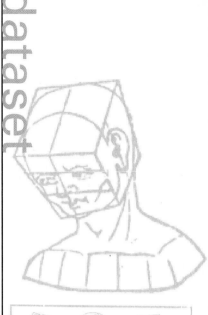

What has come to be known as the **virtual** image, the image that does not physically exist, is nothing new. Imagine another kind of container: "Square, smooth, red, about one foot on each side." We, the writer and reader, have collaborated to make a cube. It had no prior physical existence, but through language and imagination we have called it into being.

To reiterate, the digital image is split in two—the data that compose it and the representation the viewer perceives on the screen. This is the reason that the products of digital creativity are so malleable. In the example of the sand mandala, changing the design after it has been created would require physically shifting the sand—a messy proposition at best. But when working with a digital painting of a mandala, the creator works not with the image, but with the numbers that compose the image, and can watch the image change as the computer constantly redraws the image on the screen as each change is performed.

Erhard Schon's woodcut from *Unnerweissund der Proportzion*, 1542, demonstrates the use of a grid as an aid to drawing the human figure.

Digital images, and the numbers that compose them, take on form and meaning only when processed by a computer and the algorithms embedded in it by programmers. Numbers have no meaning individually, only when placed in relation to one another. A word or symbolic sign has no intrinsic relation to what it represents[3]. Words are arbitrary signs because there is no organic reason why $c + a + t = cat$. Similarly, the zeros and ones that make up an image have no worldly connection to the object represented. In this sense they function much the same way that letters of the alphabet do within the context of a written and spoken language system.

Wild carrot from the Garden of L,
generated by mathematical formula

Most datasets are created in one of two ways. The first is by creating
a virtual trace of the physical world such as taking a picture with a digital
camera or recording a musical composition. The second method uses computer
programs, or algorithms, to synthesize its content. For example, so-called 3-D
rendering software can be used to create realistic digital photographs of objects
that have no basis in the physical world, much in the same way that a painter in
a studio creates a landscape from nothing more than canvas, brush, and pigment.
What is so powerful and controversial about these programs is their ability to
make images that are indistinguishable (to the naked eye) from traditional
photographs. Traditional photographs require not only a camera and film but
also a physical referent (the thing-in-the-world that is photographed). Digitally
rendered photographs do not require a physical referent—the referent can be a
fiction created from zeros and ones that perfectly simulates something real. This
ability to synthesize photographs has created the crisis in notions of photographic
realism and photographic "truth" (but digital photographs are no more fictitious
than traditional ones).

Although the zeros and ones of the digital computer are the contents of the
dataset, it is the program that turns data into information, that is, something that
is recognized as information or an image. If the dataset is the raw material of the

realm of the circuit, **computer programs** are its tools. Programs, quite simply, are sets of instructions for the computer to perform a particular series of operations. Today's computer programs are composed of hundreds of millions of instructions. The interaction of program and data is the foundation of all computing; it is this interaction that allows for the almost infinite potential of digital creativity. It is much easier to rewrite a computer program than it is to "modify" a violin (although it may be no less easy to write an effective program than it is to build a good violin).

The tools of the new digital creator are the computer programs that are capable of shuffling the digits of the dataset and bestowing meaning on them and through them. Instead of the limits of the physical world, the realm of the circuit is limited only by the imagination of those programmers who write its rules, and those who ply its byways.

Instead of the limits of the physical world, the primary constraint in the realm of the circuit is the imagination and the ingenuity of the programmers who write the rules. Is the programmer then the artist? Who, in fact, is the author of a piece of Web-based art? Is it the person who created the work, the person who wrote the web browser, or Tim Berners-Lee, who pioneered the development of the World Wide Web? The very nature of digital creativity is so profoundly different from earlier forms of creativity that an entirely new vocabulary for the role of the creator as well as a definition of the audience is necessary.

The production of the creative act, and for the time being the experience of it as well, exists within a single location: the computer, or whatever that desktop box will evolve into. This shift of the creative act into the realm of the circuit reflects a tremendous difference in our notions and applications of creativity. We will discuss this topic in depth in the next section, Multimedia. The term we use for what the creative interlocutor creates "with"–its medium–is "metafora," introduced in Chapter Two. Unlike the materials of physical media (painting, sculpture, the book, film), metafora is not limited by venue: It moves freely through the circuit. Museums, for instance, are limited by their physical architecture in what they can present, yet the digital museum may contain anything (a.k.a. metafora) when reduced to a dataset. Digital books can hold text, image, sound, and moving pictures, and even three-dimensional virtual objects. With its virtual writing spaces, the computer positions us to transcend physical restraints and to combine experience within these spaces.

Atari's Mindlink, a video game controller that purported to allow users to control the game with their minds. It was never commercially released.

Up until now, the "medium" (i.e., film) has determined the audience for the message, its destination, and how the work is evaluated critically. For example, a film requires a screen to project onto, people to fill seats, and a critical review of two thumbs up to succeed. The fundamental absence of an object is what separates the age of the digital from the age of analog production. This major transformation presents new problems for the artist in terms of his or her ability to sell work, or even to maintain control over copyright. But it may also be the case that imaginative systems will develop using digital networks that give the "artist" greater control over his or her work. Creative ways to access lucrative systems for payment and royalties may also be introduced. The foundation for these changes are in place. So what do we need? Some creative interlocutors who are visionary enough to put it all together.

Elements of the Computer

Today's digital computer is the culmination of thousands of years of human mathematical thought. This section describes that process.

Mesolithic bone tool found at Ishango, thought to have been made about 9000 B.C.E. by a hunting and gathering society. Three rows of engraved marks are thought to represent time, and the bone a form of calendar.

The Univac computer

...emporary model, built after
...s Babbage's nineteenth-century
...ints for the Difference Engine.
...ers were stored as the positions
...gears.

Numbers

The term "dataset" appeared in the 1960s and refers to what we now call a computer file. It was initially coined by **mainframe** programmers at IBM to describe a specific type of collection of numbers. Though dataset is a modern term, the concept of using numbers to describe things is much, much older. Counting, and its companion, numbering, are as old as humankind itself. Animal bones that date back to 15,000 B.C.E. have been found with notches in them, which are thought to be tally marks. These marks directly signify the things they represent: one mark for each bison, for example. Numbers, on the other hand, are an abstraction of these tally marks. Compare the number 5 to the five lines carved on a wall or a tree, made familiar by movies that show someone marking time in a prison or on a desert island. Numbers are a precursor of the modern process of digitization: the description of concrete reality by abstract number.

Early numbering and calculating systems, such as those developed in Mesopotamia in the fourth millennium B.C.E., depended on direct physical analogs: one pebble for one sheep, two pebbles for two sheep. By the third millennium B.C.E., the Egyptians and the Sumerians had developed the written digit. Once numbers had entered the abstract world of writing and were independent of the objects they represented, numbers could be manipulated in new ways. Concepts of manipulating numbers developed into addition, subtraction, and so forth.

In order to count, we must understand that things exist discretely from one another: An individual rock is complete in and of itself, and separate from the other rocks in a pile. Digital systems, those that rely on numbers or digits, are said to be discrete, such as whole numbers or integers. Analog systems are continuous; they have no breaks or steps: Just think of thermometers used to take people's temperature. An analog thermometer has a band of mercury that extends itself continuously as the temperature rises, whereas a digital thermometer shows a changing series of numbers.

Elements of the Computer

Signals can be represented in digital or analog form, terms that refer to the methods used for encoding and storage. Analog refers to a process through which a physical trace of the signal is made. In the digital method, the signal is reduced to digits or numbers, which represent aspects of signal or information.

Digital encoding is infinitely reproducible: Copies can be made without any loss of quality because the process entails nothing more than the transcription of a set of numbers. Analog duplications lose clarity—it is almost impossible to duplicate a physical object perfectly.

An analog representation of a signal is made by allowing the signal to act directly on a physical substrate, such as light on photographic film. The quality of an analog image is determined by the sensitivity of the film and the quality of the optics of the camera.

It was Thomas Edison, in the late nineteenth century, who developed the analog process used to cut tracks in a record album. He discovered that sound caused a diaphragm in a microphone to vibrate, which in turn moved a stylus that physically cut into the surface of a rotating wax cylinder. Sound unfolds through time, and with the phonograph, the time of the sound is mapped onto the space of the cylinder through its rotation. Through the stylus, sound acts physically and continuously on the surface of the album, creating a physical analog. Playback is the reverse process: A stylus is placed in the groove of a record and then vibrates according to its irregularities. The vibrations of the stylus are physically carried to a speaker, which produces sound. The analog recording is very deeply tied to its physical existence; when its medium changes (for example, from album to tape), the sound changes quality.

In the production of compact discs, analog waveforms are converted into numbers, which are encoded in digital form.

To produce a compact disc, sound is represented by numbers that are then written onto the disc in binary notation. The sound is first fed into a computer, where it is sampled and converted into numbers that denote various elements of the sound, such as frequency, timbre, and amplitude. The frequency of sampling increases the size of the dataset and improves its quality. These numbers are then written onto the CD in binary format. In order to play a CD, the disc player must read the numbers off the surface of the CD, then interpret them and translate them back into analog signal to be carried to the speakers. A compact disc is physical and stores its information physically, but it does so as numbers. The medium that contains the digital information is irrelevant; it could be a disc, a tape, or even paper.

Both analog and digital methods must in some way create a souvenir of the event, a trace of the sound. Whereas analog record albums were stored in libraries and public or private collections, the process of digitization has moved music into the virtual network, accessible to everyone.

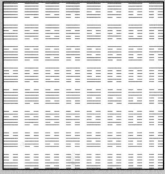

The Chinese Confucian book *I Ching*, or the *Book of Changes*, discusses a system of divination. Casting yarrow sticks or coins six times allow the sixty-four possibilities shown above.

Elements of the Computer

$$0 \quad O$$

Numeric zero, as opposed to the letter "O" (the 15th letter of the English alphabet). In their unmodified forms they look a lot alike, and various kluges invented to make them visually distinct have compounded the confusion. If your zero is center-dotted and letter-O is not, or if letter-O looks almost rectangular but zero looks more like an American football stood on end (or the reverse), you're probably looking at a modern character display (though the dotted zero seems to have originated as an option on IBM 3270 controllers). If your zero is slashed but letter-O is not, you're probably looking at an old-style ASCII graphic set descended from the default typewheel on the venerable ASR-33 Teletype (Scandinavians, for whom Ø is a letter, curse this arrangement). (Interestingly, the slashed zero long predates computers; Florian Cajori's monumental "A History of Mathematical Notations" notes that it was used in the twelfth and thirteenth centuries.) If letter-O has a slash across it and the zero does not, your display is tuned for a very old convention used at IBM and a few other early mainframe makers (Scandinavians curse this arrangement even more, because it means two of their letters collide). Some Burroughs/Unisys equipment displays a zero with a reversed slash. Old CDC computers rendered letter O as an unbroken oval and 0 as an oval broken at upper right and lower left. And yet another convention common on early line printers left zero unornamented but added a tail or hook to the letter-O so that it resembled an inverted Q or cursive capital letter-O (this was endorsed by a draft ANSI standard for how to draw ASCII characters, but the final standard changed the distinguisher to a tick-mark in the upper-left corner). Are we sufficiently confused yet?

The New Hacker's Dictionary

Golden Mean

Mathematics is the search for and recognition of pattern, and rhythm, and plays a vital part in our art and architecture. In ancient Greece, Pythagoras and his followers observed the relationship between fractions and musical scales, by quantifying the correspondence between the length of a string on an instrument and the note it produced.

Pythagoras also expanded thinking on proportions, especially the golden mean, or golden section, a proportion whereby the smaller dimension stands to the larger dimension as the larger dimension stands to the whole. The proportion can be expressed as the decimal number 1.618. It was used by Greek architects to design temples and by fine artists from the Renaissance to the present.

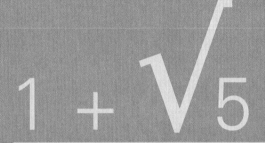

$$\frac{1 + \sqrt{5}}{2}$$

Formula for golden mean

Pythagoras

The roots of cyberspace can be traced as far back as the sixth century B.C.E., in Greece, where Pythagoras developed an elaborate cosmology based on number. He saw number as the first principle of the universe: Each thing had a particular algorithm, which not only described it but composed it as well. Pythagoras' follower, Philolaus, remarked: "Nothing about existing things, neither they themselves or their relation to one another, would be clear without number and the essence of number. It is number which takes things that we apprehend by sense perception and fits them harmoniously into the soul, thereby making them recognizable and capable of being compared with one another." Echoes of this idea can be seen throughout history to the present day, from the Chinese Taoist notion that the universe is composed of binary opposites (yin and yang).

Nautilus shell

Modulars are a scale of proportions whereby the bad is made more difficult and the good easier.

Albert Einstein

Elements of the Computer

Decimal and Binary

Our decimal counting system (base 10, using ten discrete symbols) is very probably a remnant of counting on one's fingers. If you add your two feet, you can count to 12, or a dozen. So our abstract, notational system of numbers is tied to the limits of our extremities, but it is not universal. The Aborigines who live in the Torres Strait near Australia use a base two (binary) system, the Sumerians used a base 60, and the Mayans used a base 20. The Chinese philosopher Shao Yung (1011–1077) proposed a mathematical system based on binary numbers that was a direct influence on Gottfried Wilhelm Leibniz's use of the binary system. In fact, Leibniz preferred binary to decimal for much of his writing.

Some early computers—notably the ENIAC of the mid-1940s—used decimal numbers, stored in complicated devices called decade counters, but their designers quickly realized several advantages to using binary numbers. A binary numbering system, composed of nothing but zeros and ones, is easier to store in an electronic circuit, as either the presence or absence of current in a circuit. More importantly, early computer designers saw that binary numbers shared many properties with the formal logic on which computer programs are based.

Gregory Meluson, *Untitled*, 2002

Components from early computers ENIAC, EDVAC, ORDSAC, and BRLESC-I

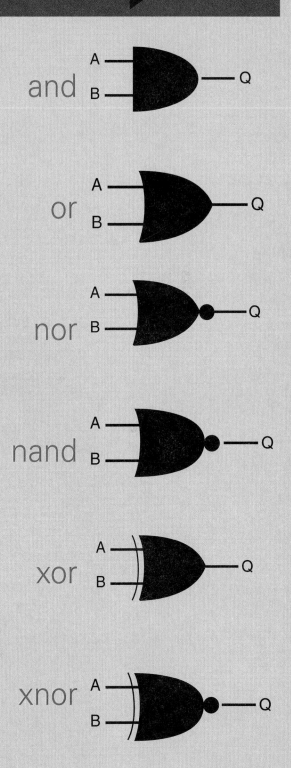

Boolean Logic

In the middle of the nineteenth century, the Englishman George Boole developed theories that would translate logic into algebra. That is, logical statements, which up until that time had been expressed through words, could be expressed in algebraic formulas, and manipulated according to algebraic laws. This was yet another building block for the modern digital computer, which uses boolean logic in its circuitry.Boolean logic is especially suited to the computer because it can be expressed in binary, and its functions can be expressed through electronic circuits. In the 1930s, Claude Shannon realized that the switches of early analog computers could be combined into circuits that could carry out logical operations. Shannon also discovered that switching circuits could make decisions, and this discovery led to the fact that programs could be used to control the actions of a computer.

Elements of the Computer

```perl
#!/usr/bin/perl

# 472-byte qrpff, Keith Winstein
and Marc Horowitz

# MPEG 2 PS VOB file -> descram-
bled output on stdout.

# usage: perl -I
<k1>:<k2>:<k3>:<k4>:<k5> qrpff

# where k1..k5 are the title key
bytes in least to most-significant
order


s'$/=\2048;while(<>){G=29;R=142;if
((@a=unqT=C*,_)[20]&48){D=89;
_=unqb24,qT,@

b=map{ord qB8,unqb8,qT,_^$a[--
D]}@INC;s/.../$/1$&/;Q=unqU,qb25,_;
H=73;O=$b[4]<<9

|256|$b[3];Q=Q>>8^(P=(E=255)&(Q>>
12^Q>>4^Q/8^Q))<<17,O=O>>8^(E&(F
=(S=O>>14&7^O)

^S*8^S<<6))<<9,_=(map{U=_%16orE
^=R^=110&(S=(unqT,"\ew\ntd\xbz
\x14d")[_/16%8]);E

^=(72,@z=(64,72,G^=12*(U-
2?0:S&17)),H^=_%64?12:0,@z)[_%8
]}(16..271))[_]^((D>>=8

)+=P+(~F&E))for@a[128..$#a]}print+
qT,@a}';s/[D-HO-
U_]/\$$&/g;s/q/pack+/g;eval
```

Algorithms

If numbers are an abstract concept that allows us to understand the world through counting, then mathematics is an abstract set of rules that allows us to manipulate numbers and so better understand and regulate the world. The ancient Greek philosopher Euclid advanced the field of geometry (literally the measurement of land) in his third-century B.C.E. work, *The Elements* (a compilation of previous thinking about algebra and geometry), as a part of a rigorous system of philosophical thought.

The Greek contributions to the field of mathematics were the notions that mathematics should be general and that mathematical statements should be proven. These proofs laid the foundation for the algorithm, building on the mathematics of the Mesopotanians, who had developed procedures for finding whole numbers.

Euclid's *Elements* contained methods for finding the common divisor of two numbers. This was an algorithm, a set of rules for finding the solution to a problem (a computer program is a type of algorithm, one translated into a code the computer can under- stand, usually through a programming language). The term "algorithm" comes from the Latin translation *(algorismi)* of the name of the Islamic mathematician Muhammed ibn Musa al-Kwarizmi. In the ninth century, he was one of many thinkers who worked in the House of Wisdom in Baghdad and was exposed to translations of Greek works. He wrote two books— *The Hindu Calculation*, which introduced Hindu notions of arithmetic to the Arab world, and the *Book of Restoring and Balancing*, which introduced algebra to the West, and from whose title the word "algebra" is derived (from the Arabic *al-jabar*, restoring).

Punched Cards

The player piano was a nineteenth-century device that could replay melodies based on encoded information. It resembled a conventional piano whose keys were controlled by an internal mechanism, which, in turn, was controlled by information encoded through holes on a paper roll or disk. As the roll turned, the holes interacted with the player piano's mechanism, which caused keys to play. This was a forerunner of the dataset: A creative act (piano music) was encoded digitally into an abstract form (the paper roll), interpreted by an output device (the player piano) to re-create the creative act.

To understand the modern dataset, one must accept that the image no longer consists of a physical trace of the object represented; instead, it is a virtual, numerical representation of that object. Following this definition, the first digital image can be traced back to 1801, when Jean-Marie Jacquard demonstrated an automated loom whose actions were directed by a program stored on punched cards, a precursor of the computers of the 1960s, which stored their programs on cards of this nature. These cards contained information encoded on them by a series of holes punched in specific locations, like those in the rolls of a player piano. The information on the cards, the presence or absence of a hole in a particular spot, would determine the movements of the loom to weave together the threads, and thus the pattern of the cloth that the loom produced. Jacquard also produced a self-portrait on the loom, encoded on 10,000 cards used to weave the portrait. We can consider this image digital insofar as it represented the image with discrete units, and required the intervention of an interpretive machine, the loom, to create the image from stored data. Charles Babbage was directly influenced by Jacquard's use of cards, and it is said that he had a portrait of Jacquard hanging on the wall of his office.

Jacquard loom, 1801

A portrait of Jean-Marie Jacquard woven into silk

Punched card

Elements of the Computer

History of the Computer

Throughout history, the computer was the mechanization of ideas about calculation.

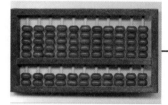

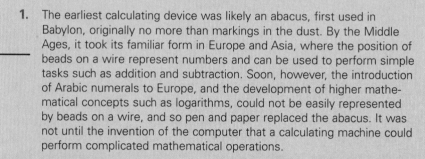

1. The earliest calculating device was likely an abacus, first used in Babylon, originally no more than markings in the dust. By the Middle Ages, it took its familiar form in Europe and Asia, where the position of beads on a wire represent numbers and can be used to perform simple tasks such as addition and subtraction. Soon, however, the introduction of Arabic numerals to Europe, and the development of higher mathematical concepts such as logarithms, could not be easily represented by beads on a wire, and so pen and paper replaced the abacus. It was not until the invention of the computer that a calculating machine could perform complicated mathematical operations.

2. In the sixteenth century, Scottish mathematician John Napier (1550–1617) developed logarithms, a mathematical concept that allowed the process of multiplication to be broken into a series of discrete steps using addition. He produced a device, known as Napier's bones, which simplified multiplication and was the forerunner of the slide rule.

3. Wilhelm Schickard (1592–1635) built the first mechanical calculating device in 1623, which incorporated a set of Napier's bones. The device could add, subtract, multiply, and divide.

4. Blaise Pascal (1623–1662) developed the Pascaline, a mechanical adding machine, in 1642. His father was a tax commissioner, and his device was a way to mechanize the labor of calculating tax tables in an age in which the dominant technology was that of clocks and gears. Numbers were represented by the positions of gears in the mechanism, and calculation consisted of physically changing the angle of the gears.

5. The Step Reckoner, invented by Gottfried Wilhelm Leibniz (1646–1716), could calculate square roots as well as basic arithmetic functions. It used gears and a movable carriage, which were also featured in later adding machines and the nineteenth-century mechanical typewriter.

6. In the mid-nineteenth century, Charles Babbage and Lady Ada Lovelace began their collaboration on the Analytical Engine, the successor to Babbage's Difference Engine, a mechanical calculating machine. The Difference Engine could perform certain arithmetic functions to twenty decimals, and its construction required a great many engineering advances, many of which Babbage developed himself. He began work on the Difference Engine as a means to calculate tide tables for the British Navy, but he abandoned the project for the more ambitious Analytic Engine, which he never completed. While most machines of the time were single purpose—designed and built to perform a single mathematical task, such as addition—the Analytical Engine was conceived to perform any arithmetic function and, more importantly, it could make decisions on the basis of its calculations. In effect, it could think for itself. While Babbage is given credit for the Analytical Engine's design, Lovelace is credited as the first programmer. An early programming language, Ada, was named after her.

7. ENIAC (Electronic Numerator, Integrator and Computer), completed in the mid-1940s, was the first general-purpose electronic computer, created by a team that was headed by John W. Mauchly and J. Prespert Eckert, Jr. at the University of Pennsylvania. Unlike earlier computers or calculating machines, it could be reprogrammed for a variety of tasks. But its programs were stored in the physical configurations of wires: It was difficult to reprogram—a process that could take days—and it could not change the program or make decisions after it had been wired. It was, in essence, a very fast and complicated adding machine, but lacked the ability to branch, and so lacked an essential feature of modern computers. During its construction, physicist John von Neumann joined the team, and together they proposed creation of the EDVAC, effectively making ENIAC obsolete before it was even completed.

8. EDVAC (Electronic Discrete Variable Automatic Computer) was an early stored-program computer completed in 1952. Unlike ENIAC, its program was stored in the same electronic space as its data, both of which were in binary format. This allowed its programs to be loaded much more quickly than ENIAC's; furthermore, the EDVAC programs could change themselves. Its architecture is the basis for all modern computing.

9. In 1948, Claude Shannon published his paper "A Mathematical Theory of Computation," which gave birth to modern information theory. His paper showed that all information media—text, voice, pictures—could be represented in binary form. That is, media could be encoded into digital files. He also coined the term "bit"—a contraction of "binary" and "digit."

The Bitmapped Image

Digital photographs and many other computer images are bitmapped, a grid system whose squares (pixels) are represented by one or more numbers that determine color, brightness, and various other characteristics of an image. The dataset for these images is mapped onto a grid on a computer screen or used to control the action of a printer. The greater the number of pixels, the greater the resolution and clarity of the image; the larger the number assigned to each pixel, the greater the number of colors that can be represented. The process of digitizing a photograph entails creating a grid and filling it with pixels.

When presented with this grid, we do not see the individual pixels: Our eyes blend them together to create a seamless, continuous-tone image. The concept of using squares of color or even numbers to create an image has developed since antiquity. The image's success depends on the squares of color remaining small enough that the viewer's eye will not be able to see each individual square, but rather blend them together.

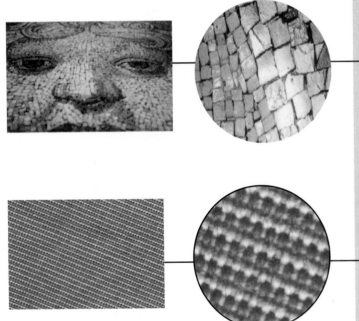

1. Throughout antiquity we can see proto-bitmaps in mosaics—small tiles of solid color—that blend to form a continuous tone image when viewed from a distance.

2. In the early nineteenth century, scientist Michel-Eugène Chevreul, the director of the Gobelins tapestry factory of Paris, had a profound effect on the Postimpressionist painter Georges S eurat, through his discovery of optical mixing. By weaving a garment from threads of two different colors, Chevreul found that the garment's color would appear to be a blend of the two: The eye could not resolve the individual threads, instead blending them into a third. Seurat, who was also familiar with the current thinking in the field of physics concerning the properties of light, used a method of painting that applied small dots of color to the canvas, in essence allowing the viewer's eye to mix the colors, rather than mixing paint on the palette. This blending in the eye is the basis for the color halftone and for the three-color cathode-ray tube monitor (CRT). The link between fabric and imagery continued into the twentieth century, as SciTex, a company that had developed machines to create fabric, marketed one of the earliest digital-imaging systems in the 1980s.

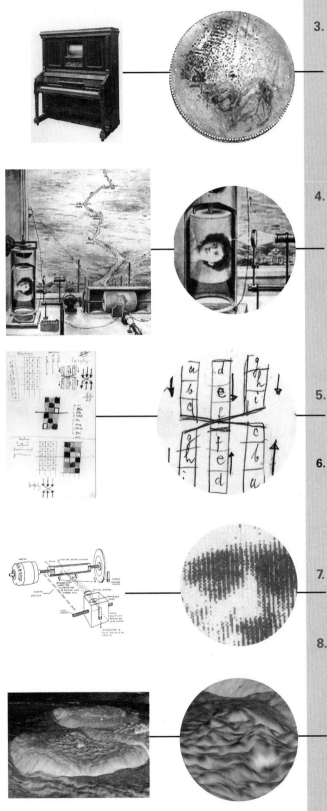

3. In the player piano, keys are activated based on information encoded in a disk. Different combinations of notes are encoded as number on the disk. This is a means of recording a sound by encoding discrete elements, which are later interpreted by the player piano and played back. Note that there was probably no "sound" present when the disk was created, merely the musical notes of the score, which can also be thought of as a discrete notational system that can be copied flawlessly.

4. Late in the nineteenth century, a process for transmitting images over the telegraph was created. In this process, a scanner moves over the image and sends an electrical pulse over the wire depending on whether the image is dark or light at a particular point. At the other end of the wire, a device darkens paper based on whether it senses a pulse. This can be thought of as the first digital image, though no provisions were made for storing it virtually, for recording the electrical pulses so that the image could be reconstructed at a later time. This would not happen until the late twentieth century.

5. Paul Klee describes a technique for painting in which a grid is drawn and letters corresponding to colors are placed in the squares of the grid. An image can then be constructed from this grid.

6. In 1951, Craft Master releases the first paint-by-numbers kit, which proclaimed, "Every man a Rembrandt." The kit contained paints and a template for a painting. Users would apply the paint inside predrawn lines. In effect, the numbers on the image encode color, a latent image that the amateur painter would complete.

7. One of the first digital images was created with a drum scanner constructed by Russell Kirsch and his colleagues at the National Bureau of Standards in the 1950s.

8. An image of Venus by the Magellan space probe. Temperatures on Venus can reach nearly 1,000 degrees Fahrenheit, making it impractical to place a camera on the planet's surface. This image was "constructed" from numerical data collected by a probe and transmitted back to Earth. Scientists then used the information to create this "photograph" through the process of ray-tracing: using imaginary rays of light to create a photographic image of a virtual object. Unlike a photograph, which this image clearly resembles, there was no "decisive moment." But it does encode time: The data were collected over a long period, mapped onto a grid, and then reconstructed.

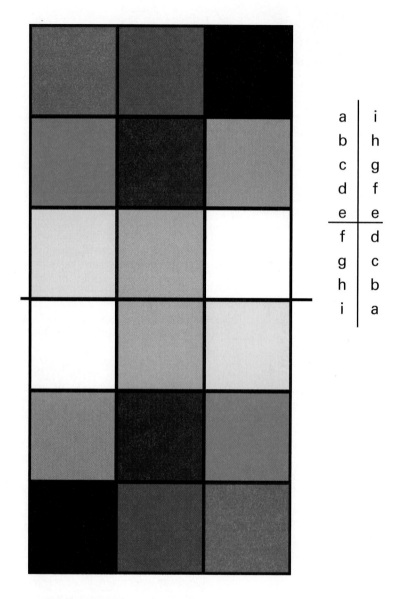

a	i
b	h
c	g
d	f
e	e
f	d
g	c
h	b
i	a

Paul Klee described a system for representing colors through letters and, more importantly, for transforming the arrangement of these colors.

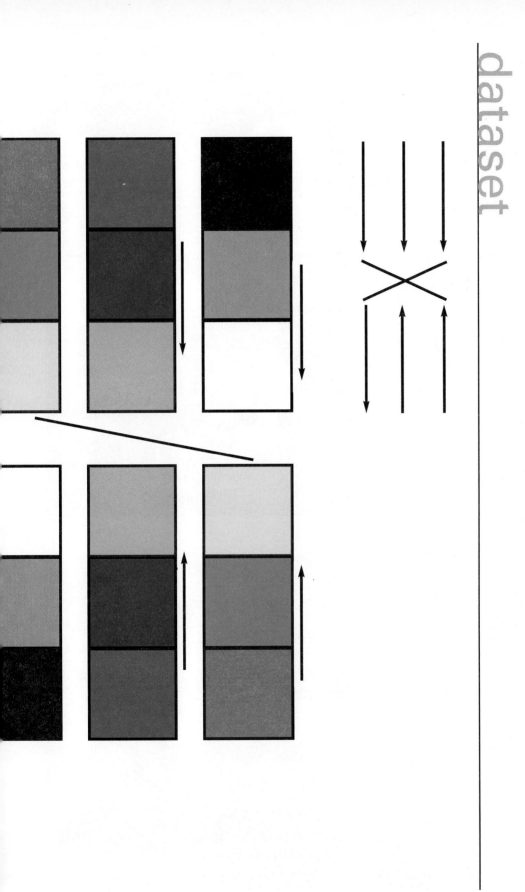

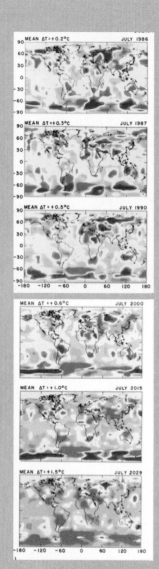

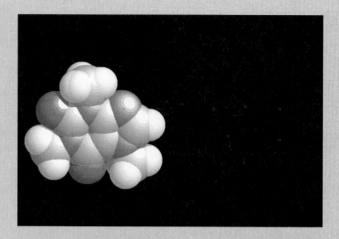

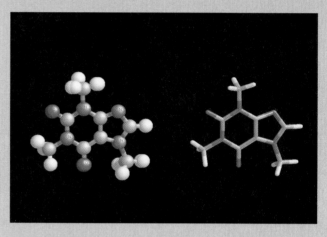

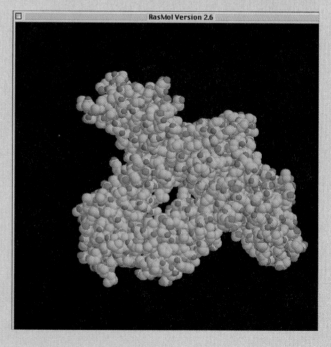

Data collected from scientific instruments, from weather satellites to MRI scanners, can be used to create imagery. Above is a representation of data on the changing surface temperature of the Earth in the years 1986, 1987, and 1990 while predicting temperatures in 2000, 2015, and 2029, generated by analyzing meterological data from around the world. Like graphs or charts, it allows scientists to analyze data in a visual fashion, to recognize pattern.

```
COMPND    caffeine
AUTHOR    Created by Dave Woodcock at Okanagan University College
AUTHOR    Date revised: Fri Sep 29 14:53:27 2000  GENERATED BY BABEL 1.6
HETATM    1  C       1      0.000   0.000   0.000  1.00  0.00
HETATM    2  C       1      1.392   0.000   0.000  1.00  0.00
HETATM    3  N       1      2.076   1.164   0.000  1.00  0.00
HETATM    4  C       1      1.373   2.321  -0.003  1.00  0.00
HETATM    5  O       1      1.978   3.365  -0.017  1.00  0.00
HETATM    6  N       1      0.017   2.344   0.003  1.00  0.00
HETATM    7  C       1     -0.710   1.202   0.002  1.00  0.00
HETATM    8  O       1     -1.915   1.218  -0.006  1.00  0.00
HETATM    9  N       1     -0.404  -1.287  -0.019  1.00  0.00
HETATM   10  N       1      1.830  -1.279  -0.020  1.00  0.00
HETATM   11  C       1      0.715  -2.048  -0.031  1.00  0.00
HETATM   12  C       1     -1.795  -1.761  -0.044  1.00  0.00
HETATM   13  C       1      3.546   1.178  -0.016  1.00  0.00
HETATM   14  C       1     -0.690   3.634  -0.013  1.00  0.00
HETATM   15  H       1      0.720  -3.138  -0.055  1.00  0.00
HETATM   16  H       1     -1.813  -2.850  -0.090  1.00  0.00
HETATM   17  H       1     -2.307  -1.428   0.860  1.00  0.00
HETATM   18  H       1     -2.302  -1.352  -0.918  1.00  0.00
HETATM   19  H       1      3.894   1.455  -1.011  1.00  0.00
HETATM   20  H       1      3.929   0.190   0.239  1.00  0.00
HETATM   21  H       1      3.911   1.904   0.710  1.00  0.00
HETATM   22  H       1     -1.557   3.583   0.645  1.00  0.00
HETATM   23  H       1     -0.027   4.428   0.329  1.00  0.00
HETATM   24  H       1     -1.020   3.851  -1.029  1.00  0.00
CONECT    1    2    2    7    9
CONECT    2    1    1    3   10
CONECT    3    2    4   13
CONECT    4    3    5    5    6
CONECT    5    4    4
CONECT    6    4    7   14
CONECT    7    1    6    8    8
CONECT    8    7    7
CONECT    9    1   11   12
CONECT   10    2   11   11
CONECT   11    9   10   10   15
CONECT   12    9   16   17   18
CONECT   13    3   19   20   21
CONECT   14    6   22   23   24
CONECT   15   11
CONECT   16   12
CONECT   17   12
CONECT   18   12
CONECT   19   13
CONECT   20   13
CONECT   21   13
CONECT   22   14
CONECT   23   14
CONECT   24   14
MASTER        0    0    0    0    0    0    0    0   24    0   24    0
END
```

Visual model of the
caffeine molecule
generated by the program
RasMol, and the Protein
Data Bank data that
generated it

Early twentieth-century fax

Pixel

The word "pixel" can refer to the physical or virtual component of an image: the smallest unit into which it can be divided. It appeared in the late 1960s as a contraction of the words "picture" and "element." Most often the term is used to describe an element of an array that describes an image: a number that denotes various information (color, hue, etc.) about that particular square of the image. A collection of pixels makes up a bitmap, a dataset. Pixels can also refer to the elements of a grid that comprise a cathode-ray tube (CRT) display. Screen pixels are usually composed of red, green, and blue phosphors that the human eye blends together, as described by the theory of persistence of vision.

Jelly Belly (enlarged below)

The images on this page and the next are stills from Karl Sims' animation *Panspermia*, which won the Golden Nica award at the 1991 Prix Ars Electronica. It takes its name from the theory that life is distributed in the form of spores or germs. The piece was modeled on Danny Hillis' Connection Machine, CM-2, and programmed in LISP, a programming language used in many artificial intelligence applications. Sims began the program with sixteen images, each composed of twenty-one randomly generated genes. Each gene controlled various aspects of the organism in LISP: growth rate, twistiness, and so forth. He then "bred" these images' genes together over many generations to produce the offspring such as those shown here.

Floor plan of the temple of Borobudur. This monument was completed in Java, Indonesia, in the eighth century. A pilgrim would circle the monument nine times before reaching the top, representing perfection.

The combination of ideas conveyed through media in a creative act is called multimedia. Metafora is an idea expressed through media (such as motion pictures or books), those channels through which we can deliver expression: movement, sound, object, image, and word (see Chapter Two). That the term "multimedia" is only forty years old suggests that we think of it as a modern practice, especially as a condition of the computer. Yet people have always combined media, realizing that the sum is greater than the whole, that by placing different media together, they can achieve a synergistic effect: New metafora is created. For composer Richard Wagner in the nineteenth century, it was the concept of the "total artwork." His essay "The Art Work of the Future"[4] proposed the unification of architecture, music, dance, and other media, which would serve drama in opera.

From the cave paintings of Lascaux to the present, multimedia is a phenomenon that is historically universal. Early Egyptian burial sites contained evidence of multimedia rituals; the Ada people of Nigeria, throughout their history have combined masks with dance and music in storytelling rituals that often satirize social behavior.

American philosopher John Dewey (1859–1952) sought to recover a continuity of being through the integration of the expressive acts with the routines of our everyday lives. In describing the Parthenon of ancient Greece, he noted, "The collective life knew no boundaries between what was characteristic of these places and operations and the arts that brought color, grace and dignity into them. Painting and sculpture were organically one with architecture, as that was one with the social purpose the buildings served. Music and song were intimate parts of the rites and ceremonies in which the meaning of group life was consummated."[5] This is what we might today give as an early example of multimedia. The realm of the circuit in the twenty-first century is at its best when it resembles the Parthenon.

In the predigital world, creativity was expressed through physical media. Books held the written word, whereas visual imagery was contained in paintings, sculptures, stained glass, photographs, and other physical objects. Even music depended on either physical instruments to create it, or tapes or vinyl albums to record it. Today, music has been liberated from the qualities of a particular instrument, or even an instrument at all: Samplers and other digital tools can fabricate sounds out of nothing more than numbers. If music once depended on the physical presence and organization of the musician and the instrument, it can now depend on the programmer and engineer.

In the digital age, photographs and words, for example, can be combined easily and quickly because they are made up of the same zeros and ones of the dataset. This was more difficult only fifty years ago, when creating a newspaper page required the layout artist physically to assemble photographs and type on a paste-board. It is precisely because the computer can hold so many forms of creative practice (metafora) that it has become the hub of multimedia practice. Although software must be purchased, it is nonetheless much cheaper to build a digital darkroom than a physical one. In addition, enhancements to the digital dark-room, such as an improved algorithm, can be duplicated and moved through the network easily and quickly. Because of this, it is likely that digital photography will evolve far beyond the limits of traditional photography.

The virtual movie studio—the computer—is the same place where digital audio tools are found. Whereas combining traditional film with traditional audio once require highly specialized tools and knowledge (at great expense), the combining of digital audio with digital video is becoming increasingly easy and affordable. In fact, every Apple Macintosh computer shipped in 2002 had preinstalled tools for the making and editing of audio, video, and photographs. Once, multimedia productions were the domain of the wealthy and powerful. The digital tools of the twenty-first century have allowed many more people to produce hypermedia and integrate it into their everyday lives. The dialog of culture has been expanded. The artifacts of this dialog can be stored in the digital repositories of the World Brain, which allow us to share them.

Goldi shaman and assistant

Performance artist Stelarc's *Amplified Body*

Caves, with drawings such as this one, were used thousands of years ago as locations for rituals that were thought to include dance, music, and performance. These were holy sites, not used for daily living, but for some sort of transcendent purpose.

Parthenon frieze, c. 438 B.C.E.

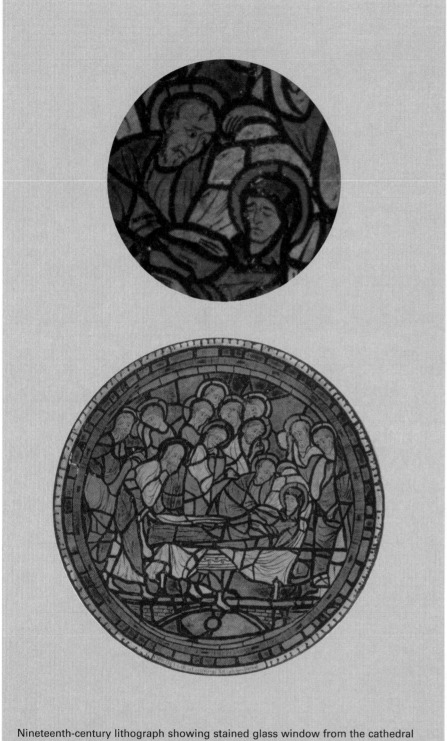

Nineteenth-century lithograph showing stained glass window from the cathedral of Chartres (detail above)

The caption to this Haitian painting translates as, "While Maxime Rémy was treating a child, the lwa [spirit] entered his head."

Facing Page Top: Detail of the Temple of the Feathered Spirit, Teotihuacan, c. 350 C.E. This temple was part of the Cuidadela, which could accommodate 60,000 people at one time.

Facing Page Bottom: The north torana of the Great Stupa at Sanchi, first century B.C.E. In this Buddhist temple, architecture is inseparable from sculpture and ritual. Visitors would circumambulate the temple through a stone path of which the stupa forms an entrance.

6

Cathedrals

The period from the middle of the twelfth century to the beginning of the fifteenth century is known as the Age of Cathedrals, due to the sheer number of these structures erected in Europe during that time. The unity of reason and faith known as scholasticism was reflected in the gothic cathedral. These massive structures, built over a span of decades or often centuries, were the mass communications technology of the time, disseminating Christian religious doctrine. A visitor to the cathedral would be presented with an often overwhelming array of media synthesized together, from the architecture of the building itself, to the music of the organ, to paintings, stained glass, written materials, and even textiles and incense.

The architectural advances of the time—most notably the flying buttress—allowed for higher ceilings, thinner walls, and larger windows. The additional light that filtered through these windows seemed to suggest the ascent to heaven (divine light), while the windows themselves were filled with stained glass that contained visual narratives from the Bible. The use of imagery was especially important in instructing and convincing the worshipers, most of whom were illiterate. The repetition of ritual was also a means of reinforcing memory. This can be found in everything from Greek epic poems up through modern rock and roll music.

Other architectural advances were the enlarged nave of the cathedral, which allowed the many pilgrims who visited churches to see the relics of the church without bothering the local congregation. The cathedral became a focal point for a variety of social and religious activities whose message was reinforced by a variety of methods of stimulating the senses. By the Reformation of the sixteenth century, visual imagery was considered distracting from direct contact with God and so was removed from the places of worship; the text of the printed Bible which developed over the previous century became more important.

Facing Page: Cathedral of Nôtre-Dame, Paris, completed in the mid-thirteenth century. The towers were added in the fifteenth century.

Cairo

Mosque

The word "mosque" comes from the Arabic *masjid*, which means a place of prostration or prayer. But it would be a mistake to think of mosques as merely that, for since the first mosque was built by the Prophet Muhammad in 622 C.E., they have served as the center of Muslim communities across the globe. The first mosque was in fact the center of the first Muslim community. The Koran describes two types of mosques: one a hub of government and social activity, and the other a sacred place. Often, mosques combine elements of both. A typical mosque today has facilities for the ritual cleansing each Muslim must perform before daily prayers, a consecrated place for prayer, a *minbar* for the *imam* (spiritual leader of the community) to conduct services, and a *qibla* wall, which is oriented toward Mecca, the historical birthplace of Muhammad. The *qibla* wall is differentiated from others by a niche or arch called the *mihrab*. The mosque served and still serves as the socioreligious center of Muslim communities. In addition to acting as the location for daily prayers, mosques have acted as libraries and schools, centers of law and politics, places for commerce, news, and proclamations; have distributed money and other aid to the poor; and have been the center of political debate. Mosques are sometimes sanctioned by the government (early mosques were built next to the caliph's residence), but just as often they serve as centers of political opposition.

There are two main activities in the mosque: daily prayers and the Friday sermon, although is not necessary to have a physical mosque in order to pray. The Prophet said that the whole world is a mosque, and Muslims can pray anywhere, as long as they face Mecca. The mosque is as much a set of rituals as a physical incarnation. The *sahn* has many uses in addition to prayer and is often used for education or as a meeting room. Thus, through architecture and social practice, the Mosque becomes the nexus for activities that weave together the lives of Muslims living across the globe.

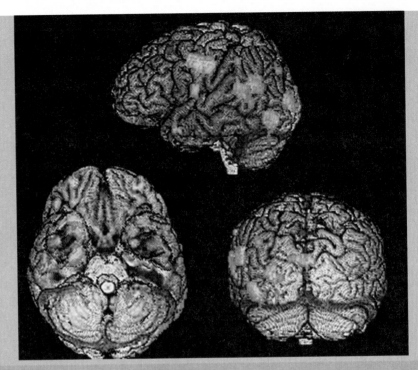

fMRI of the brain experiencing auditory hallucinations

When is synaesthesia not synaesthesia? When it's metaphor.

John Harrison

Synaesthesia and Perception

Synaesthesia, an abnormal condition of the brain, causes sensory perceptions to blend. Thus a synaesthete may smell a color. To study this condition is to understand some of the unique connections the digital network can create in multimedia. The phenomenon undermines the notion that the impulses that trigger these senses are distinct or different. Thus, who is to say that sound waves create sound instead of vision? Under normal conditions, a sense organ such as the eye or ear stimulates nerves, which send impulses to a particular region of the brain. Like a number in a dataset, this pulse is not the color blue, or the "dot dot dot dash" of Beethoven's *Fifth Symphony*; rather, it is merely electric energy, a representation of the color or sound in the nervous system. What makes one impulse indicate smell and another indicate touch is dependent on which neural pathways are stimulated. The condition of synaesthesia suggests that the path from stimuli to sensation can be altered.

Synaesthesia has been a recurrent theme of the modernist movement. Wassily Kandinsky, the early twentieth-century Russian abstract painter, actively attempted to depict music in color. The Italian Futurist group Art of Noise; the Bolshevik use of Agitprop layering of media; Vladimir Nabokov's autobiography *Speak, Memory,* wherein he saw the sound of each letter as a different color or texture; all attempt to blend media together. The electrical impulses of the brain are similar to those of the dataset: They have no implicit value until interpreted.

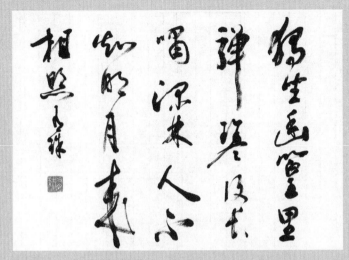

Calligraphy by Ru Young Cui

Chinese Painting

The Chinese written language is composed of pictograms, which represent words themselves and are thought to have evolved from pictograms that were used in divination around 2000 B.C.E. It is perhaps the closeness of image to word, and because traditionally the same brush was used to paint and to write, that have contributed to the coexistence of word and image in Chinese literature.

Around the turn of the first millennium, Chinese painters began combining written characters with images on narrative scrolls and wall paintings. By the thirteenth century, the scholar-official began to paint and to write poetry as a means for developing a moral and disciplined inner self. During the Northern Sung Dynasty (960–1127 C.E.), painting turned from narratives of human history to portrayals of nature. By the Southern Sung Dynasty (1127–1279), the scholar-officials turned their attention inward, away from realistic representations of nature in painting to more symbolic ones.

The computer's dataspace tools are much like the brush of the Chinese scholar: They make no delineation between word, image, sound, or statistical analysis.

By nature, human creativity is multimedia.

Facing Page: Buddhist mandalas are symbolic representations of the universe (Katmandu, Nepal).

New technology is meaningless unless we can reassess the metaphors for its use. In the digital age, the museum and the library are new social and cultural spaces.

We have borrowed the term *world brain* from the science-fiction writer H. G. Wells, who, in 1937, wrote an essay by that title. He proposed a universal encyclopedia, a populist work. His notion was of a massive collection of creativity, constantly updated, that would allow for the intellectual unification of the peoples of the world.

"Both the assembling and the distribution of knowledge in the world at present are extremely ineffective, and thinkers of the forward-looking type whose ideas we are now considering, are beginning to realize that the most hopeful line for the development of ... intelligence lies rather in the direction of creating a new world organ for the collection, indexing, summarizing and release of knowledge, than in any further tinkering with the highly conservative and resistant university system, local, national and traditional in texture, which already exists. These innovators, who may be dreamers today, but who hope to become very active organizers tomorrow, project a unified, if not a centralized, world organ to "pull the mind of the world together," which will be not so much a rival to the universities, as a supplementary and coordinating addition to their educational activities—on a planetary scale."6

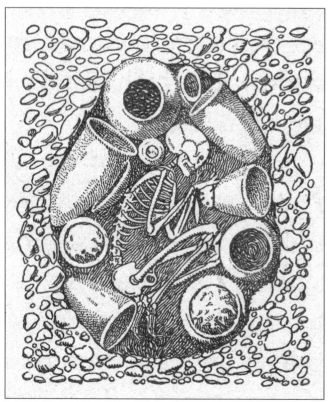

Nineteenth-century interpretation of ancient grave site

Wells' vision of a microfilm-based endeavor was never completed, but new technologies of the circuit and dataset have made his dream possible. The Web is an incarnation of what he called the "Permanent World Encyclopedia," thanks to the visionary work of people from Vannevar Bush to Tim Berners-Lee, who were building on an intellectual foundation laid by those such as Babbage, Lovelace, and the African griot. Today, online catalogs are available from libraries around the world, along with indexes of the collections of the major museums and every conceivable piece of information one might want.

One problem is navigation and validation. Jorge Luis Borges' story "The Library of Babel" describes a nearly infinite library, filled with books composed of every possible combination of words and letters. The protagonist spends his days wandering and searching for the one true catalog to the library. He is defeated by his realization that he has no means to differentiate the true catalog from the many false ones.

The impulse to collect is an important component of our humanity, and we can see evidence of it before recorded history. Collections of objects were buried with the Neanderthal and included decorated tools and trophy skulls. The burial of the dead with these objects, and the intentional positioning of the bodies, indicates the beginning of an aesthetic sense, one that is not directly concerned with physical survival, but with cultural survival.

The World Brain, or universal library, connects us all to a repository that could conceivably contain civilization's myths and tales. Anyone can visit this library, can rearrange its contents, or add pictures or sounds of his or her own. A new class of people is mandated by our ability to interact through the dataset and the circuit. They must help us facilitate this ideal in order to assure the continuation of the dialog in the most democratic ways. The postindustrial age is measured by the effectiveness of what we create and how we manage it to help us continue the dialog of culture.

Equal to our urge to collect is our urge to record and archive our thoughts. As our ancestors developed technologies to write, they could create rudimentary libraries, often the hub of centers of learning and inquiry. The first written collections are thought to have started in Sumer around 3000 B.C.E. Whenever thoughts and creativity are gathered together in a repository, they serve as an incitement to those who seek to be creative.

The digital age provides an amplification of our ability to collect and to share, and perhaps more importantly to make relationships between collections and the objects within them. Traditional collections, from works of art to Barbie dolls, were, of course, collections of physical objects. Even the abstract ideas contained in the books of a library needed to take physical form. Today, our laptops are virtual repositories of our personal collective enterprises, from the documents of our workday to the pictorial family album to music to the catalog of the collections of our interest.

The library or museum itself can become a network, provided it is organized in a sufficiently imaginative way by the someone who, beyond merely scanning and cataloging content, can create links between information and even new systems for comprehending and viewing it. The Visible Human Project created a digital library of human anatomy in the early 1990s and provided the scientific community with new visual methodologies for exploring it. The computer can manage an active library, one that can gather, evaluate, disseminate, and qualify data and experience in usable and meaningful organizations through emerging filtering and pattern-recognition software. The World Brain is a living organism of connected synapses, provided by creative interlocutors, which can grow in **rhizome**-like ways.

I dream of a new age of curiosity. We have the technical means for it; the desire is there; the things to be known are infinite; the people who employ themselves at this task exist. Why do we suffer? From too little: from channels that are too narrow, skimpy, quasi-monopolistic, insufficient. There is no point in adopting a protectionist attitude, to prevent "bad" from invading the "good." Rather, we must multiply the paths and the possibilities of comings and goings.

Michel Foucault, *Politics, Philosophy, Culture*

A periodical arcade, nineteenth century

Apple Computer's iPod, a digital jukebox

Peer-to-peer sharing systems—networks of people linked together by pro-grams such as Napster or Gnutella—have moved music out of the library and into the networked world brain. One interesting consequence of this is the peculiar phenomena called "smash-ups." Users mix songs together using inexpensive digital tools, then release them out into the World Brain. Other people can download and listen to them, or even take the smash-ups and remix them again, creating second- and third-generation smash-ups. The notion of originality is becoming more complicated.

Erik Desmazières, *La Salle Labrouste de la Bibliothèque Nationale*

Libraries arose from the desire to gather together the thinking and writing of a range of scholars, poets, and storytellers: to know the world through writing. Museums arose from the desire to gather together meaningful objects—paintings, photographs, butterflies—that carry insight into the inner workings of the human spirit, or the larger cycles of the natural world. These collections, private libraries, and other possessions of European royalty, were gradually opened to the public at the end of the eighteenth century; even then they were limited to those with the ability to physically travel to an exhibition and pay its admission fee.

Physical museums and libraries have inherent limitations: When paintings, books, and utilitarian objects are removed from the context in which they arose—the ebb and flow of everyday life that gave them richness and meaning—they suffer. The iconography of a Nigerian ritual mask is vastly diminished when hung on the wall of a museum. When scarcity was based on limited physical quantities, museums were a reasonable way to share a painting of which there were only one copy. But this hardly makes sense when works of art can be duplicated infinitely: Collections of digital art or writing are contained within the very context from which they are rooted.

Museums organize material based on certain criteria: The act of curating is the choice of what work to show and in relation to what else. Once an exhibition has been presented in a traditional museum, it is difficult to re-organize. What would happen if every museum visitor could curate his or her own exhibition?

Traditional libraries hold books and museums hold objects: not so for the new digital museum or library, which will hold creativity in an accessible, networked realm. The network itself is the context from which digital creativity arises, and by presenting these works in the digital realm, they are not decontextualized. The electronic library allows us to reorganize knowledge and to change the very notion of taxonomy.

The genesis of the library, the museum, and the encyclopedia are rooted in our desire to understand the world. We create categories and attempt to fit the contents of the world within them. Once these taxonomies become established, by academic or other scholarly standards, it is difficult to change them or the thinking that produced them. Because we are influenced by taxonomy, those who set the boundaries between fields—academics, curators, librarians, and so forth—are very powerful indeed.

Traditional libraries are managed according to a variety of organizational schemes, such as the Dewey Decimal system or the Universal Decimal Classification system. These systems are fixed and unmoving, as the tomes of these libraries must be housed on shelves. Yet in the digital realm, information is fluid. The computer enables users to formulate their own hierarchy of meaning, and so the electronic library, containing electronic books, articles, and even pictures or music, may provide new understandings of our cultural history. The digital library shifts the boundaries in a world where postmodern theory, multiculturalism, and identity politics, as well as many other new theories of knowledge, have attacked the very notions of truth and fixity.

Thomas Jefferson's eighteenth-century study chair incorporated a desk, inspiring furniture design to this day.

Interior of Vatican Library with arched, decorated ceiling

Thomas Jefferson's rotating bookstand

Erik Desmazières, *La Salle des Planètes*

Like the physical library that collects concrete tomes of abstract ideas, the traditional museum collects objects not so much for their own sake, but for the reflection of larger, more universal concepts. A natural history museum does not collect rocks for their individual qualities as rocks, but because they are useful in demonstrating concepts of the ordering and structuring of the universe. The art museum, on the other hand, gathers together the representational expressions that it prizes most highly, as examples of the best of the idiosyncratic expressions and challenges in a given age.

To amass and juxtapose objects may initially have personal motives, but eventually the collector feels the need to show the collection to others. When a collection is shared, a sense of community is formed between collector and viewer. Collections help establish the cultivation, power, and achievement of the collector, and are also a means for society itself to refine and redefine its notions of culture and history. Throughout history, collections have reflected every imaginable personal whim, scientific curiosity, and historical need to archive. The earliest collectors were an elite: people of position, education, and wealth. Today, almost everyone collects something, whether it is fountain pens or Pokéman cards.

Wonder Cabinet

During the mid-fifteenth to mid-sixteenth century in Europe (known as the Age of Discovery), a newfound curiosity about the natural world led to an increase both in exploring it and collecting objects from locations abroad, activities that were intimately tied together. Various factors conspired to encourage exploration of the globe by sea and the "discovery" of the new world of America (which had been settled as our ancestors crossed the Bering Strait 20,000 years ago). In addition to technological, social, and political advances (sailing and royal patronage), a new age of curiosity spurred European civilization to travel in search of new worlds. This curiosity in travel was part of a larger intellectual curiosity that sought new forms of knowledge in the natural world (and in the new printed book), rather than in the ecclesiastical one. These curiosities would lead to the spirit of rational inquiry and would lay the groundwork for the Renaissance, the scientific method, and the Enlightenment. As the network of exploration brought Europeans beyond the continent, they sought ways to share their discoveries with those back home. Because photography had not yet been invented, the explorers could not bring back visual records of the new world (in fact, one of the most popular uses of photography in the nineteenth century was postcards from Egypt); the explorers brought back the objects themselves. The nobility, those who could afford both exploration and collection, placed their foreign treasures into *wunderkammern* (cabinet of wonders) for contemplation.

The *wunderkammern* was more than a collection of souvenirs; it was symbolic of a view of the universe as a great chain of being, in which planets, people, animals, vegetables, minerals, and metals are linked together in complex hierarchies of correspondences, with the Christian God at the top. This view encouraged the belief that every existing thing is in some measure a symbol or reflection of something else, and each item containing to some degree an emanation of divine unity.

In the West, *wunderkammern* had roots in the collections of feudal lords; but by the sixteenth century they were widespread among the princes and members of the professional classes. The "cabinet of wonders"(also known as the cabinet of curiosities) reflected the belief that a human being had the ability to achieve universal knowledge and represented a change in perception with the compartmentalization of knowledge in the Middle Ages.

Tangible or virtual collections are often placed together disjointedly, putting an active demand on any user or viewer. To make associations, one cannot be passive; the eye must seek to create relevancy and meaning between objects. If these cabinets of wonders reflected the notion of the universe as a great chain of being, what then does a digital cabinet of wonders reflect?

Because physical space is integral to memory, recollection is intimately tied to the physical world because we situate meaning in a spatial and temporal order. If the physical library uses its tangible architecture as a means to organize its volumes, how do we organize a nonphysical library? We need help to manage the information overload that is already confronting us in the digital library. We need guidance to find our preferences through great quantities of data, in order to qualify that which is most useful to particular needs and situations. The deployment of intelligent agents throughout the network, along with imaginative search engines, may further our quest for meaning in the circuit.

Hopefully, the electronic library will further democratize the management and distribution of knowledge and, in so doing transgress boundaries of subject and content heretofore separated by physical and conceptual constraints. The creative interlocutors or knowledge managers of the datasets of today's culture will surely be the heroes of the knowledge revolution because of their abilities to facilitate discovery within the library of cyberspace.

Jacob Lawrence, *The Library*, 1960

Sir Thomas Egerton's 1615 Traveling Library: An early laptop computer?

The *Encyclopédie* was published in France in 17 volumes, the first appearing in 1751, and comprising 72,000 entries by 1772, compiled primarily by Enlightenment philosopher Denis Diderot (1713-1784), with help from Jean le Rond d'Alembert. The *Encyclopédie*, subtitled the *Analytical Dictionary of the Sciences, Arts and Trades*, was the embodiment of the Enlightenment and of the Philosophes—French thinkers of the eighteenth century who put faith in human reason. Among them was Jacques de Vaucanson, who constructed a precursor to the Jacquard loom. Unlike philosophical tracts of the time, the work was dedicated to more than the arts and sciences; it also had sections on the trades in an attempt to break down the barriers between the "liberal" and the "mechanical" arts. Diderot made comparisons between the workings of machinery and those of the human mind. Further, the work contained a complicated series of cross-references between entries, intended to challenge the fixed knowledge structures of the Church. This resulted in much controversy, and its publication stopped for years at a time.

In truth the aim of an encyclopedia is to collect all the knowledge scattered over the face of the earth, to present its general outlines and structures to the men with whom we live and to transmit this to those who will come after us, so that the work of the past centuries will be useful to the following centuries … it could only belong to a philosophical age to attempt an encyclopedia.

Denis Diderot, *Encyclopédie*

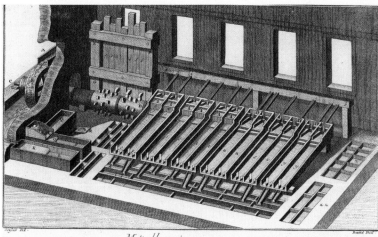

Page from Diderot's *Encyclopédie*

The Louvre, Paris

Treasure Box

The Emperor Ch'ien-lung's eighteenth-century collection held more than one million objects. Small objects were often placed in treasure boxes, microcosms of the larger collection, which held objects from the Chinese Empire spanning its reach in time and space. This may be seen as an earlier attempt to deal with what we today call information overload.

Illustration of the signs of Persian alchemy

Charles Willson Peale, *The Artist in His Museum*

Commerce

The phenomenon of online auctions has changed the very nature of collecting and selling, giving the pursuer a window on eclectic and rarified objects amassed for review and the ability to purchase in ways previously not conceived. Ebay has become a twenty-first-century flea market, where more than two million members wander among millions of items for sale, often for the mere pleasure of looking. It has opened up a truly global marketplace for goods, at the same time giving new meaning to the phrase "buyer beware" as several types of fraud develop in the digital market.

Historically, the cupboard housed utilitarian items in the common household from plates and dishes to important documents to clothing and memorabilia. Like a chair, bed, and table, it became the primary locus of exchange and discourse between family and friends. But unlike other furniture, the cupboard contains a private world for storage, archiving, and comparison. Unlike a chair, bed, or table, it is not designed to interact directly with the human body; rather, its purpose is that of a repository for the artifacts of human interest. It stored the first manuscripts and folios, codices, and the like, and was a fixture in early libraries. The cupboard was a device for physical organization of objects through one's cognitive management scheme: an everyman's "cabinet of wonders" and a prototype of an interactive computing system.

Bahia, 1984

What happens when a new work of art is created is something that happens simultaneously to all the works of art which preceded it. The existing monuments from an ideal order among themselves, which is modified by the introduction of the new (the really new) work of art among them . . . whoever has approved this idea of order . . . will not find it preposterous that the past should be altered by the present as much as the present is directed by the past.

T. S. Eliot, *Tradition and the Individual Talent*

The 2001 attack on the World Trade Center was witnessed and photographed by more people than any other event in history, perhaps because we understand things, or at least try to understand them, through the act of witness. The ultimate irony of the events of September 11, 2001, is that we may never fully grasp them, no matter how much we see of them.

The collective witness of thousands of image-makers, photographers from all walks of life, from professional to amateur, became an instant memorial in a small Manhattan storefront in a show titled "Here Is New York." A small group of volunteers quickly responded to the need to gather testament to this tragedy through the implementation of technology for a public catharsis.

Information was transmitted through the Internet and other networks, telling all who were interested that they could bring their photographs to this site, have them digitally scanned and printed, and then displayed, as a means of laying a stone at the grave. Within days, several thousand images were collected, archived, and circulated, through the wonders of digital data organization and dissemination. People came to reaffirm and contemplate the events in their own time. Easily duplicated digital prints were sold to visitors, allowing them to take home a part of the show, and raising money for the families of the victims of this tragedy.

Digital technology dispatched thousands of photographs beyond the original site and duplicated them in both physical and virtual form. In essence, the show was composed of digital information, allowing duplication in ways unavailable to traditional photographs, and so the exhibition went up in many sites across the world within a matter of days. Each exhibition site was, in some ways, a physical manifestation of the ideals of the Internet—community, spontaneity, democracy, interactivity, replication—and likely would not have come to pass without the Internet as a model. "Here Is New York" brought technology to bear directly on humanist needs: Its importance lay not in the technology, but in its imaginative application. The virtual data of the images were brought to the real experience through the realm of the circuit.

George Eastman Kodak's box camera simplified the act of photography so that anyone could take a photograph as a souvenier of a journey or a likeness of a loved one.

The garden of L

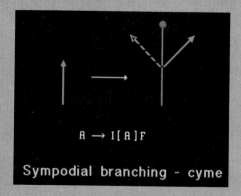

Plant development

productions

Visual Models of Morphogenesis

In the late 1950s, botanist Aristid Lindenmayer began his postdoctoral studies with the logician J. H. Woodger in England. He began to develop mathematical formulas to model biological growth, known as morphogenesis. His formulas—algorithms—were similar to those used by cellular automata, or a Turing machine: They proceeded from one state to the next based on a set of rules. At each time frame, the system would consult its formula on how to change in the next time step. In fact, the first model of morphogenesis was proposed by Turing, known as the reaction-diffusion model. Lindenmayer looked to formal language theory because biological growth was based on the grammar of DNA, which used a four-letter alphabet as the building blocks of life.[7]

He proposed his theories (L-systems) purely as a means to describe plant growth mathematically, but two of his graduate students began to use his algorithms to actually draw plants using computers. "The L-systems themselves don't generate images. They generate long strings [of numbers] . . . you must interpret the string as branches." Here we see an algorithm generate a set of numbers, which is then interpreted by a computer: A dataset becomes an image.

A → I[A]F

Sympodial branching - cyme

Network and Visualization

The very nature of networks and their uses change how we think about time and distance, our relation to each, and, inevitably, our approach to representing ourselves in these dimensions. The birth of the twentieth century saw a multitude of discoveries that would change the nature of time, space, and perception, and provoke artistic responses. Einstein's theory of relativity and Heisenberg's uncertainty principle annihilated previous conceptions of a fixed, predictable grid of time and space; Sigmund Freud's notions of the unconscious mind showed that we were not in control of our thoughts; advances in communication and travel networks changed our relation to the physical surface of the globe.

In the visual world, the invention of photography in the mid-nineteenth century (and its network of replications) freed painting from verisimilitude and gave rise to stronger interpersonal, emotional appeal. Impressionist landscapes were facilitated by the artists' abilities to travel by rail to the countryside and record their fleeting impressions of nature. The Japanese Ukiyo-e woodblock print recorded and reproduced artists' travels across the countryside bringing images from the "floating world," to an increasingly mobile public that was already engaged with the transitory nature of existence. The later developments of Cubism and Futurism came with an understanding that both speed and time changed the position from which everyday people—and by extension the artist—could interpret an object. Rail travel offered the city-dwelling painters travel to the countryside for the day to paint, as the Barbizon School painters did, and to observe the landscape rushing past them from the window of the train.

A great age of exploration was brought into the living room of the bourgeoisie through the eyes of the itinerant photographers and their ability to travel the world, to witness faithfully the great natural and human-made wonders of the globe, and to bring them back to eager audiences. The camera, which enabled observation to be recorded and also disseminated allowed everyone to collect a cabinet of curiosities.

Claude Monet and J. M. B. Turner, in their nineteenth-century depictions of the railroad, conveyed a dazzling impression of this new technology as a spectacle. Ukiyo-e artists were fond of creating series of prints that considered, say, Mt. Fuji in thirty-six views—an acknowledgment that a single instant or image is not sufficient to fully understand a scene. Later, Cubist painting technique responded to the new speed of the railroad by portraying the object from many points of view simultaneously, moving the spectator around the object. The Futurists, on the other hand, saw that one actually perceived things differently as one sped past them on the train, anticipating or implying a feeling of kineticism.

In the computer, the imagery is a kinetic experience, as we can move any object and ourselves in any direction in real time. Both Cubism and Futurism understand intuitively what we now know: The networked organism is constantly moving. The computer need not imply movement: It can embody it. Viewers can navigate their way through the creative act, from video games to virtual sculpture to images that can shift and change over time.

An example from the world of medical imaging is the Visible Human Project, which, in 1991, digitized a human body, and gave viewers the ability to rotate this body 360 degrees, while simultaneously peeling away layers of skin, viscera, and musculature to reveal the underlying structures. Furthermore, the viewer was given the ability to "fly" through the cavities of the body. In the mid-1990s, choreographer Merce Cunningham popularized the choreographic software Lifeforms, which transforms the vocabulary of dance by allowing him and others to interact with the figure in new and unexpected ways. Whereas the digital network opens up new vistas across the globe, and even into the larger universe, so, too, have the spaces of the human body become new arenas for exploration.

B.C.E.

7000–3000 Cities begin to appear in Mesopotamia.

4500 Sailing ships are used in Mesopotamia.

3200 The wheel is invented, facilitating movement and trade.

3500 Horses are domesticated in Kazakhstan.

2350 Homing pigeons are used by Mesopotamian kings.

2300 Domestication of the horse by Indo-European speakers in Central Asia and Eastern Europe.

2000 Egypt establishes a courier system, the beginning of written communication from a distance.

1700 The first postal system is established in Babylon.

1300 The Shang Dynasty in China uses an elaborate drumming system to sound alarms.

1200 The Egyptian army uses homing pigeons to communicate in battle.

1000 Seafaring vessels are constructed that include a keel, hull, and stern.

900 The Zhou Dynasty in China establishes a postal system for government communication.

900 China uses smoke signals as a means of communication.

776 The first dated Olympic games are held in Greece. Pigeons are used to communicate news of the various events.

6th century Xenophon, in his *Cyropaedia* [8.6.17], notes that Cyrus, founder of the Persian Empire, has developed a system of interconnected post stations; riders carry messages from station to station, similar to the nineteenth-century Pony Express. The distance between posts was based on how far a horse could run without tiring. Cyrus uses this system to manage his empire, which spans nearly three thousand miles from the Aegean Sea to the Indus River. Confidential messages to Cyrus are sewn into the belly of a rabbit, and the rabbit is offered as a gift to the emperor. Herodotus notes that this is a precursor to the envelope.

500 The Greeks develop an elaborate communication system using smoke signals, fires, trumpets, and loud noises.

500 A courier system develops in Persia using horses to carry messages long distances.

490 The news of the Athenian victory over the Persians is carried by messenger from Marathon to Athens, a distance of approximately twenty-six miles. The modern marathon footrace commemorates this.

4th century In Greece the position of keryx–a personal messenger who operates within and between cities–is developed. Hermes is the keryx of the Olympian gods.

3rd century Chinese couriers travel as far as Persia.

chronology: circuit

200 The Silk Road is established, connecting Asia and Eastern Europe.

146 A complex torch-signaling system is employed in Greece.

50 The European Amber Route emerges, with amber traded from northern Europe to northern Italy.

C.E.

45 Saint Paul begins his missionary journeys to spread Christianity.

circa 200 The earliest Christian pilgrimage to Jerusalem takes place. Pilgrimages become increasingly popular in the Middle Ages; in addition to local shrines, the most popular pilgrimages are to Rome, the Holy Land, and Santiago de Compostela in Spain. Often composed of elaborate systems of support, pilgrimages account for a major source of travel in the Middle Ages. Pilgrimages are also fundamental to Buddhism, Hinduism, and Islam.

313 Emperor Constantine allows Christianity into the Roman Empire after his conversion in 312.

476 The fall of Rome and the final blow to the Roman Empire. After the fall of the Roman Empire, its system of roads falls into disrepair.

650 Muslim caliphs in Persia establish a regular carrier pigeon system.

900 Over 1,000 courier stations are used as part of an elaborate courier system in China.

980 Norse settlers reach Greenland and shortly thereafter land in North America.

1154 Al-Idrisi, a Muslim geographer living in Spain, creates a world map.

1280 Kublai Khan founds pony courier system in China.

1346 The beginning of the Black Plague in Europe. Believed to originate from rats carried on Italian trading ships, the plague spreads rapidly throughout Europe via trade networks and through travel, killing thousands.

15th century The three-masted sailing ship is invented.

1441 Portuguese sailors capture African slaves and begin the Atlantic slave trade and the African diaspora.

1464 France establishes an official postal system.

1492 Christopher Columbus leaves Spain and lands in the Caribbean, marking the beginning of the European conquest of the Americas.

1500 The Chinese postal system begins delivering letters to private citizens.

1501 African slaves are brought to the New World.

1540 The horse is introduced to North America by Vásquez de Coronado. The horse facilitates movement and travel and supports existing trade networks.

1560 The Spanish create a maritime convoy system that periodically travels across the Atlantic trade routes in an attempt to deter piracy, which is on the rise.

1588 The English use signal fires to warn of the arrival of the Spanish Armada.

1627 A registered mail system is established in France in order to send money via post.

1661 The American colonies establish a postal system.

1662 England publishes its first newspaper, *The Weekly News.*

1663 Turnpikes, roads funded by tolls, are established in England.

1700 Emperor K'ang Hsi reigns (1661–1722) and communicates with officials through written documents known as palace memorials. This is another example of using written messages to control a large empire.

1755 A regular mail service between England and the North American colonies is established.

1759 John Harrison invents an accurate clock that allows mariners to compute a ship's longitudinal position, which greatly facilitates sea travel.

1765 The British Post Act makes it a crime to carry the mail at a speed of less than six miles per hour.

1769 James Watt patents the steam engine.

1780–1860s The Underground Railroad helps escaped slaves travel from the South to places of safety in the northern United States. Neither a railroad nor underground, it is a network of individuals who oppose slavery.

1784 England develops the use of a horse-drawn coach system to deliver mail. The system keeps to a strict timetable, which is made all the more difficult because time is not standardized in all the towns in England. Travel through England is made easier through the tarring of many roads.

1790 Claude Chappe d'Auteroche begins experimenting with a visual telegraph, which conveys information from tower to tower visually, an innovative means of communication for use throughout the newly formed French Empire. Each tower has a set of articulated arms that can move in various positions to indicate a letter of the alphabet. An observer in a nearby tower records the message and relays it to the next tower in the network. The arms are eventually outfitted with lamps to send messages at night. Although this visual telegraph system is used primarily for military and government purposes, it is also used for important civilian business, such as the transmission of lottery numbers.

1790 The British adopt a secret flag code. Using ten colored flags, the British Navy employs this code to communicate during battles.

1791 Projected light messages relay coded financial information from Philadelphia to New York.

1794 The North American colonies' postal service becomes widespread, employing letter carriers throughout its network.

1804 The first railroad powered by steam engine is built by Richard Trevithick near Wales, and is used to transport iron ore.

1814 Newspapers are printed by steam-powered presses at a rate of one thousand papers an hour.

1819 A sail-powered ship, the *Savannah,* crosses the Atlantic in twenty-six days.

1820 Hans Oersted discovers electromagnetism.

 chronology: circuit

1836 Samuel F. B. Morse builds his first functioning telegraph instrument.

1838 The *Sirius* makes the first transatlantic voyage using steam power only.

1839 Electric telegraph wires are set up in India by the British colonial government.

1840 The English standardize postal rates at one penny per letter.

1842 Alexander Bain invents the chemical telegraph.

1844 Samuel F. B. Morse sends the message "What hath God wrought" through the telegraph from Baltimore to Washington.

1853 The first pneumatic tube system is created at the London Stock Exchange.

1860 The founding of the Pony Express, which covers an 1,800-mile route from St. Joseph, Missouri, to Sacramento, California. It was made obsolete by the transcontinental telegraph system and went out of business in 1861.

1863 The world's first underground railroad opens in London.

1863 Fax messages are sent between London and Liverpool via typotelegraph.

1864 James Clerk Maxwell publishes a new theory of electromagnetism, which describes the shape of electromagnetic fields and how electricity and magnetism interact. Any change in an electrical or magnetic field starts a series of waves that radiate out into space; these electromagnetic waves travel at the speed of light. The only difference between electricity and light is the length of the wave.

1866 A steamship, the *Great Eastern*, lays a transatlantic cable between the United States and Great Britain.

Laying of the transatlantic cable

1866 Steamships make the transatlantic journey in seven days.

1869 The Union Pacific Railroad links the East and West coasts of the United States when the rail lines from each coast meet at Promontory Point in Utah.

1869 The Suez Canal opens, connecting the Mediterranean Sea and Red Sea. The canal helps to facilitate travel and trade between the Middle East and Europe.

1870 The first elevated subway opens in New York City. By 1894, work begins on an underground subway system. In 1902, the Interboro Rapid Transit Company builds additional lines. The subway is seen as a way to ease over-crowding in the city's older neighborhoods, where it is feared that Bolshevik agitators are fomenting revolution. Real estate developers who own land in the Bronx are also anxious to see inexpensive transportation from the places of work to land they can develop. By 1930, the system carries more than two billion passengers a year. The current shape of the city is tied to the shape of the subway system.

1870 Microphotographed messages are carried via pigeons during the Franco–Prussian war.

1876 Alexander Graham Bell demonstrates the telephone at the World's Fair.

1883 The Brooklyn Bridge opens on May 24 and is widely proclaimed the "eighth wonder of the world." Designed by John Roebling, the bridge inspires painters and poets, though Henry James characterizes it as a soulless mechanical monster. It links Brooklyn and Manhattan, allowing for the flow of goods and people. Roebling's research and development of braided steel cables is used in the construction of the elevator, which then allows the construction of the skyscraper. The concentration of skyscrapers in lower Manhattan is tied to the growth of the subway and the ability to move large numbers of people quickly.

1884 The invention of the Linotype allows movable type to be created by machine.

1885 Karl Benz invents a 1.5-horsepower automobile that is powered by petrol. A precursor to the Model-T, Benz's invention helps launch the automobile revolution.

1890 Herman Hollerith, founder of IBM, conducts the United States census using machines that encode information on punch cards. These cards form the basis of IBM's early computing machines.

1892 The telephone network moves from manual to automatic switching.

1896 Guglielmo Marconi begins experimenting with radio transmission: the wireless telegraph.

1900 Wilbur Wright builds his first glider.

1900 Reginald Fessenden broadcasts his voice over the radio.

1900 George Eastman's Kodak introduces the Brownie camera, which becomes available to the general public.

1901 The first transatlantic radio signal, from Poldhu, England, to Newfoundland, Canada, is sent by Guglielmo Marconi. The radio can transmit only morse code.

1902 The United States Navy installs radio telephones on all its ships. The Trans-Pacific telephone cable is established between Australia and Canada.

1902 Dr. Arthur Korn develops phototelegraphy. A precursor to the fax machine, Korn's invention allows users to send photographs via telegraph wires.

1903 Orville and Wilbur Wright successfully fly the "Wright Flyer," a glider with a propeller, at Kitty Hawk, North Carolina.

1904 Sir John Ambrose Fleming invents the vacuum tube diode, which helps to improve radio communication.

1906 The invention of automatic dial telephone switching by Fessenden.

1907 In the Soviet Union, Boris Rosing proposes some early theories on the possibility of television.

1907 The Breguet gyroplane becomes the first helicopter to fly successfully. Models and plans for helicopters can be traced back to Leonardo da Vinci in 1486.

 chronology: circuit

1908 Henry Ford begins mass producing the first modern gasoline-powered automobile, the Model T, in Detroit.

1914 Robert Goddard begins early rocket experiments in the United States.

1915 The electric loudspeaker is invented.

1918 Regular airmail deliveries are established between Washington, D.C. and New York City.

1919 The shortwave radio is invented.

1920 The world's first commercial radio station, KDKA-AM Pittsburgh, begins broadcasting.

1925 The Federal Aid Highways Act of 1925 creates the U.S. Highway System. The system facilitates travel across the U.S. through its standardization of signs and route numbers.

1925 The Leica camera is introduced. A small handheld range-finder camera, the Leica greatly improves the speed and ease of photography and is crucial to the advent of modern photojournalism.

1927 Charles Lindbergh becomes the first person to fly nonstop across the Atlantic Ocean alone. He flies the *Spirit of St. Louis* from Long Island to Paris.

1927 Philo Farnsworth assembles the electric television and transmits its first signal.

1928 The transatlantic telephone line is created.

1928 IBM begins using the 80-column punch card.

1934 The Federal Communications Commission (FCC) is established to oversee broadcasting in the United States.

1934 The Associated Press of the United States establishes a countrywide phototelegraphy network.

1935 As part of the New Deal, the Rural Electrification Administration is established and helps bring electricity, telephones, and other essential services to the rural United States.

1935 FM radio is introduced.

1936 Great Britain has its inaugural television broadcast.

1937 Chester Carlson invents the photocopier, using the xerography process.

1939 Transatlantic airmail is established on a regular basis.

1941 Using perforated 35mm film to store information, Konard Zuse's Z3 becomes the first computer controlled by software.

1945 Vannevar Bush proposes the memex as a means to reorganize and distribute information. He envisions that it can be operated remotely.

1947 Vacuum tubes are replaced with the invention of the transistor.

1948 Community access television (CATV) is established in Pennsylvania. For a monthly fee, CATV offers television access to remote rural homes.

1950 Phonevision, an early pay-per-view, is introduced.

1954 The Soviet Union launches *Sputnik*. Approximately the size of a basketball, *Sputnik* orbits the Earth in about 90 minutes. Designed to relay information about the Earth's upper atmosphere, *Sputnik* launches the race between the United States and the USSR to gain supremacy over Earth's sky.

1954 Color television begins to broadcast regularly in United States.

1956 Dwight D. Eisenhower approves funding for the Federal Aid Highways Act, which will improve and complete the nation's interstate highway system.

1957 Funding for the Advanced Research Projects Agency (ARPA), which will lay the groundwork for the Internet, is approved by Eisenhower.

1958 The United States launches *Explorer I*, the first U.S. artificial satellite. Later in the year, NASA (National Aeronautics and Space Administration) is created.

1959 Xerox creates and manufactures a photocopier.

1960s John Kemeny, computer scientist and philosopher, implements a system of time sharing for the computers at Dartmouth College. In 1963, the college makes computer literacy part of its liberal arts program and needs to accommodate a large number of users. The time-sharing system allows a user in one location, say a classroom, to access a computer in another location, say the computer building.

1960 *Echo 1*, a balloon in orbit, becomes the first communications satellite, reflecting radio signals to Earth.

1961 The Soviet Union launches the first human into space (Major Yury Gagarin) in the *Vostok I*. Later that year, the United States launches *Freedom 7* and the first U.S. manned spacecraft.

1961 FM stereo broadcasts are approved by the FCC.

1961 Leonard Kleinrock completes research that proves essential to the creation of the Internet. Published in 1964, *Communication Nets* reveals the basic workings of packet switching, a fundamental aspect of Internet technology.

1963 President Lyndon Johnson receives the first telephone call from a space satellite, AT&T's *Telstar*.

1963 Postal ZIP codes are introduced in the United States.

1964 Intelsat, an international satellite organization, is formed.

1965 *Early Bird*, the first Intelsat satellite, is launched.

1966 The telecopier, a modern fax machine, is sold by Xerox.

1968 The Soviet Union builds and flies the first supersonic passenger jet, the *Tupolev TU-144*.

1969 "One small step for man, one giant leap for mankind"–Neil Armstrong's remark as he becomes the first human to walk on the moon.

1969 ARPANET (Advanced Research Projects Agency Network), a network developed by ARPA and a precursor to the Internet, is established by the U.S. Department of Defense.

 chronology: circuit

1970 Research into fiber-optic technology begins, which will eventually allow the transmission of telephone signals around the world almost instantaneously.

1970 Barcodes are introduced. Information is encoded into wide and narrow lines, which translate the zero and ones of binary code to indicate the manufacturer and type of product.

1972 *Landstat 1*, the "eye in the sky" satellite, is launched. The *Landstat I* and its successors gather data from space that is transmitted back to Earth and is used to form color images of Earth's surface. *Landstat* data prove extremely useful for the prediction of weather patterns, droughts, forest fires, and crop management.

1975 The Concorde jet begins regular service from North America to England. With a cruising speed of Mach 2, this revolutionary jet travels from New York to London in a record time of three hours and forty-four minutes.

1979 The first cellular phone network is established in Japan.

1980 CNN, the first 24-hour news channel, begins broadcasting.

1980s New York pop group They Might Be Giants distributes their music through "Dial-A-Song," no more than their music recorded on an answering machine, anticipating downloadable music.

1981 The French introduce the TGV (Train à Grande Vitesse), a train that travels at a speed of 181 miles per hour.

1986 Desktop publishing begins with the introduction of Aldus PageMaker.

1987 NSFNET (National Science Foundation Network) replaces ARPANET.

1988 The longest undersea railroad tunnel (approximately thirty-four miles long) opens in Japan connecting Hakodate in Hokkaido with Aomori, Honshu Island.

1989 Tim Berners-Lee begins working on the World Wide Web, a set of protocols that allows for the publication and retrieval of information using the Internet.

1993 Mark Andreessen at the National Center for Supercomputer Applications releases Mosaic, a web browser.

1994 Approximately thirty-one miles in length, the Chunnel crosses the English Channel, connecting England and France.

1999 Amtrak introduces the Acela Express train, the first high-speed passenger train in the United States. Limited to the northeastern United States, the Acela travels at approximately 150 miles per hour.

2001 Satellite radio is introduced.

B.C.E.

28,000–10,000 Walls of caves are painted with figures of humans and animals. These caves are not used as living areas, but as places for social gatherings.

3000 Sumerian people bury tools and pottery with their dead.

2700 Imhotep builds the funerary complex at Saqqâra for King Djoser. Egyptian mythology posits an afterlife, to which the dead would bring the possessions from their tombs.

1270 Early encyclopedia complied by Syrian scholars.

715 Reign of King Hezekiah, who amasses riches in his treasure house (II Kings 20:12–19)

7th century The institution known as the library has its roots in ancient Mesopotamia. The unearthing of the palace of Ashurbanipal reveals thousands of clay tablets, each bearing stamps of ownership. Catchwords reveal that a well-developed cataloging system is in existence.

575 Jewish scholars begin organizing the books of the Hebrew Bible.

4th century Aristotle lays out the epistemological basis in the West for the division of knowledge into areas.

4th century The earliest written record of the Hindu epic, *The Ramayana*. Although codified in Sanskrit, *The Ramayana* is part of a sacred mythic tradition and has thousands of different versions depending on the region, village, and narrator.

350 Early cookbook appears in Greece.

350 The Athenian Speusippus, nephew of Plato, attempts to collect all human knowledge in one tome.

335 Aristotle founds the Lyceum in Athens—a school and research center devoted to teaching logic, metaphysics, and other topics.

284 Demetrius Phelereus founds a library at Alexandria, inspired by the Library of Athens, which will be maintained by a succession of Egyptian rulers until it is destroyed by civil war late in the third century C.E. It is believed to have held 40,000 volumes and established the Alexandrian canon of Greek poets. A bibliography is created, and the library is responsible for dividing the work of the poets into "books," probably the length of the scrolls on which they were recorded. Envisioned as a universal library, it attempts to collect all the significant texts and works in existence.

239 Lu Pu-Wei, minister of the state of Ch'in, invites scholars from across China to his estate in Wei. He then asks his guests to record all they know in a collection of volumes that contains more than 20,000 words.

2nd century The Rosetta stone is carved. Written in Egyptian hieroglyphics, Greek, and demotic (a cursive form of Egyptian hierogylphics), the Rosetta stone later provides the key to unlocking and translating Egyptian hieroglyphics.

105 The first technical college is founded in Alexandria.

chronology: collections

1st century Liu Hsang compiles a bibliography, a catalog, of Chinese literature.

39 Rome establishes a public library.

77 Pliny the Elder, a Roman administrator, writes his *Natural History*, comprising 2,500 chapters in thirty-seven volumes. His notions of collecting specimens for observation would lay the foundation for natural history museums.

100 Tsai Lun (50 C.E.–121) invents fiber-based paper.

540 Cassiodorus, a Roman monk, founds the monastery Vivarium, where he preserves many works of Christian and pagan authors. He attempts to persuade his monks not only to study sacred works but to copy them as well. He also compiles one of the earliest guides to libraries, a work known as *Institutions*. It lists manuscripts for understanding the Bible and others for understanding the liberal arts. The guide circulates throughout Europe for hundreds of years and is probably decisive in drawing attention to authors whose books might otherwise have perished.

600 Two types of encyclopedias come into being in China. The *Ch'u hsüeh chi* (*Manual for First Steps in Learning*) is analogous to what we think of today as an encyclopedia: a collection of articles on a wide range of subjects. Ou-yang Hsün compiles the *I-Wen Lei Chü* as a study guide. His work contains choice quotations from literature to help candidates with application essays for the civil service examination.

716 The Hebrew and Christian Scriptures are compiled in the *Codex Amitianus*.

8th century Arab philologists collect bits of Arabic writing in order to better understand obscure passages of the Koran.

9th century The caliph al-Ma'mun founds the Bayt al-Hikmah (House of Wisdom) in Baghdad, where Greek texts are collected and translated into Arabic. This early library nurtures the great Arab thinkers of that era, including al-Khawarizmi, who develops the algorithm.

983 Chinese statesman compiles the *T'ai-p'ing yü-lan*, a collection of abstracts.

1000 The beginning of the Great Zimbabwe civilization. At its peak in the thirteenth century, Great Zimbabwe's capital contains almost 20,000 people. A thriving cultural center in southern Africa, Great Zimbabwe becomes a center for learning, scholarship, and rich cultural activity.

1068 Cairo's Fatimite Library is destroyed by invading Turks.

1125 *The Pi-yen lu*, or *The Blue Cliff Records*, is compiled by Yüan-wu in China. Although containing only 100 zen koans, Yüan-wu's work is one of the best printed collections of Buddhist koans.

1126 A large fire in Korea destroys the Royal Library, containing thousands of books and manuscripts.

1151   Paper arrives in Spain from China. Previously, texts were written on a variety of materials including vellum, parchment—both forms of animal skins—and papyrus, a reed, all of which were more expensive and less durable than paper.

1253   First college library founded at the Sorbonne in Paris. From the thirteenth century on, with the rise of the universities, a lay book trade emerges to copy and distribute new kinds of literature and scholastic, civil, and canon law. Private libraries rise among the nobility, as symbols of status and power.

1321   Dante completes work on his *Comedia*, later named *The Divine Comedy*. This was the first work of literature written in Italian rather than in Latin, making it available to a wider audience.

1362   Petrarch plans a national library in Venice, but nothing comes of it.

1368   The Bibliothèque Nationale is initiated when Charles V moves his private collection into the Louvre. By 1373, the library contains over a thousand volumes.

15th century   Sankore mosque is built in Timbuktu as part of the Mali Empire in Africa. Sankore mosque becomes the center of a rigorous and highly developed Islamic educational system in Africa. Often called the "University of Timbuktu," the loosely structured system pairs students with imams, or Muslim masters, in different schools. Although the primary focus of study is the Koran, the approximately 25,000 students also study a wide range of subjects from astronomy and mathematics to history and medicine.

15th century   The town library in Germany is housed in the church. Most rulers thereafter become competitive in expanding their libraries. The Gutenberg press has transformed the notion of collecting books, and private libraries appear. The early collectors have very few ways of organizing their collections short of putting them in cupboards. A typical papal library in the Middle Ages such as that at Avignon has only a few hundred books. By the late 1960s the British Museum accessioned in excess of 130,000 volumes per year; today the Library of Congress holds over 115 million volumes. Thus, the major issue of libraries is their growth and size, which has a relation to the expansion of knowledge over the centuries.

1410   Emperor Chu Ti compiles the largest encyclopedia ever, consisting of more than 11,000 volumes totaling nearly one million pages. It takes two thousand scribes to copy the work into three editions.

1453   Invading Turks destroy most of the Constantine Library.

1455   Johannes Gutenberg prints his forty-two-line Bible. He brings together many existing technologies—paper, ink, metallurgy, sculpture, and the screw press—to make printing possible. From this point on, the number of books available expands at a terrific rate.

chronology: collections

1484 Early sea manuals appear in Portugal and contain detailed charts and tables to help sailors navigate and determine latitude.

16th century Li Shih-chen compiles the *Pen-ts'ao kang-mu* (*Great Pharmacopeia*).

1503 Pope Julius II della Rovere begins the Vatican Museums.

1545 Conrad Gesner of Zurich writes the *Bibliotheca Universalis*, listing 1,800 works by author, with annotations and opinions about the quality of each entry. A doctor and lecturer by trade, his early writings include a book on the virtues of milk, and in 1548 he publishes *Pandectarum sive Partitionum universalium Conradi Gesneri*, an attempt to compile all current knowledge in twenty-one books. He would die after having written nineteen.

1559 Pope Paul IV's *Index of Prohibited Books* condemns Eramus and other writers' works.

1603 Federico Cesi, the Duke of Acquasparta, founds the Academy of Lynxes, the first modern scientific academy.

1604 Containing about 3,000 words, Robert Cawdry's *A Table Alphabeticall* is the first English dictionary.

1620s Cassiano dal Pozzo (1588–1657), a Jesuit priest and scholar, begins collecting drawings, manuscripts, and watercolors for his *Paper Museum*. Containing thousands of documents and illustrations, the *Paper Museum* becomes an exhaustive archive of scientific knowledge.

1626 Le Jardin des Plantes, Paris's first botanical garden, is established by Louis XIII.

1638 Hortus Botonicus Amsterdam is established in Holland. One of the oldest botanical gardens in the world, the garden serves as an herb and medicinal garden for local physicians and pharmacists.

1683 The Ashmolean Museum is founded in Oxford, England.

18th century The Enlightenment seeks to make learning simpler and less burdensome, and the concept of the public library is initiated, its contents limited to "useful" books. Other books might readily be discarded, and in many cases the ones thought not to be useful are destroyed. Libraries come under control of elitism; private libraries preserve the "unuseful," which may in fact be useful. The French Revolution secularizes ecclesiastic libraries as well as encouraging public patrician collections.

1731 Benjamin Franklin founds the Philadelphia Library Company, a subscription library, which provides access only to members.

1732 Franklin begins publishing *Poor Richard's Almanac* (1732–1758). Written under the pseudonym Richard Saunders, Franklin's almanac, like others produced at the time, contains a calendar, weather predictions, astronomical charts, and miscellaneous data. *Poor Richard's Almanac* was a best-seller in the American colonies.

1735 Start of the reign of the Emperor Ch'ien-lung, who had a collection of over a million objects. Smaller objects were often placed in treasure boxes, often microcosms of the entire collection—holding old and new objects, objects from far and near—that is, the reaches of the empire in both time and space. "All objects are accorded the same treatment, be they authentic relics of antiquity or copies of masterpieces of calligraphy. Implicit in this ordering of works of art is the value system which puts the secondary function of art objects—as possessions to please the owner—on an equal footing with or above their value as expressions of the human spirit."[8]

1751 Publication of *Encyclopédie*, or *Analytic Dictionary of Sciences, Arts, and Trades,* which had been compiled by philosopher Denis Diderot and mathematician Denis Jean d'Alembert under the direction of publisher André le Breton. It lays out a comprehensive philosophy of the branches of knowledge, postulating that there is nothing that cannot be reasoned—the cornerstone of Enlightenment philosophy. Seen as an attack on the Church, it is widely condemned by conservative religious and government officials.

1753 The British Library is established in London.

1755 Samuel Johnson publishes his dictionary, *A Dictionary of the English Language.* Although not the first dictionary, Johnson's exhaustive volume becomes the model for subsequent dictionaries such as the *Oxford English Dictionary* (*OED*).

1756 Beginning with the collection of Sir Hans Sloane (1660–1753), the National History Museum in London is founded. Containing everything from dried plants and snakes to skeletons and books, Sloane's museum becomes one of the first natural history museums in the world.

1759 The Royal Botanical Gardens are founded in Kew, England.

1768 The first volumes of the *Encyclopedia Britannica* are published.

Late 1700s Napoléon himself envisions the universal library, the Bibliothéque Nationale, which manifests a wholesale requisitioning of all volumes that it does not own. This vision becomes the idea for the national libraries of the nineteenth century in the West.

1793 The Revolutionary government opens the Louvre, once a private museum for the French royalty, and its collections to the public.

1798 Lithography is invented by Alois Senefelder. Employing large stones and grease-based ink, Senefelder initially prints sheet music. Lithography is quickly adopted and used in printing book illustrations, posters, and artists' prints.

1800 The Library of Congress is established. Initiated by President John Adams, it began as a legislative library for members of Congress. Believing that the library and American legislators need more than legal books to nourish a grow-

 chronology: collections

ing democracy, Thomas Jefferson later expands the role of the library during his presidency to include a wide range of books in many different languages.

1806 Noah Webster publishes the first American English dictionary, *A Compendious Dictionary of the English Language*.

1812 Jacob and Wilhelm Grimm publish the first volume of *Kinder und Hausmärchen* (*Children's and Household Tales*), a collection of eighty-six folktales and stories. The second volume is published in 1814.

1814 The Library of Congress is burned down by invading British troops.

1828 London Zoo becomes one of the world's first scientific zoological collections, opening its doors to the public in 1847.

1846 The Smithsonian Institution is founded in Washington, D.C.

1851 The first World's Fair in London gathers the latest inventions and cultural offerings from around the world.

1855 John Bartlett publishes the first edition of *Familiar Quotations*.

1859 Chartered under the Philadelphia Zoological Society, the Philadelphia Zoo becomes the first zoo in the United States.

1870 The Metropolitan Museum of Art in New York is founded.

1872 The great treasures of the Tokyo National Museum, founded in the late nineteenth century, come from shôsôin repository, which consisted of the emperor's personal belongings dedicated to the great Buddha, and implements of the temple Tôdai-ji. Detailed descriptions were given in scrolls noting these donated objects on the death of Emperor Shomu in 756 C.E.

1880s Andrew Carnegie uses his wealth to endow countless libraries and educational facilities.

1882 Cornell University acquires the Reuleaux Collection of Kinetic Mechanisms from Franz Reuleaux (1829–1905). Considered the father of kinematics, Reuleaux was also a mechanical engineer, collector, and expert on the modern design theory of machines. Containing over 200 machines, Reuleaux's collection not only is one of the largest collections of nineteenth-century kinetic machines in existence, it represents Reuleaux's systematic attempt to categorize and catalog the language of machines.

1884 The Pitt Rivers Museum is founded in Oxford, England, following a donation by Lt. General Pitt Rivers of his collection of anthropological and ethnographic objects from around the world.

1887 Montgomery Ward begins distributing its 500-page catalog. The Sears-Roebuck catalog follows shortly thereafter, in 1895. Exhaustive in scope, these catalogs offer a virtual mall at their customers' fingertips.

1893 The Field Museum is founded in Chicago to house the biological and anthropological collections displayed at the Fair.

1894 Paul Otlet and Henri la Fontaine obtain a copy of Melvil Dewey's Decimal Classification system and resolve to set up an International Institute of Bibliography. They enter 400,000 items into their Universal Bibliographic Repertory, whose purpose is to contain an international bibliography stored on three- by five-inch cards.

1895 Otlet and la Fontaine found the International Institute of Bibliography (IIB).

1900 The first volumes of the *Oxford English Dictionary* are published. Beginning in 1857, Professor James Murray of Oxford University oversees the compilation and writing of the *OED*. Compiled from thousands of public submissions, the dictionary represents a unique and exhaustive effort to archive the entire English language.

1906 The first edition of the Yellow Pages is published.

1906 Paul Otlet establishes the Universal Iconographic Repertory.

1912 The Universal Iconographic Repertory contains 250,000 items.

1913 The first list of most popular songs is published by *Billboard* magazine

1919 Otlet and la Fontaine found the Mundaneum in Belgium. By 1934, they have collected more than fifteen million entries.

1926 Book-of-the-Month Club starts. Its slogan: if you have a mailbox, you can have a library.

1928 The *Oxford English Dictionary* is completed.

1929 The Museum of Modern Art in New York opens to the public.

1931 Irma Rombauer self-publishes *The Joy of Cooking*. In the years to come, *The Joy of Cooking* becomes a definitive compendium of American cooking and cuisine.

1948 Alfred Kinsey publishes *Sexual Behavior of the Human Male*. In 1953, he publishes *Sexual Behavior of the Human Female*. Compiled from years of interviews, the results of both books shock the largely conservative American public.

1955 The first edition of *The Guinness Book of World Records* is published.

1960s Ted Nelson develops his Xanadu hypertext system that although visionary, is never completed. The system is planned to be a compendium of all human creative endeavors—writing, photography, film, music, and so forth—and to offer all users universal access through a web of hypertextual links. Authors would be paid a small fee, which would be charged to the users each time they accessed a work. Thus, more popular artworks would earn the authors more money.

1963 The Musical Museum is established in London, England, by Frank Holland. Holland's unique museum houses hundreds of automatic musical instruments from all ages.

chronology: collections

1971 Michael Hart begins Project Gutenberg at the University of Illinois. Deciding that the greatest value of computers is not computing but storage, he sets a goal of distributing free electronic versions of texts that are in the public domain. To date, the project has scanned nearly three thousand books, including the Bible and the complete works of Shakespeare.

1987 Tufts University founds the Perseus Project, an evolving digital library of the ancient world. It contains the full text of thousands of works from Greek and Roman antiquity through the Renaissance, as a means to "connect more people through the connection of ideas."

1990 The Human Genome Project (HGP) is initiated by the DOE Human Genome Program and the NIH National Human Genome Research Institute (NHGRI) in an effort to uncover the estimated 35,000 human genes and their sequencing for biological study.

1990 The second edition of the *Oxford English Dictionary* is published. It is now available on CD-ROM.

1993 John Mark Ockerbloom at Carnegie Mellon University starts the On-Line Book page, a Web bibliography of more than 10,000 free online books.

1994 Established by Steven Spielberg in Los Angeles, the Survivors of the Shoah Visual History Foundation documents and archives thousands of hours of interviews and testimonials of Shoah survivors. The vast digital archive preserves over 50,000 recorded interviews drawn from survivors and witnesses.

1998 The Open Directory Project (ODP)—maintained by a loose community of volunteer editors, or "net citizens"—is one of the largest human-edited directories of the Internet and World Wide Web. Unlike search engines, ODP offers an unprecedented effort to edit and catalog the voluminous contents of the WWW.

2001 A working draft of the Human Genome Project is published in *Science* magazine. Although only a draft, the complex sequencing of DNA provides a veritable instruction manual for the workings of the human body. By providing detailed instructions and information on our genetic makeup, this revolutionary information not only allows us to understand ourselves even better, but also opens new doors of scientific inquiry and investigation.

2002 The Bibliothéca Alexandrina opens in Alexandria, Egypt. Connected with Alexandria University, the library includes a planetarium, conference center, school, and museum. Reviving the global vision of knowledge fostered by Alexandria's ancient library, the new Bibliothéca Alexandrina updates and expands on this tradition and carries it forward into the digital age.

B.C.E.

10,000 The shaman explores society's relation to the world through rites that include music, dance, and painting.

3500 Pictographic writing systems develop in Mesopotamia.

3000 Egyptian hieroglyphic writing system is developed.

3000 Chinese shadow puppet theater is developed.

2000 Chinese pictographic writing system is developed.

1027–256 (Chou Dynasty) The classic period of Chinese culture produces a book of odes, the *Shih-Ching*, which implies the use of drums, bells, and music as a part of the celebration of agricultural harvesting. It will lay the basis for Confucian philosophy in the middle of the first millennium.

540 The development of Greek drama—incorporating the actors, dancers, and a musical chorus into a narrative performance.

449–432 The Parthenon, the main temple to Athena in the city of Athens, is constructed as part of the Acropolis. Architecture, dance, painting, and song are combined in rites that reinforce the sense of community.

100 Posters are used in ancient Rome.

100 Mayan civilization adorns pyramids with elaborate wall paintings, depicting local mythology and ritual practices.

C.E.

5th century to 15th century During the Middle Ages, the cathedral comes to occupy the center of religious and social life in Europe. It combines music, text, spoken word, painting, stained glass, and incense.

7th century The mosque is the center of Islamic religious practice.

Late 8th century Picture books appear in Japan.

1150 Ankor Wat in Cambodia is completed. A massive city-temple complex, Ankor Wat becomes the religious, cultural, and civic center for the Khmer Empire in Cambodia.

1200 French troubadours sing love songs and tales of chivalry.

1200 Mystery plays are performed throughout Europe by itinerant troupes out of portable wagons that move from town to town. They portray biblical events—principally the lives of the saints—as a way of conveying morality through entertainment. A truly popular art, they are performed in the vernacular, rather than chanted in Latin. Interactive as well as mobile, performances are staged with laypeople and props found on location.

1418 Earliest surviving woodcut in Europe.

chronology: multimedia

1435 *Della Pictura*, written by Leon Alberti, describes the basic laws of perspective.

1450 Johann Gutenberg develops a printing press that uses movable type and revolutionizes printing.

1581 Catherine de Médicis commissions a ballet, the first choreographed dance set to music, for her daughter's wedding. The ballet, *Comique d'elle Reine*, which combines pantomime, dance, song, and poetry, is six hours in length.

1599 The Globe Theatre is completed.

Early 17th century Kabuki theater develops in Japan. Combining singing, mime, dance, and music, kabuki is one of the most popular forms of theater in Japan.

1646 Athanasius Kircher, a Jesuit monk, builds a primitive slide projector using a lantern.

1702 The first daily newspaper is published in England—the *Daily Courant*.

1789 Igniting a new entertainment fad, the first panorama is exhibited in London. Often depicting rural or historic scenes, panoramas consist of large paintings hung inside a curved room that engulfs the viewers' field of vision.

1807 The camera lucida is invented.

1817 Sir David Brewster invents and patents the kaleidoscope.

1823 Louis Daguerre exhibits a diorama in London. Enormously popular, the diorama contains a constructed scene (often based on historic events) that incorporats sounds and lights to heighten the drama and narrative.

1834 The invention of the zoetrope—using several drawings on a drum, the zoetrope gives the illusion of movement.

1834 Louis Braille creates raised text, allowing the blind to read.

1838 Charles Wheatstone describes the principles of stereoscopy to the Royal Society in London. By placing two similar images in a viewfinder, the stereoscope gives the illusion of three-dimensionality to the photographic image.

1839 Louis Daguerre publicly announces his invention of the daguerreotype—introducing photography to the world. Later that year, Henry Fox Talbot introduces his paper negative process—the calotype.

1839 The publication of magazines with woodcuts, text, and lithographs that are copied from daguerreotypes.

1842 *Illustrated London News* begins publishing text with engravings.

1849 Glass-plate photographic slides become available.

1851 Sir David Brewster introduces the Lenticular Stereoscope at the Crystal Palace in London. Queen Victoria is fascinated.

1870 P. T. Barnum's Grand Traveling Museum, Menagerie, Caravan, and Circus debuts. In 1887, Barnum collaborates with James A. Bailey and forms Barnum & Bailey's Circus—the "Greatest Show on Earth."

1877 Thomas Edison invents the phonograph.

1877 Eadweard Muybridge begins photographic experiments with motion. Photographing horses and people, Muybridge's experiments foresee the developments of motion pictures.

1880 Muybridge demonstrates his Zoopraxiscope, a zoetrope that projects his images in motion.

1881 Visitors to the Paris Exposition listen to opera over telephone wires.

1881 The halftone process, which allows the reproduction of photographs in newspapers and magazines, is invented.

1882 Étienne-Jules Marey invents the chronophotographic gun—which takes twelve photographs a second—and begins his photographic motion studies.

1886 The photographer Paul Nadar interviews the French scientist Chevreul on his hundredth birthday. Using still photographs of the interview to accompany the transcribed text, Nadar creates a precursor to modern reportage and interviewing.

1888 The first motion picture camera, the Kinetograph, is invented by Edison and William Kennedy-Laurie Dickson.

1888 Phonographs become widely available.

1889 Edison and Dickson introduce the Kinetoscope, an improvement on the Kinetograph. They also introduce the Kinetophonograph, which synchronizes sound from a phonograph with images from a Kinetoscope.

1890 Theatrephone is introduced in France. For a small fee, subscribers can listen to live concert performances.

1890 The first jukebox appears.

1890 William Edward Green develops the kinematograph camera and projector— an early movie camera.

1895 Louis and Auguste Lumière create the first motion pictures. Georges Méliès also invents stop animation.

1896 The first comic book, Richard Felton Outcault's *The Yellow Kid*, is published by the *New York American* and sold for 5 cents.

1897 The *New York Tribune* publishes the first halftone photograph in a newspaper.

1907 Carl Hagenbeck creates the first zoo with simulated and constructed habitats in Hamburg, Germany.

1921 The word "robot" is introduced in Rossum's "Universal Robots," a play by Karel Capek.

1922 Revolutionizing concepts of time and narrative, James Joyce's *Ulysses* is published in Paris.

1925 John Logie Baird invents the mechanical television—an early predecessor to modern television.

1926 The invention of the Vitaphone system allows film and sound to be synchronized.

chronology: multimedia

1927 Philo Taylor Farnsworth invents a complete electronic TV system and transmits the first television image. Technicolor is also invented.

1927 Advances in film technology allow for the addition of sound to what had previously been silent film. Al Jolson's *The Jazz Singer* ushers in the era of the "talkie."

1928 Disney releases *Steamboat Willie*, Mickey Mouse's second short, and the first cartoon with synchronized sound.

1928 E. L. Lissitzky designs a multimedia exhibition for Pressa incorporating sculpture, drawing, graphic design, and painting.

1928 On September 11, "*The Queen's Messenger*," the first television drama, is broadcast from Schenectady, New York station WGY.

1933 Black Mountain College is founded. For the next twenty years, faculty members such as Josef and Anni Albers, Merce Cunningham, R. Buckminster Fuller, Robert Rauschenberg, and John Cage turn Black Mountain College into a radical center of artistic production and interdisciplinary experimentation.

1936 *Life* magazine debuts.

1938 *Superman* ushers in the golden age of comic books.

1940 Peter Goldmark invents modern color television.

1941 Although delayed by World War II, NBC and CBS launch the first commercial stations. Television enters the home, allowing moving images and sound to be viewed outside of the theater for the first time .

1945 Vannevar Bush proposes the memex, the memory extender, a personal computer–like device that would store and play back images and text.

1947 Edwin Land introduces the Polaroid camera.

1951 Computer flight simulator.

1952 *Bwana Devil*, the world's first 3-D film, is released.

1952 Cinerama's wraparound screen alters movie goers' visual experience.

1952 John Cage debuts "4'33"." One of the most important pieces of twentieth-century avant-garde music, the piece involved the pianist silently sitting in front of the piano for four minutes and thirty-three seconds.

1956 Bell Telephone Laboratories begins testing the Picturephone.

1956 Morton Heilig invents Sensorama Simulator. Through the use of sounds, motions, smells, and breezes, Heilig's arcade-style console simulates such experiences as riding down a city street on a motorcycle or watching a belly dancer perform.

1961 Ivan Southerland develops Sketchpad, a computer interface that uses windows, icons, and a graphical user interface.

1961 Steve Russell writes the computer game Spacewar! on a PDP-1 mainframe computer, the first to use a cathode-ray tube (CRT) screen and a typewriter keyboard rather than punch cards. The game is distributed as freeware and very likely reaches every research computer in the United States. It reaches the arcades as Computer Space in the 1970s.

1961 Smell-O-Vision debuts.

1963 The introduction of CAD (Computer-Aided Design).

1963 Nam June Paik's first solo exhibition, "Exposition of Music–Electronic Television," a video-television sculpture, is displayed in Germany.

1965 Super-8 film becomes available.

1965 Douglas Engelbart develops the computer mouse, which links the position of the cursor on the screen to human movement.

1965 Ted Nelson coins the term "hypermedia."

1969 Alan Kay builds a model of his Dynabook, a tablet-sized computer with a graphical interface (previous interfaces had been all text). He refines his vision at Xerox's Palo Alto Research Station, including his idea for Smalltalk, a program that would allow users to create on their own.

1970 Building on the legacy of the panorama and Cinerama, the first multiscreen IMAX film is displayed at the Expo '70, Osaka, Japan.

1970 *I Seem to Be a Verb* is written by R. Buckminster Fuller.

1971 Steina and Woody Vasulka found *The Kitchen*, a multimedia performance space in lower Manhattan.

1972 Pong, the first home computer game, becomes available.

1972 The Magnavox Odyssey, the first home video game system, is introduced.

1972 Sony Port-a-Pak, the first portable video camera, is introduced.

1972 Laurie Anderson, a multimedia performance artist, performs one of her first pieces, entitled "Automotive." Like many artists during the mid-1970s, Anderson begins staging performance pieces that incorporate music, film, sculpture, and theater.

1972 Philips introduces the laser disc.

1973 Xerox creates a local area network called ethernet.

1974 The Altair, one of the first successful home computer systems, is released.

1974 Dolby surround sound is introduced.

1975 Bill Gates and Paul Allen reconfigure BASIC to run on the Altair 8800.

1977 The Apple II becomes the first PC to incorporate color graphics.

1978 Texas Instruments introduces the Speak and Spell game.

1978 MIT demonstrates the Aspen Movie Map, combining video, text, and sound.

1979 Sony introduces the Walkman, a portable cassette tape player.

1980 Atari 2600, a cartridge-based home video game, is released.

 chronology: multimedia

1980 Atari Pac-Man is released.

1981 MTV begins airing on cable television. The first video shown is the Buggles' "Video Killed the Radio Star."

1982 An early digital camera is developed in Japan.

1982 The first all-digital computer special effects are displayed in *Star Trek II: The Wrath of Khan*.

1982 Apple releases the Macintosh, the first truly multimedia-capable personal computer. It allows the user to manipulate text, sound, and images, and combine them through HyperCard (released in 1987), a hypertextual multimedia authoring system based on Smalltalk.

1983 Apple introduces LISA, the first commercially available computer with a GUI (graphical user interface).

1984 Compact Disc Audio is released by Sony.

1985 3-D television that does not require glasses is introduced in Japan.

1987 Apple releases HyperCard, a multimedia, hypertextual authoring system.

1988 Director, a multimedia design program, is released by MacroMind (now Macromedia).

1995 Disney's *Toy Story* becomes the first feature-length movie completed solely with computer graphics.

1995 The introduction of RealAudio allows streaming sound via the Internet.

1999 Napster debuts and allows users to download and share MP3 music files via the Internet.

CHAPTER TWO

METAFORA

gesture ▭ sound ▭ object ▭ image ▭ word

Creativity is the process of giving form to vision that is otherwise unrecognized by everyday perception. Creative expression was once limited by the tools that were used to translate imagination into physical form. In the computer, the creative individual is presented with tools that are constantly in flux. This chapter investigates creativity as a vehicle for the translation and transformation of ideas, and discusses the new forms of creativity facilitated by the computer: metafora.

Parthenon, Athens

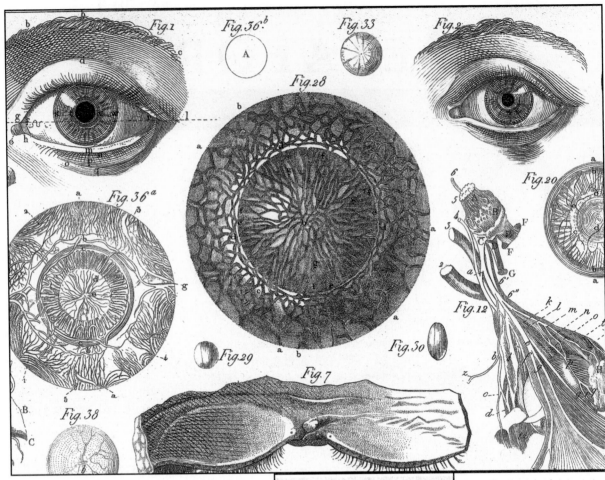

> *The activity of art is based on the fact that a man receiving through his sense of hearing or sight another man's expression of feeling, is capable of experiencing the emotion which moved the man who expressed it.*
>
> Leo Tolstoy, *What Is Art?*

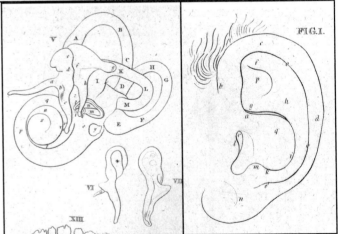

Anatomy diagrams

Creative expression is the process of conveying meaning from one person to another: It assumes there is a maker and a receiver. Metaphor is its primary vehicle. The word "metaphor" refers primarily to a figure of speech in which one idea or representation of an object is used to describe something else: "And what is love but a rose that fades?"[1] The root of "metaphor" is the Greek word metafora, which means to transfer and transform.

We have used the word "metaphor" to represent: (1) the basic element of creative formulation; (2) the new expressive possibilities that can be generated with the aid of the computer. Traditional creative forms are determined by their physical characteristics. Photography could be described in terms of how the camera and lens focus light onto film, or the ways photographic paper can be used to print an image. But the computer presents the user with a dazzling array of tools, and tools that change seemingly day to day. There is no physical substrate to describe.

We have chosen to discuss the creative potential of the computer in terms of the most basic level of communication: gesture, sound, object, image, and word. All of these forms have existed before and are given new meaning in the computer. Gesture is primary to the formation of metafora. Sound requires motion, but not necessarily a physical object, to form expression. Objects hold our ideas in physical form. Image is the graphic representation of idea, and words help us to communicate and to think. These elements have always interacted with one another in the formation of imaginative human endeavor, and all creative acts use one or more of these elements. Dance combines gesture with sound and often includes objects in the form of props. Painting uses movement to create image and objects, and music combines movement, sound, and words. All of these share the fact that they are a means of transferring creative intent from the creator to the audience. In the computer, the container for creativity is always shifting.

Boogie Down Productions is somewhat an experiment

The antidote for sucka MCs and they're fearin it

It's self-explanatory, no one's writin for me

The poetry I'm rattlin is really not for battlin

But if you want I will simply change the program

So when I'm done you will simply say "damn"

So this conversation is somewhat hypothetical

Boogie Down Productions attempts to prove somethin

I say hypothetical because it's only theory

My theory, so take a minute now to hear me

Boogie Down Productions, *Poetry*.

Metafora is a vehicle for carrying ideas.

The computer mimics existing forms (photography, for instance) and enables us to create meaning in forms we might never have imagined, such as hip-hop music or architectural structures such as Frank Geary's museum in Bilbao. Furthermore, it is the very fluidity of digital media and tools that has allowed continuous innovation, as in hip-hop, whereby each new rapper creates a "fresh new style." There is no canon of hip-hop, nor for that matter of digital media.

The computer allows us a new hub for the combination of these multimedia forms, whereby activities are no longer contained in discrete media. The realm of the circuit has made it possible to mix and transform a creative message into many permutations, because the creator is no longer limited by the physical forms of metafora.

In addition, the very speed of the computer—both in how it helps us formulate ideas and how we can deliver them—changes the creative act. On the most basic level, just think of how email has changed the nature of writing, and how the ease of sending a photograph with that message is further changing the illumination of even the most banal events in our lives.

Soon it will be hard to imagine any form of creative expression that is not affected by the computer, whether in opposition to it (as painting was changed by photography) or formed within it (as photography has morphed into digital imaging). The future holds the potential for forms of expression we have yet to imagine.

DJ Funkmaster Flex

Movement is a fundamental act of expression, perhaps the most fundamental. We cannot communicate without it. We resort to gesture when language fails. Everyone understands a shaking fist or a baby's pointing finger. Winston Churchill raised two fingers in a V for victory, buoying the British nation during World War II, while across the English Channel Adolf Hitler saluted with an upraised arm.

Not all movement conveys meaning. Although we may infer from a twitch that someone is experiencing a nervous tic, it is not an intentional act. Movement is metafora when it acts as a conduit between two people, when it acts to convey expression.

Like spoken language, gestures require a common understanding between the sender and the recipient of the message; sometimes a gesture means different things in different cultures. Touching your thumb and middle finger together means "OK" in the West, while in Arab countries, it suggests the evil eye. Such gestures depend on an arbitrary relationship established by culture. They are not, in the terms of Charles Peirce's theory of semiotics, indexical like a grimace. Indexical signs indicate the presence of something else: Smoke indicates fire, a grimace indicates pain. Systems of gestures can become languages, as in the case of highly structured, nonverbal American Sign Language, in which gestures have agreed-upon meanings by those who understand ASL.

Children's games often involve movement in ritualized form. Pat-a-cake is a series of rhythmic gestures, accompanied by a short chant. These interactive amusements form bonds between those who participate, be it a parent using the game to teach the rudiments of speech and rhythm, or children who amuse themselves with it. Mime is another ritualized form of movement, thought to have begun in ancient Greece as ribald comedy and at about the same time in India with the *bharata natya*, a Hindu dance accompanied by music. *Bharata natya* includes long sections of pantomime through a series of ritualized hand gestures. Whereas mime today is silent, dance implies music, and most music triggers some kind of movement and very often dance.

Certain formal dances are choreographed and follow rules, such as the waltz or the Country and Western contra, whereas others such as punk music's slam dancing are generally improvised. But it is the application of the elements of structure (see Chapter Four), most notably rhythm and style, that separates dance from spasm. By moving rhythmically, dancers align themselves to the beat of the music, joining others: Dance is a fundamentally social activity. The term "wallflower," a person who is socially awkward, comes from the sight of women waiting along the walls of dance halls, waiting to be asked to dance. A woman who was not asked was a wallflower.

If we accept that gesture and dance are the primal examples of expressive movement, further investigation reveals how they evolve in other forms. Think of the power of abstract painter Jackson Pollock as he thrusts paint onto a blank canvas or the precision of stroke in the hand of a calligrapher. The integration of eye, hand, and mind is an integral part of the intentional act of writing. Theater is an obvious extension of primitive dance and storytelling; and cities and their architecture grow out of the necessity to enable movement, even though they sometimes fail. We can see the beauty of movement in everyday acts or in the grace of Michael Jordan as he moves the ball to the basket.

Though the computer itself does not move (in most cases, although digital circuitry controls all manner of self-moving devices), it can depict movement, and it demands a physical dexterity. Interactions with early computers such as ENIAC required direct physical manipulation of the computer's wires in order to program it; later computers allowed interaction through a keyboard. The computer mouse, invented by Douglas Engelbart's Human Factors Research Center in 1965, transferred the motions of the user's arm into the virtual space of the computer screen. This electrification of motion is one of the great inventions of the twentieth century, as it enables us to convert human intention directly into the realm of the circuit.

Around the same time, an attempt to teach children computer programming used motion as a teaching tool. In the 1960s, Seymour Papert designed a programming language called LOGO. By the 1970s, the program had been adapted to run on personal computers, including the Apple II, and could control the actions of a robotic turtle attached to the computer. The child programmer could issue commands to the turtle by writing a program on the computer, using simple commands such as "forward 10" and "right 90," then running the program. These two commands would cause the turtle to move forward ten inches, then turn right ninety degrees. Repeating this sequence four times would cause the turtle to move in a square. There was also a pen attached to the turtle, so its motion could be used to draw shapes. Eventually, the turtle moved from the floor to the screen. The programs no longer moved a physical creature around the floor of the classroom, but a virtual turtle around the computer's screen.

Presently, there are a variety of devices that enable the user to interact physically with the computer. VR headgear and gloves interpret the motion of the users' head and hands, converting it into signals that the computer can understand. In most applications, the users' hands control their motion through a virtual space, whereas turning the head changes the view from the headgear, giving the impression that the user is immersed in the space. Motion capture devices, meanwhile, can be attached to every joint on a person's body and can record its motion. These are commonly used to animate figures in the computer for video games or animated films in which realistic human motion is needed.

The computer can simulate motion: Perhaps the most familiar is in video games known as POV or first person shooter, whereby the screen approximates the character's view. iD software's Doom was one of the huge commercial successes of the 1990s, spawning dozens of competing products. The scene is pulled past the players' point of view as they navigate this rudimentary **virtual reality**. These screen-based forms of entertainment are just a starting point. There is no telling what future digital environments might use as an interface to suggest motion.

Today, the vistas of cyberspace stretch before us like so much unexplored territory. Our motions through them and in them have the potential, if they are thoughtful, to create meaning through the ways we move, and so interact, with others.

Apple computer's mouse, c. 1984

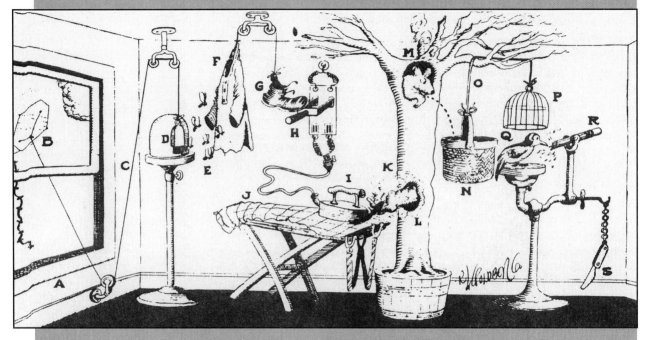

Rube Goldberg was a cartoonist and sculptor, best known for his comic strips that show elaborate contraptions to perform simple tasks. This is a pencil sharpener (note the woodpecker on the rotating perch).

James Seawright's House Plants, 1986, could flash its LEDs and move the flip disks on the domed plant in response to the level of light in the room.

The work of Kazushi Nishimoto, at his laboratories in Kyoto, Japan, illustrates the new potential of motion in cyberspace. His design of a wearable system of sensors allows a person to create and play music through the motion of his or her body, and to further share these impromptu performances with others over wireless networks. These so-called 'costunes' translate motion into electronic signals that can be used to control sounds in any space or across great distances. For instance, a DJ at a disco might be able to synchronize the beat of the music to the motion of the crowd.

Designer Tomas Egger used Lifeforms and Electric Image software to create a dancing robot for a music video.

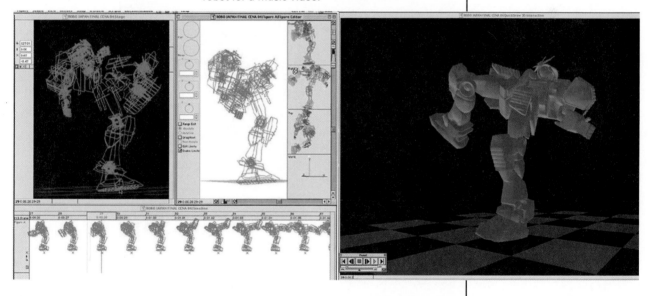

I taught her how to dance and all when she was a tiny little kid. She's a very good dancer. I mean I taught her a few things. She learned it mostly by herself. You can't teach somebody how to really dance.

J. D. Salinger, *Catcher in the Rye*

Photography, as exemplified by the work of Eadweard Muybridge, allowed a new appreciation of the act of motion through creative interpretation. These are Muybridge's photographs from the 1887 series "Animal Locomotion."

Portraying Movement

Many of the inventions of the nineteenth century were technologies of movement: Railroads moved people from country to city; telephones projected voices across a continent; film projectors brought entire worlds of static images to life. Photography, which was born in 1839, was a visual medium uniquely qualified to portray motion.

The realism of photography is heightened by the concept that the decisive click of the shutter stops movement, thus allowing us to observe that which we normally cannot—a splash of milk or a bullet piercing an apple. Eadweard Muybridge's photographic studies of animal motion began when he was asked to settle the question of whether all four of a horse's legs left the ground in a gallop. Scientists of the nineteenth and twentieth centuries continued to use photography to study motion, while artists such as Henri Cartier-Bresson and Garry Winogrand used photography to juxtapose the elements that passed before their eyes.

Motion pictures achieve the precision of the photographic moment in a repetitive sequence, allowing us to archive and study the nature of our movements through it over and over again. In the earliest films, the camera sat fixed on a tripod and recorded staged dramas—essentially plays. Eventually, directors realized that the camera could be moved to show action from multiple perspectives like those implied in Albert Einstein's theory of relativity or the Cubist painter's canvas.

The computer, arriving mid-century, enters into and influences a world in which information, images, and identities are in constant flux. There is no moment of stasis when working within the frame of the computer because objects can be scaled, rotated, or penetrated. This is especially apparent in scientific applications such as the program RasMol, which takes a description of a biological molecule and presents it on screen for a researcher to rotate, enlarge, and even "fly-through."

We declare that a new beauty has enriched the world's splendor: the beauty of speed. A racing motor car, its hood adorned with great pipes like snakes with explosive breath, a roaring motor car that runs like a machine gun, is more beautiful than the Winged Victory of Samothrace.

F. T. Marinetti, *The Futurist Manifesto*

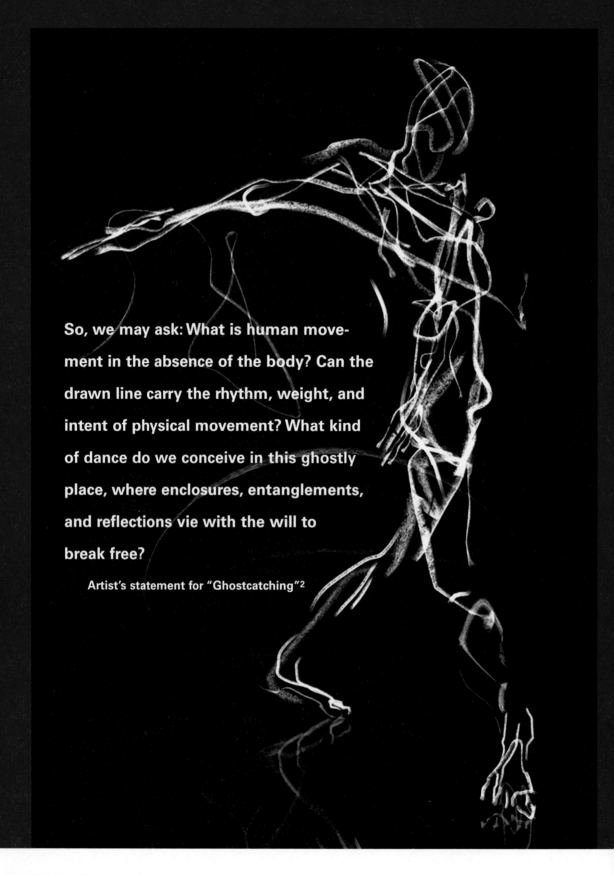

So, we may ask: What is human movement in the absence of the body? Can the
drawn line carry the rhythm, weight, and
intent of physical movement? What kind
of dance do we conceive in this ghostly
place, where enclosures, entanglements,
and reflections vie with the will to
break free?

Artist's statement for "Ghostcatching"[2]

Computer Dance

Contemporary choreographers have begun to use a new generation of computer tools to create dances in virtual realms. In 1998, computer artists Shelly Eshkar and Paul Kaiser collaborated with choreographer Merce Cunningham to create the work "Hand-drawn Spaces." The programmers provided Cunningham with virtual characters and a stage to create with. "The dancers appear as life-size drawings emerging from the darkness and moving in an apparently limitless three-dimensional space. Though the dancers are visible on three screens, they move through a much larger virtual area, and so travel in and out of the projected image, often traversing the spectators' space."[3] The following year, Eshkar and Kaiser helped Bill T. Jones create the work "Ghostcatching." Jones' motions were captured with motion sensors and used to animate wire frame figures in the computer, which were then drawn over in order to create abstract dancing figures. In both cases, the final product was not the result of the work of either the choreographer or the programmer alone, but instead of collaboration between all of the participants as creative interlocutors.

The computer potentially liberates dance and motion from the constraints of gravity. In video games, such as Sonic the Hedgehog and Super Mario Brothers, players are able to control the actions of avatars which can leap and soar to physically impossible heights, because their gravity is no more than an algorithm. Because motion in the computer is controlled not by the unchanging rules of the physical world but by infinitely malleable algorithms, a programmer can change a dance by literally changing the gravity in the computer simulation.

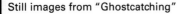

Still images from "Ghostcatching"

Bill T. Jones

Dancing and building are the two primary and essential arts. The art of dancing stands at the source of all the arts that express themselves first in the human person. The art of building, or architecture, is the beginning of all the arts that lie outside the person; and in the end they unite. Music, acting, poetry proceed in the one mighty stream; sculpture, painting, all the arts of design, in the other. There is no primary art outside these two arts, for their origin is far earlier than man himself; and dancing came first.

Havelock Ellis, *The Dance of Life*

The practitioners of zen Buddhism move toward enlightenment by sitting motionless.

The Sufi dervish meditates through motion—whirling and dancing.

THAI ELEPHANT ORCHESTRA

DAVE SOLDIER & RICHARD LAIR

The Thai Elephant Orchestra
performs on specially designed
instruments.

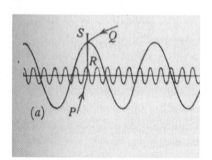

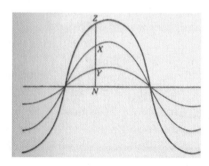

All art aspires to the condition of music.

Walter Pater, *Studies in the History of the Renaissance*

Music is a means of bringing order to chaos, and to "endow our highest moments of awareness with enduring form and substance."[4] In musical compositions, so long as we hear only single tones, we do not hear music. Listening, the act of deciphering sound, depends on the recognitions of the in-betweens of tones, of their placing and spacing, of the application of the elements of structure to noise. Anthropologist Franz Boas said that the two significant traits that distinguish man from other animals are the use of utensils and the organization of articulate speech—the use of sound to convey meaning.

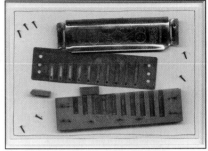

David Brown, *Harmonica Collage*, 1980

Marshall McLuhan wrote in *The Gutenberg Galaxy* that in preliterate societies, before the development of the alphabet or the written word, the ear was the dominant sense organ, not the eye: Hearing was believing. "The phonetic alphabet forced the magic world of the ear to yield to the neutral world of the eye. Man was given an eye for an ear." Writing, then printing, were two preeminent means of the development of Western culture. They were apprehended through the eye. McLuhan goes on to point out that "visual space is uniform, continuous and connected. The rational man in our Western culture is the visual man." McLuhan believed that electric technology returns us to the preliterate, previsual, aural world of our ancestors. We can be selective in the way we experience the visual image. Hearing, on the other hand, is less easy to control. Sounds are everywhere. Short of stuffing our ears with cotton, it is virtually impossible not to detect them.

Remember dancing in those electric shoes? Remember? Remember music and beware.

Anne Sexton
The Wonderful Musician

Audible vibrations (oscillations) include both noise and sound. The distinguishing factor is that the latter has communication purpose. Noise is random, although one person's noise may be another person's **Industrial Music**. Sound can be represented by sine waves; complex, but still relatively simple forms—such as notes played on musical instruments—can be represented by more complex harmonic curves, with numbers of harmonic tones or overtones superimposed on the fundamental tone. The complexity of a sound wave can become so great that no particular pitch can be discerned; white noise, so called by analogy with white light (a mixture of all frequencies, or colors, of visible light), is an example. In an age of media-driven information overload (what William Gibson calls "information sickness"), it has become increasingly difficult to be selective and turn the visual and aural noise around us into knowledge.

In his textbook on applied media aesthetics *Sight, Sound and Motion*, Herbert Zettl divides motion picture sound effects into two categories: literal and nonliteral. Literal sounds convey a specific meaning and refer to the source that produced them, such as a car crash. Nonliteral sounds are more abstract and are used to evoke feeling or mood, such as music. Certain sounds can cross into either category, depending on the context in which they are used. Literal sounds are referential or source-connected. Nonliteral sounds appear to be source-disconnected and do not produce literal visual images. When we hear a car crash, we envision the crunch of steel. A violin concerto should draw the listener's attention away

Ron Carter

from the instrument itself to a state of transcendence. When a violinist hits a wrong note, the spell is broken, and attention is brought back to the literal sounds of the violin.

The love of music is a fundamental feature of the human species and is found in every society; it is one of the things we do for pleasure alone. It is embedded in the complex workings of the human brain and the ways in which it comprehends and processes sound. The music instinct, our ability to organize and manipulate sound as a means of expression, is thought to predate the evolution of the homo sapiens. As the species evolved, music-making tools were among the first fashioned: Recent research indicates that our ancestors created musical instruments as early as fifty thousand years ago.

Music is not unique to human beings: Analysis of birds and whales indicates that their "singing" abides by the same laws of compositions as those we produce. For example, the humpback whale produces sounds that follow rudimentary rhythms (such as A B A B A) and range seven octaves.

Until recently, most music could be recorded in an allographic system of notation: The notes of its composition could be written in a score. Whereas musical notation produces a record of songs or composition that can be studied, modified, and replayed at a later date, notation refers only to what can be played on an instrument.

The writing of digital files can represent instrumental music along with any type of sound. This created forms of music such as Industrial and hip-hop, which are often produced without what we might call "traditional" instruments. Hip-hop relies heavily on sampling for its musical repertoire, and not traditional instruments. Sampling enables the musician to record a short bit of sound and play it back as if the sampler were an instrument. Rap artists have appropriated everything from drums and bass lines to environmental noise. "We did not come to make music, we came to destroy it," said Chuck D of Public Enemy, whose 1988 album *It Takes a Nation of Millions to Hold Us Back* brought sampling to a new level of artistic achievement. Digital music is not the trace of sound, as a recording is, but sound made into trace. It is not the sign of a sound, but a sound that has become sign.

Twenty-first-century music has been radically transformed by digital technology. We can see the beginnings of digital music in the 1960s and 1970s with the use of the electronic synthesizer to create musical tones, and the sampler to record short sounds and play them back as music. This technique was used extensively by early pioneers of hip-hop music such as Kool Herc, who extended the "break" (the part of a song where only the instruments played) by cuing up two copies of the record, playing one break, then switching to the second when the first was finished. He called this continuous, looping sound the break beat. Grandmaster Flash, an engineering student in the 1970s, improved the technique by building a device that would let him hear what was playing on one turntable while the other played simultaneously. These are among the pioneers who predate today's sampling and mixing with digital technology.

The contemporary music library is a pocket-sized device or laptop that stores digital music. The contemporary turntable is the laptop equipped with software such as Pro Tools that provides musicians a range of effects and ways to mix songs together that is entirely unlike any analog technology. Instead of hauling crates of vinyl records to a club, today's DJs bring their laptops filled with music and commercial or even custom-written software.

In the late 1980s, the musician Moby began his career spinning records at clubs in New York City, playing one song after another from vinyl albums, or mixing them together through analog stereo equipment. By 2001, he had released five albums of digitally produced music. Unlike a traditional musician, Moby uses no instruments, instead creating his music bit by bit (literally) in the computer. His songs consist of samples of other people's music, run through the computer and recombined to create an aural collage. A traditional CD contains a recording of a live musical performance (or several performances or takes mixed together in the studio). But Moby's music is not so much performed as it is assembled. The result is a music (or sound) that is entirely unique to the digital medium and sounds unlike anything before it. Moby and others such as hip-hop artists DJ Funkmaster Flex, DJ Spooky, Reflection Eternal can work this way because they are working with digital files. When ambient music pioneer Brian Eno wanted to repeat a piece of music, he literally had to construct a loop of magnetic analog tape and feed it into a tape player (as early hip-hop musicians physically had to manipulate the LP albums on turntables). Digital music artists need only make use of the computer's ability to replicate and combine.

Learning music in a conservatory is well suited to preserving existing musical forms, but is no longer necessary for musical innovation. The radical changes wrought by Louis Armstrong came about because he learned his craft on the street and in the saloons of New Orleans. Today, the heyday of jazz has passed; it is the new spontaneity of hip-hop music, taught and played in the streets, that captivates the youth who adapt and mutate the music.

Performance in the future is not likely to be the product of performers as we have come to know them. Rather, the future of creativity with sound may lie with the genius of a programmer, a composer of the dots and dashes of the digital realm, who has been freed from reliance on the musician.

Sound cannot exist without motion: A still object is silent.

Ours is a brand-new world of allatonceness. "Time" has ceased, "space" has vanished. We now live in a global village ... a simultaneous happening. We are back in acoustic space. We have begun again to structure the primordial feeling, the tribal emotions from which a few centuries of literacy divorced us.

Marshall McLuhan,
The Medium Is the Massage

In the early 1960s, the TX-0 computer "had an audio output: when the program ran, a speaker underneath the console would make a sort of music, like a poorly tuned electric organ whose notes would vibrate with a fuzzy, ethereal din. The chords on this 'organ' would change depending on what data the machine was reading at any given microsecond; after you were familiar with the tones, you could actually hear what part of your program it was working on."

Steven Levy, *Hackers*

Talking Heads

Whereas theater is primarily a verbal medium, film and television are visual (compare the monologues of Shakespeare's plays to the sparse dialog of today's movies). A news item that may have been given thousands of words in a newspaper is now reduced into a ninety-second spot, condensing the events of the world and removing us further from the word and the text in terms of its mediation of our language and thought. Who today really has time to read the newspaper cover to cover? Is it that we lack the ability to concentrate, or the fact that the television has conditioned us to think only about the surface of things?

Louis Armstrong

There is perhaps no better reaction of music to the hustle and bustle of the early twentieth century than in the jazz pioneered by Louis Armstrong. Gary Giddens noted: "He created modern time. The approach to time that was completely divorced from marching band time . . . . The rhythms are going to be changed in all kinds of ways but they're always going to proceed from where Armstrong created so that not only jazz but pop music, rock and roll, rhythm and blues, anything you want to talk about that has a modern rhythmic feeling goes back there. ... He makes rhythm as important as melody and harmony." It was his relaxed playing over the frenzied rhythm of his accompanists that suggested a response to the heyday of modern, industrial life.

In his 1927 recording "Hotter Than That," Armstrong's playing drifts away from rhythmic patterns, which stands in contrast to Johnny Dodd's more precise clarinet solo. Armstrong further plays with the rhythm with his scatting (singing nonsense syllables) in the piece, his placement of notes on the beat and silences off the beat, contrasting guitarist Lonnie Johnson's more strictly rhythmic playing. Armstrong's reach extends throughout the range of twentieth-century music, all the way to contemporary hip-hop music, which has as its main concern rhythm instead of lyrics or melody. If rock music tells you a story, hip-hop lets you feel it.

Ludwig von Beethoven

Beethoven's sketchbooks, many of which have been preserved, reveal a lot about his methods of work. The man who could improvise the most intricate fantasies on the spur of the moment took infinite pains in the shaping of a considered composition. In the sketchbooks, such famous melodies as the adagio of the *Emperor* Concerto or the andante of the *Kreutzer* Sonata can be seen emerging from a trivial and characterless beginning into their final form. It seems, too, that Beethoven worked on more than one composition at a time and that he was rarely in a hurry to finish anything that he had on hand. Early sketches for the Fifth Symphony, for instance, date from 1804, although the finished work did not appear until 1808. Sometimes the sketches are accompanied by verbal comments, perhaps as a kind of *aide-mémoire*. Sometimes, as in the sketching of the Third (*Eroica*) Symphony, he would leave several bars blank, making it clear that the rhythmic scheme had preceded the melodic in his mind. Some of the sketches consist merely of a melody line and a bass—enough, in fact, to establish continuity. But in many works, especially the later ones, the sketching process is very elaborate indeed, with revisions and alterations continuing up to the date of publication. If, in general, it is only the primitive sketches and jottings that have survived, it is because Beethoven kept them beside him as potential sources of material for later compositions. The working out of a musical composition in all its detail ceased to interest him once the piece had been completed.

The first movement of his Fifth Symphony, marked with allegro con brio, springs out of the rhythmic three shorts and a long (dot dot dot dash) that dominate the entire symphony. In the relaxation of the second theme, this rhythm does not slacken and is repeated. Beethoven achieves a contrast of colors in his changes in mood: The first movement is in a somber minor; the second, with its classic serenity, is in major; the third, save for a jovial trio, returns to the minor. And then the dark C minor is dispelled with the upsurge of the finale. The fourth movement expresses monumentality in its sonata form, to which Beethoven adds an ending that sustains the tension of what has gone before.[5]

Seymour Lipkin

bang

sound

If a tree falls in the forest, and no one is there to hear it, does it make a sound?

Often attributed to George Berkeley

In 1917, **Dadaist** Marcel Duchamp signed a urinal with the name R. Mutt, titled it "Fountain," and entered it in a gallery show. By doing this, he called attention not only to the beauty of the sculptural form of the urinal, the beauty inherent in the industrial form, but also to the sanctifying power of the gallery, which gives meaning to objects that they do not inherently have.

In the Renaissance, Michelangelo believed the process of sculpture was that of freeing the form (the eventual sculpture) from the rock. The difference between a rock (raw, unformed material) and a sculpture is the intention of the artist, the use of the rock as a metaphor to convey an idea or feeling.

Objects have the potential of creating a permanent record, whereas movement endures only in the memory of those who observe it. Likewise, sound endures only so long as it is being created, and there is someone to hear it. This profound question, posed by the philosopher George Berkeley in the eighteenth century, takes on new meaning when one considers the digital encoding of any creative act. Does the virtual world need a physical trace to exist?

We know that the digital file that encodes sound can be burned onto a compact disc, encoded onto a portable MP3 player, or even written in longhand (as zeros and ones) on a sheet of paper. Yet, these objects are only "carriers" for the encoded act. They are not the originals. In contrast, the spiritual importance of the Shroud of Turin depends on the fact that it is the original cloth that wrapped the body of Jesus Christ. Representations and copies can be made, but they are not equal to the original. Likewise, sound can be recorded either in analog form (as an old-style vinyl album) or in digital form. Analog information is hard to duplicate, but digital information is not. This is why piracy of music is so widespread in the digital age.

Much of what occurs in the computer is fleeting, in existence for no longer than a moment, changes in the voltage state of millions of microscopic switches. Computer-based creativity achieves permanence less as a traditional, stable object, than in its ability to transfer from one computer to another, much like a computer virus (think of the rapid spread and reach of the nimda or code red viruses). In Western culture, beginning with Giotto in the thirteenth century, paintings were principally representations of other objects: The frame of the painting was the metaphoric window frame; the canvas represented the scene beyond. The object of the painting was meant to be a mirage, a simulation of the process of human vision, a record of an actual or historical event, or even an allegorical event, one that never happened. In the nineteenth century, photography took the burden of representation from painting: Painting needed to change to survive. At the turn of the twentieth century, Modernist painters broke with the depiction of reality. Painters no longer painted representations of reality, but moved toward formalism and abstraction. Paint and brushstrokes themselves became imbued with meaning, and the painting was no longer a metaphor for vision, a window to another world, but an object to be looked at. It became an exploration into our fantasies, and the nature of paint and canvas became substance, cultural icons in and of themselves.

Photography democratized representation by allowing anyone to make an image, and became a window on the world for practically everyone. Because the image was so easily duplicated, the photograph itself had little value as a unique object.

MICROSOFT INTERNET EXPLORER, VERSION 5.0, AND SOFTWARE RELAT-
ED COMPONENTS.

END-USER LICENSE AGREEMENT FOR MICROSOFT SOFTWARE

IMPORTANT-READ CAREFULLY: This Microsoft End-User License Agreement
("EULA") is a legal agreement between you (either an individual or a single
entity) and Microsoft Corporation for the Microsoft software product(s) identi-
fied above which may include associated software components, media, printed
materials, and "online" or electronic documentation ("SOFTWARE PRODUCT").
By installing, copying, or otherwise using the SOFTWARE PRODUCT, you
agree to be bound by the terms of this EULA. If you do not agree to the terms
of this EULA, do not install or use the SOFTWARE PRODUCT. If the
SOFTWARE PRODUCT was purchased by you, you may return it to your place
of purchase for a full refund.

The SOFTWARE PRODUCT is protected by copyright laws and international
copyright treaties, as well as other intellectual property laws and treaties. The
SOFTWARE PRODUCT is licensed, not sold.

1. GRANT OF LICENSE. The SOFTWARE PRODUCT is licensed as follows:

* Installation and Use. Microsoft grants you the right to install and use copies
of the SOFTWARE PRODUCT on your computers running validly licensed
copies of the operating system for which the SOFTWARE PRODUCT was
designed [e.g., Windows(r) 95; Windows NT(r), Windows 3.x, Macintosh, etc.].

* Backup Copies. You may also make copies of the SOFTWARE PRODUCT as
may be necessary for backup and archival purposes.

* Components. Certain software components of the SOFTWARE PRODUCT
are subject to the following additional provisions:

DCOM95. You may only use copies of the DCOM95 component on
computer(s) for which you have licensed Microsoft Windows operating
system platforms.

NetMeeting. NetMeeting contains technology that enables applications to be
shared between two or more computers, even if an application is installed on
only one of the computers. You may use this technology with all Microsoft
application products for multi-party conferences. For non-Microsoft applications, you should consult the accompanying license agreement or contact the
licensor to determine whether application sharing is permitted by the licensor.

Software License

Software is generally sold as a license, not a tangible object.
Although you may take home a box from the store, it is not the CD
inside that you are paying for, but the right to use the software
encoded on the CD. When you purchase software, you do not
acquire an object so much as you enter into a relationship with the
program's creator, which gives you license to use the software.

Once an image is reproduced and disseminated to culture at large, it begins to take on iconographic meaning: representation of significant cultural values. Today, as objects, vintage photographs take on financial value.

Better design in the computer results from thinking less like graphic designers or painters and more like product designers, people who have to consider physical form and function, as well as movement and time. The control of processes on the computer is different than that in traditional two-dimensional design. It involves relationships that are neither flat nor linear and are always metaphors. Finally, and most importantly, the end result of the creative act on the computer is infinitely malleable: It is process. In the realm of the circuit, there is no longer the need for any physical substrate in the creative process, although it is not precluded.

Unlike our dealings with everyday objects, we have no direct experience with a corporal substance in the realm of the circuit; everything is mediated. What we see or experience in the circuit are merely interpretations of data by software (3-D modeling programs) and hardware (computer screen, virtual reality goggles). Objects in the computer are experiential; we cannot interact with them in the way we are used to interacting with physical objects: they have no tangibility, color, shape, or smell. We perceive them only as they are interpreted by output devices: monitors, speakers, VR headgear, and so on.

Diaz de la Pena, untitled, nineteenth century

Architecture is the moulding and altering to human needs of the very face of the earth itself.

William Morris

شنیدم که در دشت صنعا جنید / سگی دید برکنده دندان صید

زنخ بر سر از ناتوانی نهاده / فرو مانده عاجز چو روباه پیر

پس از عزم آهو گرفتن بسی / شده جور از گوسفندان حی

چو مسکین و بی طاقت و بینوا دید / بدو داد یک نیمه از نان خویش

شنیدم که می‌گفت و خوش می‌گریست / که داند که بهتر ز ما هر دو کیست

به ظاهر من امروز از او بهترم / به که ناچیز باد لعنت خدا بر پدرم

گرم پای ایمان بلغزد ز جای / به سر برنهم تاج عفو خدای

و گر کسوت معرفت در برم / نماند به بسیار از این کمترم

که سگ با همه زشت آیینی خویش / مرو را بد و زخ نخواهم هم پیش

ره اینست سعدی که مردان راه / بغیرت نکردند در خود نگاه

ازان ملایک شرف داشتند / که خود را به از سگ نپنداشتند

کرا ز حاکمان سخت آید سخن / تو بر زیر دستان درشتی مکن

حکایت جنید و سیرت او در تواضع

Sixteenth-century Islamic poetry. In some Islamic cultures, religion forbids representational images and so writing as gesture is imbued with ritualistic meaning.

Ananova, the world's "first virtual newscaster," 2001

Rand, South Africa, 1976

Ritual Objects

All cultures have rituals through which they communicate with a greater spiritual whole. In the West, there is Catholic mass or Jewish seder. In much of central and western Africa, ritual masks create a connection with the spirits of ancestors or of those who inhabit the spiritual world. The practice of using masks to create culture in rites spans the length of the African continent and the breadth of its history. Masks are more than *objets d'art* to be hung on a wall. They are actively used in multimedia rituals as a means to communicate with the spirit world, as part of rites of passage rituals, and as initiation into sociopolitical organizations. An intricate and vital part of the organization of society, masks are employed in a variety of ways to understand and shape the society that creates them.

During these social rituals, masks transform an individual from representation of spirit to actual spirit incarnate, and are treated accordingly. In Cameroon, priests sprinkle ritual masks with water in order to "cool" them down, lest they overheat. The ritual is a creative act brought about not only through the mask, costume, dance, and music but also through the participation of the audience, the greater social body for whom the ritual has meaning.[6]

During sociopolitical and traditional rituals, the values and customs of the society are passed from one generation to the next, and are reinforced for current generations, either implicitly or explicitly.

It is increasingly clear that cyberspace is creating new social spaces that will form their own protocols and interactions, which then will become the building blocks of new cultural traditions. For example, visual chat rooms enable participants to interact as avatars, visual representations of the self, onto which they can add a virtual mask of their own making. The image to the left is Ananova, the self-proclaimed first virtual newscaster. Perhaps an unintentional parody of the network news anchors, she is a computerized talking head who reads the news over the Internet. Ananova is not imitating human beings. Instead, she is a personification of newly created "lifeforms" evolving out of the digital network.

The act of creativity is putting yourself into an object, then separating the object from yourself.

Scholar's Rock

In China, rocks are often used as objects of contemplation. Named "Scholar's Rocks," they are found objects, prized for their beauty, awkwardness, as well as their representational qualities—the ability to suggest figure, their wrinkling, a suggestion of age or texture and moisture, a suggestion of tactility. The creative act here lies not in shaping the rock, but in recognizing its meaning and amplifying it by changing its context from field to table.

The world within a world is a consistent theme in Asian art. The idea of a space or cosmos floating within another form is often seen in Chinese landscape painting. As the sculptor and cyberartist Richard Rosenblum has noted, "Cyberspace itself has the ability to take us into microcosmic worlds that become whole entities in themselves, new aesthetic experiences."[7]

Architecture

Everything designed has an architecture, from a teapot to a web site. Architecture reflects the positioning of the object as a statement of human intercourse in space, revealed through its masses and lines, and the light and shade of spaces. Geoffrey Scott, in his 1914 classic *The Architecture of Humanism*, notes two principles: (1) We have transcribed ourselves in terms of our architecture. It is a statement of our humanness and our aspirations. We identify with it as an object. (2) Conversely, we transcribe architecture in terms of ourselves. It reflects our moods and our evolving needs. Thus it is a projection of the image of our functions into concrete forms and a manifestation of our creative design on the world. Architecture uses the object of the building to communicate its message.

Architecture can do more than communicate: It is the stuff of life itself. It was the design of the stairways and safety exits of the World Trade Center that permitted its evacuation and saved thousands of lives, although some say its engineering hastened its collapse. A fire chief once remarked that fire safety codes were holy books: Each rule had been bought at the cost of human life.

```
void _MD_InitGC(void) {}

extern void *
_MD_GrowGCHeap(PRUint32 *sizep)
{
    void *addr;

    if( *sizep > MAX_SEGMENT_SIZE ) {
        *sizep = MAX_SEGMENT_SIZE;
    }

    addr = malloc((size_t)*sizep);
    return addr;
}

HINSTANCE _pr_hInstance;

int CALLBACK LibMain( HINSTANCE hInst, WORD
wDataSeg,
                WORD cbHeapSize, LPSTR lpszCmdLine )
{
    _pr_hInstance = hInst;
    return TRUE;
}
```

Excerpt from the source code for Mozilla, Netscape's open-source, or free, browser

Object-Oriented Programming

<programming> (OOP) The use of a class of programming languages and tech-
niques based on the concept of an "object," which is a data structure (abstract
data type) encapsulated with a set of routines, called "methods," which operate
on the data. Operations on the data can be performed only via these methods,
which are common to all objects that are instances of a particular "class." Thus
the interface to objects is well defined and allows the code implementing the
methods to be changed so long as the interface remains the same.

Free On-Line Dictionary of Computing

The discussion of the image is part of contemporary analysis in many discourses, from literary criticism to cultural studies, from media critique to communications theory. The word "image" suggests a bigger family of mental constructs produced by language, sound, and movement, and to explore its meaning is to explore the nature of reality itself. W. J. T. Mitchell divides images into classes: graphic, optical, perceptual, mental, and verbal.[8] We will discuss what he refers to as the graphic representations, those that can be displayed as a rendering, drawing, or photograph of the real or virtual world. As a specific form of metafora, we use image in contrast to those things signified by gestures, sounds, objects, or words. It is the content of what is often referred to as the "visual arts." The visual may be so powerful that language, in the words of Roland Barthes, can only attempt to mirror it, and yet representational images are dependent on the word for description.[9] Further, the distinctions between Mitchell's categories are not cut and dried, and no image can exist purely in one category. All images provoke thought, stimulating the imagination of both the maker and the viewer. They record, if nothing else, our attempts to hold memory in a graphic form. Photographer Jacques-Henri Lartigue quipped that the camera was his memory's eye.

If I could say it in words, I'd write a book.
Painter Joan Mitchell

The history of the visual image began somewhere in the caves of our ancestors. It is impossible to know what the intentions of their makers were, though it is clear that the images serve as a chronicle of some sort: Underneath these gestural marks lies a spirituality, the artifact of a creative endeavor. Archaeologists saw two types of images in these caves. The first were figures of animals and human beings. The second were inverted handprints, thought to have been produced by placing a hand on the wall, then spraying charcoal—perhaps from the mouth—to reveal its outline. The first type of image is what Charles Sanders Peirce would call an icon, a sign that resembes its referent.[10] The second type of image, the handprints, are indexical: They have a direct trace of the referent, or indicate its presence as smoke indicates fire. Paintings are iconic, since they do not necessarily indicate the presence of their subjects: A painting of a unicorn does not demonstrate the existence of the mythical beasts. Photographs are the most common form of indexical images, those images that have a one-to-one correspondence with the scene in front of the lens. People believed for a long time that photographs were "true" that they were accurate depictions of the world. Although fakes and forgeries abounded, it was not until the spread of digital photography that the public at large came to accept that photographic images could be manipulated, that they were equal parts iconic and indexical.

The camera and other devices for making images (including the growing use of the computer to generate images) drive communication in the realm of the circuit. The computer extends the reach of the lens and of representational images to such a degree that the picture or constructed rendering of the object becomes more important than the thing it represents. We live in a society in which a great deal of our reality is that which we perceive through images. Jean Baudrillard described modern culture as the hyper-real world of simulations,[11] a world in which the image refers not to an external object or referent but to itself. Reality becomes circular—Disneyland?

Having your image reproduced and distributed through social, electronic, or other circuits can produce fame. The physical appearance of a celebrity becomes unimportant, as it is the media image that produces his or her identity. Our cultural fascination with Marilyn Monroe has little to do with her physical body and everything to do with an aura created by a multitude of representations, and the knowledge that other people were acknowledging her as well.

In the 1980s, Madonna demonstrated an innate understanding of how to manipulate the media image to create a series of identities, from the downtown bad girl to the sophisticated Marilyn clone, each one a new avatar that was propagated through the media environment. Recently, Britney Spears reversed Madonna's "bad girl" vocabulary, plasticizing every aspect of her own persona into that of a sexualized child. For what do we really know of Britney Spears? Is she not just a figment of the lens?

We are the only creature that does not know what it is to be itself. . . . We are the only creature that must perceive of itself through images. The limits and possibilities implied by these images, then, are the limits and possibilities for our perceptions of ourselves. And because we can hardly be expected to exceed the morphology of our perceptions, it's clear that our images of ourselves determine the morphology of our very lives.

Russell Banks, *Hamilton Stark*

Pictures portray things.

They grasp and render qualities of perception,

shape, color, and movement.

All pictures have a certain degree of abstraction

about them in that they are

representations and not reality.

In the words of Rudolf Arnheim,

A picture is a statement about visual

qualities, and such a statement can be

complete at any level of abstraction.

Only when the picture is incomplete,

imprecise, or ambiguous with regard to

these abstract qualities is the observer

called upon to make his own

decisions about what he sees.

Art and Visual Perception

Gutenberg Bible

In the beginning was the Word;
And the Word was with God
And the Word was God.

John 1:1

In the beginning was Brahman, with whom was the word. And the word is Brahman.

Vedas

Like images, words stand in for ideas. René Magritte's painting that depicts a smoking pipe includes the words *Ceci n'est pas une pipe* (This is not a pipe) on the canvas. He titled the painting "The Treachery (or Perfidy) of Images." By juxtaposing image and word, coupled with the title of the work, Magritte brings the viewer's attention to the fact that the object of the painting is not the same thing as the object it represents. Magritte also loved to comment on the arbitrary nature of language: His painting also implies that the connection between the word "pipe" and the class of objects it represents (things you put tobacco in and smoke) is entirely arbitrary. We could just as easily call them "windows." Language depends on our ability to divide the world into categories we use words to represent. We can say that those two objects are similar in function, so we will call them both chairs. Much in the same way that the organization of sounds creates music, the organization of words through grammar makes language. Linguists such as Noam Chomsky posit the existence of an innate human ability to form language through grammar.

Language is known as a discrete combinatorial system. Elements in such a system can be combined but they remain separate, unlike paints, whose color cannot be individually discerned after they are blended. Linguist Steven Pinker notes that DNA is also a discrete combinatorial system, whereby different nucleotides combine to create our unique genetic code.[12] Within the Judeo-Christian tradition, the "word" is equated with a kind of divine origin, as in "In the beginning was the word." There is also "I give you my word," which is more than an oath, but a promise, a swearing to a self that is unwaveringly honest and sincere. In the 1980s, "word up" became shortened to "word," indicating the speaker's agreement with something just said.

Language is our most fundamental form of communication; mastery over language is the very condition that makes us human. Although many have tried, none have yet taught a chimpanzee the logic of language, nor a computer its poetry. Through the structures of language, abstract notions of words, and grammar, we evolved a higher level of consciousness. The reflexive sounds that any animal makes, such as gasps, are not language. They are elementary and so do not need attention, neither to be made nor to be understood. Language, however, requires focus and agreement by both speaker and listener; interactivity is implicit. This agreement, and a common experience through it, creates a culture.

The first time

I read the dictionary

I thought it was

a poem about

everything.

Comedian Stephen Wright

We travel on the Internet virtually and in a sense have removed ourselves further from the origins of "the thing itself." We are continually caught in the dilemma of trying to locate ourselves in an intangible and ever-changing sphere of stimuli. Although this condition may have foreboding overtones, the extension of human experience and observation into a virtual world presents us with a creative ability limited only by our imaginations, and the imaginations of those who have created the hardware and software that we use to create.

Can we really use words as indexes for things we do not experience? For example, we have no direct contact with subatomic particles and the laws of quantum physics that describe them. Are there words sufficient to mirror these phenomena? Perhaps not, but computer algorithms can represent concepts in new metaphorical ways that may not be limited by language. Thus, they might be able to model phenomena and allow us metaphorically to see what we could not previously comprehend.

Communication through speech requires a commonality of experience. Whereas a painting of a horse has a certain resemblance to a particular animal and therefore can be understood by speakers of any language, the word "horse" refers not to a particular subject but to a class of things. It is only through a shared language and a common set of cultural metaphors that we can understand this term.

Speech developed before writing, and what of all the metaphorical language have we lost since the time when ideas and knowledge were communicated orally? African tradition says that the earliest archives and libraries were held in the memories of the storyteller. How much more expressive might the fundamental myths of civilization have been when heard with voice and inflection, gesture and performance of the great orators and storytellers that every civilization anointed as the keepers of their knowledge?

The horror of the Middle Passage, the slave trade of the sixteenth to the nineteenth centuries, brought African slaves to the United States. Though brutalized by the practice of slavery, Africans blended their cultural traditions with those of the New World. Henry Louis Gates, Jr. notes that this tradition of storytelling, which maintains a dialog with the tradition that precedes it, lives in African American literature from the mid-nineteenth century until the present.[13] It can also be seen in calypso music, hip-hop culture, and rap music, which are heavily centered around storytelling and reflection on culture.

The digital age and a new orality made possible by video streaming and real-time interactivity, as well as voice recognition and language translation, may suggest the dawn of an age in which meaning is infused back into sound and is also

> *Words are not just wind. Words have something to say. But if what they have to say is not fixed, then do they really say something? People suppose that words are different from the peeps of baby birds, but is there any difference or isn't there?*
>
> Chaung Tzu, *Basic Writings*

> I am not yet so lost in lexicography as to forget that words are the daughters of the earth, and that things are the sons of heaven. Language is only the instrument of science, and words are but the signs of ideas; I wish, however, that the instrument might be less apt to decay, that the signs might be permanent, like the things they denote.
>
> Samuel Johnson, *Dictionary of the English Language*

amplified by gesture, image, and performance, held in permanence within the digital libraries of the computer, distributed across vast electronic networks. The effects of this new orality may be seen from the courtroom to the boardroom and from the news report to the class report. This could be a grand resurgence, a renaissance, of multimedia, one that will require new examination, critical analysis, an assessment of loss, and a change in the way in which things are remembered.

Joseph Kosuth's 1965 installation "One and Three Chairs" consists of a photograph of a chair, a chair, and the dictionary definition of a chair. It is an exploration of the relation between image, word, object, and the more abstract ways we categorize the world.

It's no use of talking unless people understand what you say.

Zora Neale Hurston, *Moses, Man of the Mountain*

People evolve a language in order to describe and thus control their circumstances, or in order not to be submerged by a reality they cannot articulate.

James Baldwin, *New York Times*

What is a word? It is the image of a nerve stimulus in sounds. But to infer from the nerve stimulus a cause outside us, that is already the result of a false and unjustified application of the principle of reason . . . . The different languages set side by side, show that what matters with words is never the truth, never an "adequate expression," else there would not be so many languages. The "thing in itself" (for that is what pure truth, without consequences, would be) is quite incomprehensible to the creators of language and not at all worth aiming for. One designates only the relations of things to man, and to express them one calls on the boldest metaphors. A nerve stimulus, first transposed into an image—first metaphor. The image, in turn, imitated by a sound—second metaphor.

Friedrich Nietzsche[14]

Greeting from an artist

Language is a virus from outer space.

William S. Burroughs

Jeffrey Shaw, *Legible City*
(see page 95)

Poetry is undergoing an experience with language.
Luigi Ballerini

Poetry

A sharpened edge of a razor, hard to traverse,
A difficult path is this—poets declare!

Katha Upanishad

If humanity conveyed its first experiences in the form of poetry, and the epic stories that early chants and rituals chronicled, it then began to create for its progeny a history or legacy. This gave homo sapiens a means of rationalizing and sharing experience, a means of forming society and community. However, the meaning we can convey purely through the literal meaning of words can be limiting: Words are no more than signifiers and labels. But poetry, which arises out of our expression of desire, is our most nonobjective use of the word. Anthropologists think that poetry began with the growth of agrarian society in the form of ritual or magic, to make the connection with some spiritual realm outside of everyday existence. Hence, the divine nature of the word. What is poetry? Is it not the beginning of the creative use of words in the evocation of concept and feeling, the expression of that which we do not know, or cannot know? It is not about equating identity to things, but thinking about them imaginatively. Perhaps we developed poetry because of the limits of language and of the representational qualities of words.

I wear the color of my skin

like a brown paper bag

wrapped around a bottle.

Sleeping between

the pages of dictionaries

your language cuts

tears holes in my tongue

until I do not have strength

to use the word "love."

What could it mean

in this city where everyone is

Afraid-of-Horses?

Sherman Alexie, *Crazy Horse Speaks*

Anyone who calls a spade a spade ought to be forced to use one.

Oscar Wilde

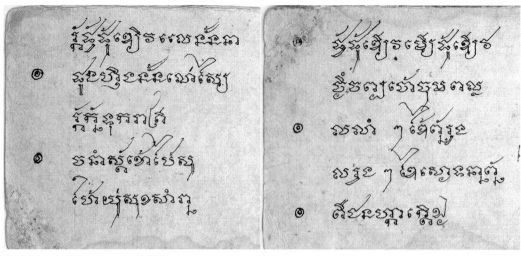

Thai calligraphy

Word (wɔ̄ɹd), *sb.* [OE. :—OTeut. **wurdom*
:—pre-Teut. **wrdho-* (cf. Lett. *wàrds,* OPruss.

word

<storage> A fundamental unit of storage in a computer. The size of a word in a particular computer architecture is one of its chief distinguishing characteristics.

The size of a word is usually the same as the width of the computer's data bus so it is possible to read or write a word in a single operation. An instruction is usually one or more words long, and a word can be used to hold a whole number of characters. These days, this nearly always means a whole number of bytes (8 bits), most often 32 or 64 bits. In the past, when 6-bit character sets were used, a word might be a multiple of 6 bits, for example, 24 bits (4 characters) in the ICL 1900 series.

Free On-Line Dictionary of Computing

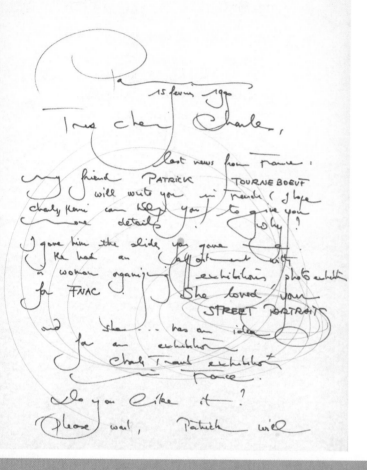

Note from multimedia artist
Frank Royon le Mée

Personal Home Pages

The early days of the Web saw a proliferation of personal home pages, sites put up by individuals for no other reason than to share their lives with other people over the Internet. Putting up a page in the early 1990s was not easy. Because it required knowing how to write a web page in HTML and how to use complicated software to transfer files to web servers, pages were usually created by those who were computer-savvy. Around 2001, a variety of sites (blogger.com, diaryland.com among others) created easy-to-use software for people to post simple web sites, known as blogs, short for web logs. These sites typically are intensely personal in nature and are updated frequently with likes, dislikes, and random thoughts. The worst are tediously boring: I had a sandwich for lunch today. But the ability to have an intimate look into people's lives and thoughts will always fascinate.

Cooking in my kitchen one recent afternoon, I was captivated by the lovely vernacular sounds of black schoolchildren walking by. When I went to the window to watch them, I saw no black children, only white children. They were not children from a materially-privileged background. They attend a public school in which black children constitute a majority. The mannerisms, the style, even the voices of these white children had come to resemble their black peers— not through any chic acts of cultural appropriation, not through any willed desire to "eat the other." They were just there in the same space sharing life—becoming together, forming themselves in relation to one another, to what seemed most real.

bel hooks, *Outlaw Culture*

1. A magic spell cast over a computer allowing it to turn one's input into error messages.

2. An exercise in experimental epistemology.

3. A form of art, ostensibly intended for the instruction of computers, which is nevertheless almost inevitably a failure if other programmers can't understand it.

The New Hacker's Dictionary

Words have a linear, discrete, successive order; they are strung one after another like beads on a rosary; beyond the very limited meaning of inflections, we cannot talk in simultaneous bunches of names. Visual forms—lines, colors, proportions—are just as capable of articulation, of complex combinations, as words. But the laws that govern this sort of articulation are altogether different from the laws of syntax that govern language. The most radical difference is that visual forms are not discursive. They do not present their constituents successively, but simultaneously.

Susanne K. Langer, "Problems in Art"[15]

Apple's 1984 Macintosh computer employed the earliest commercially successful graphical user interface (GUI). Users interacted with the computer by manipulating icons on the screen. For instance, instead of typing the arcane UNIX command "mv letter.txt ../documents/" to move a file, users could simply drag a picture of the file into a picture of a folder.

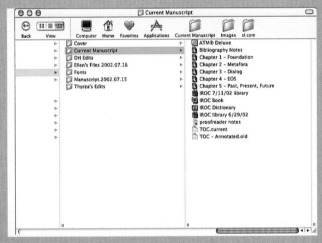

Apple's OSX operating system

Darwin, the UNIX underpinning for OSX, has a command-line interface.

Assyrian cuneiform

Writing

For the last five thousand years, writing has been a cryptic means for humanity to preserve and transmit its memories. Writing codifies what we have learned, how we act, and how we organize ourselves into functional societies. Texts such as the Koran or the **Upanishads** guide behavior by codifying thought to form an agreed culture. It is no coincidence that the rise of cities, around 3000 B.C.E., occurred with the development of writing that was capable of handling their bureaucratic systems and the codification of laws and rules. Throughout the last five millennia, slow but constant development of technology from the Phoenician alphabet to the development of paper in China and the Anglo-Saxon steel-nib pen, improved our ability to communicate. Each new mode of writing has affected the way in which written thought is structured.

Humans have always made marks to record emotions and creative expression, yet it was not until around 3000 B.C.E. that written language developed in Egypt and Sumeria, an early Middle Eastern civilization that flourished where Iraq now stands. The earliest written symbols were—to use Charles Sanders Peirce's word—iconic. Egyptian hieroglyphs and Sumerian cuneiform were pictographic in nature; they resembled the objects they represented. The cuneiform pictogram for a bowl was a simplified drawing of a bowl. Later, cuneiform would become more abstract, and hieroglyphs eventually became phonetic, representing sounds rather than whole words. This was an important development, as Eric Havelock notes in *The Literate Revolution in Greece*: The development of a phonetic alphabet simple enough to be learned in childhood is necessary for the development of widespread literacy (and perhaps democracy) in a culture.

Both the early Egyptian and Sumerian systems were composed of thousands of characters and required years of study to learn and memorize. As a result, only a privileged few could read and write. Around the eighth century B.C.E., the Greeks developed an alphabet that was entirely phonetic. The Greeks were probably influenced by the Phoenicians, though some iconic or pictographic roots are evident: In Hebrew, the second letter of the alphabet is beth, which also means house. It is thought to have derived from the Phoenician pictogram for house, which resembles the letter B on its side. Writing began as something that resembled painting, iconic in nature, and then evolved into something wholly symbolic and abstract.

Writing and literacy became means to transmit ideas through language, over greater reaches of time and space. Yet, like an oak cask that ages wine, writing changes the character and content of the words it holds. In *Of Grammatology*, postmodern philosopher Jacques Derrida developed a philosophy known as deconstruction. Deconstruction is a philosophy first but has also been immensely influential in literary theory as well. Deconstruction challenges the very core of Western metaphysical thought, which depends on the creation of meaning via binary oppositions. For example, when one opposes speech to writing (or spirit to flesh, man to woman, human to animal, nature to culture), the first term, "speech," representing oral communication, is the pure, truer form; writing is secondary, a supplement; that is, it comes off not as mediated. Does writing transcribe some ideal concept hidden in speech or is speech really not already a kind of "writing"? Is "speech" like breath—natural, unmediated, utterly present—whereas writing is not? Derrida's point is to deconstruct the metaphysical premise behind such a notion: "I think on the contrary that oral language already belongs to writing." In other words, to Derrida all speech is contained in a system called writing; there is no access to an unmediated "truth."

After the conceptual shift from pictograms to the phonetic alphabet around 1400 B.C.E., the primary force that affected the written word was its physical substrate. In cuneiform and hieroglyphic cultures, the expressive quality of an oral tradition become lost, subsumed into the act of recording. With the invention of the alphabet, a more reflexive language emerges, one that can be recorded and that allows for the investigation of abstract concepts. It can represent concepts, which cannot be pictured: What would the pictogram be for love? Every technological advance brings with it both formal and conceptual changes. The medium is the message—as Marshall McLuhan said. Societies have always been shaped more by the nature of the media by which they communicate than by the content of communications. Initially writing was done on stone and clay tablets, columns, and other

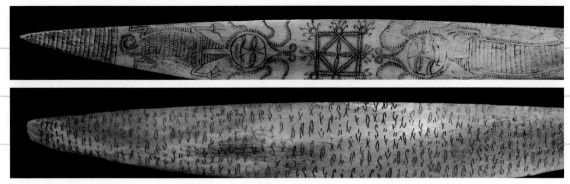

Indonesian divining rod, bone, nineteenth century.

objects. The Egyptians developed a process for weaving the reed papyrus into the mat-like material, which bears its name. Papyrus was as portable as clay tablets, while at the same time less fragile and lighter. Parchment, thought to have been developed around the second century B.C.E., was made from the skins of animals, and the ability to write on both sides of it led to the development of the codex several hundred years later. The codex was a major shift in the preservation of the written word. It consisted of sheets of vellum bound together in a form that resembles the modern book (see the History of Hypertext section), a new interface to the written word.

Paper was invented by the Chinese around 100 C.E., but did not reach Europe by way of the Middle East until around 1300. Each development of writing surface made it easier to carry (lighter and increasingly less expensive), thus allowing the written word (and therefore knowledge) to spread more easily, quickly, and broadly across society.

Printing evolved in the fifteenth century, and the words in a printed book follow one another, forming sentences that create the linear structure of the book. This stresses logical arguments that can be expressed in linear ideas. But there is also a long tradition of nonlinear writing and thinking. For example, Leonardo da Vinci readily combined image, text, and notation on a single sheet of paper. We can see other nonlinear notations in the nonprinted calligraphic forms of the East, in which text and image coexist on a page. It is not until the twentieth century and the invention of the computer that we have been able to combine the mass-production capabilities of the printing press with the nonlinear hypermedia writing spaces. The twenty-first century will surely be formed by a new organization of our thoughts and perceptions wrought by the digital networks. The computer has created a space for the text that is not only nonlinear and nonsequential but also devoid of surface entirely.

Written language developed from an iconic to a symbolic system, but the way in which we interact with the computer has moved in the opposite direction. All operating systems, which enable the user to interact with data files and programs, are abstractions. Instead of dealing directly with the zeros and ones of the computer's memory, users manipulate symbols that refer to them. Early computer interfaces used written language as an interface and then evolved into more iconic ones. For example, the UNIX operating system or DOS resembles nothing if not a conversation. Although later, more advanced operating systems such as the Macintosh or Windows are mostly iconic, the user interacts primarily with visual symbols (GUI) rather than words.

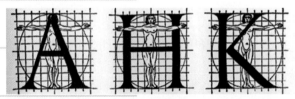

Geoffrey Tory's Champ Fleury Alphabet of 1529 was influenced by the proportions of the human body.

A shprakh iz a diyalekt mit an armey un a flot.

(A language is a dialect with an army and a navy.)

Attributed to
sociologist
Max Weinreich

The typography of industrialism when it is not diabolical & designed to deceive will be plain; and in spite of the wealth of its resources—a thousand varieties of inks, papers, presses, and mechanical processes for the reproduction of the designs of tame designers—it will be entirely free from exuberance and fancy. Every sort of ornament will be omitted; for printers' flowers will not spring in such a soil, and fancy lettering is nauseating when it is not the fancy of type founders and printers but simply of those who desire to make something appear better than it is. Paradoxical though it be, the greater the wealth of appliances, the less is the power of using it. All the while that the technical and mechanical good quality is increasing, the de-humanizing of the workman is also increasing. As we become more and more able to print finer and more elaborate & delicate types of letter it becomes more & more intellectually imperative to standardize all forms and obliterate all elaborations and fancifulness. It becomes easier and easier to print any kind of thing, but more and more imperative to only print one kind.

Eric Gill, designer of Gill Sans, in which this type is set,
An Essay on Typography

Programming Languages

When we interact with the computer, we do it through symbols. Programming the earliest computers, such as ENIAC, was done through physically rewiring the mammoth machine. Based on the theoretical work of mathematician Alan Turing, the ENIAC was the first electronic general-purpose computer, which meant that it could be reprogrammed to execute more than one program. Another mathematician, John von Neumann, realized that a computer that could store its programs electronically would be easier to reprogram; the computer could modify its program as it went along. In effect, it could make decisions. The earliest programming languages were written in machine language: zeros and ones. Eventually, programming allowed the use of more natural human speech through the introduction of assembly language and then high-level programming languages, such as FORTRAN, which was developed in 1956.

Western history was shaped for some three thousand years by the introduction of the phonetic alphabet, a medium that depends solely on the eye for comprehension. The alphabet is a construct of fragmented bits and parts which have no semantic meaning in themselves, and must be strung together in a line, bead-like, and in a prescribed order. Its use fostered and encouraged the habit of perceiving all environment in visual and spatial terms—particularly in terms of a space and of a time that are uniform,

c,o,n,t,i,n,u,o,u,s

and

c-o-n-n-e-c-t-e-d

The line, the continuum—this sentence is a prime example—became the organizing principle of life. "As we begin so shall we go." "Rationality" and logic came to depend on the presentation of connected and sequential facts or concepts.

Marshall McLuhan, *The Medium Is the Massage*

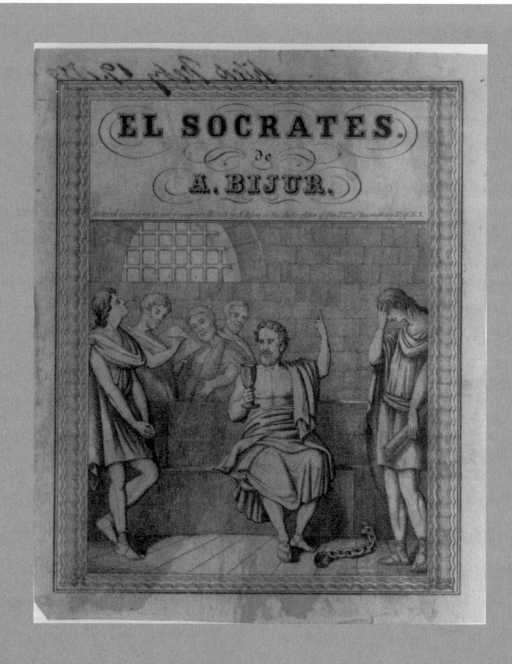

Plato and Writing

When exactly the Greeks began to use writing is still under debate, but most agree it was probably sometime in the last half of the eighth century B.C.E. Plato (428–347 B.C.E.) was quite interested in the roots of Greek culture in an oral tradition and the effect writing had on the development of rational thought. Plato perceived writing as a tool to advance his notions of the rational mind. He, and Socrates before him, saw Greek society trapped in an oral mode of discourse and learning that was based on emotion, subjectivity, and memorization rather than rationality, thought, and objectivity. No less than the soul of Greek culture and the notion of

Western individuality were at stake. Until that time, Greek cultural tradition had been transmitted by means of "rhythmic narratives," according to Eric Havelock in *Preface to Plato*. Rhythm was a means of helping the teller and listener remember what Marshall McLuhan called the "cultural encyclopedia," whereby learners had to surrender themselves to the spell of the oral poetic performance. But memorization came at a price—the diminishing of the rational in thought and in society.

To break this spell, Socrates developed the dialectic method, a means of philosophical inquiry in which listeners interactively engage the speaker in a dialog. This was a radical tool, but not radical enough for Plato, who turned to the newly developing technology of writing. For him, writing was a battering ram to break long-standing traditions of Greek culture; those locked in the poetic traditions that he felt stifled thought and prevented the development of the individual.

Poetic methods of learning depended on certain tools, because the learner had to memorize long texts. These tools—rhythm and emotional identification—take a great deal of psychic energy, which could be redirected and used for rational thought. By using writing as a means to aid memory, the mind could be freed. Thus education is not only learning knowledge through memorization but also the cultivation of rational thinking facilities of the mind. Plato did not completely abandon oral tradition: In *Phaedrus*, he records Socrates as he reasserts the power of oral memory and dialectic as a philosophical tool:

> I cannot help feeling, Phaedrus, that writing is unfortunately like painting; for the creations of the painter have the attitude of life, and yet if you ask them a question they preserve a solemn silence. And the same may be said of speeches. You would imagine that they had intelligence, but if you want to know anything and put a question to one of them, the speaker always gives one unvarying answer. And when they have been once written down they are tumbled about| anywhere among those who may or may not understand them, and know not to whom they should reply, to whom not: and, if they are maltreated or abused, they have no parent to protect them; and they cannot protect or defend themselves.

Some have interpreted this as an attack on writing, yet it is not. It is merely an assertion that writing is not enough: Once written, thought needs to be probed.

> But nobler far is the serious pursuit of the dialectician, who, finding a congenial soul, by the help of science sows and plants therein words which are able to help themselves and him who planted them, and are not unfruitful, but have in them a seed which others brought up in different soils render immortal, making the possessors of it happy to the utmost extent of human happiness.

Socrates advocates a kind of living writing, one that evolves through dialog and exchange. This is precisely the kind of writing made possible by the computer, through hypertext and the ability of multimedia to juxtapose image, text, and other media, and for the reader to interact with the text by changing the words in it.

Guglielmo Marconi

The computer is unlike other forms of expression; it is a container that carries ideas without the necessity of a tangible base.

I n the nineteenth century, the telegraph key was at first the only way to communicate electronically—to encode information into a digital signal (dot or dash, zero or one) that could be received and deciphered. Today there are countless input devices that allow us to translate nearly any form of human creativity—from painting to dance to moving pictures—into electric metafora. The rise of the electronic message has so fundamentally changed the experience, that is, the translation of idea from creator to audience, that we have coined the word "metafora." The term denotes the potential of expression in a transmedia form of limitless possibilities for interaction and communication across great reaches of time and space.

Prior to Samuel F. B. Morse's invention of the telegraph in the nineteenth century, perhaps nothing but the beat of a drum allowed communication over great distance without a physical presence. Morse's invention gave communication the speed of light, and it traveled across half the world with the installation of the transatlantic cable in 1865. The magnitude of this innovation notwithstanding, it was still necessary to be connected through the telegraph cable, a connection that was limited by topography.

Guglielmo Marconi's discovery and harnessing of the radio wave allowed for wireless telegraphy, the transmission of the dots and dashes of Morse code through the air: "Here is nothing but space, a pole with a pendant wire on one side of a broad, curving ocean, an uncertain kite struggling in the air on the other—and thought passing between."[16]

Communication was now liberated from the physical and from the limits of peer-to-peer communication as well. Messages could be sent to multiple receivers—the next step in the evolution of the mass audience and mass communication. By 1906, the work of a number of inventors, such as Alexander Graham Bell, Eliot Gray, Nikola Tesla, and Reginald Fessenden, culminated in the first voice broadcast by radio. After the telegraph was invented, its use quickly spread in the West. (Asian cultures whose writing could not be alphabetized so easily were slower to adopt the telegraph. The emperor of China was for a time interested in the Pantelegraph, which could transmit rudimentary images and so the pictographs of the Chinese language.) As telegraphy spread, it wrought profound changes, amplified all the more by the advent of the telephone, which came shortly thereafter (1876). Although the telegraph allowed one to broadcast one's own words, it was still a notational system, lacking the inflection of the human voice. The telephone allowed people to broadcast their voices in real time, connecting one person to another in virtual space. Our word "call," applied to the use of the telephone, came from the phrase "to call on" or to pay a visit. People could now visit from afar and interrupt the daily routine at any time. This marked the first instance of the virtual self, the ability to interact with others in unexpected new ways.

The upper classes worried that such unexpected interruptions would break down the carefully crafted etiquettes that held the class system in place, and they did. Today, we similarly fear the uninvited intrusion of unwanted calls and email, though newly developing filtering technology may offer some relief. Technology's presence is a constant condition of our waking life: The cell phone, pager, and wireless email leave no one unconnected. As Avital Ronell says in *The Telephone Book*, "Technology is always on."

The telephone and its accompanying technologies changed the configuration of the physical spaces of living and work, and so the nature of our community. Managers could now oversee the mill from a distant location using the telephone, and their offices began to congregate in downtown business districts. This led to the skyscraper and the necessity for the elevator and the subway to transport large masses of people to and from these centralized locations. The advent of telecommuting, related perhaps to the spread of the suburbs, may move the location of the office entirely out of centralized locations. The physical and time boundaries between office and home, and public and private, have lessened, while no physical boundary need limit the reach of the realm of the circuit.

John Roebling's invention of braided steel cable in the nineteenth century allowed new types of bridges that spanned great rivers. Cable-assisted elevators made skyscrapers practical, subways necessary, and modern cities possible.

The Line Gang

Here come the line-gang pioneering by.
They throw a forest down less cut than broken.
They plant dead trees for living, and the dead
They string together with a living thread.
They string together an instrument against the sky
Wherein words whether beaten out or spoken
Will run as hushed as when they were a thought.
But in no hush they string it: they go past
With shouts afar to pull the cable taut,
To hold it hard until they make it fast,
To ease away—they have it. With a laugh,
An oath of towns that set the wild at naught,
They bring the telephone and telegraph.

Robert Frost

All art is the suspension of disbelief.

Henry David Thoreau remarked, "We are in a great haste to construct a telegraph from Maine to Texas. But Maine and Texas, it may be, have nothing important to communicate."[17] Clearly, today one does not doubt the humanity of a grandmother in Maine who talks to her granddaughter in Texas. What we lament is the loss of content in that conversation.

Highbrow Lowbrow Middlebrow

Liberace and the Guggenheim Museum. Which is which brow?

The boundaries between what was once thought of as high culture and what has become known as popular culture have blurred. Fashion and design are no longer separate in the magazine or gallery. The notions of highbrow, middlebrow, and lowbrow, once useful to delineate and analyze culture, are no longer valid. The electronic circuit so completely changes the context in which a given form is created that it can be rapidly transformed from simple vernacular expression to high art in a simple keystroke. What was once available only to an elite class is today subject of the popular talk show or chat room. The music of Beethoven, once heard only in the concert hall by the most privileged, is now played anywhere at any time. If he could hear his Ninth Symphony in a digital recording, would he be thrilled or might he be aghast at the liberties taken in perfecting the sound and removing from it the subtleties of imperfection? How might he have responded to Jerry Lee Lewis's Roll Over Beethoven (or the seventy-five other artists who recorded the song, from Chuck Berry to the Electric Light Orchestra) or a symphony performed on a device the size of a keyboard and produced by a kid on a street corner with a ring in his nose?

History of Hypertext

The history of hypertext is a history of the organization of written expression.

In the beginning ARPA created the ARPANET.

And the ARPANET was without form and void.

And darkness was upon the deep.

And the spirit of ARPA moved upon the face of the network

and ARPA said "Let there be protocol"

and there was protocol.

And ARPA saw that it was good.

And ARPA said, "Let there be more protocols,"

and it was so.

And ARPA saw that it was good.

And ARPA said, "Let there be more networks,"' and it was so

Danny Cohen, Internet pioneer[18]

Networks are more than ways of connecting people and places; they also organize thoughts and information. We can think of the ways in which we write, the ways we place words on a page or a screen, for instance, as a network. The mind itself is a network of associations of thoughts, feelings, and memories, and although the larger social networks are best when they freely share information across the globe, the smaller networks of writing are best when they facilitate and amplify our thinking processes.

Over the millennia, thought in the form of the written word has been organized in a variety of ways. These forms have been influenced by technology and, conversely, they influence the ways in which we think and write. The book, with its regularly sized sheets, bound into a codex, where the story often moves uninterrupted from start to finish (such as a novel), seems to us as though it has been around forever, and so its influence on our thinking patterns and creativity has gone largely unnoticed and unquestioned until recently. The book is the norm against which all other forms of writing, especially modern-day hypertext, are measured. Yet, a look over the last few thousand years shows that the written form has undergone profound changes over time. If it is true that the forms of writing we use shape the way we think, then the form in which we write is important indeed. (See also History of Printing on page 172.)

Most books are linear; they are intended to be read from the first page through to the last page, one page after another. Today, the computer has spawned the peculiar term "nonlinear," referring to text in which the author has prescribed no fixed order, and readers are free to choose their own path through a story. This ability for readers to discover or even create their own meanings in the text—as Roland Barthes posits in his notion of the **death of the author**, or in Umberto Eco's concept of the **open text**—has become electrified and embodied in the realm of the circuit. Yet, we should be careful not to simply devolve into chaos: Not all readings of a text are useful or even interesting. Not all pathways through knowledge are worth traveling. It is the role of the creative interlocutor to discover worthwhile journeys and to facilitate their access.

Our eyes move over the printed page in a radically different way than they move over an image. In the English language, text is read from left to right, top to bottom (some languages read right to left, others arrange words in columns and read top to bottom), and although this may influence the way we look at images, we do not move our eyes over an image in a proscribed manner. Because of this, visual artists and graphic designers use tools of composition to direct the viewer's eye around the page. Colors and other aspects of the image such as balance, stress, pattern, and contrast direct the eye through the image. Perhaps rules once applied to visual composition might be applied to the new nonlinear writing, which may at times seem to be without structure.

The computer will work best when it enables us to organize our thoughts in a manner consistent with the workings of our mind. Will the computer kill the book, as many predicted and feared in the early 1990s? The question is perhaps better asked by pondering whether the new nonlinear, hypertextual writing styles will enhance or hinder our creativity. If, over the next few decades, we find that they are a hindrance, it is up to the community of programmers to allow writing to evolve to the next level, one that surpasses both linear and nonlinear writing. Whereas authors create the content of these new writing spaces, it is the programmers who will create an imaginative algorithm to give writing new forms.

1. The earliest writing, around 3000 B.C.E., consisted of marks made on clay or stone tablets in Mesopotamia. The Egyptians were the first to process the papyrus plant into a paper-like substance, which they rolled into scrolls to write on. Until the fourth century C.E., most text was written on scrolls and in some instances, such as the Torah, still is. The scroll presents a certain way of interacting with text. One reads from beginning to end without skipping forward or back. It is difficult to present a table of contents as an overview, or an index as a guide, because there are no page numbers, and physically maneuvering within the text is difficult. Today, we see the scroll return in computer programs that present files in windows. When the window is too small to present all of the information in the file, the user is forced to "scroll" through it. This way of traveling through a text is limiting and permits the user little facility for interaction.

2. Whereas contemporary written languages are always read in one direction, left to right, top to bottom, and the like, hieroglyphs are not. They are often read right to left, but the symbols were commonly oriented toward statues of important gods or pharaohs, or run around architectural features. The architecture of space interacts with and influences the "layout" of the words.

3. In Judaism, the very manner of reading the Torah is proscribed by holy law: A portion of the Torah is read at temple each week, and on the last day of Sukkoth, Simhath Torah, the cycle begins again. The physical form of the text presents a model for a social ritual that has repeated itself for centuries and offers the reassuring notion that it will continue into the future. In China and Japan, scrolls hold not only text but also paintings, and the viewer experiences the painting as a journey through the depicted landscape as it is unrolled. If the computer can change our experience of reading a text by presenting it in nonlinear fashion, how might it change our experience of viewing an image? Is there such a thing as a nonlinear image?

4. The Talmud is an early example of a nonlinear, hypertextual writing system. It is the transcription of the Jewish oral law, first written down around the same time as the development of the codex: the fourth century B.C.E. As a transcription of an oral tradition, the Talmud lays down commentary over and next to other commentary like the complex conversation of many voices. In the Middle Ages, North African Talmudic scholars began to point out the relationship between different sections of the text in what is called the tosafot. Printings of the Talmud have the main text in the center, flanked by the commentaries of Rashi on the left and the tosafot on the right.

5. Ephraim Chambers' *Cyclopedia*, published in London in 1728, is a two-volume work describing the arts and sciences, and thought to be the precursor to the modern encyclopedia. It was cross-referenced: Related articles were linked to one another, thus designed to be read in a nonlinear fashion. This cross-referencing created a network of meaning within the text. The *Cyclopedia* would also use supplements to keep it up-to-date: Chambers accurately perceived that information needs to grow and to change if it is to remain vital. Inspired by the success of the *Cyclopedia*, André le Breton began work on a French version. The *Encyclopédie* would be no less than a written embodiment of the ideas of the Enlightenment, primarily that of knowledge through rational inquiry.

6. In the mid-eighteenth century, Thomas Jefferson designed a book stand which allowed new ways of storing and accessing the information in books. (See page 67.)

7. Toward the close of the nineteenth century, the Belgian lawyer, bibliographer, pacifist, and socialist Paul Otlet, along with his friend Henri-Marie la Fontaine, developed radical ideas about the organization of knowledge. (la Fontaine would later win the Nobel Peace prize for his work in the development of the World Court in The Hague.) They proposed a universal repository that would contain all human creative endeavors and would bring about no less than world peace. In 1895, the two founded the International Bureau of Bibliography partially as an attempt to solve some of the problems associated with the nineteenth-century information overload. Otlet proposed that bibliographic information be stored and collated using an innovative technology available at that time: three- by five-inch index cards. Links between these cards and the objects and books they represented were created as well, a sort of proto-hypertext. Otlet proposed that the repository store not only words but also images, sounds, taste, and more, for any sense organ could convey meaning: "The book is only a means to an end. Other means exist and as gradually they become more effective than the book, they are substituted for it." [19]

Otlet also speculated on the means to access information through a "scholar's desk," a precursor to the memex, itself a precursor to the networked computer. It would have multiple surfaces to work on numerous projects at once, similar to today's multiple-windowed |operating systems. It would have easy access to remote filing cabinets that contain information accessed through a telephone and seen on a television screen. Readers would be able to annotate texts as well.

8. Otlet's system was limited by the unwieldiness of physical objects. A library containing all human knowledge in print would be enormous, and location and retrieval of documents would have been difficult, to say the least. Vannevar Bush provided a solution to this problem in his conception of the memex in 1945. The memex would enable the user to store unlimited amounts of information, which could be either purchased on "enhanced microfilm" or added through a keyboard, a scanner, and presumably other devices. Like a computer, it could be operated and accessed from a distance. But the most important and interesting aspect of the memex was the ability of the user to create "knowledge trails" through information. These trails would enable a reader to interact with texts and to create meaning and enhance understanding through the juxtaposition of ideas. A reader interested in a particular topic would be able to tie together various texts on that topic, adding notes and annotations as needed.

The brilliance of the memex, short for memory extender, lay in the reconception of the organization of knowledge. Bush's imaginative administration countered the predominant organizational metaphor, which had been in place since the nineteenth century: that of the filing cabinet in which bits of information are stored in alphabetical order. As thinkers from Aristotle forward have noted, the mind organized knowledge in quite a different way: "It operates by association. With one item in its grasp, it snaps instantly to the next which is suggested by its association of thoughts." Bush's vision of the memex's ability to scan information enabled the user to recombine information, to recombine art and knowledge: To become a creative interlocutor. [20]

Bush's mechanism is now as common as the desktop computer, and yet his essential idea of the memex, that users can be empowered by hypertextual trails through information, is unfulfilled. The World Wide Web, the most prevalent implementation of hypertext, is essentially a one-way distribution system, in which the user has little facility to be creative. We foresee the use of the computer networks to facilitate and empower the creative interlocutor.

9. In the early 1960s, Theodore Helm Nelson began work on his Xanadu project, which he never completed. An eccentric thinker, and diagnosed during his childhood with attention deficit disorder (ADD), Nelson did poorly in traditional academic settings. Partially to counter his inability to read traditional books, he developed a nonlinear reading and writing system. In a paper presented at the Association for Computing Machinery in 1965, Nelson coined the term "hypertext" to refer to his nonlinear, nonsequential authoring program: "Let me introduce the word "hypertext" to mean a body of written or pictorial material interconnected in such a complex way that it could not conveniently be presented or represented on paper."

Nelson's complex system would create a worldwide repository for human expression, in which readers would make miniscule payments to authors each time they read their text, ensuring easy access for users as well as compensation for authors. Like the memex, Xanadu was an idea conceived before there was adequate technology to implement it. It could be argued that it spurred the development of technology that would later allow incarnations of hypertext to develop.

10. In 1965, Ivan Sutherland developed a computer language called Sketchpad, the first computer-assisted design (CAD) prgoram. It operated in real time, allowing true user interactivity. Previously, users would have to submit programs or designs to be processed at a later time. Sutherland's program was also the first to integrate a graphical user interface (GUI), which enabled users to see and interact with the results drawn on the screen.

Building on the developments by Engelbart and Southerland, Alan Kay worked on the Dynabook computer—a "knowledge manipulator"—throughout the 1970s at Xerox's Palo Alto Research Center (PARC). Kay was struck by Marshall McLuhan's dictum "The medium is the message" and developed the notion of the "user illusion," of the computer as an interface to knowledge. His computer was to be networked and portable, and would work with multiple media. The technology of the 1970s would not support such a computer and the Dynabook was never completed; however, Kay's ideas would profoundly influence the designers of the Macintosh computer.

11. Douglas Engelbart demonstrated his NLS (oN Line System) in 1968, which was influenced by Bush's memex. He saw NLS as a system to augment human intelligence. It had a mouse to track the movement of the user's hand, hypertext to connect documents, and integrated multimedia.

```
I20   (U) +H20*12                                    C19

  A           G          H          I
1 HOME BUDGET, 1979
2 MONTH         NOV.        DEC.        TOTAL
3 SALARY      2500.00     2500.00    30000.00
4 OTHER
           -----------------------------------
5 INCOME     2500.00     2500.00    30000.00

6 FOOD         400.00      400.00     4800.00
7 RENT         350.00      350.00     4200.00
8 HEAT         110.00      120.00      575.00
9 REC.         100.00      100.00     1200.00
10 TAXES      1000.00     1000.00    12000.00
11 ENTERTAIN   100.00      100.00     1200.00
12 MISC        100.00      100.00     1200.00
13 CAR         300.00      300.00     3600.00
           -----------------------------------
14 EXPENSES   2460.00     2470.00    28775.00

15 REMAINDER    40.00       30.00     1225.00
16 SAVINGS      30.00       30.00      360.00
```

12. VisiCalc, developed by Dan Bricklin and Bob Frankston in the late 1970s for the Apple computer, was the first "killer app"—an application so good that users would buy a computer just to be able to use it. This program enabled users to lay out numerical accounting data in a table, effectively creating a front end, or interface, for the data. Numbers could be put into visual relationship with one another, enabling the user to visualize new relationships. VisiCalc did not require new technology; it was merely a means of reconceptualizing an approach to knowledge.

13. In the late 1980s and early 1990s, Tim Berners-Lee developed the World Wide Web. Unaware of the work of predecessors such as Bush or Theodor Holm Nelson, Berners-Lee created his system as a computer scientist at CERN, a European research facility in Geneva. Although it had many fewer features than Nelson's Xanadu, it was simple enough to be implemented. The Web began as an attempt to share information among the scientists at CERN (a network of minds) across their computer network. The scientists used a variety of different computers spread across its huge campus. Berners-Lee wrote a protocol (a set of parameters for computing) that would enable a scientist anywhere on the campus to access a file on the computer of any other scientist. Based on the success of his system at CERN, Berners-Lee adapted it for use on the ever-expanding Internet and founded the World Wide Web Consortium to oversee its development.

Jeffrey Shaw's 1990 Legible City consists of a bicycle connected to a video projector and a computer. By pedaling the bicycle and turning its handlebars, the viewer of the work is able to navigate through a representation of Manhattan in which buildings are composed of letters that form one of several narratives. By choosing different paths, the user will be brought through different paths through the texts. Unlike traditional artwork that represents space, Shaw's work becomes the space.

History of printing

Printing's ability to store and reproduce information can be thought of as a direct precursor to the computer. It was (and is) a technology for the organization and storage of discrete bits of information into storage units (books), which contain thoughts and ideas (metafora) so that they can be distributed across networks. It is the mechanization of what was once a hand craft (just as photography is the mechanization of drawing). The development of printing technology transformed the written word from something created laboriously, by scribes who copied documents by hand to a mass-produced book. By mass-producing writing, printing made the book into a consumer item, a commodity to be carried through networks of commerce and culture. Today's electronic books move writing into the realm of the circuit, where bits and bytes can travel at the speed of light through the network.

Words and books, as repositories of thought (and therefore power), have been moved through networks since they were first created. Over the years, texts have become smaller, lighter, cheaper, and easier to reproduce. Early texts were large, cumbersome, and rare, because they were copied by hand before the advent of printing. As printing technologies developed and gradually improved, the availability of the written word exploded, flooding the networks with new words and ideas. Today, the capabilities of the computer for storage and distribution of text provide resources, as yet barely tapped, to foster the literary and intellectual life of our culture. Computer visionary Stewart Brand once remarked, "Information wants to be free."[21] Printing began the journey toward freedom, and the electronic network may be the last step.

Before printing, literacy was largely confined to royalty and clergy or to an elite class of scribes. Because of the high cost of writing materials, from papyrus to vellum, and the time it took to reproduce a book by hand, writing was not an efficient means for transmitting information. Until the advent of movable type in Europe, most books were handwritten, and so fantastically expensive, often made of vellum, cured animal skin.

Printing as we know it today developed over several centuries. By the second century B.C.E., technologies for printing existed in China: ink, paper, and words carved into a surface. Pilgrims visiting Buddhist holy sites created souvenirs by painting ink onto scriptures carved into pillars and then placing sheets of paper onto them to receive the impression, much in the same way that visitors to the Vietnam Veterans Memorial in Washington, DC, bring rubbings of names home with them. In the late eighth century C.E., an early printing technique using wood blocks had developed in China. The text to be printed was carved into a block of wood. The block was then inked and paper placed on it to receive the impression. In Buddhist practice, repetition takes special significance, whether it is the speaking of a phrase or mantra over and over, the repetition of the basic building unit of a pagoda, or the circumambulation of the nine steppes of Borabudur. Thus,

Gutenberg with a screw press, as depicted in a nineteenth-century print

The fact that we still use paper today is testament to its usefulness. It is flexible, inexpensive, and can be easily sorted into stacks, pinned to bulletin boards, spread across a desk, or made into an airplane. The invention of Post-its and sticky notes shows that paper continues to evolve: These items are a paper-based way to multitask, a kind of windows-based paper operating system.

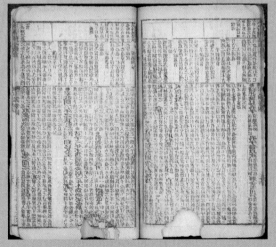

Teachings of Confucius, twentieth-century printing

A Thai samut manuscript showing the Buddha contemplating a corpse

The Diamond Sutra

the multiplication of the Diamond Sutra had significance beyond the mere act of copying. Printing with woodblocks, in which a piece of wood is laboriously carved by hand, continues to this day, and was extensively used in the nineteenth century in ukiyo-e printing in Japan, for example. This process, though revolutionary, was time-consuming, but it would take several additional factors to make books inexpensive to produce and so widely available.

In 1455, Johann Gutenberg printed his forty-two-line Bible by bringing together several existing technologies—movable type, metallurgy, papermaking, ink, and the screw press—to create the first inexpensive, portable written document, a precursor to today's laptop computer in its ability to store and transmit information. During the early Middle Ages, the Christian Church was a network of religious officials who held close control over the interpretation of the scripture. Paramount to their hold on power was keeping the Bible a Latin text, contained in precious few volumes, and so inaccessible to the laity. Religious doctrine was dispensed only by clergy in cathedrals, that is, from fixed locations.

Trade networks opened toward the end of the Middle Ages, exposing Europe to new ideas, as merchants and Greek texts flowed from Arab countries, over trade routes pioneered by Crusaders returning from their pillaging of the Middle East. At the end of the twelfth century, monks began to collaborate with secular scribes, redrafting ancient texts as well as documents of commerce for the new merchant bourgeoisie, who plied the trade routes of Europe and the East. By the mid-fifteenth century, the Bible had become a printed document and no longer had to be laboriously copied by hand. There are those who argue that printing developed in part to satisfy the thirst for knowledge created by new trade routes, new networks of commerce. By the early seventeenth century, King James I commissioned a translation of the Bible into English (the vulgate or vulgar), and the closed network of the Medieval Church became destabilized. At the same time, the novel as a popular form of literature emerged, as printing created a mass audience for literature. Book prices continued to drop in the nineteenth century, as industrialization lowered the price of paper and mechanized the printing press. This allowed for books to be mass produced and, in the absence of international copyright agreements, even created the earliest cases of piracy, as English and American presses reprinted books from overseas, often only days after they arrived on the shores. (We see similar concerns today with the legal battles over music piracy.)

One of the most significant changes in publishing would come with the rise of the computer. In 1971, Michael Hart started Project Gutenberg with the intention of repaying a gift of computer time that he valued at 100 million dollars. For him, the great value created by computers was the storage and distribution of information, and so Hart set out to distribute electronically books that had passed into the public domain. At first, he simply typed the Declaration of Independence into the computer, hoping to distribute it in electronic form to everyone connected to the Internet. By 2000, he and a loose network of volunteers had digitized more than two thousand five hundred texts: everything from the Christian Bible to the Egyptian Book of the Dead to Victor Hugo's *Les Miserables*. These texts are stored on computers connected to the Internet, encoded into the most universal file format—ASCII text. There is no charge to download the texts; and as they are in the public domain, there are no royalties to pay to the authors and thus no cost to the users. Project Gutenberg moved the text from the library to the network.

Renaissance print shop

The ability to duplicate a digital file would infinitely extend the reproduction power of the printing press. In the mid-1980s, Adobe Systems developed the PostScript printing language, which, when combined with Apple's LaserWriter printer and Aldus System's PageMaker, brought printing and publishing into the home. For an investment of no more than a few thousand dollars, anyone could create newsletters, pamphlets, and even books. By the next decade, the Web enabled anyone with nothing more than a personal computer and access to the Internet to publish a personal "home page." As thousands of amateur sites sprang up, the naive design of the pages (which coincided with a rise in the appreciation for "outsider art") created a new primitive aesthetic.

Although printing allows the dissemination of ideas through books, it freezes their content. In some cases, this is what the author wants, but in many other cases the content of the text wants or needs to change. Newspapers could once update news only as often as they were printed and distributed (eighteenth-century newspapers came out only once every few weeks), but online journals can change instantly. Perhaps more importantly, digital texts can be changed by anyone, enabling potentially any-body to collaborate in authoring. How might religious doctrine change if the parishioners could interact with and even change Scripture? The Jewish Talmud, the civil law, has changed over millennia, as successive generations have added interpretations and commentary to the text. How might a digital Talmud serve its community, when it can be placed in an online library, accessible and potentially changeable by anyone?

Television 1934   Radio 1897

one-to-one

one-to-many

Interactive

hello alo diga me ciao hello alo diga me ciao hello alo diga me ciao

Do Wop She Boom Sho Be Do bie

010101010101001101

Wireless Telegraph 1898

Phonograph 1877

What hath God wrought?

hello

The Bell Magneto telephone in 1877

Telephone 1876

Motion Picture 1895

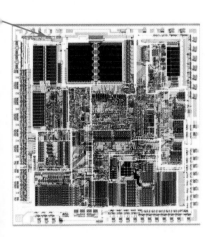

Integrated Circuit 1958

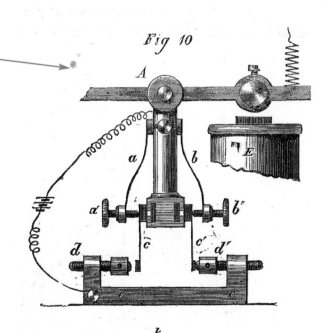

Fig 10

Telegraph 1844

CHAPTER THREE

DIALOG

identity ▭ survival ▭ learning ▭ advertising
love ▭ amusement

Human beings are social animals, and dialog in its broadest sense is the means through which we relate, how we define ourselves to others and through others. New dialogs enabled by the computer consist of the exchange of metafora, the creative potential of the computer. Creativity is an encounter, and as the realm of the circuit produces new ways of interacting, of encountering other people, it produces new fields of creativity. The first two chapters provide the how of creativity; this chapter provides the why.

Susan Litecky and Jeanine Hausler, *Untitled* 1992

Previous page: Silver denarius of Nerva (emporer of Rome 96–98 C.E.), minted in Rome in 96. Roman currency was inscribed with the words "CONCORDIA EXERCITUM." The coin signifies the state of harmony between the emperor and the armed forces.

There are only two or three human stories, and they go on repeating themselves as fiercely as if they had never happened before.

Willa Sibert Cather, *O Pioneers!*

Culture is the story we tell about ourselves, using **narrative** to transform information into knowledge and knowing into telling. No matter what medium we choose, creativity inevitably engages the maker and the audience in a dialog, one that has been changed through the evolved digital tools of the twenty-first century. Today, television broadcasts entertainment to the mass audience, but provides little opportunity for interaction, save perhaps changing channels. The fundamental process of digital creativity (described in the first chapter) enables the audience to engage the artist and the work in an exchange of ideas that enriches both parties. By definition, dialog refers to a conversation and we generally think of conversations as verbal. In the realm of the circuit, dialog reaches beyond verbal transactions to include all performances of the creative act.

Each new creative work is a way to understand and to create our sense of self and relation to others, as well as to contribute to the canon of understanding. Once we recognize ourselves, we become concerned with survival and then with improving our condition through learning. Having accomplished something of value, we then want to promote it, to share it with others and make an indelible mark. Our drive to propagate is the way to assure the continuation of ourselves. All the while, these acts are made more pleasant by the amusements we create. The interactivity of exchange and dialog delivers us from banal solitude.

Creativity is a process of continuing an ongoing story of our essential myths—how we survive or the love stories we have created—embellishing them and creating new ones. All cultures perpetutate themselves through storytelling in one form or another. Digital stories are always in process, acted on by the class of creative interlocutors to which we are all challenged to join. The growing power of the personal computer provides almost everyone the ability to produce new creative artifacts; we can all add to the story. The discipline of desktop publishing, nearly two decades old, affords anyone with something to say the tools to produce a pamphlet or even a book. Creativity is a bottom-up affair. We can conduct a romance across formerly insurmountable boundaries or join in amusements once unimaginable in realms of the past.

By placing inexpensive production tools in the hands of a broad range of people (primarily, though not exclusively, the middle class of developed countries), the dataset and circuit give us the potential to extend the narrative. Culture need not emanate only from the museum, the lyceum, or the dictates of unseen authority. Rather, culture is a social intercourse that calls for new forms of exchange, dialog, and commerce. The question is whether the individual who seeks community

No human society has yet been found in which such mythological motifs have not been rehearsed in liturgies; interpreted by seers, poets, theologians, or philosophers; presented in art; magnified in song; and ecstatically experienced in life-empowering visions. Indeed, the chronicle of our species, from its earliest page, has been not simply an account of the progress of man the toolmaker, but—more tragically—a history of the pouring of blazing visions into the minds of seers and the efforts of earthly communities to incarnate unearthly covenants. Every people has received its own seal and sign of supernatural designation, communicated to its heroes and daily proved in the lives and experience of its folk. And though many who bow with closed eyes in the sanctuaries of their own tradition rationally scrutinize and disqualify the sacraments of others, an honest comparison immediately reveals that all have been built from one fund of mythological motifs—variously selected, organized, interpreted, and ritualized, according to local need, but revered by every people on earth.

Joseph Campbell[1]

The idea is a sign of things; the image is a sign of the idea, sign of sign. But from the image, I reconstruct, if not the body, the idea that others had of it . . . true learning must not be content with ideas which are in fact, signs, but must discover things in their individual truth.

Umberto Eco, *The Name of the Rose*

and interaction can keep from being co-opted by bigger systems that may be antithetical to his or her original intentions.

Historically, it may be technology that has created the rift between society and the creative energies that lie at its foundation. Techniques of mass production that heralded the process of specialization, factory production, and the assembly line, while greatly increasing the output of a factory, obliterated groups of artisans who took pride in their craft. These craftsmen were transformed into a working class that drudgingly repeated a single task over and over again, becoming alienated from the final objects they produced. Workers no longer gave value to their imagination, only the volume of their output. The appreciation of imagination became a thing of leisure, for the elite. The common man lost control of his own story, those links in the production process that once allowed him to connect the past with the future by creating his own narrative. Today, the possibility of reversing this alienation lies in the creative application of digital technology.

The integration of culture and creativity can be reborn in the realm of the circuit. We may all be able to weave our personal narratives into the culture at large. The content of the dataset is not fixed, and our ability to change it easily almost requires us to do so. Tying a computer into a network means that creativity can, and must, be shared with others in the process of ongoing dialog, which builds culture.

Audience expectations have changed. We are not the same society we were ten years ago, able or willing to sit passively through a concert or stroll through an exhibition. The audience may now demand a greater interaction with the creative act.

Of all affairs, communication is the most wonderful. That things should be able to pass from the plane of the external pushing and pulling to that of revealing themselves to man, and thereby to themselves; and that the fruit of communication should be participation, sharing, is a wonder by the side of which transubstantiation pales. When communication occurs all natural events are subject to reconsideration and revision.

John Dewey, *Experience and Nature*

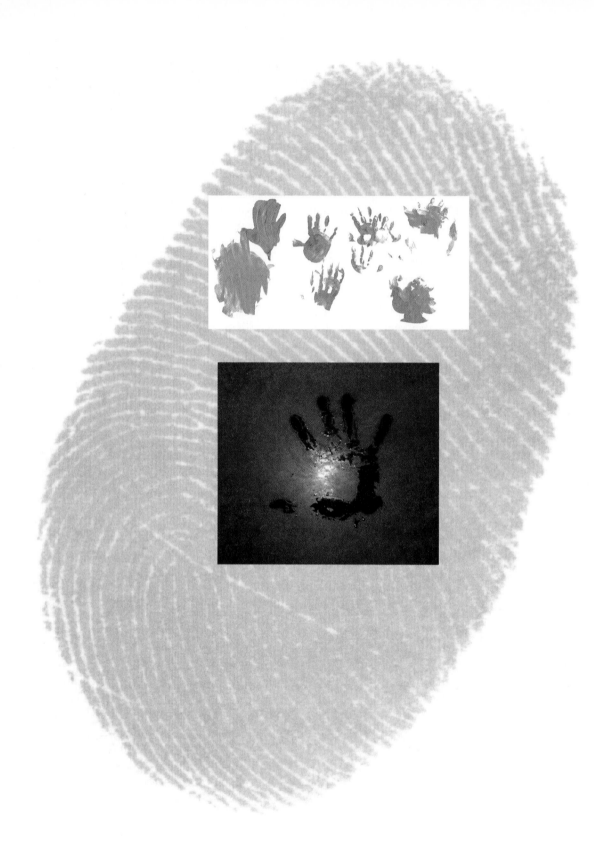

identity ▭ survival ▭ learning ▭ advertising
love ▭ amusement

The nature of identity is the subject of many areas of inquiry: from psychology to philosophy, sociology to religion. There is little agreement, except for the fact that identity is usually formed in relation to others, that interaction with the group confirms or distorts it. In part, a sense of identity is formed by the individual's perception of the universe and a search for a place in it. We seek affirmation by asking such questions as, Who am I? Where did I come from? Psychologist Erik Erikson said that our sense of identity is "the accrued confidence that one's ability to maintain inner sameness and continuity is matched by the sameness and continuity of one's meaning for others."[2] This condition connects us; it is the origin of humanism that allows us to form a group, a society, and a culture. In essence, we are constantly striving to create bonds with others whether through religious or cultural beliefs, moral or ethical laws, expressive or didactic communication. Our creation of metafora carries the messages that enable us to form these bonds. Through it, we define ourselves and others in the scheme of the world.

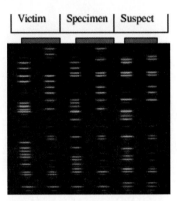

DNA samples can be used to establish identity.

Identity in the twenty-first century includes how we project ourselves into the circuit. In describing and defining the "projected self" in the digital form, early computer hackers coined the term *avatar*, from the Hindu notion of the incarnation of a god in earthly form. This term was widely used to describe the ways in which a person "existed" in the computer, especially in text-based games known as **MUD**s. In a MUD, you appear to others as a description; you can choose your identity in how you write that description. Sociologist Sherry Turkle documents the ways in which players would carefully construct their online identities.[3] But, if you can manipulate your identity, how do you maintain a continuity of self? Some claim that the ability to customize an "electronic" identity holds the promise of removing, or at least mitigating, the prejudices often associated with race, class, and gender from social interaction in the digital sphere. Conversely, individuals can more easily conform to the creeping homogenization fostered by global media. Instead of looking within oneself, it is all too easy to forge an identity composed of consumer items: Marlboro cigarettes and Coca-Cola. With the anonymity available in the digital realm, are we more apt to forge our identities to a cultural ideal, or might this anonymity provide us a forum whereby we can allow ourselves more vulnerability in sharing and forming our "true" selves?

This may produce a fear that we become alienated from our families, communities, or societies by the technological distortion of our identities into something unreal, a virtual self that is dissociated from our "real" self. If one finds sanctuary in projecting an idealized identity through the network, might this force an individual to analyze his or her perception of this fantasy and pave the way for real self-evaluation and introspection?

Every creative act requires that the maker place a little bit of him- or herself into what he or she creates. By looking at something a person has created, we can better understand who that person is and also who we are. Our values are stirred

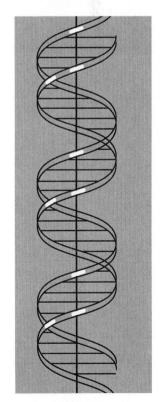

DNA is composed of four base pairs that encode information.

bob n.

At Demon Internet, all tech support personnel are called "Bob." (Female support personnel have an option on "Bobette." This has nothing to do with Bob the divine drilling-equipment salesman of the Church of the SubGenius. Nor is it acronymized from "Brother Of BOFH," though all parties agree it could have been. Rather, it was triggered by an unusually large draft of new tech-support people in 1995. It was observed that there would be much duplication of names. To ease the confusion, it was decided that all support techs would henceforth be known as "Bob," and identity badges were created labeled "Bob 1" and "Bob 2." ("No, we never got any further," reports a witness.)

The reason for "Bob" rather than anything else is due to a user calling and asking to speak to "Bob," despite the fact that no "Bob" was currently working for tech support. Because we all know "the customer is always right," it was decided that there had to be at least one "Bob" on duty at all times, just in case.

This silliness inexorably snowballed. Shift leaders and managers began to refer to their groups of "bobs." Whole ranks of support machines were set up (and still exist in the DNS as of 1999) as bob1 through bobN. Then came alt.tech-support.recovery, and it was filled with Demon support personnel. They all referred to themselves, and to others, as "bob," and after a while it caught on. There is now a Bob Code describing the Bob nature.

The New Hacker's Dictionary

in response to the creative act of others: recognizing our commonality and our differences. Teenagers form a sense of who they are through the music they listen to. It is no wonder that they form communities with other teens based on similar musical interests.

The accounting of our selves is maintained through the codes that pervade our world. Our social identity is constructed through the codes of our social security numbers, personal identification numbers, bank accounts, and the answers to multiple-choice personality inventories administered by psychologists. This becomes worrisome when we consider how easily information which has been collected can be shared without our consent or even knowledge. When statisticians use this information to group us with others, judgments can be made about us in a formulaic manner, which often leaves out the subtleties of human existence. On the other hand, our ability to project ourselves into cyberspace may allow us to interact with the codes of others to create a collective identity.

This is happening with the parents of children with rare genetic disorders. The Internet has given them the ability to share information—including their children's raw genentic code—with others in an attempt to further research. The Internet has also provided them with access to vast amounts of information: The National Library of Medicine has estimated that private individuals, not doctors, performed one hundred twenty million searches in 2001. Handwritten newsletters mailed by parents have given way to websites accessed by parents, researchers, and health care professionals around the world.[4] One of the problems for parents is being able to collate and decipher the information they receive: Much of it may be suspect. A creative interlocutor might develop a way to sort through the information, providing valuable information to all those concerned.

Identity is the process of organizing materials, experience, and information into form, through narrative and other creative strategies. In the digital age, information and form are plastic, changeable. This can work for us or against us. The process of identification—to oneself and to others—is a product of our creativity. But identity is constructive only if it enables us to survive as responsible members of a community.

Above: Walker Evans, *Penny Picture Display*, Savannah, 1936
Below: Passport, First Irish State, 1927

Memorial mural, Brooklyn, 2000

The IS of identity, assigning a rigid and permanent status, was greatly reinforced by the customs and passport control that came in after World War I. Whatever you may be, you are not the verbal labels in your passport any more than you are the word "self." So you must be prepared to prove at all times that you are what you are not.

William S. Burroughs,
The Electronic Revolution

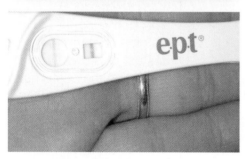

Top: Author's mother
Middle: Designer's son
Bottom: Author's daughter

Langton's Loops

The development of artificial life depends on establishing and reproducing identity through information. In 1979, Chris Langton set out to create a computer program that would mimic the basic functions of biological life: That it contain information that could be copied or used as instructions, just as a cell's DNA could. He began by creating a cellular automata—a hypothetical organism first proposed by John von Neumann that would exist on a grid—on an Apple II computer. He then created the "creatures," which consisted of a sheath (the blue cells) surrounding core cells (red, white, green, and black). The color of a particular cell on the grid would determine its behavior as the simulation progressed from state to state (von Neumann was building on Turing's notion of a finite state machine, the conceptual basis for modern computers). Langton's loops are able to reproduce and to form colonies: "as the loops on the outer fringes reproduce, the inner loops—blocked by their daughters—can no longer produce offspring. These dead progenitors provide a base for future generations' expansion, much like the formation of a coral reef."[5]

I am an invisible man. No, I am not a spook like those who haunted Edgar Allan Poe; nor am I one of your Hollywood-movie ectoplasms. I am a man of substance, of flesh and bone, fiber and liquids—and I might even be said to possess a mind. I am invisible, understand, simply because people refuse to see me . . . nor is my invisibility exactly a matter of bio-chemical accident to my epidermis. That invisibility to which I refer occurs because of a particular disposition of the eyes of those with whom I come in contact. A matter of the construction of their inner eyes, those eyes with which they look through their physical eyes upon reality.

Ralph Ellison, *The Invisible Man*

identity

cogito ergo sum

Descartes

From the film *It's Good Business*, Illinois State Chamber of Commerce, 1953

Laurie Anderson tells us, in her album *United States,* that children become used to the notion of the virtual self at an early age. They are handed telephones and told, "It's Grandma, speak to Grandma. "The "it" in this sentence, the "it" they are handed, is not a person, but an electronic device which allows Grandma to project her voice.

The definition of personhood [in Japan] is distinct from the prevalent Western definition, in which individual personality is defined as a discrete ontological entity or monad. Rather, personality in Japan is defined as basically interactive, shaped by the context within which it acts and by its obligations in such contexts. This does not, of course, entail— as some critics have claimed—the denial of individual responsibility. Rather, it denotes a specific mode of formulation of the basic parameters of selfhood and of human relations.

    S. N. Eisenstadt

Matthew Courtney, 2002

A poet is the most unpoetical of anything in existence, because he has no identity; he is continually informing and filling some other body.

John Keats, *Letter to Richard Woodhouse*

Chinese altar

Julia Cowing, *Two Generations, One American,* 1998

Therefore the sage holds in his embrace the one thing (of humility), and manifests it to all the world. He is free from self-display, and therefore he shines; from self-assertion, and therefore he is distinguished; from self-boasting, and therefore his merit is acknowledged; from self-complacency, and therefore he acquires superiority. It is because he is thus free from striving that therefore no one in the world is able to strive with him.

Lao Tse, *Tao Te Ching*

By the late twentieth century, our time, a mythic time, we are all chimeras, theorized and fabricated hybrids of machine and organism; in short we are cyborgs. The cyborg is our ontology; it gives us our politics . . . the relation between organism and machine has been a border war . . . [this is] an argument for pleasure in the confusion of boundaries and for responsibility in their construction . . . unlike the hopes of Frankenstein's monster, the cyborg does not expect its father to save it through a restoration of the garden . . . it is not made of mud and cannot dream of returning to dust.

Donna J. Haraway

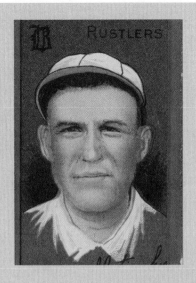

Edward Abbaticchio,
1911

Our sports heroes have been celebrated in one form or another since before the first Olympic games. In modern times, the star is often little more than a compilation of statistics. A drop in those numbers and his or her fifteen minutes of fame is over.

EDW'D J. ABBATICCHIO

Edward J. Abbaticchio, the infielder whom the Louisville American Association team got from the Boston Nationals late in 1910, decided to go into business for himself, and Louisville fans were greatly disappointed. "Abby" had 14 years' experience in professional base ball, having commenced in 1887 with the Greensburg, Pennsylvania, team. He spent 1898 with the Boston Nationals, 1899 and 1900 with Minneapolis, 1901 and 1902 in Nashville, and then three seasons each with the Boston Nationals and the Pirates.

	G.	B.	F.
1908	144	.250	.969
1909	23	.230	.965
1910	48	.243	.907

BASE BALL SERIES 400 DESIGNS
SWEET CAPORAL
CIGARETTES
The Standard for Years
FACTORY Nº 42 4TH DIST. N.C.

MISSING WTC
FITZROY ST.ROSE
(718) 652-2414

Memorial wall, New York City,
September 15, 2001

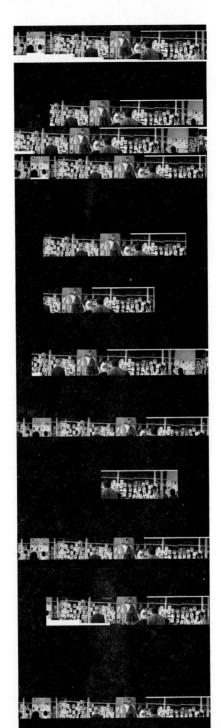

identity

Grateful Dead concert, Meadowlands, New Jersey, 1986

Self is the lord of self, who else could be the lord? With self well subdued, a man finds a lord such as few can find.

The Dhamapada

The spirit is the true self.

Cicero

The computer game Spacewar!, written as a program for mainframe computers in the early 1960s. This was perhaps the first
instance of an "avatar," a manifestation of a user in a shared virtual reality, in this case a computer screen on which each player
controls a ship that fires torpedoes at the other player's ship.

This self is the
honey of all beings,
and all beings
are the honey
of this Self

Chandogya Upanishad

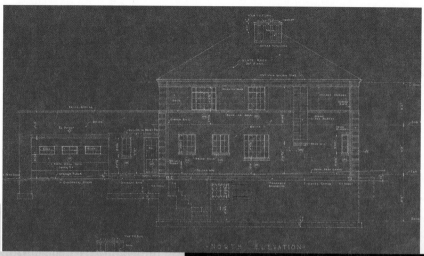

Gilgamesh, why doest thou
run about this way?

The life that thou art seeking,
thou wilt never find.

When the gods created man,

They put death upon mankind,

And held life in their own hands.

Fill thy belly, Gilgamesh;

Day and night enjoy thyself;

Prepare each day some
pleasant occasion.

Epic of Gilgamesh

Above: Blueprint, Louis Stamberg, 1937
Right: Stelarc, "The Third Hand"

*We are survival machines—robot vehicles blindly programmed
to preserve the selfish molecules known as genes.*

Richard Dawkins, *The Selfish Gene*

The field of biology holds that survival is the most fundamental quest of our existence. Not just survival of our physical bodies, but of our genetic makeup as well—our dataset. Our ancestors survived not only by cheating death from day to day but also by passing on their genetic legacy from generation to generation, making copies of their program. It is no wonder, then, that survival is a central theme of our formulation of metafora, from literature to the graphic arts. Everything that we leave behind is a testament to survival, that we were there. Our personal survival came to depend on economic survival, the ability of our society to produce those goods and services that met our basic needs. Societies form culture through the production of creative work, and the survival and evolution of societies depends on passing on this creativity from generation to generation.

The sciences describe the process of evolution as what theorist Donna Haraway would call an origin myth—a story we tell to describe how we came to be who we are. Each culture has its own origin myth, from the Bible to the Zuni stories that tell how humans came from deep in the Earth: Each culture needs a story to reconcile unknown beginnings. Origin myths create a narrative out of the facts of the past, and Haraway's work has consisted of trying to rewrite that narrative.

Evolution is the process of change a species undergoes over time, based on the pressures the environment puts on it. In the nineteenth century, Charles Darwin posited the theory of natural selection as the means through which evolution occurred. Our ancestors survived as a species by passing on adapted genes. If a particular trait, say the ability to see farther, allows an individual to anticipate oncoming danger, then he or she is more likely to survive, and pass on this trait to offspring through genetic code. Changes in the gene pool are brought about by random mutation in DNA, or through the process of sexual reproduction whereby two sets of genes combine to form a third unique code.

Over the last few thousand years, advances in technology have provided for our needs. Medical science has advanced to the point where we can implant devices into our bodies, from insulin pumps to artificial hearts that pump blood. Haraway declared that today we are **cyborgs**, that the boundary between human and machine is shifting and uncertain. We co-evolve with technology, increasing our abilities, including the possibility to make more technology. (*Co-evolution* is the term given to the mingling of biological destinies of two species.) We might consider whether we have become too dependent on technology.

Survival once depended on the ability to adapt to a world that was physically demanding: Our ancestors had to forage for food and provide shelter from inclement weather. They banded together, united for protection, and were

Will the species of computers turn out to be a parasite or a symbiote? I would argue that the answer to that question is entirely up to man. He is the dominant partner in the relationship. If human beings collectively have enough understanding and enough foresight, they can assure that the interaction between the two species will be totally beneficial to mankind.

John G. Kemeny,
Man and the Computer

The computer is the single most important invention since fire.

John Perry Barlow

Our loyalties are to the species and the planet. We speak for Earth. Our obligation to survive is owed not just to ourselves but also to that cosmos, ancient and vast, from which we spring.

Carl Sagan, *Cosmos*

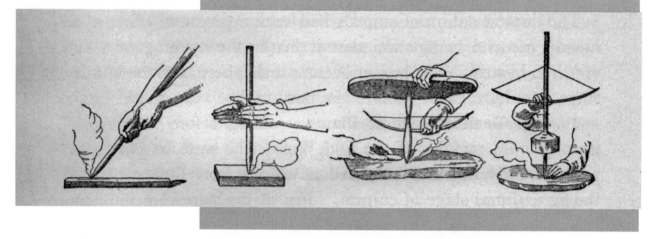

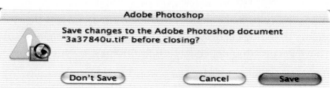

agressive in their quest for territory. Today, the technologies we have developed have largely taken care of our needs for food and shelter; it is failures in the political and economic systems that for the most part produce poverty and starvation. Political and economic factors determine the successful application of the technology: Creativity is the key to survival.

Our creative endeavor becomes a lasting testament in the quest for immortality. Survival is measured not only by the deeds of a lifetime, but also in the legacy of our works. Artifacts of our creativity acknowledge that we are in fact not immortal, that we are leaving something that we hope will outlast us. When combined with the works of others, our metafora help to shape and to define the culture. As we move into the realm of the circuit, in which there is greater access to tools of creativity, and in which the network and World Brain allow us greater access to the works of others, our culture will evolve. By extending our ability to preserve and share, the realm of the circuit brings new meanings to our survival.

Taipei, Taiwan

Space is the stuff of human life. We design it for protection, balancing between shelter and freedom of movement and spirit. Our essential designs are those that protect us.

Fairy Tales

Fairy tales are never about what they are about. Instead, they are a means for teaching through telling stories, for allowing cultures to survive from generation to generation. All cultures have fairy tales: They are a means of teaching and protecting continuity in a culture. They serve to pass our sense of culture from one generation to the next. Learning is essential to the continuation of the symbolic language that is culture.

The relationship of image both as visual symbol and as metaphor is perhaps best understood in the stories particularly fundamental to Western culture, which revolve around the apple. Clearly its symbolic origins are linked to bliss and to the vulva shape of its cross-sectioned core. From the beginning of time as we know it, the apple was used as a symbol of fertility, springtime, youth, and even immortality. Greek, Nordic, and Celtic mythology refer to it as the sustaining fruit of the gods in the story of the Apple of Discord, also known as the Apple of Hesperides and the golden apple tossed by Eris set off the Trojan War. The tree of knowledge in Scripture is the source of the fall of humankind, and thereafter the apple becomes a principal metaphor in all Western religion. Eastern cultures similarly attribute beauty and renewal to the apple blossom and its fruit.

Once the story begins and cultural meaning is attributed to the iconic apple, the potentials and creative uses of the metaphor are endless. One need only think of these other great stories of the apple: the apple of Sodom; the myth of Atalanta; Newton's apple; Johnny Appleseed's legacy; William Tell's arrow; Camelot, the Arthurian tale located in Avalon (an apple orchard); and finally Snow White and the Seven Dwarves and the poisoned apple. The great power of such storytelling and the great symbolic meaning attached inspired Steve Wozniac and Steve Jobs to name their icon-driven computer the Apple.

Fairy tales are stories told for enchantment of youth, set in a place and time that are geographically and temporally vague. The heroes and heroines are a-historical, allowing each individual to transpose on them their unique interpretation; they are archetypical. Snow White, a widely known tale, probably found its origins in central Europe and became disseminated throughout the continent in varying forms and incarnations. For example, Italo Calvino, in his story "The Apple Girl," retells the classic Italian version. Its magic lies in its use of the metaphor of the apple and the evocation of freshness pertaining to the Snow White–like heroine.

A common African myth is that of the perverted message, in which God promises humanity eternal life, but the message is changed by the greed or stupidity of the messenger. A more global myth is that of the trickster animal, who practices deceit and magic, and may be anything from a hero to an evildoer. Most likely, these myths represent a fundamental human interest in deception and trickery. Native American trickster tales tell of everything from the coyote to the raven. In South America and Japan it is the fox. African tales have tricksters in the form of spiders, hares, or tortoises, while the fifteenth-century Chinese literary classic, *The Journey to the West*, also known as *The Monkey*, tells of the exploits of the monkey trickster-god. The tale is thought to have originated in India and traveled to China through stories passed on in the oral tradition.

Many of today's European folk tales originate in preliterate times and were comprehensively and exactingly documented by the Brothers Grimm, German philologists, in their collection *Kinder und Hausmärchen* in 1812. They collected material through interviews with peasants who had preserved these stories by retelling them over generations. By collecting preliterate peasant tales in one volume, the Grimms believed that they were reconnecting a cultural identity that had been fragmented when the Medieval church suppressed their telling. They felt that their exactness in documenting the tales would help to glorify values that had endured in their cultures through the ages, and that each tale was a cultural artifact.

An apple a day keeps the doctor away   Smooth Apple—A suave person   Wise Apple—Impertinent youth   The Big Apple—New York City   Them Apples—Breasts   Apple Head—Stupid person   Apple Knocker—Fruit picker   Apple pie—Neat and orderly   Apple Polisher—One who curries favor   Don't go under the apple tree   Apple of my eye   Don't turn over the apple cart   Apple pie   The Apple is Harlem

Hoboes, homeless men who traveled the country by rail in the early twentieth century, developed a series of signs to communicate information necessary for survival.

In the twenty-first century, digital technology is allowing us to become increasingly nomadic, carrying our lives with us in our laptops and connecting to the Internet and other networks through wireless technology. The practice of warchalking recalls earlier nomads, hoboes, the itinerant workers who traveled the United States by rail. Hoboes communicated with one another with signs and symbols they left chalked on buildings, warning of danger or providing useful information. Warchalking is the process of providing information that describes the wireless networks people have found by using sophisticated scanning equipment. These networks are typically set up by home users or corporations, and their range often extends into public spaces, where wanderers-by can tap in with (or without) the permission of the owners. The symbol above indicates the presence of a network with the SSID of "Kynance" and a bandwidth of 1.5 megabits.

Warchalking Pocket Reference

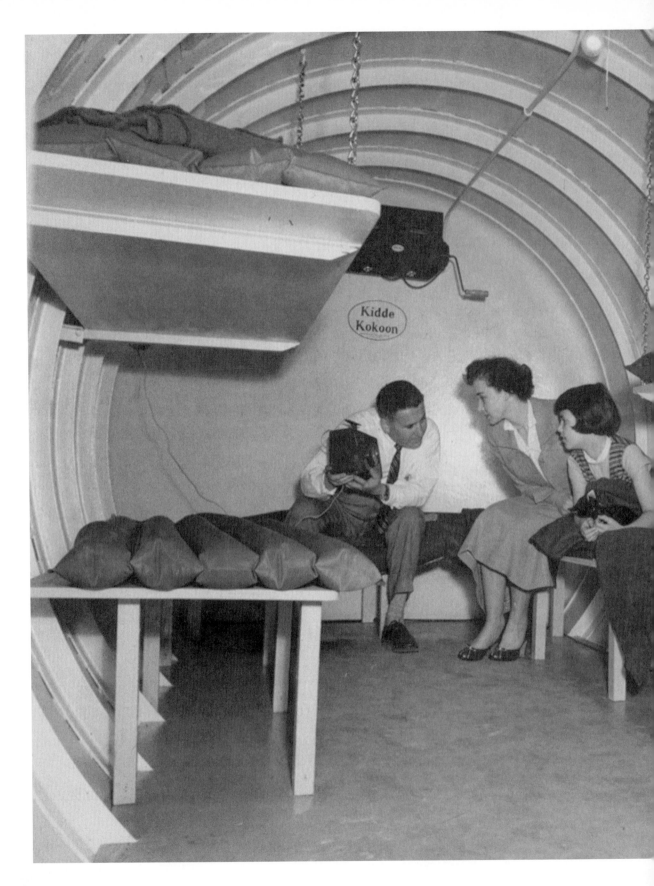

Destiny's Child
Survivor

Now that you are out of my life,
I'm so much better,
You thought that I'd be weak without ya,
But I'm stronger,
You thought that I'd be broke without ya,
But I'm richer,
You thought that I'd be sad without ya,
I laugh harder,
You thought I wouldn't grow without ya,
Now I'm wiser,
You thought that I'd be helpless without ya,
But I'm smarter,
You thought that I'd be stressed without ya,
But I'm chillin',
You thought I wouldn't sell without ya,
Sold nine million.

I'm not gonna give up (what),
I'm not gon' stop (what),
I'm gonna work harder (what),
I'm a survivor (what),
I'm gonna make it (what),
I will survive (what),
Keep on survivin' (what).

H-Bomb hideaway

Edward Curtis, *Pomo Lake*

When our ancestors discovered fire, they built a hearth, which became the center of their survival. Families were created and communities evolved from that circular pit. When shelter could not be found, it was constructed.

Architecture, like all evolutionary concerns, changes along with our human behavior. Shelter is primary, but as we develop the ability to rearrange nature, through farming and technology, so too do we rearrange the structures that give us shelter and that we occupy to conform to our development.

Our species has adapted to the external world through our ability to understand it through symbols and then use these symbols to communicate with one another and to further our survival. By making symbols concrete, through painting them on a rock or a canvas, we allow our ideas to survive through time. Carl Jung noted our attraction to stone as a medium for communication because of its endurance over time.[6]

What will come of communication when it has no physical substrate, composed of no more than the fleeting bits and bytes of metafora? How will creative works survive for future generations as the computers or operating systems that are required to run them become obsolete? Many critics have commented on the fleeting nature of so-called "net art," which has been created for a web browser that is likely to become obsolete in a year or two.

Arthur Rothstein, *Farmer and Sons Walking in the Face of a Dust Storm.* Cimarron County, Oklahoma, 1936

Mount Rushmore

Red Crescent poster: Your Blood Saves Lives.

While, with your pencil and with your colors,
you had already made art the equal of nature,
and had, in fact, diminished her glory in part,
since you gave her beauties back to us more beautiful,
now that you've set yourself, with your learned hand,
to the worthier task of putting pen to paper,
you've taken from her, by giving life to others,
even that part of her glory that you still lacked.
For any age that ever vied with her in making
beautiful works, had to yield to her, since all
things must come to their ordained end. But now,
by rekindling memories of others, long extinguished
you make both them and yourself live for eternity,
despite their fate.

    Michelangelo, *Lives of the Painters*

Written on the Stela of Hammurabi are the civil, economic, and criminal laws of Babylon. It was carved long after Hammurabi's death in 1750 B.C.E., and the laws had evolved long before his reign began. They created the cornerstone of Babylonian society.

Law, Symbol, and Culture

The concept of law is fundamental to society. The attempt to put it into code and to understand its meaning is a defining issue of civilization and its survival. Laws are the rules of conduct of a community that are recognized as binding by its members. Sign, symbol, and the oral and written word chronicle the law's existence, define its evolution, and allow the interpretation that defines the continuity and exchange between people, allowing the humanizing conditions for the survival of the species. In Judaism the Torah is called the Law of the Pentateuch; traditionally they are the books received by Moses on Mount Sinai. Symbolically they have been kept through the ages preserved in all Jewish synagogues as handwritten scrolls of parchment residing in a special place of reverence known as the ark of law. All law in Judaism, commentary and interpretations, is considered an extension of the sacred oral tradition that defined the culture, and is the basis for not only the Jewish but also the Roman Catholic and Eastern Orthodox churches. Similarly, the Koran is not only the word of the prophet Muhammad, but also law, governing both religious and secular conduct. The act of writing the law is itself holy. Maybe politicians should remember this.

Although the law may come from divine sources, its meaning in a democratic society is, by definition, a collaborative act of faith. In the contemporary sense, the code of law is a hypertextual, interdisciplinary organ of continual exchange, growth, and evolution acted on by many different parties including the legislature, the constabulary, and the voting populace. In a constitutional democracy, such as that in the United States, a short handwritten text—the Declaration of Independence—is the basis for all its governing principles.

Moses receiving the Ten Commandments

could the dead feel any interest in Monuments or other remembrances of them, when, as
Anacreon says: Ολιγη δε κεισομεσθα
Κονις, οστεων λυθεντων
the following would be to my Manes the most
gratifying.
On the grave
a plain die or cube of 3.f without any
mouldings, surmounted by an Obelisk
of 6.f. height, each of a single stone:
on the faces of the Obelisk the following
inscription, & not a word more

Here was buried
Thomas Jefferson
Author of the Declaration of American Independance
of the Statute of Virginia for religious freedom
& Father of the University of Virginia.

because by these, as testimonials that I have lived, I wish most to
be remembered. to be of the coarse stone of which
my columns are made, that no one might be tempted
hereafter to destroy it for the value of the materials.
my bust by Ciracchi, with the pedestal and truncated
column on which it stands, might be given to the University
if they would place it in the Dome room of the Rotunda.
on the Die of the Obelisk might be engraved
Born apr. 2. 1743. O.S.
Died ——

In designing his own tombstone, from its shape to inscription to position, Thomas Jefferson created a tangible relic of his life.

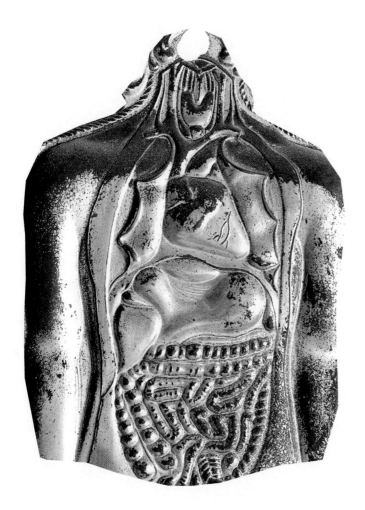

Ex votos are brought to Catholic churches and hung on altars either in gratitude or in the hope for a cure to the depicted organs.

Learning is the process of transmitting culture from one generation to the next; Marvin Minsky defines learning as an omnibus word for all the processes that lead to long-term changes in our mind.[7] Our minds apprehend the world symbolically; this is what makes us human. Teaching is the process of making the world comprehensible to another through symbol or abstract form. Our capacity for symbolic thought and expression were evident long before we perfected any particular technology. Thought is the process of dissecting the world so another can reassemble it. By breaking the world into parts, teachers allow pupils to rebuild it in their own style. Teaching is a constant process of enabling us to retell the stories of culture. The interactive process of learning begins in infants when they understand, at about six months of age, that there is a world outside of them. In order to learn about this world, we need to engage it. The interaction of parent and child is the first time a child gets meaning from others—it is an exchange, a dialog.

Great teachers are arguably our greatest resource, for they nurture talent and genius through their interlocution. The process of learning cannot take place without dialog, for students cannot simply absorb information. They have to process information into knowledge in order for learning to take place: Learning and teaching are two sides of the same coin. In the circuit, we can learn by becoming teachers; teaching is a fundamental creative act, a responsibility each of us owes to the survival of his or her community.

Our old methods of learning and teaching seem deficient in the digital age. Culture expands the "extensions of man,"[8] our inventions from the elementary pencil and paper to the complicated digital computer. As we have discussed in this book, these inventions require a corresponding visual and linguistic literacy, a mastery of the elements of structure. As we evolve new metafora through the computer, we must develop corresponding literacies. In the nineteenth century, German writer, philosopher, painter, and statesman Johann Wolfgang von Goethe was said to be the last man to know everything, not because he was any smarter than we are today, but because now there is more to know. A generation raised on learning with and through the computer may not need to rely on old metaphors to understand the new medium (our computers today use a graphical interface based on paper files and folders). Rather, we may create new metaphors that will enable us to reconceptualize the process of learning and teaching entirely.

In the twenty-first century, one cannot hope to grasp all of the details, even within a specialization of a given field. We can better understand the information overload by using the computer to filter and negotiate the fields of data. We all become a new kind of student. No longer can we act as sponges that soak up information, but we must become more proactive in exploring new networks of possibilities, creating systems and programs to enhance our own capabilities. Education is no longer the process of learning the answers, but of learning how to ask the right questions. The World Brain holds the answers, if we can navigate.

Today's child is growing up absurd, because he lives in two worlds, and neither of them inclines him to grow up. Growing up—that is our new work, and it is total. Mere instruction will not suffice.

Marshall McLuhan,
*The Medium Is
the Massage*

There is a world of difference between the modern home environment of integrated electric information and the classroom. Today's television child is attuned to up-to-the-minute "adult" news—inflation, rioting, war, taxes, crime, bathing beauties—and is bewildered when he enters the nineteenth century environment that still characterizes the educational establishment where information is scarce but ordered and structured by fragmented, classified patterns, subjects, and schedules. It is naturally an environment very much like any factory set-up with its inventories and assembly lines.

Marshall McLuhan, *The Medium Is the Massage*

The toys children play with are an integral part of their learning process.

Many, many men have been as troubled morally and spiritually as you are right now. Happily, some of them kept records of their troubles. You'll learn from them—if you want to. Just as someday, if you have something to offer, someone will learn something from you. It's a beautiful, reciprocal arrangement. It isn't education. It's history. It's poetry.

J. D. Salinger, *Catcher in the Rye*

It appears that rhetoric is an offshoot of dialectic, and also of ethical studies. Ethical studies may also be called political; and for this reason rhetoric masks as political science, and the professors of it as political experts— sometimes for want of education, sometimes for ostentation, sometimes owing to their own human failings.

Aristotle, *Rhetoric*

The Master said, "He who aims to be a man of complete virtue in his food does not seek to gratify his appetite, nor in his dwelling place does he seek the appliances of ease; he is earnest in what he is doing, and careful in his speech; he frequents the company of men of principle that he may be rectified—such a person may be said indeed to love to learn."

Confucius, *Analects*

According to my view, any one who would be good at anything must practise that thing from his youth upwards, both in sport and earnest, in its several branches: for example, he who is to be a good builder, should play at building children's houses; he who is to be a good husbandman, at tilling the ground; and those who have the care of their education should provide them when young with mimic tools . . . . the teacher should endeavor to direct the children's inclinations and pleasures, by the help of amusements, to their final aim in life. The most important part of education is right training in the nursery. The soul of the child in his play should be guided to the love of that sort of excellence in which when he grows up to manhood he will have to be perfected.

Plato, *Laws*

Education

Vittorino da Feltre created one of the greatest schools of the Renaissance in Montua Italy. Among his students, which included both men and women taken from all social classes, were the great leaders and creators of the time. He advocated the integration of the body and the mind as well as the development of the spiritual pursuits. As a humanist, he sought to develop the virtues of his students, emphasizing that fulfillment of their obligations to others was a means for them to reach greatness. The school itself was an environmental that replicated the comforts of home, creating an atomsphere that was joyous and pleasant for learning. We cite him here because his educational methods anticipated those we advocate. Education today must be interdisciplinary and enjoyable. Above all, it must take into account the notion that values which help to develop well-rounded humanists are served not by accumulating information, but by nurturing the ability to think through the creative process.

"There are no educators. As a thinker, one should speak only of self-education. The education of youth by others is either an experiment, conducted as one yet unknown and unknowable, or a leveling in principle to make new character, whatever it may be, conform to the habits and customs that prevail: In both cases, therefore, something unworthy of the thinker—the works of parents and teachers, who an audaciously honest person has called 'nos ennemis naturels.'"

Friedrich Nietzsche, *The Wanderer and His Shadow*

"I believe that school is primarily a social institution. Education being a social process, the school is simply the form of community life in which all these agencies are concentrated and which will be most effective in bringing the child to share in the inherited resources of the race, and to use his own powers for social ends. I believe that education, therefore, is a process of living and not preparation for future living."

John Dewey, *My Pedagogical Creed*

"A wholesale literacy seemed at first to open new and happy vistas for everyone. But paradoxically, mass distribution of schooling accomplished a negative miracle. The speed of dispensation of eduation for immediate use neglected biological orientation without which the urge for creative activity was lost and with it the most important aid to maturity and judgment. It provided the mass with a quick training but threw overboard its purpose, that 'not knowledge but the power to acquire knowledge was the goal of education.'"

László Moholy-Nagy, *Vision in Motion*

"Good teachers know what size to make each step and can often suggest analogies to help the child's mind to use what it already knows for building larger scirpts and processes. . . . Each child learns, from time to time, various better ways to learn-but no one understands how it is done. We tend to speak about 'intelligence' because we find it virtually impossible to understand how this is done from watching what the child does. The problem is that we can't observe a child's strategies for 'learning how to learn'—because those strategies are twice removed from what we can see ... Perhaps our educational research should be less concerned with teaching children particular skills and more concerned with how we learn to learn."

Marvin Minsky, *The Society of the Mind*

"Throughout my years as student and professor, I have been most inspired by those teachers who have had the courage to transgress those boundaries that would confine each pupil to a rote, assembly-line approach to learning. Such teachers approach students with the will and desire to respond to our unique beings, even if the situation does not allow the full emergence of a relationship based on mutual recognition. Yet the possibility of such recognition is always present."

bel hooks, *Teaching to Transgress*

Top: Advertisements for gladiators and poets, Pompeii, first century B.C.E.
Above left: Patent medicine advertisement, nineteenth century
Above right: Cartoon by Arthur Young: Big Advertiser breaks pen of Ye Editor

I am whatever you say I am.
If I wasn't, then why would I say I am?

—Eminem

Commerce is an essential component of survival and largely dependent on advertising. What we call popular culture is often dispersed as a by-product of advertising and public relations. One need only look at the designer logo on anything from a computer to a T-shirt to realize that corporations create their identities through advertising: If you do not advertise, you do not exist. The word *advert*, from the Latin *ad* and *ver*, means to turn to one's self or to another favorably. This suggests something of the origin of the concept. Once our ancestors found that they could make a mark, they realized that they could project themselves through symbols and by doing so make others turn their attention to them. Metafora is in some sense advertising, in the sense that each creative act contains a piece of our identity and will cause its viewers to pay attention to it.

Media, from newspapers to television, and now the Internet, are largely driven by their advertising revenues. Advertising and communication are intertwined in all spheres of our mass media. For good or bad, the dissemination of information—our identities, nationalities, politics, likes, and dislikes—is defined in response to the paid-for image. Our individuality is created by our resistance to or acceptance of advertising or propaganda (that is, advertising we dislike). When we see an ad for Gap chinos, do we run out and buy them, or pierce our noses in defiance?

If myth is the story we tell about ourselves, in the modern age advertising is the story told to us by commerce. Advertising is a very careful construction of a story, one we are invited to join through the act of purchasing a product. When a consumer buys an SUV, he buys the story told in the advertisement, and by doing so he can add to his identity. Baudrillard has referred to these imaginary constructions, the tokens of advertising, as simulacra, the image of a reality.[9] The story advertising tells allows the viewer to participate only through buying a product. The only exchange is of money, not dialog.

Advertising is camouflage, presenting one thing as another. In many ways, it is a creative construct that often disguises banal issues in the form of glamour. Beautiful women have nothing to do with the mechanics of an autombile, only with creating an aura around it. As the advertising motto goes, "If you have nothing to say about your product, have a celebrity say it." The media have exploited our need for mythic heroes so that we venerate actors to the point where they actually get elected to public office. As Samuel Johnson put it, "Promise, large promise, is the soul of advertising."[10]

Iranian revolution propoganda

Propaganda

Propaganda is yet another form of metafora. It implies a recipient, usually a mass audience, for its message, who is to be moved by the packaging of an idea in an often rousing manner. Adolf Hitler, a master propagandist, employed the swastika as part of the regalia and staging that mimicked the imagery of the all-conquering Roman Empire. It should be remembered that he was a creative interlocutor in his own right. Hitler aspired to be a painter and dabbled in commercial and architectural arts as well as writing. In his book, *Mein Kampf*, Hitler explored the power of the visual symbol. He understood the emotional and persuasive power in creating a new identity for a depressed culture, and even studied the psychological effects of the colors symbolically employed by his Nazi party. To complete his dominance over the minds of the German people, he aspired to control all the arenas of German culture and media from the schools to radio to fine and visual arts, using the power of electronic media as a tool for propaganda. It is no surprise that he surrounded himself with the likes of the architect Albert Speer; the filmmaker Leni Riefenstahl; coordinator Joseph Goebbels, an orator and journalist, who was appointed the head of the National Ministry for the Public Enlightenment and Propaganda. Nothing but humanity's watchful eye can safeguard against creativity being used for the most evil ends.

The Nazi swastika, the most powerful and most negative icon of the twentieth century, was the rallying sign reinterpreted by Adolf Hitler. Ironically in all of its previous incarnations across many cultures, the symbol was one of life and of regeneration. To the Buddhist, it is a symbol of reincarnation and the cyclical nature of life. In the Mesopotamian culture, it was linked with the female reproductive organs and appeared on the pubis of the Goddess Ishtar and where it implied 'life force' was found throughout China. In the Roman catacombs it was used as a sign of Christ; the Scandinavians used it to symbolize thunder and lightning and the god Thor. Finally, it was found in the Babylonian symbol of the sun's energy and, finally, in the Native American culture of the four winds or the four seasons.

Certain symbols of political or religious nature are the visible manifestation of propaganda—advertising for a doctrine. They include the rose, for socialism and for Islam; the fascia for Italian Fascism; the American bald eagle; the Jewish Star of David and the Chinese Red Star. In the modern sense, propaganda has become the entire apparatus by which a public opinion is molded through the media. The appeal through subtle persuasion and often-reductive simplistic idealization—even to mythic origins—is used to stir essential wants, prejudices, projections, and unconscious complexes and desires. Primarily, propaganda appeals to what Carl Jung termed "the collective unconscious and the will for survival or betterment manifest in buying into someone else's 'word' and finding community in it."[11]

As much as in any other realm, computer technology shows its imprint upon the change in how we conceive and think about propaganda. All political campaigns since popularization of the Internet in the mid-1990s have been affected by the profuse dissemination of commentary, fact, exaggeration, and satire. A shift in who produces the propaganda has occurred. It no longer emanates solely from the "central organizing committee" but from the keystroke of whoever may seek to sway the tides of sentiment. There is hardly an email user who is not affected on a daily basis by the distribution of unsolicited jokes and commentary aimed at either swaying or reaffirming one's views.

Propaganda exists only by contrast; it is what the other guy says. One person's propaganda is another person's education.

Leni Riefenstahl filming *Triumph of the Will*, a masterpiece of Nazi propaganda

Olympics, 1984

Police brutality protest,
New York City, 1989

Mao Tse-tung

B.C.E.

9000 Paintings seem to have been signed indicating the identity of their makers.

Circa 3500 Public criers are used in ancient Babylon. Public criers are one of the earliest forms of advertisements and appear throughout the ancient Mediterranean. They are often used to announce the arrival of a new shipment of trade goods, extol the virtues of a particular shop or product, advertise slaves, and so on. Romans later incorporated musical accompaniment and singing to attract the public's attention.

Circa 3000 Around this time, the first appearance is made of symbol-signs above stores and businesses. Advertising food for sale, these early signs are essentially clay slabs with symbols pressed into the surface.

Circa 3000 Early advertisements on papyrus posted on temple doors for runaway slaves appear in Egypt.

Circa 900 Assyrian Brick Stamp is used to identify the maker of a brick.

Circa 5th century In Greek mythology, Venus asks Mercury to descend from the heavens to find Psyche, who has run away without permission, and spread the word of her flight to all who will hear.

5th century Shop signs in Rome are used to communicate to the largely illiterate public. The most common signs included a bush (a symbol for wine) to indicate the presence of a tavern, a cherub with a shoe for a cobbler, the phallus (symbol of life) for a bakery, and three golden balls to mark a pawnbroker's shop. Similar signs were also widespread in ancient Egypt and Greece. At a time when streets lacked names, signs also become important landmarks for stores trying to lure customers.

2nd century The Rosetta Stone is carved in Egypt, whose ruler at the time, Ptolemy V Epiphanes, commissioned similar edicts and stone monuments to communicate with his people.

C.E.

circa 150 150 Painted signs containing text appear in Pompeii. Still largely limited to symbol-based advertisement, signs with handwritten text appear as literacy increases. Often posted near public places such as bath-houses, early signs announced upcoming sporting event, theatrical performances, and gladiator events. Election signs are also discovered in the excavation of Pompeii.

247 King Asoka of India (Maurya Empire) adopts the tenets of Buddhism. Asoka commissions stone monuments carved with messages of his conversion and religious tolerance and has them placed throughout his empire.

12 century In England, theatrical troupes stage large processions with music and dancing to advertise their plays and performances.

1141 Public criers in Berry, France, organize and petition Louis VII for exclusive access to advertising in local county.

15th century Posted advertisements become widespread in England and Europe. In England, these handbills are known as "siquis," after the Latin *si quis* for "if anybody"—a phrase that began all Roman advertisements or handbills.

chronology: advertising

Subway station, Tokyo, Japan

1450s Johann Gutenberg's invention of the movable printing press allows merchants to print flyers advertising their wares.

1480 The first printed advertisement appears in England. William Claxton, who helped introduce printing to England, posts advertisements for his book on local church doors.

Early 16th century Publishers begin including price lists along with testimonials for other books in their books.

1525 One of the first printed advertisements in a published document appears in Germany advertising a medical book by a Dr. Laster.

early 17th century Newspaper advertisements begin to appear in Europe.

17th century Illustrated shop bills become widespread. Known as "trade cards" or "tradesman's cards," these flyers become an important way to reach customers. Among the earliest and most successful illustrators is W. Hogarth (1697–1764).

1612 The *Journal Général d'Affiches* appears in France. Still in print, the *Journal of Public Notices* is essentially a list of classified ads and public notices.

1704 The first newspaper advertisement in the United States appears in the *Boston News-Letter*.

1760 Early advertising jingle for shoe polish appears in England.

19th century Billboard advertisements flourish in the United States and elsewhere. Generally handpainted, the signs initially advertised available wares within the building—it was only later that billboards were located separately from the store they were advertising.

1830s Large wagons are used to carry painted advertisements throughout New York City.

1840s Gaslight signs are used to illuminate storefronts and entertainment halls in New York City.

1850s P. T. Barnum becomes a master of self-promotion through publicity stunts and clever advertising. Featuring animals, clowns, and other circus entertainers, Barnum commissions the largest color lithograph poster ever made. In 1884, Barnum leads twenty-one elephants across the Brooklyn Bridge to prove its safety in a highly publicized stunt, which also promotes his circus.

1855 Often covering municipal buildings and private residencies, bill posters use the cover of night to plaster London with advertisements. Londoners agitate for reform as the city is overrun with handbills and posters. Public pressure leads to the creation of designated advertising posts. Control is also placed in the hands of regulated bill posting agencies.

1860s During the Civil War, the United States government begins widespread advertisement to obtain army recruits and volunteers.

1860s The modern poster advertisement is created in France.

Mid-19th century United States advertisers turn their attention to women. As women attain more economic resources and access to the workforce, advertisers begin to target them through women's magazines and other venues. Although advertisements have always had a perceived audience, this marks an important shift from general advertisement to targeted advertisement.

Mid-19th century Patent medicines dominate the marketplace in the United States. Although not entirely new, and present in England and Germany as early as the sixteenth century, patent medicines become widespread in the United States after the Civil War. Largely unrestricted, purveyors of patent medicines make sweeping claims about the potency and healthful qualities of their products. Enormously successful, patent medicines not only make their creators wealthy, but also help finance many of the major newspapers through their advertisement fees. Although legislation eventually stops the false claims of patent medicine advertisers, the advertisers help introduce a new age of persuasive advertising—offering a new life and transformative personal effect rather than a necessity.

1886 Coca-Cola is invented in Atlanta, Georgia. The flowing script used for Coca-Cola becomes one of the most successful and recognizable logos in advertising history.

1887 Montgomery Ward begins distribution of its first catalog in the United States. These catalogs are essentially created to reach the large numbers of Americans living beyond major U.S. commercial centers. Filled with pictures and descriptions of hundreds of items, the catalogs allow anyone in the United States to purchase goods and have them delivered to their door.

1890s Color advertisements are introduced as magazine inserts.

1890s Advertising slogans become widespread—among the earliest and most memorable is Kodak's "You push the button, and we do the rest."

1891 The first outdoor electrical sign appears on Broadway in New York City. Containing 1,457 lamps, the sign was visible for blocks up and down Broadway and Fifth Avenue.

 chronology: advertising

Late 19th century The caricature "Uncle Sam" begins appearing in U.S. political cartoons and is later used on U.S. Army recruitment posters.

1920s Radio becomes a key source of advertisement in the United States and elsewhere.

1920s Celebrity endorsements and testimonials become widespread in the United States.

1922 Skywriting is developed by J. C. Savage, an English aviator. Flying at heights of 10,000 to 17,000 feet, skywriting planes were employed to write out slogans and brand names above popular destinations, such as beaches, amusement parks, and baseball fields.

1923 Neon signs are introduced in the United States.

1950s Television joins radio as a major outlet for advertisement.

1989 The Internet is opened to commercial traffic.

Romeo and Juliet

The dataset may have sped up the mating game but it has made it no less complex. One need surf the Internet only momentarily before a matchmaking site appears. The quest for human contact, for love, has always been undertaken through the wiles of the imagination in employing whatever artifice might enhance the courting ritual. The development of technology and its metaphors may have been as much a result of the need to spread romance as that of commerce, from the hand-delivered love letter, or the flirtation of the chat room. We pursue that more base drive, sex, through everything from phone sex to the creation of digital surrogates. It is remarkable that after the so-called "dot-bomb," the crash of technology stocks at the turn of the third millennium, that pornography was the most (and nearly the only) profitable endeavor on the Internet.

True love, whatever it may be, remains the elusive quest of the poet. We continue "looking for love in all the wrong places," as the popular song says. There is such a thing as unrequited love, but the best kind is interactive.

It is not our task here to define love, but what would love be without metafora, and what would metafora be without love? Cultivation roots itself in the innate biological need to procreate, to create a personal bond between mate, family, colleague, friends, and community. We constantly seek the other, to bring him or her into the realm of our knowledge and familiarity, and even control as an object, as the ancient Greeks would have it, of our fulfillment. We have evolved our most elaborate jesters' rituals, dances, dramas, words, and images about the subject. It is the story we most love to hear. The ancient Hindus even equated cultivation of love and lovemaking to that of a science; today few would doubt it is an art, yet one that is never complete and always in process.

The civilizing forces of most societies are centered in the notion that the creator is love, and that we are required to love all as we love the greater deity and ourselves. Such love is of the most enlightened form. Herein lies the great dilemma—are we really capable or have we created enough understanding to be able to accomplish such a feat? It is always easier to love that which is familiar and more like one's self, whereas anything foreign—the other—often disrupts our complacency and provokes opposite reactions, those of aggression and hatred.

Humanity has made great steps in the development of technology to serve these negative reactions in the development of war machines. It is a sad irony that many of our greatest leaps in technology were fostered by the engines of conflict. All nations need to be watchful over their military-industrial machines whose preoccupation with weaponry may drain resources from the direct development of humane technology. Hopefully, we are driven to create as a means of fulfilling our desires: the quest for love in all of its guises, and the promise of technology may be that it can narrow the gaps of our alienation, our inability to connect.

Love . . . interrupts at every hour the most serious occupations, and sometimes perplexes for a while even the greatest minds. It does not hesitate . . . to interfere with the negotiations of statesmen and the investigations of the learned. It knows how to slip its love-notes and ringlets even into ministerial portfolios and philosophical manuscripts. . . . It sometimes demands the sacrifice of . . . health, sometimes of wealth, position and happiness.

Arthur Schopenhauer,
The World as Will and Idea

Mexican calacas figurines from the Day of the Dead festival

Love, the cause of my torment, now brings me joy
Like a day when the low lying dark clouds
Though add gloom to the discomfort of heat
Relieve both by their inevitable showers.

Your heart I do not know, but mine, day and night,
Sets my limbs on fire in a cruel longing for you.
Love tortures your body but mine he burns to ashes
Like the daylight that hides the moon but not the lily.

Kalidasa, *Shakuntala*

In the shorthand of text messaging through cell phones and beepers, by which the small keypad forces an economy of characters, 143 means I love you. Each number represents the number of letters in each word of the declaration.

Prisoner of Love

Romeo brand chewing tobacco

Padua, Italy

Then raising from their lacquered gloom

Old keepsakes, tokens of undying love,

A golden hair-pin, an enamel brooch,

She bids him bear them to her lord. One-half

The hair-pin still she keeps, one-half the brooch,

Breaking with her dim hands the yellow gold,

Sundering the enamel. "Tell my lord,"

She murmured, "to be firm of heart as this

Gold and enamel; then, in heaven or earth,

Below, we twain may meet once more." At parting

She gave a thousand messages of love,

Among the rest recalled a mutual pledge,

How on the seventh day of the seventh moon,

Within the Hall of Immortality

At midnight, whispering, when none were near,

Low in her ear, he breathed, "I swear that we,

Like to the one-winged birds, will ever fly,

Or grow united as the tree whose boughs

Are interwoven. Heaven and earth shall fall,

Long lasting as they are. But this great wrong

Shall stretch from end to end the universe,

And shine beyond the ruin of the stars."

Po Chu-i, *A Lute of Jade*

& Love is an evil word.

Turn it backwards/see, see what I mean?

An evol word. & besides

who understands it?

I certainly wouldn't like to go out on that kind of limb.

Amiri Baraka, *Eulogies*

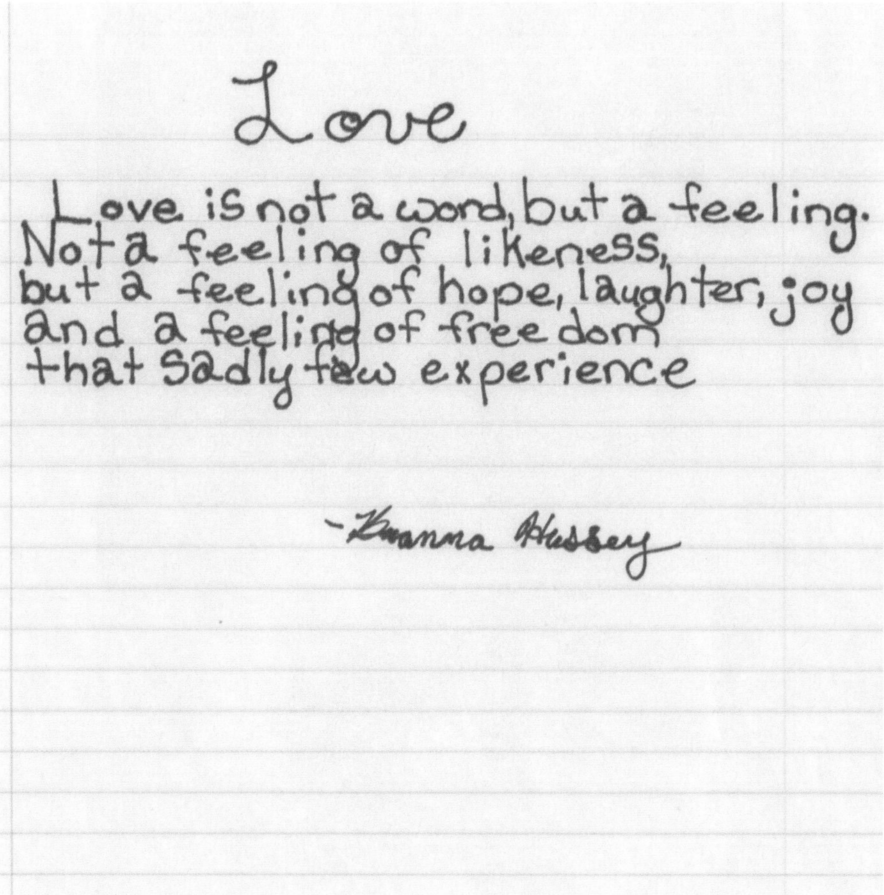

Love

Love is not a word, but a feeling.
Not a feeling of likeness,
but a feeling of hope, laughter, joy
and a feeling of freedom
that sadly few experience

~Kwanna Hussey

It is very easy
to love alone.

Gertrude Stein

IN THE REALM OF THE CIRCUIT 235

To be human, we need play: To create counterpoint to the tensions of our lives. Play refreshes us, reframing our pursuits in games, sports, entertainment, and recreation. In fact, entertainment is the largest component of what most communities call culture.

The activity of play is integral to the creative act. The ability to fail, to try out variations, allows the individual to explore the possibilities of any particular gesture and to fit gestures together, thereby forming new experiences. Play allows us to get events and objects out of order, to structure the narrative in new ways. It does not follow sequences, because it is an end to itself. This is the process of discovery in any field, from the arts to the sciences. The first time a child drops an object it is an accident, but he or she repeats the act over and over to explore gravity and the limits of the parents' patience.

To entertain someone literally means to hold that person's attention, so it is by definition an interactive process. We can entertain each other through performance, or any creative act that occupies us in the exercise of our minds and bodies. The entertainer and audience participate in a process of creating an entity that is more than merely the act itself—performance is by nature interactive. This exchange serves to draw the participants into a dialog in which the audience's attention might be brought to some new or unexpected facet of the world. The audience may also be made aware of its own potentials and limitations, say through the grace of a dancer.

This process of interactivity is perhaps most apparent in what may be the oldest form of entertainment—storytelling. The bard or griot engages a small audience, who, in turn, participate by asking questions, suggesting plot, and actively altering the course of the tale. The best comedians tell stories, engaging the audience: Laughter is a social activity. It is very hard to laugh alone, and it takes a great deal of discipline to amuse one's self without the interaction of others. Like the comedian, the coach or the director, the conductor or the curator, and the editor engage us as players, audience, actors in an orchestration of talents.

Games are among the most pervasive means of play, usually involving more than one person. They are simply played with an agreed-upon set of rules or structures that create the values of the game. Winning may be a matter of finding new structures within the rules: It may be that the best poker players win by understanding the game as a narrative of our human frailties. Play may be a sublimation of other agressive traits—domination and competition—allowing us to turn them into creativity. We have a vicarious identification with the champions of the sports we watch. Professional wrestling and stock-car racing are the two most popular spectacles in the United States. Their champions become cultural heroes, state governors, and the subject of all forms of iconography.

Aaron Siskind,
Savoy Dancers, 1936

Al Gore or the Unabomber?

Ken Crossman's "Al Gore or the Unabomber" quiz presents twelve excerpts from writings by the two men, although it doesn't identify the speaker of each particular quote. Visitors to the site are challenged to match Gore or the Unabomber to each. This is among the thousands, if not millions, of sites on the Internet that serve no purpose but to amuse. They carry no advertising, nor sell products, nor act as official spokes-sites for any political party. They are simply quirky, funny.

The Gore/Unabomber Quiz[12]

Did Al Gore say it? Or was it the Unabomber?

It may be more difficult to decide than you think.

Each quote below is either from Al Gore's book *Earth in the Balance* or from the Unabomber's "Manifesto."

There may or may not be an equal number of quotes from both thinkers.

The twentieth century has not been kind to the constant human striving for a sense of purpose in life. Two world wars, the Holocaust, the invention of nuclear weapons, and now the global environmental crises have led many of us to wonder if survival—much less enlightened, joyous, and hopeful living—is possible. We retreat into the seductive tools and technologies of industrial civilization, but that only creates new problems as we become increasingly isolated from one another and disconnected from our roots.

1—Gore – Unabomber

Again, we must not forget the lessons of World War II. The Resistance slowed the advance of fascism and scored important victories, but fascism continued its relentless march to domination until the rest of the world finally awoke and made the difference and made the defeat of fascism its central organizing principle from 1941 through 1945.

2—Gore – Unabomber

It is not necessary for the sake of nature to set up some chimerical utopia or any new kind of social order. Nature takes care of itself: It was a spontaneous creation that existed long before any human society, and for countless centuries, many different kinds of human societies coexisted with nature without doing it an excessive amount of damage. Only with the Industrial Revolution did the effect of human society on nature become really devastating.

3—Gore – Unabomber

Play is recreation—literally the ability to recreate, either through amusement or by emulating our cultural heroes. As first lady, Jacqueline Kennedy stood out in many ways, but as a fashion icon, she had no peer. She brought style, as a cultural phenomenon, into the homes of the average woman. In the 1960s, fashion watching became entertainment, and so buying clothes became a way of playing with roles and identity. By the end of the century, Madonna was master of role-playing, changing identity as often as some people change clothes. Artist Barbara Kruger summed it up in her work *I shop therefore I am.*

The electronic circuit provides its viewer with a new set of cultural and pop references and preferences, which in many ways construct the identity of the individual youth today, as it is prevalent in the worldwide exchange of information (can you imagine a teenager who would not watch MTV if he or she could?). From **infomercial** to **infotainment**, television blends all forms of performance into what may be a medium that is far too passive.

The twentieth century melded all forms of expression—and the amusement gained from them—into the electronic circuit. The differentiation between high and low culture became stigmatized by class distinctions, racism, and economic divisions. Postmodern assessment of our culture has reenlivened the alignment between those things that we seek for pleasure and diversion. Only in this past century did the lines blur between what was felt to be "art" and the more common entertainment. The world of fashion incorporated art into every aspect of its activities from promotion to production. Graffiti could as easily hang on the gallery wall, as the graceful movements of a pickup basketball game could be studied by classical dancers. The artist today might just as well create a commercial as a museum piece.

If, in the electronic circuit, activities of all levels of culture are collaged into the sites of play, then there exists the potential for a true collaboration among creative energies, irrespective of their origin. Once again, the great responsibility is placed on the audience-interactor to assess the value and meaning of these activities: to teach scrutiny. Every work of creativity, in time, escapes from its maker's intentions. The success of its subsequent aura to move audiences may well determine its cultural value.

Images from *Myst III*.

Video and Computer Games

The most intense thing about Missile Cmmand, though, was the weird crazy moment at the end, when the ICBMs are raining down and you knew you were about to lose it, that was totally euphoric. Because you knew you were going to die. . . . And after the fireworks display, you get to press the restart button and you're alive again.[13]

> J. C. Herz, Joystick Nation

In one way or another, all games involve interaction. In most games this interaction is with another player, but even in single-player games, the rules stand as a framework for the behavior of the participants. In the card game Solitaire, the player's actions are guided through an interaction with the way in which the game is designed. John G. Kemeny, former president of Dartmouth College and computer pioneer, wrote in 1972: ". . . for many inexperienced users, the opportunity of playing games against a computer is a major factor in removing psychological blocks that frighten the average human being away from free use of machines."[14] The growth and proliferation of inexpensive video games in the late 1990s meant that most children's first interaction with a computer (because video game consoles are in fact sophisticated computers) comes at a very early age. Computer games serve as recreation and also, in the case of multiplayer games, as a means for interacting with other people. When a video console or a computer is connected to the Internet, players can interact with other players anywhere in the world.

Games have always been a part of human interaction and activity. The game Go is thought to be nearly twenty-five hundred years old. More recently, computer and video games began as computers started to allow more complicated human interaction in the late 1950s. One of the earliest computer games can be traced back to 1958, when William Higinbotham—eager to create a demonstration for the public of Brookhaven National Laboratory's facilities—made a multi-player game of electronic tennis. Although immensely popular with visitors, Higinbotham's game never made it out of Brookhaven.

The game that would introduce computer games to the world was created four years later at MIT. Called Spacewar!, it was driven by Steve Russell's fascination with pulp science fiction, but was in fact the result of many people's work. Spacewar allowed two players to control spaceships that flew through an imaginary space and fired torpedoes at one another. It ran on the PDP-1, one of the earliest mainframe computers that had a screen (earlier computers used either punched cards or a teletype to communicate with its users). Although again wildly popular with anybody who played it, the group at MIT figured its creation had no real commercial viability (and the practice of selling a software was not widespread) and so gave the code away to anyone who wanted it. It eventually was installed as standard software on the PDP computers it ran on. It was even used as a diagnostic tool by those who repaired the computer. By the mid-1960s, it had spread across college mainframes and spawned hundreds of variations.

Shortly after Spacewar! came a generation of text-based games, beginning with Hunt the Wumpus, in which players moved from room to room in a quest to find a monster. A more sophisticated game soon followed. Adventure, using only text, created a richly detailed world for players to explore. In his book, *Hackers*, Steven Levy wrote, "In a sense, Adventure was a metaphor for computer programming itself—the deep recesses you explored in the Adventure world were akin to the basic, most obscure levels of the machine that you'd be traveling in when you hacked in assembly code."[15] Many contemporary games follow the same structure as Spacewar! and Adventure: so-called twich or arcade-style shoot-em-ups like Asteroids and adventure or exploration games like Ultima.

It would take almost ten years after Adventure was written for video games to catch on with the world outside of college mainframes, when less expensive chips allowed the creation of smaller and more economical machines. Although PONG was not quite the first arcade game (Computer Space, an adaptation of Spacewar! preceded it by a year, in 1971), it was the first successful one. Nolan Bushnell created PONG, and it attracted a wide variety of people to its simple "avoid missing ball for high score" instructions. Atari became a household word, and games such as Space Invaders, Asteroids, Defender, and Pac-Man followed. While simple consoles were available for home use—the Atari 2600, Coleco, and others—games with sophisticated graphics and play were found in the video arcade, a collection of single-purpose freestanding games, whose roots can be found in the penny arcades and nickelodeons of the end of the nineteenth century.

As the personal computer became common in homes, video games lost some of their appeal (and revenue). Whereas early video games were almost entirely about physical prowess and pattern recognition, owing as much to pinball as to Spacewar!, computers of the time had less intuitive controls and encouraged slower, strategy-based games. More often than not, computer games were offering a sort of primitive virtual experience as Adventure had done: Take on the role of a character and explore a new, unique world. Indeed, the popular game Zork was no more than a more sophisticated rewrite of Adventure. Whereas Adventure had used a limited two-word vocabulary to allow interaction with the world, Zork permitted the player to enter full sentences to describe their actions, and the game would respond with equally verbose descriptions. Completely text-based, the heart of Zork was still solving puzzles and collecting various treasures, but the game was also trying to create a compelling, novelistic world.

Similar in its attempt to create another world was the Wizardry series. Wizardry had a point-of-view perspective as players wandered a three-dimensional maze seeking to kill an evil wizard. A few years later came the Ultima series, which opted for an overhead, God's-eye view, and was noteworthy not only for its attempt to create an entire world (complete with mountains, cities, and oceans surrounding the ubiquitous caves and dungeons) but also for its efforts to present moral quandaries for the player. The cushioning distance of video games was challenged when players found that not only did their actions have lasting, ethically-based consequences in the game, but also that these ethical dilemmas were the heart of the game.

Things were still progressing on campus mainframes in a different direction. Despite not having the new graphical frills of personal computer games, MUDs (Multi-User Dungeon) had a lasting popularity. MUDs allowed groups of people to interact in their primitive dungeon environments, offering up the first seeds of a style that would not fully catch on until the 1990s and the commercial dominance of the Internet.

By the late 1980s, more sophisticated console games such as Nintendo and Sega revitalized the market that Atari had started long before. Console systems, with their sophisticated graphics capabilities, dominated the more action-oriented games and home computers, with their better storage capacity, offered simulations, strategy games, and virtual worlds.

And then there was Doom, a first-person computer game whose players roamed around an alien planet killing demons. It was as fast-paced and dynamic as any video game, as immersive and frightening a world as anybody had offered, and perhaps most importantly, Doom was a return to the sort of hacker philosophy of those earliest days at MIT. Doom could be played as a network, allowing multiple players to wander the game together or against each other—a virtual arena for the digital age. Additionally, Doom allowed its players to modify the game, creating their own levels, graphics, and weapons. People did not just play Doom; they became a part of it.

Since then, games have only become more complex and more immersive. Their graphics are amazingly detailed, their sounds comparable to big-budget movies, and entire teams of people labor at creating them. No doubt inspired by the Internet, most games now allow some form of networking option, and entire virtual worlds have been created for people to play online. Ultima itself has evolved into Ultima Online—a huge networked world in which players can still run around killing monsters, in addition to buying houses, opening up shops, and joining organizations of like-minded players.

At this point, computer and video games are more than just a cultural phenomenon: They are culture. As an industry, they make more money than movies, music, or any other form of entertainment. The military has used them for training and to recruit soldiers, politicians have used them as a scapegoat, and people routinely barter their online properties for real-world dollars. Most importantly though, generations have been raised on them and can now relate through the shared cultural experience of their first game of Pac-Man or Doom. Built on a principle of sharing information, virtual experience, and creating new modes of interaction, video and computer games offer us a glimpse of the creative potential of society.

```
You are in a 20-foot depression floored with bare dirt.  Set into the
dirt is a strong steel grate mounted in concrete.  A dry streambed
leads into the depression.

The grate is locked.
north

You're at slit in streambed.
go south

You're outside grate.

The grate is locked.
look

You are in a 20-foot depression floored with bare dirt.  Set into the
dirt is a strong steel grate mounted in concrete.  A dry streambed
leads into the depression.

The grate is locked.
```

Above: Adventure

Below: Dixie, Ted, and Timmy from the interactive video game *A Bad Day on the Midway* by the Residents and Jim Ludtke.

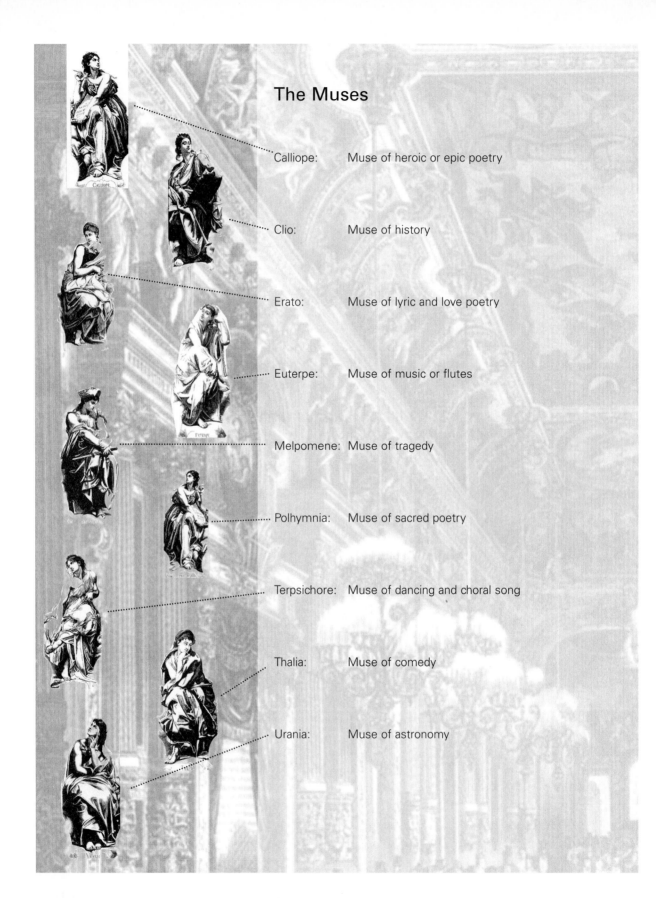

The Muses

Calliope: Muse of heroic or epic poetry

Clio: Muse of history

Erato: Muse of lyric and love poetry

Euterpe: Muse of music or flutes

Melpomene: Muse of tragedy

Polhymnia: Muse of sacred poetry

Terpsichore: Muse of dancing and choral song

Thalia: Muse of comedy

Urania: Muse of astronomy

Tea Ceremony

The Japanese ritual tea ceremony is a highly formalized and aesthetic way of entertaining guests. The highly structured ritual serves (no pun intended) to relieve the participants from the distractions of everyday life. As in other Zen Buddhist practices, the form of the ceremony is its most important aspect.

Double Dutch contest, New York, 1986

The boundaries of perception are defined not only by perception but also by action.

Charles Sanders Peirce

Do not take the entire world upon your shoulders. Do a certain amount of skylarking, as befits people your age. Skylarking, incidentally, used to be a minor offense under Naval Regulations. What a charming crime. It means intolerable lack of seriousness. I would love to have had a dishonorable discharge from the United States Navy—for skylarking not just once, but again and again and again.

Kurt Vonnegut[16]

Discus thrower

Above and facing Page: Asymptote, *NYSE 3DTF Virtual Reality Environment*

In 1998, the New York Stock Exchange commissioned Asymptote, the architectural firm of Hani Rashid and Lise Anne Couture, to envision a means to manage the vast complexity of data that traders were confronted with, from real-time information like stock quotes, to news stories and archived data. Asymptote created a "Virtual Trading Floor," one that can exist only in the realm of the circuit, where the computer ushers the visitor to this new architectural space to navigate information that is drawn from the World Brain. Visitors can configure the environment to suit their needs, drawing on the abilities of the computer to envision data in meaningful ways.

S tewart Brand, media critic and founder of the WELL (Whole Earth 'Lectronic Link), once said that information is a verb.[17] By this he meant that, like a shark, it needs to move to stay alive. Ideas are given meaning as they pass from person to person in a dialog. Metafora, too, is a verb, not a noun. It has value, as a catalyst, in the spaces that connects people. Information lives in the digital network; metafora lives in the dialog. Our achievements are given new meaning because the computer affords a greater facility for creation in the exchange of information. If metafora is a virus, society is its host.

The subject of interactivity is the end point of this chapter as it connects people through metafora. Metafora is given life in the realm of exchange, whether it be for identity, survival, learning, advertising, love, or amusement. Indeed, this inter-activity becomes metafora, which in turn nourishes interactivity. This symbiotic relationship guarantees reciprocal and continuous growth. Creativity allows and anticipates interaction—the love act. This process of give and take is as essential to human affairs as mating itself. It defines our humanness. Our ability to create metafora is the *inter* in *interactivity*. Meaning is held in metafora, and the measure of communication is how successfully the metafora engages its target. It bridges the gap between our desire for expression and its formation: "The essential characteristic of the nexus is that every action of one person is expected to have reference to, and influence everyone else. The nature of this influence is expected to be reciprocal."[18]

Creativity lies not only in what you make but also in where you put it. The pop singer Bjork has given her songs new and greater meaning by posting them on her website and allowing anyone to download and remix them, and then repost them to her site for anyone to download and remix (and so on). Originality resides with what the receivers do with metafora, how they use digital tools to rework metafora in relation to oneself or the community.

The dialog described in this chapter is the activity of the multimedia cathedral, which amplifies interaction between people, and between its contents as well, changing the very forms of dialog in an ongoing process. The speed of interaction through the realm of the circuit may change its nature, as the speeds of the tele-

"The bell didn't work."

"That's what made it art."

Man Ray, commenting on his work "Self-Portrait," in which the viewer was to push a button that rang a bell

graph and telephone changed the nineteenth century. Further, we can interact with the tools themselves, shaping them, through programming, to suit our particular needs. Last, new communities can be formed through the imagination of the creative interlocutor, extending the story.

Clearly, the creative act in the realm of the circuit does not rest with a single person. It is no longer a concern of producing artifacts or endings. Instead, the substance of metafora in this new realm is the creative process itself. Metafora is a vehicle for expression, for the transmission and transformation of creative thought. The very act of communication is interactive: It requires that the receiver actively interpret (and transform) the message. Interaction, dialog, and exchange lie at the core of our social structures. The realm of the circuit and the creative interlocutor have value only as they enhance the dialog.

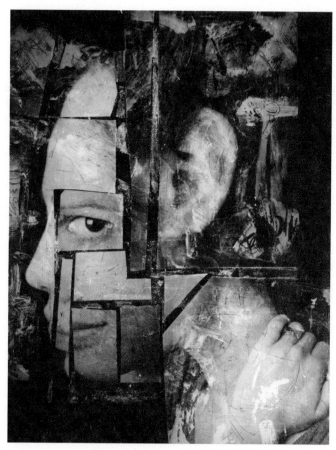

Anonymous, *Untitled*

B.C.E.

circa 5000 Earliest archeological record of African music and dance. Although numerous instruments are used, the drum forms an integral part of African life, music, and culture. For the Anlo-Ewe people of Ghana, like many modern and ancient African tribal groups, dance-drumming plays a central role in communal life. Highly interactive and participatory, Anlo-Ewe dance-drumming engages and incorporates everyone in a communal ritual.

460 Pericles (c. 495–429), a wealthy Greek politician and Athenian leader, helps introduce democracy to Greek society and city-states. Literally translated as "people rule," from the Greek *demos*, "people," and *kratos*, "rule," democracy introduces a new level of public involvement and interaction in their social and political lives.

C.E.

12th century Zen koans (Chinese, *kung-an*) are used by the Japanese Rinzai sect of Buddhism. Originally introduced from China, koans are paradoxical questions and statements drawn from the life of Buddhist masters and used to facilitate a spiritual awakening in a Buddhist novice. Designed to exhaust the monks' intellect and test their capacity for intuitive thought, koans are often selected to fit the needs of a particular monk and are solved only through deep contemplation and interaction with the monk's master.

13th century Ramon Llull (c.1235–1316), a Catalan mystic and poet, creates some of the first movable books. Llull's books contained movable discs and flaps, all of which were used to illustrate his complex ideas about truth and existence. By moving these discs and flaps, readers could interact with and creatively explore Llull's ideas.

1435 Leon Alberti's "Della Pictura" formally introduces the laws of perspective. Alberti's systematic approach to drawing three-dimensional images alters the audience's visual experience and creates new interaction with the visual image.

1545 First dated performance of Commedia dell'arte—an Italian theatrical form that thrived from the sixteenth until the eighteenth century. As popular theater, the commedia dell'arte relied on ensemble acting and improvisation. Often drawing on stock characters and classical literary stories, the commedia dell'arte actors often change and alter their performances depending on their audience.

1553 Hans Holbein (1497–1543) paints "The Ambassadors." The picture contains an optically distorted skull on the floor that can only be visually corrected when the viewer looks at the picture from an odd angle. Like many artists of the time, Holbein used optical illusions and tricks to engage and question the viewer's sense of visual representation. This tradition of illusionistic and interactive painting continues in the twentieth century with the paintings of René Magritte (1898–1967) and M. C. Escher (1898–1972).

Early 17th century Kabuki theater in Japan develops. Performances are highly interactive and often incorporate audience participation. Actors stop and address the audience, who respond in kind in a ritualized interaction of questions, applause, and verbal praise.

chronology: interactivity

Mid-17th century African American spirituals in the United States incorporate call-and-response patterns in hymns and religious music in which the preacher would practice "lining out," or reading the largely illiterate audience's line, the call-and-response pattern becomes an integral part of religious hymns and spirituals. It is believed this pattern developed from a close interaction of African musical traditions and white folk-music elements.

Early 1880s The first vending machines appear in London, England.

Early 1900s Drawing on African musical traditions, jazz emerges from New Orleans. Fusing musical improvisation with swing, musicians such as Louis Armstrong help invent modern jazz.

1905 The jukebox debuts. Initially offering twenty-four choices, the jukebox allows users to choose the music they want to hear. By the 1950s, jukeboxes were ubiquitous in bars, restaurants, and other popular hangouts.

1917 Marcel Duchamp creates "Fountain," his most notorious "ready-made." Stressing the viewer's role in completing the artwork, Duchamp's ideas explore the roles of the artist and the viewer, and helps revolutionize the arts.

1929 Early flight simulators developed by the U.S. government. Constructed with a disassembled plane fuselage, the simulator allows the user to interact and learn the basics of plane operations. In the 1960s and 1970s, flight simulators incorporate VR (virtual reality) graphics in attempts to create more realistic flight simulation.

1930 The beginning of call-in radio shows allows audiences to participate and interact with radio programs.

1931 Bally Hoo, the first coin-operated pinball machine, is introduced. Enormously popular, pinball requires the user to push, tilt, and shove the machine to achieve the highest score.

1932 Bertolt Brecht writes about the communicative and interactive potentials of radio in *Radio—eine vorsintflutliche Erfindung?* In this text and others, Brecht envisions an age in which radio will allow us, as "listeners-speakers," both to receive and to transmit messages—fostering a new age of public communication and interaction.

1946 ENIAC (Electronic Numerical Integrator and Computer) is designed. Occupying a whole floor at the University of Pennsylvania, ENIAC responds to human programs to complete complex problems in record time, thereby advancing human-computer interactivity.

1948 Norbert Wiener (1894–1964) publishes *Cybernetics, or Control and Communication in the Animal and Machine*. His pivotal research and theories form the basis of our study of artificial intelligence in computers and machines.

1949 Dan Robbins, illustrator and employee of Palmer Paint Company, invents Paint-by-Numbers. Fun and interactive, Palmer's idea allows users to re-create paintings simply by following instructions.

Handbills, Oakland, California, 1994.

1962 Steve Russell completes Spacewar!—the first computer game—while at MIT. Played over the earliest server, ARPANET, Spacewar! is also the first multiplayer video game. Later, Russell helps create the first joysticks with his colleague Alan Kotok and others.

1963 Ivan Southerland, at MIT, develops Sketchpad, which allows the user to draw on a screen and see the results in real time, instead of having to write a program, then feed punched cards into a the computer, and wait for the output.

1963 A. Michael Noll writes computer programs that create drawings influenced by Cubism. He insists that the work of art is the program, not the drawing.

1963 The mouse is invented by Doug Engelbart. Along with the GUI (graphical user interface), the mouse helps bring about a new form of interactive computing.

1969 Myron Krueger, a computer scientist and artist, begins creating the first interactive computer art. Influenced by John Cage's notions of indeterminacy and audience participation, Krueger helped pioneer interactive computer art with pieces such as *GLOWFLOW*.

1969 Nicholas Negroponte and the Architecture Machine Group at MIT use a computer-controlled arm to build a maze for gerbils out of blocks. As the gerbils navigate the maze, the machine, called Seek, rearranges the blocks in response to their movements.

1969 Don Wetzel, Tom Barnes, and George Chastain invent the first successful ATM (automatic teller machine). By allowing customers to interact and conduct their own banking transactions, Wetzel and his colleagues change the nature of banking.

1970 James Seawright installs Network III in the Walker Art Center, where lights hanging from the ceiling flash on and off in reaction to the movement of people in the room.

1971 One of the first email messages is sent via the U.S. Department of Defense's ARPANET. Email introduces a new level of instantaneous communication and interaction.

1971 Sam Hurst, founder of Elographics, invents touch-screen technology while teaching at the University of Kentucky. Central to museum displays, information kiosks, and ATMs, touch-screen technology introduces a new level of digital interaction and interface to everyday life.

1972 The first successful computer arcade game, PONG, ushers in the age of video gaming.

1972 Krueger coins the term "virtual reality" in his dissertation, later published in 1983.

1978 Texas Instruments introduces Speak and Spell. Its combination of voice simulators and keyboard uses a simple interactive interface to teach children how to spell.

 chronology: interactivity

1978 Architecture Machine Group (AMG), later the MIT Media Lab, makes the first demonstration of interactive video. Using a laser disc, viewers are allowed to explore a 3-D rendering of Aspen, Colorado.

1979 "Choose-your-own-adventure" series makes its debut with *The Cave of Time*. Hugely successful, the books guide young readers through various adventures, letting them choose the course of the narrative.

Late 1970s Hip-hop music arises in the South Bronx. Scratching and sampling records while rhyming over the beats, DJs interact and deconstruct existing songs, creating a whole new genre of music.

1980 James Pallas completes his "Progmod," a sculpture that stands nearly seven feet high. It contains a computer workstation and a popcorn popper. It creates abstract patterns on its screen in response to sounds and visual stimuli.

1980 Richard Bartlee and Roy Trubshaw, of the University of Essex, write a program to create the first MUD (Multi-User Dungeon), an online virtual environment in which users can interact with one another and with the computer. The interaction takes place entirely through text, because computers of the time have limited capacity for graphics. The reliance on text requires an additional level of interactivity on the part of the players, or mudders. The MUD form continues to be popular to this day.

1980 Smalltalk is created at Xerox's Learning Research Group. The first object-oriented programming language and a predecessor to Hypercard, Smalltalk is a key inspiration for the graphical user interface that would become integral to Apple's Macintosh computer. Smalltalk introduces drag-and-drop file manipulation and pop-up menus and windows.

1983 Myron Krueger creates *Videoplace: Critter Interaction*, one of his Responsive Environments, sculptures that change based on the behavior of the viewer and that can learn and change its behavior. *Videoplace* consists of computers, video cameras, and video screens. As viewers enter the exhibition, their images are projected on the screen, accompanied by an electronic "critter," which attempts to avoid contact with the viewers' image.

1983 Apple introduces LISA, the first computer with GUI. In addition to being one of the first multimedia computers, LISA also introduces new levels of interaction with the mouse and easy graphic interface.

1986 James Seawright's "House Plants I" can move based on the level of light in a room.

1987 Apple Hypercard is introduced. Incorporating graphics, text, and animation, Hypercard allows users to interact and explore authored programs.

1988 Director is released by Macromind (now Macromedia). Director allows users to create elaborate interactive CD-ROMs.

1989 Multimedia artist Jeffrey Shaw exhibits "Legible City." Sitting on a bicycle, the user can ride through a virtual urban landscape comprised of words and letters.

1991 "Hypertext Hotel" at Brown University. The Hypertext Hotel is a collaborative fiction project that was started by Robert Coover. Similar to a MUD, the Hypertext Hotel is a MOO, or object-oriented MUD, which allows numerous users to alter, adapt to, and interact with their environment.

1991 Compact disc interactive (CD-I) is introduced by Philips.

1994 Broderdund's MYST becomes one of the first successful 3-D interactive video games.

1996 The introduction of DVD technology. Written on CD format, the DVD (digital video disc) greatly improves sound and resolution. DVDs also allow unparalleled viewer interaction in the form of movie chapters, deleted scenes, actor/director interviews, and so forth.

1996 Tamagotchi toys are introduced in Japan. Loosely translated as "lovable egg," Tamagotchis are virtual pets that require constant attention in order to stay alive. By pressing certain buttons, the user needs to console, feed, and nurture them.

1997 Ultima Online (UO) is introduced by Origin software. Although not the first multiplayer online game, UO expands the popularity of MUDs by allowing thousands of players to interact, fight, and compete in a highly detailed 3-D fantasy world.

1997 Reigning world chess champion Gary Kasparov plays IBM's Deep Blue Supercomputer in a chess match and loses.

1998 Taking interactive toys to a new level, Tiger Electronics introduces the Furby—a furry creature that uses infrared sensors to respond to outside stimulation. Furbys interact with other Furbys, move, sneeze, learn, and talk to their owners.

1998 Sega releases the Dreamcast system—one of the first home video gaming consoles with online Internet capabilities. In addition to basic web access, the Dreamcast allows users to play interactive multiplayer games via the Internet on their home televisions.

2000 Antoinette LaFarge's plaintext players perform *The Roman Forum*, directed by Robert Allen. Their daily online and stage performances, set in Imperial Rome, respond to events at the Democratic National Convention.

chronology: interactivity

CHAPTER FOUR

ELEMENTS OF STRUCTURE

narrative ⧉ spacetime ⧉ form ⧉ color ⧉ rhythm
perspective ⧉ style

All creative acts have a structure that is built from many elements. Understanding the elements covered in this chapter enables us to use them to stretch our imaginations and the imagination of others. Because the computer manages metafora in multiple forms, it is necessary for those who creatively engage this tool to understand these fundamentals.

Anne Ryan, *Untitled*

Alexander Bing, *Untitled,* 1954

Today's multimedia forms of creativity change at a dizzying pace. Computer programs—tools for shaping metafora—are released at an ever-increasing speed. Because datasets are mutable and mutating, the ability to manage structure is essential to being adaptable to these changes. In order to be able to work effectively today, creative individuals must have a grasp of the underlying principles that give meaning to the creative act, of its elements of structure. Narrative is the way in which events in an artistic work unfold, and space and time are the environments in which they unfold. Form and rhythm are concerned with the arrangement of the parts, whereas color affects the intensity of the act. Perspective is (sometimes literally) the artist's point of view, and/or the way in which audiences orient themselves to the work. Finally, style is the successful management of all of these elements, giving the distinction to the creative act.

Roman Jakobson, an early twentieth-century Russian formalist, stated that all communication is conveyed from one person (an addresser) to another (an addressee) based on a shared context and code.[1] The elements described in this chapter form that context and code. Language is a set of arbitrary sounds that we agree upon to have certain meanings, whereas our appreciation of a photograph depends on our having had a common experience of the object depicted. Some elements are innate; others are acquired. Each of us has a natural rhythm, but may never learn the graces that allow it to have style.

Humanity's need to express is not merely an accounting of information, fact, or figure: Those acts are simply translation. Creativity, on the other hand, is an embellishment in our quest to comprehend the unknown and unknowable, and in so doing to create new vehicles of understanding. As we sharpen our skills to manage metafora, we extend the abilities of our senses. We are then interpreting and reinterpreting experience, creating new styles. In the creation of writing, music, dance, painting, and sculpture, we constantly seek to integrate the countless combinations of the elements of their structure into powerful expression. Art, science, and technology pursue the same concerns of establishing our place on earth. But the role for creative people in any field is constantly to challenge existing structures, re-arranging their elements into new configurations.

ADDRESSER

Contact
Message
Context
Code

ADDRESSEE

Metafora is the vehicle that contains and carries the message formed by the elements of structure enabling us to express ourselves through representation.

All art may be a kind of story that humanity attempts to tell itself, and narrative is the underlying structure of that endeavor. Henry Louis Gates, Jr. says that "people arrive at an understanding of themselves in the world through narratives."[2] The creation of metafora is integral in the production of narrative in the many forms of creativity. Roland Barthes wrote: "Narrative is present in every age, in every place, in every society; it begins with the very history of mankind and there nowhere is nor has been a group of people without narrative. All classes, all human groups have their narrative, enjoyment of which is very often shared by men with different opposing cultural backgrounds. Caring nothing for the division between good and bad literature, narrative is international, transhistorical, transcultural; it is simply there, like life itself."[3]

The creative use of metafora gives the inflection that allows us to transcend the simple telling of events one after the other. Storytelling allows us to move into new realms of interpretation and stimulation of the imagination that defy the pat conventions of chronology. E. M. Forster defines story as "a narrative of events, arranged in their time sequence."[4] Each new teller or artist brings to the underlying narrative new translations and meaning, and each new audience receives this act of creativity in new ways, carrying it forward as it is meaningful and useful in new forms to yet newer audiences. Thus, the myths that underlie our culture evolve over time, as our quest for understanding continually moves forward. The finesse of the story or myth, whether told in word, movement, or image, is in the creative use of metaora, or the inventions of new forms of it.

Time itself is the story, a sequence into which we put the narrative of our passing through space. We construct a beginning, a middle, and an end to events that we tell in order to give shape to our lives. Paul Ricoeur states that narrative is inseparable from temporality. He takes temporality to be the structure of existence that "…reaches language in narrativity and narrativity to be the language structure that has temporality as its ultimate reference."[5]

Despite the fact that time moves forward, we seem to need closure in narrative. Each audience brings its own sense of an end to its engagement of the story or the creative idea, whether it is finished in the formal sense or not. Spectators or readers carry the experience with them, opening it and closing it as their own imagination engages and reengages the experience. In one sense, there is no definitive closure to the stories that society tells itself with narrative, as we are constantly dreaming it forward. The only finality that an individual can really know is death; otherwise our narrative is the legacy we leave by being creative.

The new interactivity of the realm of the circuit adds further dimension to the issue of closure, the narrative, and the story. If in more conventional narratives there was a beginning, middle, and end, in cyberspace everything is to be continued. The viewer or operative can disrupt: reconfigure the meter of the poetry, edit the film, and transform the music to his or her own ends. Once the audience can perform these measures, the so-called closure made by the author is in a state of flux. The new technologies bring us back in a way to the early form of story-telling, that of sitting in a circle, listening to the griot, in taking away from that experience one's own adaption for a new cultural legacy.

Can a narrative acted upon by those who receive it in cyberspace, and who in turn become authors, ever stop evolving? Absolutely not: It is in our very nature, in the creative license we individually have in the thoughtfulness of our interactions produce culture, evolving the narrative into new metafora only a new kind of temporality occurs.

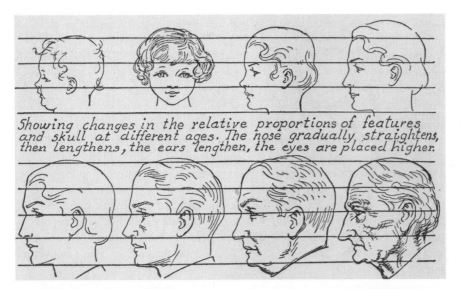

Showing changes in the relative proportions of features and skull at different ages. The nose gradually straightens, then lengthens, the ears lengthen, the eyes are placed higher.

We understand our lives as stories.

Engraving, after stained glass in Chartres Cathedral depicting scenes from the life of Jesus Christ

Television dramas, those that continue from week to week, often weave several stories together in a single episode, intersplicing different times of the story to unfold within the sixty-minute time slot. Often, plots will extend from week to week, or even season to season, in what is known as an "arc," thus keeping the viewers interested so they will tune in again. It is a feature of most film and television storytelling that these arcs, or smaller plot lines, which Alfred Hitchcock used to call "McGuffins," are resolved at some point. Recent dramas, though, have left them unresolved, much as real life does not always answer the questions it raises. Time is a part of our creative drama. We construct it, as we do space, through whatever medium our ingenuity desires.

The narrative of the circuit is yet to be denied. Our experience and expectation of the world are greatly complicated by the constant exchange with events, their depiction and their mediation in a scenario in which it is practically impossible to delineate the distinctions between what is real and what is unreal. "Once upon a time" changed to "A long time ago in a galaxy far, far away" or "Insert quarter to continue." The expectations of the creative audience are no longer conditioned by a defined space nor a defined time. Our aspirations are defined in a collage of experience that multimedia and hypermedia creativity casts on us all. Time intertwines in curious ways. Endings are nullified by new beginnings: Space is always changing.

Rimini, 1990

Our creative endeavors fall into different categories based on how they exist in space and time. If you look at it while standing still, it's a painting. If you move around it, it's a sculpture. If you pass it around, it's a snapshot. If you live in it, it's architecture.

Our history can be seen as the struggle to define our relationship to the world through time and space. We can see evidence of this struggle in the placement of tools, food, and other artifacts in prehistoric burial sites. Anthropologists believe that this indicates some belief in an afterlife, as the dead were prepared for their journey through the future. Paintings of the hunt found in caves dating from 20,000 B.C.E. also indicate some sort of engagement with time: They are either a commemoration of a past event, an attempt to influence future events, or both. Handprints near these paintings seem to be an attempt by the painter to give him- or herself some sort of permanence by leaving a record of his or her identity: "Yo, man, I did this."

Our experiences of space and time are so intertwined that we cannot understand one without the other: They are fundamental units of exchange in the ongoing intercourse of society. Creativity is the management of the dimensions that embrace us.

By the turn of the twentieth century, Albert Einstein (building on the work of earlier physicists) proposed that time and space are relative to the observer–they stretch and change–and are, in fact, two sides of the same coin. One cannot be considered separate from the other. The notion of the space-time continuum is perhaps the most remarkable metaphor of the twentieth century, though Einstein's concept is under constant scrutiny and challenge.

Culture concerns itself with the exploration and modulation of time. However imperfect, these explorations help us to establish our place in the universe. Notwithstanding the growling of our stomachs and the drooping of our eyelids, we have no specific physical relationship to time. We can note its passage through other perceptions: the ticking of a clock, the motion of the sun, or the foliage of the seasons. If our closest physical orientation to time is the clock of the stomach, then it is perhaps through such an essential urge that we began the metaphorical quest to understand time and space. Other cycles of the human body–menstruation, pregnancy, and aging–relate the body to longer durations of time.

All creative acts take into account the time and space in which the viewer will experience them. Performing arts unfold over a prescribed period of time, in a prescribed space. In the fine arts, the audience determines the time spent on viewing a piece and in what manner they move their eyes over the piece. Creative management of time and space in the performing arts and film lies in how the work unfolds during the performance, how the other elements of structure affect the viewers' sense of the passage of time. We may be better able to understand the way viewers look at a web page by examining how they examine a static work such as a painting. Because the viewers have greater choice in how they interact with a static piece, its creator can better guide their attention by careful management of the elements of structure. Such things as color, balance, and tone can be used to direct the attention of someone looking at a painting. Web designers use the same compositional elements within a single page, but should also be aware that the user interacts with the entire site over a period of time.

Space and time are experienced in a fundamental way through architecture. The design of buildings—from skyscrapers to temples—controls our movement through space, and consequently our experience of the ediface as we travel through it over time. An aesthetic appreciation of good architecture rests in how it tells a story—where it stops us, how it moves us, and our interaction with the ornament that makes our passage a meaningful event. It is our interaction with the building over time that shapes our memory of it. Time is at the core of this experience, for it is how we spend our time with the space that determines its utilitarian as well as its social and aesthetic value. Finally, how those values measure up over a larger period of time determines the greatness of the construct of this physical narrative itself. Perhaps the addition of time to space allows us to create a narrative out of our journeys. It is not surprising that the stories of many of the earliest computer games—Adventure and Zork, for instance—followed the physical movement of the player through an imaginary cave.

Architecture is interactive. A good architect will anticipate the needs and movements of those who use the space. In the late 1950s, for example, the University of Toronto would adjust the pathways on its campus by carefully observing students' footsteps in freshly fallen snow. Rather than laying down paths in an attempt to anticipate students' movements, the university's planners decided to allow the students to determine how they wanted to walk through the campus, and then moved the paths to accommodate them.

Cyberspace is a new public architecture. It is conditioned on timing, as physical distance gives way to the distance between network points, measured in the wait time as a web page downloads. Cyberspace extends the notion of all of our institutions—the cathedral, the courthouse, the building, and the city—to a temporal relationship in narrative time and image space, webbed in designs and patterns that are constantly in motion. We can move from one institution to the next, from one country to the next, in a stroke of the key, no longer making time the limiting factor of our travel or experience. This unites us in Marvin Minsky's "society of the mind."

Just as our minds actively construct vision from disparate bits of sense information, they also construct a sense of flowing, continuous time from our perceptions of all that goes on around us. We can measure time, but we can never fully grasp it, because its passage is seen only through memory. Just as we cannot stand still in time, likewise we rarely are motionless in space, and so our perception of space is also created through memory and change. Experience itself is flux: We cannot perceive passage from one point to another without recollecting our position in the past.

Though our experience of time varies, we attempt to construct a uniform, temporal world to live in, composed of regular hours and minutes. Time is not measurable by tangible objects. To standardize time, we turn to what we think of as uniform: Space, because space can be measured by physical things such as a tape measure. Our models of time are quite often spatial, such as the notation we make to represent the tempo or beat in a musical score, days on a calendar, or the expression "high noon," when the sun is at its apex. Scientist William Friedman believes that there is some intrinsic mental mechanism responsible for the nearly

spacetime

Space alone, or time alone is doomed to fade into a mere shadow; only a kind of union of both will preserve their existence.

Hermann Minkowski[6]

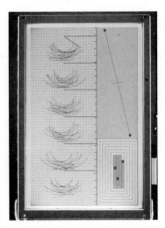

John F. Simon, Jr.,
Clock Piece

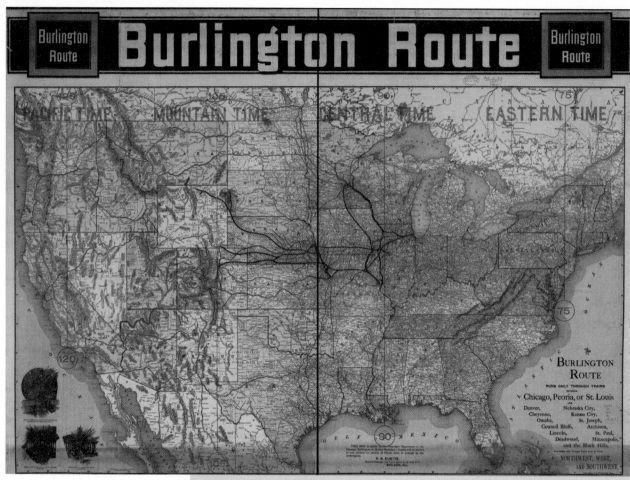

Burlington Route

In 1884, a conference in Washington, DC established twenty-four time zones across the globe. This development was spurred in part by the need for standard railroad schedules, and its implementation was made possible by the telegraph, as the time was transmitted from telegraph offices.

Metaphors of Space

Steven Pinker writes that all human languages share common metaphors of space and force. For example, in the phrase "the meeting is at 3:00" the word "at" is a spatial metaphor. We use concrete terms to express abstract concepts. In this case it is the correspondence of an event (the meeting) with a time (3:00). Pinker postulates that this is because our ancestors had evolved sophisticated reasoning mechanisms for space and force, and as language developed, the pressures of evolution reused these neural circuits to help us reason more abstract concepts such as time. But this points to a failure in language noted by philosopher Friedrich Nietzsche, that in fact all language is abstract and that we cannot ever hope to know the outside world through language.

universal use of these spatial models.[7] Perhaps we think of time in the same way we think of space, as continuous and uniform (or at least we used to before Einstein) because it is reassuring to do so.

Any form of static art–from painting to photography–is an attempt to compress space and time into the plane of a picture or the frozen essence of a sculpture. To some extent, all creativity is a narrowing of focus, a drawing of the viewer's attention to particular aspects of reality, but it is especially salient to representational work such as painting and photography.

Both representational and abstract images suggest the passage of time. An abstract canvas such as those of Lee Krasner cannot help but suggest the movements of the artist as she splattered paint. The representational image has a more complicated relation to time. Because they endeavor to show the physical appearance of the world, representational images seek to freeze time as they remove the scene they represent from reality. Such images can show a past event, a time of myth, or an allegory of some hoped-for future.

In the theater, the time of the performance unfolds in real time, yet the time of the story may cover several days or even years. Jumps in time in the story are usually accomplished through the changing of scenes or acts in the play, or denoted by changes in lighting or dress. Nonetheless, the audience experiences time in the same way that the actors experience it. Motion pictures portray time in an entirely different way. Early "movies," like many new art forms, imitated older art forms, in this case theater. Movie cameras recorded skits and plays, and the film was played back at a later time. The audience became one step removed from the actors, but there is no interpretation by the medium, merely replication.

As filmmakers gained experience with the new medium, they explored its ability to distort the viewers' experience of space and time through editing. By splicing together lengths of film, the illusion of the passage of time could be given. But the time of the film is a fiction; a film whose duration is two hours may depict the lifetime of its characters. The cutting and splicing of the editor's table tells a story by creating a new object. The narrative is not held in the abstract words of a book, but in the physicality of the emulsion to be viewed and experienced in a totally new time and space. Space, too, is manipulated in powerful ways. With photography, telephoto lenses can compress space and wide-angle lenses can expand it, but editing can also move the viewer's perspective in impossible ways. The most common example of this is a conversation between two people, whereby the camera cuts from one face to another. The camera can jump from one face to the next because the scene has in fact been filmed twice, by two cameras in two different places, and the film is later spliced together. This creates a change of perspective that is not possible in the normal unfolding of time and that requires a suspension of disbelief on the part of the viewer.

Postmodern French critic Paul Virilio emphasizes that speed, the lightning transmission of information, or shift of perspective, collapses the dimension of space and hence the dimension of time.[8] Walking across Sibera is one thing, flying across it is another, and watching a news conversation between a correspondent in Siberia and a television anchor in Berlin is yet another thing entirely.

spacetime

The nineteenth-century zoetrope was one of many mechanical devices that could portray moving images that unfold over time from a sequence of still images.

Turing's man is the first who actually works with time. Like space, time is a commodity provided by the computer, a material to be molded, insofar as this is possible, to human ends. This intimate contact with time promises success in time (progress) but also an awareness of ultimate temporal limitations . . . . The CPU (and each program it executes) is a consumer of time, of the abstract, electrical pulses handed out by the sequencing mechanism; it therefore must be constructed to be a wise consumer. Time is a resource, perhaps the primary resource, by which the computer operates.

Jay David Bolter, *Turing's Man*

For classical scholar and computer scientist Jay David Bolter, time is the raw material of the computer.[9] At the heart of every computer lies its clock, which acts as coxswain, sending out millions of pulses each second that serve to coordinate the actions of all of the components, from the central processing unit to the memory to the hard drive. Computer engineers choose how many pulses each instruction or action can consume. They have literally constructed the computer out of time.

Built according to rigid and fixed rules that describe and control their actions, computers use a time that is continuous and discrete, though our experience of time on the computer is anything but—it can seem slow or amazingly fast, and sometimes it is truncated by our own stupidity in hitting the wrong key.

Whether in the design of a computer game or in the composition of a symphony, the management of the viewers' attention remains a major concern of the artist. Some works unfold in a predetermined sequence, such as in a film or a musical composition wherein the pace and rhythm serve to mediate the viewers' sense of time, just as the composition of visual images mediates our sense of space.

Consideration of space and time is crucial for those who seek to create in the realm of the circuit. Even before the digital age, it was not possible to create outside of time, nor without a careful consideration of space. Today's electronic culture has seemingly obliterated previous concepts of space and time, and simultaneously created entirely new spaces and time frames. The circuit enables us to enter cyberspace almost whenever and wherever we like. We can move through imaginary spaces, held in the nearly unlimited memory of the computer, having removed the need for conventional movement of the body from one tangible object to the next. In cyberspace, our physical bodies stand still (in **meatspace**), while our minds move from metaphor to metaphor.

William Gibson described cyberspace: "The Matrix . . . a two-dimensional space war faded behind a forest of mathematically generated ferns, demonstrating the spatial possibilities of logarithmic spirals . . . a consensual hallucination experienced daily by legitimate operators, in every nation by children being taught mathematical concepts . . . a graphic representation of data, abstracted from the banks of every computer in the human system. Unthinkable complexity. Lines of light arranged in a non-space of the mind, clusters in constellations of data."[10]

Cyberspace is modulated space whose very essence is design, a design to help users navigate from one space to the next. It is an experience entered mentally and is delineated by metaphors drawn from all aspects of our creativity—whether sound, image, or word. Our memory reverberates with metaphors that allow our minds to move through this new creative space. The space itself becomes metaphor and carries with it the signals for functioning inside and outside of it.

Cyberspace is nothing but a play between zeros and ones. Its design draws on the historical foundations of negative space and so allows the ground for composition and contemplation. The "space between" creates a counterpoint to what is said or drawn, as in music, where the pause between notes carries as much weight as the note itself.

In his article "Liquid Architecture in Cyberspace,"[11] Marcos Novak draws compelling parallels between cyberspace and poetry. If poetry is an undergoing of experience with language and the quest for creating new metaphors that defy conventional logic yet give us new ones, then cyberspace is the mathematical conjuring of new experience through the algorithm, forcing on us an experience

The Lagoon Nebula, as captured by NASA's Hubble telescope

Immersant in head-mounted display

with no equivalency in the tangible world. Novak notes that poetry enables an inflection of language that produces an inflection of meaning, a push and pull that are applied to both syntax and symbol. In cyberspace, we push and pull together. Although this domain has fallen largely under the control of the technologists, is it not through creativity that the imagination renders space, challenging conventional perceptions of the world, thereby leading us to new insight?

Is cyberspace Cartesian or Einsteinian? In a sense, it is both. Its initial coordinates are laid out as a Cartesian grid—points in a systematic, repeating space. Yet the grid can mutate and shift in a relativistic manner to suit the point of view of the cyber pilot. Cyberspace is the blank interval between areas of our intelligence. We compose it in a multimodal act, and each movement in this virtual ether is a composition requiring us to design, and so define, space.

The circuit enables a serialization of image, sound, and text that allows for infinitesimal manipulation of time and space. While one used to navigate through space, one now navigates through time. Digital editing has responded to the pace of our lives in an age of speed, and editing has become faster and easier. Filmmakers no longer need to struggle with tape and scissors to restructure the time of their work: Digital editing tools have given the editor, and even the viewer, great facility in changing nearly any aspect of the work by doing no more than shuffling around its zeros and ones. The lack of physical substrate in the electronic media of video and television presents time as unfolding in a seemingly more direct, unedited manner. So-called reality TV strives to avoid the appearance of artifice or even editing, though certainly it is compressed to fit the needs of advertising or the attention span of the viewer. Perhaps this is a reaction to the hectic pace of images in the music videos of MTV, whereby the music provides a temporal framework for seemingly disjointed images. Television confuses temporal focus by leaving us hanging in anticipation and by further disrupting and punctuating the narrative according to its own agenda, with commercials. Disruption is unfortunately a condition of our time.

If we understand that the formations of time are metafora, we can better decipher the significant implications of creative practice in cyberspace. We cannot separate our sense of who we are from our sense of time and space. Today we understand our sense of causality, the relationship between the past, present, and future, in the context of the dataset. Our sense of the past and of history is archived in the networked library and helps us to tell stories about who we are in the present, while our concept of the future is dependent on our hopes, dreams, and aspirations and the creative management of the metafora of time and space in the dataset.

"Tree Pond." Digital frame captured in real-time through HMD (head-mounted display) during a live performance of immersive virtual environment Osmose (1995). Tree Pond is one of many environments the immersant travels through.

Char Davies, in collaboration with programmers at SoftImage, created a virtual reality environment called Osmose in 1995. The user or immersant enters the "space" by putting on headgear that contains goggles showing the space on tiny CRT monitors, and a vest that helps the user to navigate. As a scuba diver, Davies knew that by breathing in while diving, the air in her lungs would create bouyancy. In Osmose, the vest enables users to move up and down through the space by inhaling and exhaling. There are a dozen "world-spaces" in Osmose, based on "the metaphysical aspects of nature." For Davies, the work is "a place for facilitating awareness of one's own self as consciousness embodied in enveloping space."

The quality of space is to give room, of dharma to cause motion, of adharma to cause rest. The quality of time is to roll on, of the self, awareness.

You should know, in short, that all these qualities are formless. Souls, aggregates of matter, dharma, adharma and space, contain innumerable dimensional points, but time has no dimensional points [i.e., no dimensions].

Pravacanasara

Jose Clemente Orozco, *Untitled*

I discovered a new analytical way of listening to music. The unheard sounds came through, and each melodic line existed of itself, stood out clearly from all the rest, said its piece, and waited patiently for the other voices to speak. That night I found myself hearing not only in time but in space as well. I not only encountered the music but descended, like Dante, into its depths.

Ralph Ellison, *The Invisible Man*

*Space has been contrived by architects
and decried by critics, filling the vacuum
created by fugitive symbolism.
If articulation is taken over from ornament
in the architecture of abstract expressionism,
space is what displaced symbolism.*

Robert Venturi, *Iconography and Electronics*

spacetime

Asymptote, Guggenheim Virtual Museum

Jeff Weiss, *Bronco,* 1997–2000. This image suggests the distortion of time through the distortion of space.

Hello, excuse me, can you tell me where I am?

In our country, this is the way we say hello.

It is a diagram of movement between two points.

It is a sweep of the dial.

In our country this is also the way we say goodbye.

Laurie Anderson, *United States*

You never know exactly when something begins. The more you delve and backtrack and think, the more clear it becomes that nothing has a discrete, independent history; people and events take shape not in orderly, chronological sequence but in relation to other forces and events, tangled skeins of necessity and interdependence and chance that after all could have produced only one result: what is. The intertwining strands of DNA that determine a creature's genetic predispositions might serve as a model for this complexity, but the double helix, bristling with myriad possibilities, is not mysterious enough. The usual notion of time, of one thing happening first and opening the way for another and another, becomes useless pretty quickly when I try to isolate the shape of your life from the rest of us, when I try to retrace your steps and discover precisely where and when you started to go bad.

> John Edgar Wideman,
> *Brothers and Keepers*

A sculpture is the thing you trip over in a museum when you are backing up to get a better look at a painting.

Contemporary joke

Mythic Time

From the days of the Greeks, Western thought has been dominated by the law of the "excluded middle" and the desire for extremes. One is either mortal or not mortal; there is no middle ground. The attempt is to rationalize away the vagaries of human existence; however, many Indian religions, such as Buddhism and especially Jainism, are based on the middle.

Buddhists seek the middle path—balance—whereas Jainsts hold to the "doctrine of maybe," a sevenfold division of possibilities. Thus, a Jainist, trained in the doctrine of many-sidedness, realizes that all things are relative to the aspect in which they are made or known, and their education is focused on knowing something as thoroughly as possible by considering it from all points of view. Space is made up of an infinite number of points and an infinite number of atomic instants, a notion that predates Einstein's theory of relativity by centuries.

Previously in China and Japan, time was a combined perception of cosmic and mundane changes in a cyclical form based on nature. The linear notion of history becomes more a matter of a utilitarian conception. Time was defined as flowing in a natural, temporal, and, above all, annual cycle. There is only one Japanese word for time, *Toki*, which translates as something like "intervals." The homogeneity of the Japanese culture, up to the twentieth century, and its rigid regard for tradition rooted in the deified emperor perhaps emanate from the fact that there was no emphasis on the discontinuity between different dynasties or stages of institutional change. Japanese history is continuous and constantly present. Because natural cycles are constant, dynasties are viewed as never-ending manifestations of a naturally repeating cycle.

For German philosopher Martin Heidegger, time was an existential experience based on the human sense of finality. We know that we die. What can we do in that span we call life? It is the "concern" of human endeavor to define the space of our existence. We are remembered by the artifacts we leave behind. "Look upon my works ye mighty and despair," said Ozymandias. The space of existence is always mediated, whether through new metaphors for the passage of time; through philosophical, psychological, or religious concepts of self; or through technology that records the events of history.

Perhaps the greatest reflections of our industry are the cities and the communities that they hold. The collective monuments and edifices we build are tributes to our ingenuity and needs for comfort and survival, our passage through space. They mark time in history through their very existence and endurance. Cities seem lifeless and static when viewed from afar but become living organisms when we encounter them in our daily activity. Their meaning can be appreciated only as we traverse their evolving narratives. The Twin Towers of New York City are enduring symbols of urban life, though their physical presence evaporated in moments.

Fixed Space

"It is a fundamental impulse in both the theory and practice of the arts to attempt to breach the supposed boundaries between the temporal and the spatial."[12]
W. J. T. Mitchell

Fixed space is a term used by the anthropologist Edward T. Hall to define the basic organizing activities of civilization. It includes material as well as internalized designs that govern our behavior as we move about from point to point.

Discussions of space raise the issue of the real and unreal in the realm of experience. How do we construct a model in our minds of an external world? Space implies something unlimited, without tangibility or definitive boundaries. Our concept changes as we move from one place to another, and with each movement we define particular spaces anew. By definition, space is that interval of time between two definitive points, denoting duration of a movement through time.

In ordinary experience the word "space" conjures up two distinct and opposing realizations. The first is metaphoric, like a box, a room, or a container where we put something, a place that holds the elements and objects of our existence. It is real, insofar as we can define it in the memory of our sensual experience. The second is boundless, that unlimited reach beyond the blue sky and the mortal plane that the Greeks called "ether." It is this latter, unfathomable area that seems to hold the very filament of existence. This concept of space is barely understood in the physics and mathematics that attempt to describe the space–time continuum, especially with the recent inroads in the field of quantum mechanics. With each quest of our genius, we move farther out in space, both mentally and physically, expanding infinitesimally the limits or the duration of its entity. If our existence on Earth is one point, is there another point? The attempt to delineate that area of our operations and creativity becomes a matter for the imagination.

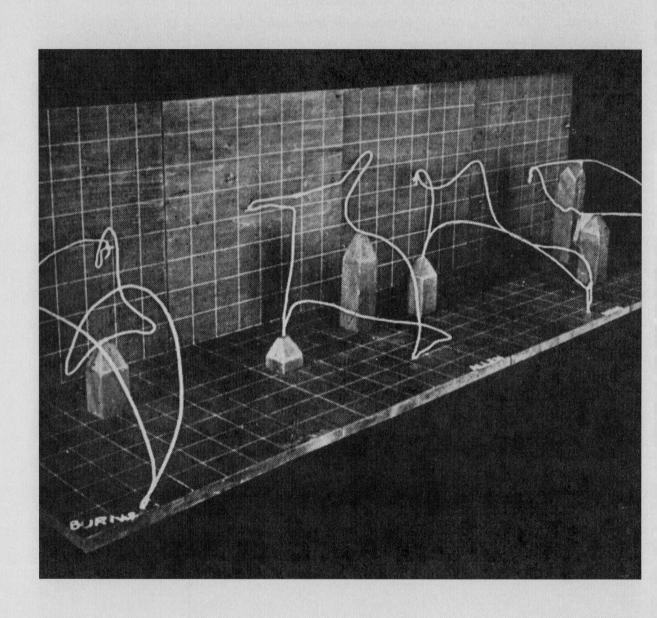

Taylorism

In the late nineteenth century, competition among factories was intense, and a young engineer by the name of Frederic Winslow Taylor began to investigate ways to improve productivity in the Midvale Steel Company. By 1906, he published "The Art of Cutting Metal," a paper that described his productivity studies, which he had conducted over more than twenty years. A complete study of the methods of production in the factory, the paper included management techniques, from the motion of the worker as he performed his job, to training and productivity incentives. Taylor thought of the factory as an organic whole, with management and labor working together in unity. His special focus was on the worker's motion and on reducing wasteful movements in repetitive tasks. Although today Taylorism is associated with the dehumanization of labor, Taylor thought of his methods as a means to aid the worker, by making his job more efficient and therefore less tiring. With more efficiency, the worker, and therefore the factory would become productive, and the worker would benefit from higher wages. Unfortunately, most managers focused only on Taylor's motion studies, ignoring his ideas that might make labor more bearable for the factory worker.

Around 1912, Frank and Lillian Gilbreth invented the "cyclograph" to study motion. They filmed workers performing tasks in front of a black background, with an electric light attached to the limb that performed the work. By showing these studies to workers, the Gilbreths hoped to improve the efficiency of the work. In *Mechanization Takes Command*, Sigfried Gideon notes that the Gilbreths' studies (which they sometimes made into wire sculptures that traced the motion of a hand), may have had a direct influence on artists such as Joan Miró and Paul Klee, and they were at the least indicative of an increased interest in motion and its depiction. All of these endeavors are, in effect, studies of space and time—that is, the relation of the object to the space it occupies and the time of its motion.

Elmer Rice's expressionist play, *The Adding Machine of 1923*, explored the life of Mr. Zero, whose humanity became trivialized in the mechanization of modern industry. Meanwhile, motion pictures such as Charlie Chaplin's *Modern Times* and Fritz Lang's *Metropolis* explored the dehumanizing effects of the factory workplace on the lives and spirits of the modern worker, while the tedium of late twentieth-century office work has been portrayed in films such as *Nine to Five* and the cartoon strip *Dilbert*.

Hansjorg Meyer

Concrete Poem

The turning of a page is an aesthetic event; or at any rate it should be. Anyone who writes will know how oddly crucial it can be that a certain page end with a certain word, that the next one begin with a certain other.

If we turn the page, space will become time. Now there is magic, the magic of technology. There is the key to the new poetry. Now you know how to read "etwas" or "LIFE." Science may be magical, but art is always logical. Imagine the "etwas" poem on a single page, as it was in the original. Extend the white space; transfer the black rectangle to the following page. What has happened is that we have developed a plot. We have added suspense—that is, time. Play with the space in "LIFE." Midway through the word, change the side of the page the letters appear on. You have altered the periodicity of the poem; you have changed the velocity, the rhythm, in which the poem must be grasped as expressing time. What the reader does is enter the time of the book.

Eugene Wildman, *Anthology of Concretism*

Memory and Space

We cannot think about space without memory, nor can we have memory without space.

Who cannot remember where they were on **September 11, 2001?**

It is in this way that psychology and the unconscious assume an important role in our organization of metafora and where we place the images of falling buildings. Time has little meaning for memory, because memory does not really record the duration of a sensation.

Calling forth the past requires an abstraction that is devoid of a specific time frame. Memories float in the vast ocean of experience and by connecting them to space, we fix them. Organizing them in a timeline is the work of biographers and historians, but personal memory does not work that way. Memory is a creative act, one the medium of space.

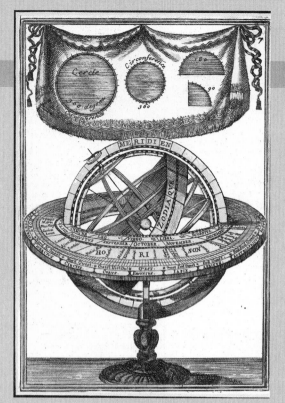

Seventeenth-century movable globe.

Einstein and Relativity

In 1905, while working as a clerk in a Swiss patent office, Albert Einstein published "On the Electrodynamics of Moving Bodies." This paper contained his special theory of relativity that would forever change how we think about time, space, and our place in the universe. Before Einstein, Europeans had long used the Ptolemaic model to explain the movement of the planets, which held that the earth was at the center of the universe inside a series of concentric spheres. Accordingly, the Earth remained stationary as the planets rotated around it. This model was challenged by the scientists of the Renaissance, including Nicolaus Copernicus, Johannes Kepler, and Galileo Galilei. They proposed that the Earth and other planets revolved around the sun. The fact that the church persecuted Galileo demonstrates just how closely related our notions of space-time are to our worldview: By challenging the idea that the sun rotated around the Earth, Galileo was doing no less than shaking the very foundations of the Catholic Church.

By the mid-seventeenth century, in the midst of the wonder of the scientific revolution, Sir Isaac Newton and René Descartes, among others, formulated laws that described motion, inertia, and other properties of space and time. The development of the visual models of perspective—paintings created from a single point of space and time—was directly related to the notion of a single, detached observer, the man who is the measure of all things. So, too, were the works of Newton and others: They created a universe that was easily comprehensible and, perhaps more importantly, easier to depict in the rules of painting that had evolved over the past three hundred years.

Newton discovered the law of gravity, from which it follows that there is no absolute standard of motion. That is, if you were in a carriage traveling along a road, there would be no way to tell you were in motion without looking out the window. The laws of physics were the same for you as they were for those outside of the carriage. Newton's law of gravity did away with the notion of absolute position in space, but not with the notion of absolute time.

Scientists as far back as the late seventeenth century had postulated that light travels at a constant speed. In the nineteenth century, James Clerk Maxwell developed a set of equations describing the electromagnetic spectrum, which included visible light. Light travels at a fixed speed, for any observer, which can be measured at 186,000 miles per second. But if there were no absolute rest, what was this speed relative to? Through a series of thought experiments involving no apparatuses, only the question "What would happen if ..." Einstein demonstrated that space was relative and so, too, was time. If two observers are traveling in relation to one another—that is, if their frames of reference are moving—they will observe time and space differently. Neither observation is correct or incorrect, only different. At the speeds we experience in everyday life, these differences are hardly noticeable, but as an observer approaches the speed of light, they become more pronounced. Einstein also showed that gravity was in fact a curvature of space-time caused by the mass of objects. Objects travel in a straight line in four dimensions (space-time), though they appear to us to travel in a curved line in three dimensions.

The Big Nurse is able to set the wall clock at whatever speed she wants just by turning one of those dials in the steel door; she takes a notion to hurry things up, she turns the speed up, and those hands whip around that disk like spokes in a wheel. The scene in the picture screen windows goes through rapid changes of light to show morning, noon, and night—throb off and on furiously with day and dark, and everybody is driven like mad to keep up with the passing of fake time.

Ken Kesey, *One Flew Over the Cuckoo's Nest*

New York City, punk style

Leary's Cyberpunk

Culture has expanded beyond the conventional perceptions of time and space in the new realm of the electronic circuit. In his 1988 essay, "The Cyberpunk: The Individual as Reality Pilot."[13] Timothy Leary suggests that a new sensibility is needed to navigate the spaces of the computer. The term "cyber" is derived from the ancient Greek word for pilot, sailors who navigated the Aegean Sea by wits and cunning, usually without a map or more advanced navigational equipment (see the Glossary for the literarary use of the term "cyberpunk"). These ancient seafarers relied on intuitive senses to find their way. The later Roman pilot, or steersman, was less experimental—a reflection of the uniformity of Roman society at that time—and followed predetermined sets of orders or paradigms. Contemporary uses of the term cyber (notably those of Norbert Weiner and his cybernetics movement) describe control, not individuality or freedom. Leary's essay reintroduces the term cyber in the contemporary context. The pilot of the twenty-first century is the cyberpunk, a person in a time when ". . . creativity and mental excellence become the ethical norm. The world has become too dynamic, complex, and diversified, too cross-linked by the global immediacies of contemporary (quantum) communication, for stability of thought or dependability of behavior to be successful . . . cyberpunks are the inventors, innovative writers, techno-frontier artists . . . all of those who boldly package and steer ideas out there where no thoughts have gone before."

Rebel Girl
Bikini Kill

Apple Computer's iTunes provides a visual analog to sound.

Sound of Space

Music in cyberspace has no acoustics in the traditional sense;
instead music spreads through tendrils across the networks, finding
its way to the computers of everyone from teenagers to college
students through quasi-legal file sharing services. Every physical
space has a unique sound. On movie sets, audio engineers record
the sound of a room for thirty seconds or so, in order to "mix" the
"room tone" into conversations when the movie is edited. John
Cage intended to have the audience listen to the ambient sounds of
the concert hall in his 1952 piece 4'33" (Four Minutes and Thirty-
three Seconds) where he sits silently at the piano: the chirp of the
crickets outside, the rustling of the audience, the buzz of the electric
lights. The piece was born from Cage's interest in the Buddhist practice of meditation as a means for understanding the self.

spacetime

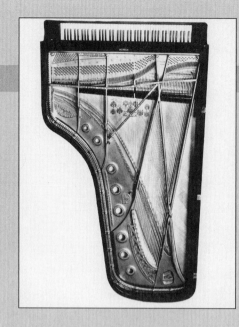

Acoustics

Acoustics is the interaction of sound and space through time. Sound rarely travels in a straight line from its source to the listener. It propagates through the air like ripples from a dropped stone in a pond and bounces off any surface it might encounter. Reverberation within a space is one of the many factors determining the quality of the sound. Sabine's law, named after the scientist Wallace Sabine (1868–1919), is a mathematical description of the interaction of sound and space. Sabine applied this mathematical concept to acoustics, which enabled him to design many great places for the performance of music, among them Boston Symphony Hall.

An important factor in the evolution of oratory and musical styles has been the nature of the building (or space) where the music is heard. The cathedral, with its long reverberation times, heightens the effect of choral and organ music. The cathedral's vault creates a transcendent environment that enhances religious worship, both visually and acoustically. Baroque chamber music was written for small spaces; Renaissance courts commissioned works that encouraged sociability, such as the waltz. Although the harpsichord and clavichord are too quiet for the cathedral, they are well suited to intimate social gatherings. The space of a performance hall also has an effect on the timing of the piece: In a building with great reverberation, the performer either has to use a slower tempo or runs the risk of having the reverberation blur the sounds together.

The increasing popularity of rock and roll music in the United States prompted promoters in the music industry to negotiate increasingly large venues, and what was once performed in the intimate atmosphere of a small club moved to the outdoor arena. As the performers moved farther and farther from the audience, their relative size changed and some, notably KISS and other glam rock bands, turned to outlandish costumes and elaborate stage shows to keep the audience interested. Rock and roll has its roots in rhythm and blues music, a tradition continued by Othar Turner, who performs with his fife and drum band in rural Mississippi. The music is loud and jarring, as befits music that must compete with and be heard over conversations at picnics where it is traditionally performed. Meanwhile, the uniquely urban hip-hop, with its booming bass beats, developed in the playgrounds and on the stoops of New York City, where it may best be listened to by blasting it from the speakers of car stereos.

Music

Music exists only in time. As events in it succeed each other through time, tension is maintained through the connection between antecedent and consequence. Rhythm in the larger sense controls all the relationships within a composition. The meter of the piece is the fixed time pattern in which musical events unfold. Within meter, rhythm is allowed to flow freely, and musical time is a beat, the regular pulse to which we tap our toes. Rhythm is an expression of the spontaneity of not only the individual who creates the music but the listener as well. This condition demands a kind of physicality on the part of the performer and a similar response of the listener's senses in an exchange of attention.

Upuntil the mid-nineteenth century, classical music was composed to hold the listener's attention in a manner similar to the narrative of a play. In theater, events, such as a murder, set up a tension. This holds the viewers' attention until a resolution occurs (the murder is solved). This is called denouement, which releases the tension in what Aristotle called catharsis. Catharsis is the release of the viewers' tension as they watch a dramatic tragedy unfold: They are able to direct their real fears and anxieties onto the fiction unfolding in front of them, thereby ease their fear.

Classical music begins with a central magnetic chord, called the tonic, which expands, pulling the rest of the composition back to it: It is established in a way so that departure from it makes you want to return to it. Like most of the world's population before the advent of modern means of travel, tonal music starts a short journey with the expectation of returning home after a short time.

Wagner and Mahler in the mid-nineteenth century began to break with this tradition, and the turn of the twentieth century broke from older considerations of time as it was previously considered, with the advent of the new classical music of Stravinsky and Schoenberg, and in jazz. According to Theodore Adorno, Stravinsky exemplified this change: "His music is devoid of recollection, and consequently lacking in any time-continuum of permanence. Its course lies in reflexes."[14] There is no narrative. The exposition, development, and recapitulation that marked the canon of nineteenth-century music are no longer elements. The music of the new space of the twentieth century lacks thematic material and is self-contained within its own progressions, patterns, and pattern breaking. Like the experiments of the futurists and the surrealists, contemporary music anticipates the time-space continuum and the schizophrenia of the postmodern era, collapsing any linear continuity. It turns us toward the sensuous world of the unconscious and our connection to the exotic and primitive. It works like our busy minds.

The older forms of music, such as chamber music, require an attention that may, unfortunately, no longer be possible for today's MTV generation, and threaten to sink into the background like the background music of tony restaurants, while the music of Snoop Doggy Dog or the Chemical Brothers dissects and reassembles time in our disjointed present. Their rhythmic structures resist narrative structuring by a cyclical repetition more akin to non-Western music than classical composition.

spacetime

Sometimes I rhyme slow

Sometimes I rhyme quick

Nice and Smooth

Q: What do you get when you play a country-western song backward?

A: You get back your wife, and you get back your truck, and you get back your dog.

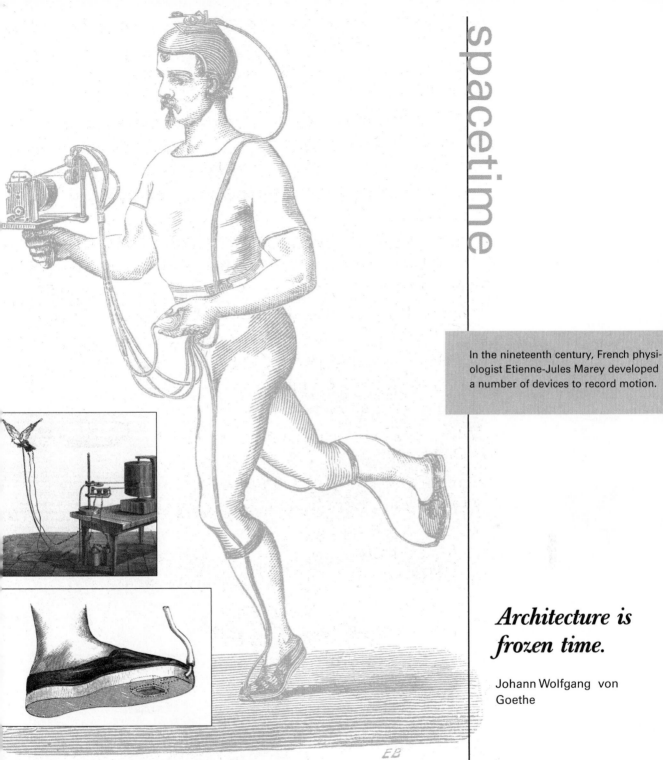

In the nineteenth century, French physi-
ologist Etienne-Jules Marey developed
a number of devices to record motion.

*Architecture is
frozen time.*

Johann Wolfgang von
Goethe

Romantic Time

Our sense of romantic love is a condition in which something from the past is idealized in such a way as to project a kind of perfect state in the future. If I meet the right person, my love will endure eternally. This emotional condition is exploited by the popular media through countless love songs and the never-ending soap operas such as *Days of Our Lives* and *As the World Turns,* which imply that there is always a tomorrow, like the classic tale of *One Thousand and One Nights*, whose never-ending story precludes time's one reality—death. (Even death is not a permanent condition in soap operas, as characters are resurrected through bizarre twists in plot.) This can also be seen in the narratives of video games, which begin anew with the press of the "start" button; life is restored and the story starts again.

Canning

Contemporary technology enables us to can and preserve the summer's harvest to eat the year round. Greenhouses and the global agricultural marketplace, combined with the network of its commerce, can deliver fresh food where once there was none. While this has led to greater health and well-being for people who can afford this bounty, it has nonetheless removed from our lives yet another connection with the natural world around us.

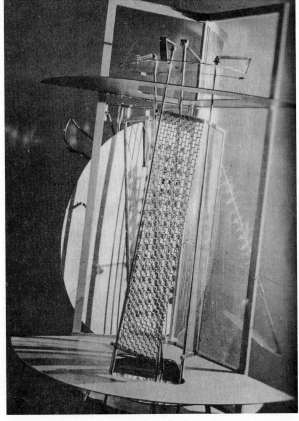

László Moholy-Nagy's *Light-Space Modulator*, 1921. Not meant as a sculpture, it was an electrically driven machine that produced a light show, sort of a moving photogram. In 1929 he used the machine to make the film, *Light Display, Black and White and Gray.* The machine was surrounded by 128 lightbulbs, switched on and off by a drum contact, and turned slowly while projecting light on the wall from its three independent sections. It was not an object in and of itself, but part of a process.

Minsky

Marvin Minsky, artificial intelligence sage at the Massachusetts Institute of Technology, makes the point that no part of the mind can completely understand or describe the processes of the other parts of the mind because, it seems, our memory control systems have too little short-term memory even to represent their own activities in much detail. An attempt to reflect on our mental state will change that state, just as physicists believe that trying to observe an electron will change it.

The mushroom, as no other form, has defined the twentieth century.

The Big Duck farm stand, Long Island. Robert Venturi coined the term *duck* to mean any architectural structure whose form suggests the service it offers.

To understand clay is not to understand the pot. What a pot is all about can be appreciated better by understanding the creators and the users of the pot and their need both to inform the material with their meaning and to extract meaning from the form.

Alan Kay, *Insanely Great*

The space of the computer is one that contains—and is composed of—nothing but abstract forms, described by the potential of the dataset; a computer rendering is a sleight-of-hand. When we travel in cyberspace, we travel in a vehicle that does not really move, but merely simulates the act of speeding from place to place, form to form, object to object. Objects in the computer have no matter; they are nothing more than abstraction, potential that may or may not be realized into the physical (in metaspace). Form is paramount: There is no matter. In the circuit, the form (or the program that creates it) changes as need demands. Creativity now lies in our ability to respond in a process of changing functions, as much as it does in the production of stable objects.

Ancient Greek philosophers initially debated the nature of the universe in terms of the matter from which it was composed. In the sixth century B.C.E., Pythagoras shifted the discussion away from the universe's constituent matter to its organization, its form. For the ancient Greeks, form gave meaning and substance to matter. Through his mathematical study of music, Pythagoras was led to the notion that number was the first principle of the universe; each object was composed of a particular mathematical formula that organized its matter into form.

Sake bottle, Japan, 1868

Modernist architecture of the twentieth century, epitimized in the work of Mies van der Rohe, developed the notion that form followed function. Analysis of the resources and needs of a building dictated its planning and organization and ultimately its physical shape. In the twenty-first century, form has become more determined by function than ever before. A contemporary automobile is styled first by aerodynamic concerns. Likewise, contemporary communication is driven by speed, efficiency, and economic pressures. For example, the language of an instant message has been reduced to the bare essentials of the letters, without the intrusion of grammar, punctuation, or spelling.

Snowflakes

The principle of form is to advance our understanding.
It is the organization of a piece which helps the listener
to keep the idea in mind. To follow its development,
its growth, its elaboration, its fate.

Arnold Schoenberg, *Letters*

Today, scientists believe that matter is energy, whose arrangement and composition into atomic elements gives structure to the universe. Although Western science once thought that the matter of the universe was solid and unchanging, we now know that it is made up of potentials and possibilities, of unstable and unknown subatomic elements. This is echoed in the virtual world, where datasets are composed of no more than zeros and ones, its elements arranged into such things as music or cyber architecture, but whose order can be easily shifted around to create new objects, whose structures are amalgams of energies. If matter is energy in constant flux, then so too are its forms. Creativity is the search for new meanings in abstract forms and their realization in material structure.

We can morph our identities, our appearance, our sexuality, and the very composition of genetic code. Everything is unstable. Images can be radically changed, text is cut and pasted across the Internet, music is likewise sampled, mixed together and constructed from nearly any sound. The distinctions that once separated races, genders, and even the human from the machine are all blurring. Finally, borders that separated states and political or economic entities are redefined on a daily basis. Once-stable assumptions are now in question. According to Jacques Derrida, the father of deconstruction, the very language we use to construct our notions of the world can be questioned.[15] Nothing is really knowable because the signs that compose language refer to nothing but one another: There is nothing outside language. This line of thought can lead to obscure thinking and chaos, but it nevertheless underlines a prevailing condition: We should question all assumption and, in so doing, create new realms of creativity.

The process of deconstruction, as provocative as it may be, enables the rediscovery of our notion of self. The deconstructed self has replaced the unified or stable being. In cyberspace, we become multifaceted and at the same time we disintegrate as we glide through the electronic ether. As we move from one node to the next, we change the space we move through, leaving parts of ourselves at web sites and in chat rooms. Our interaction with people on the Internet changes us, changes them, and ultimately changes the spaces for interactions. Online games present players with an arena for interaction, virtual worlds created by text or images that construct medieval landscapes, for example. In some of the games, players can interact not only with one another but also with the landscape of the game itself, as they are enabled to create new maps, characters, and scenarios. Some go so far as to write stories based on the games themselves.

A new problem arises: In the process of continuous change and the evolution of ideas, will we be able to find a stable context? Maybe the answer lies in the Hindu notion that om, or spiritual energy, is the underlying principle of the universe; it is the container for all of its aspects—time, space, matter, and so on. Through the practice of yoga, yogins attempt to achieve enlightenment by liberating their personhood from matter; that is, to recognize their true form.

The concept of form is indispensable to the practice and criticism of many disciplines and is inherent in all design and creative acts. The perception of form may be an issue that connects us as human beings, because it has some consistency across people. In the creation of metafora, form is the logic or illogic we assign to the thread that weaves our creative endeavors. Creativity is a function of the growth and mutation of the form.

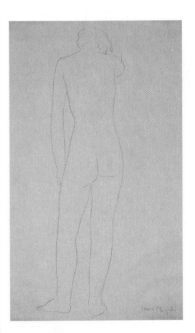

Isamu Noguchi

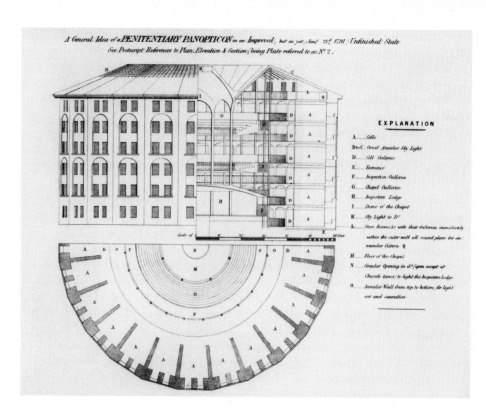

A General Idea of a *PENITENTIARY PANOPTICON* in an *Improved*, but as yet, Jan.ᵈ 23ᵈ 1791 (*Unfinished*) *State*
See Postscript References to Plan, Elevation & Section (being Plate referred to as N.º 2)

EXPLANATION

A ..... Cells
B to C .. Great Annular Sky Light
D ..... Cell Galleries
E ..... Entrance
F ..... Inspection Galleries
G ..... Chapel Galleries
H ..... Inspectors Lodge
I ..... Dome of the Chapel
K ..... Sky Light to Dº
L ..... Store Rooms &c with their Galleries, immediately within the outer wall all round place for an annular Cistern. Q
M ..... Floor of the Chapel
N ..... Circular Opening in dº (open except at Church times) to light the Inspectors Lodge
O ..... Annular Wall from top to bottom, for light air and separation.

Tetraktys diagram

Pythagoras regarded numbers and shapes themselves as holy (as do many religions, such as Hinduism and Christianity), especially the *tetraktys* of the decad, a triangle made up of ten dots. An emphasis on number led to several well-known geometric theories, including the Pythagorean triangle and the Harmony of the Spheres, the notion that the planets were arranged in the heavens based on musical harmonies and intervals. Shortly after Pythagoras, Plato developed the concept of an enduring form, which gives an object its identity. These forms were permanent and unchanging—unlike matter, which was unstable—and existed in a spiritual realm independent of their physical manifestation.

The Hindus consider the syllable om to be sacred, part of meditation and other holy rituals. It is composed of the sounds A, U, and M, representing the trinities of three major Hindu gods and of heaven, atmosphere, and earth.

Evolved Beam

This is a simplified two-dimensional model of a truss designed by Andrew Keane and his staff at Southampton University's Computational Engineering and Design Center. Keane developed a piece of software called Options, which was used to improve the traditional design of the truss in its transmission of vibration energy. The initial design and testing were done with the computer, and a physical model was eventually built and successfully tested. This has become a standard procedure—models are created and optimized with the computer, then built and tested in the physical world. The interesting thing about Keane's program is that no human intelligence intervened in the design process, except in the design of the software. Options uses an algorithm called Genetic Algorithm (GA), which simulates biological evolution to optimize a problem.

Danny Hillis pioneered GAs in the 1980s, to "evolve" a computer program that sorted numbers. Hillis started with a primordial stew of computer programs—randomly generated snippets of code. He then allowed them to "breed" by combining parts of one program with another, in a process much like biological reproduction—in which offspring get attributes of each parent. He also allowed for random mutation, whereby code could change at random during reproduction. After each generation, he evaluated the pool of computer programs to see if they could sort. He chose the best 20 percent of these programs, discarded the rest, and repopulated his simulation with the top 20 percent. He ran this simulation over many, many generations and eventually created a program that was as good as any that a human being had written.

The beam Keane developed (though it is not accurate to say he developed it; perhaps it is better to say he guided its evolution) bears an uncanny resemblance to a biological form.

He would see faces in movies, on T.V., in magazines, and in books. . . .
He thought that some of these faces might be right for him. . . . And
through the years, by keeping an ideal facial structure fixed in his
mind....Or somewhere in the back of his mind. . . . That he might, by
force of will, cause his face to approach those of his ideal. . . . The
change would be very subtle....It might take ten years or so....
Gradually his face would change its shape. . . . A more hooked nose. . . .
Wider, thinner lips. . . . Beady eyes. . . . A larger forehead.
He imagined that this was an ability he shared with most other
people. . . . They had also molded their face according to some
ideal. . . . Maybe they imagined that their new face would better
suit their personality. . . . Or maybe they imagined that their
personality would be forced to change to fit the new
appearance. . . . This is why first impressions are often correct. . . .
Although some people might have made mistakes. . . . They may have
arrived at an appearance that bears no relationship to them. . . .
They may have picked an ideal appearance based on some childish
whim, or momentary impulse. . . . Some may have gotten half-way
there, and then changed their minds.
He wonders if he too might have made a similar mistake.

Talking Heads
Seen and Not Seen
1980

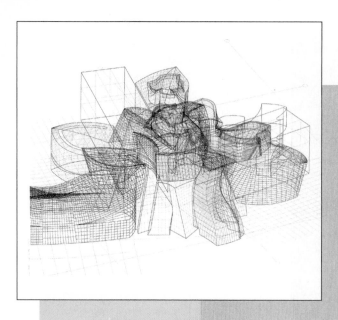

3-D Modeling

In computer programs that model three-dimensional objects, a variety of abstract schemes are used to enable the designer to translate his or her ideas into reality. But the virtual shapes created by these programs are not real in the traditional sense of the word. They are nothing more than descriptions, a combination of algorithms that suggest the potential of being rendered into a form in which we can experience them—whether on a screen or as an actual physical object. These programs provide the designer a new facility, and the ability to create shapes that he or she might never have imagined or been able to fashion using traditional tools that work with physical materials.

Computer-aided design (CAD) programs provide the designer or architect a new language to translate ideas into a form that can be built. Architect Frank Gehry used the CATIA system to create the plans for the Guggenheim Bilbao. The computer gave him a new language, a way to model shapes and non-Euclidean curves that traditional tools were not able to represent.

Black and white cookie

Changing Forms

In all of the arts, form often shows itself in a dualistic way. It is the selection of detail on the one hand, and the rejection of it on the other. Perhaps form is binary. Creativity lies in the discernment of when this balancing act works best. Art-making carefully considers the relationship of all the parts that constitute the whole form. Good design requires a balance between entities of unity and variety, symmetry and asymmetry, movement and repose, and so on. A good work may be one that exhibits a continuity of tensions that keeps stimulating our senses, drawing us back to the work—again and again.

Position is the prime element of form and from position are derived all elements of structure and form.

Frederick Sommer, *Selected Texts*

Shape

Johannes Itten, the Bauhaus designer and theorist, deduced that there are three basic forms—the square, the triangle, the circle—which in turn are typified by four directions in space: The square is horizontal and vertical; the triangle diagonal; and the circle a tautology, never-ending and with no clear beginning. These abstract forms enable us to categorize the shapes (the mark we make or the outline of an object) we experience in everyday life. Each of the basic forms has its own character and each denotes meaning in and of itself, based on our psychology. The square is nondynamic; hence a dullard is called a "square." A triangle's diagonal lines create motion and tension and so it is the shape of a warning sign. The circle, like the mandala, is spiritual, warm, and endless, like a wedding ring. In any graphic representation we build the organizing structures for the gestalts we seek to create from these shapes, their compound shapes, and their negative spaces, the shapes between them. We use shapes in combinations, and truncate and multiply them to create a language of architecture and metaphor.

Shape refers to the external outline of an object. Through geometry, we can define shapes mathematically in terms of points and lines. A triangle may be defined by its three corner points, a circle by its center and radius. By combining fundamental geometric shapes, we can give form to space—what we often call architecture or design. Thus, in the world of the circuit, the complex geometry that creates virtual shapes is a matter of representations that are primarily experienced through the eye. Shape is one of the elementary characteristics of a perceived object: We decipher visual stimuli in terms of shape, motion, location, and a few other primary characteristics. Our concept of universal forms enables us to recognize a particular shape as a subset of a larger class of shapes. A chair, for example, takes many shapes and forms, but if we recognize one, we have no problem recognizing others.

From the moment we get up in the morning to the moment we drift off into sleep, everything we interact with is designed. There is nothing human-made that has not been designed, although many things are designed poorly. But human creativity is only one special case of giving shape to form. Although the creative drive is unconscious, its enactment is conscious and deliberate. Shape can be created by the human hand or what biologist Richard Dawkins calls the blind watchmaker—nature. D'Arcy Thompson noted nearly a century ago that nature's designs are truly beyond our comprehension and yet exist with many of the formal qualities that give shape to our creativity.

An understanding of the visual world is all the more critical in the realm of digital expression, as we become more attuned to the symbolic functioning of shape by heightening our visual sensibilities. Our experience with the computer is almost exclusively through visual symbol (though our input is tactile); and although we hear it through a multitude of sounds, we cannot experience it as a transforming space without engaging its shapes. Repeated uses of certain shapes become icons, and those icons are the building blocks of the architecture through which we navigate within our computers, like the familiar shape of the Macintosh's trash can.

Success in the marketplace depends on shapes becoming trademarks and ubiquitous cultural status symbols. Through advertising, the Nike "swoosh" logo has become a symbol that carries a plethora of cultural meanings. Shapes have meaning beyond their literal appearances and become metaphors more powerful than the words that describe them; think of the almost visceral reaction we have to the shape of the Nazi swastika. The problem for creativity is that the frequent use of such shapes inhibits the creation of new paradigms for exploration. We tend to use existing entities rather than creatively or logically extending our metaphors in building new architectures.

In the field of graphic design we can speak of geometric shape as opposed to organic shape. Geometric shapes are based on simple rules of geometry, whereas organic shapes tend to be more complicated and less easy to reproduce. It is easier to draw a circle than a face. Until recently, computers had difficulty drawing organic shapes, though they could very easily be programmed to create geometric ones. Early computer art, such as the work of Vera Molnar, was based on the computer's ability to create multiple iterations of simple forms. In 1986, she programmed a computer connected to a plotter to modify the arrangements of a square, carefully and systematically exploring the possible permutations of composition. Recently, the introduction of fractal-based algorithms and the availability of massive computational power have enabled computers to model organic forms realistically, and thus produce convincing images of "reality" out of thin air, synthetic images generated by 3-D modeling software.

Apple's OS X has updated its classic trash can icon.

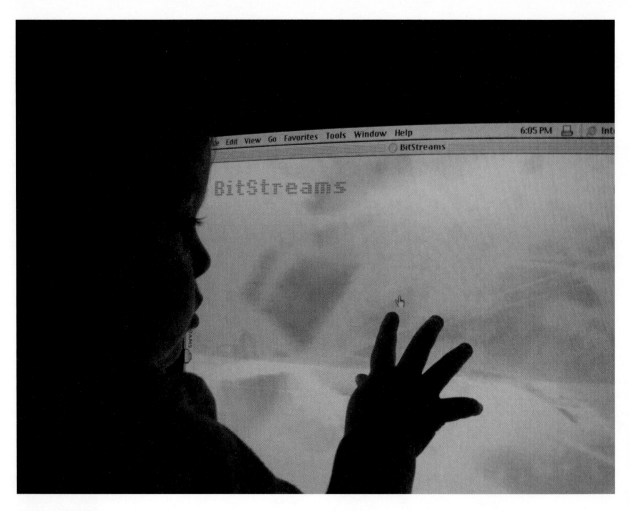

Author's daughter, again

The soul is the important thing.
Form will follow.

Kazuo Ohn, founder of Butoh

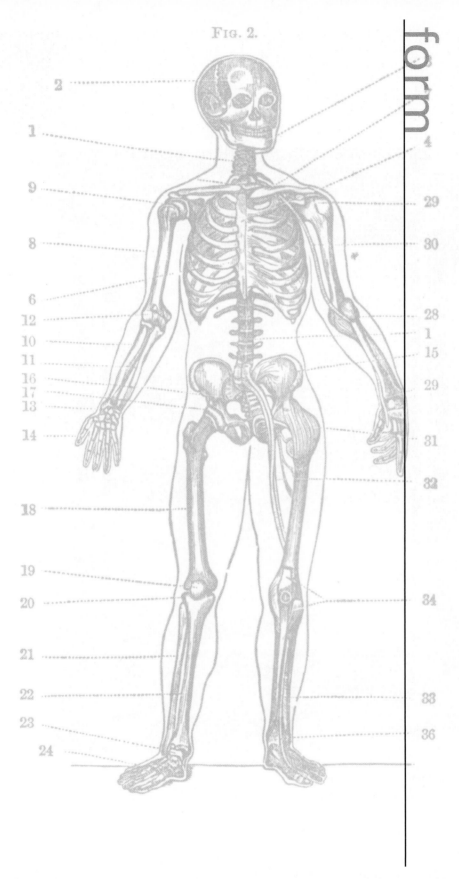

FIG. 2.

2
1
9
8
6
12
10
11
16
17
13
14
18
19
20
21
22
23
24

form

4
29
30
28
1
15
29
31
32
34
33
36

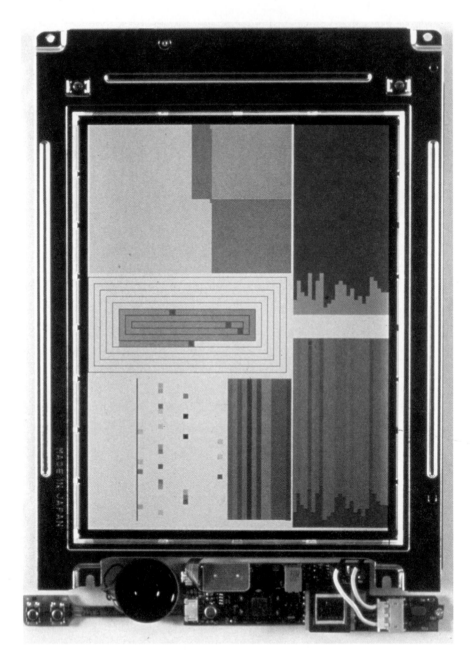

John F. Simon, Jr., *Color Panel*, 1999

Color is particularly plastic in electronic media. No longer bound by the physical constraints of cost or scarcity of exotic pigments or dyes, artists can indulge in whatever colors they wish. However, the facility of change and speed of manipulation are not substitutes for a deeper understanding of the grace and harmony necessary to use color as a means to convey expression.

In visual creative practice, color has three basic dimensions to which values can be systematically given. (1) Hue corresponds to the wavelength of the light reflected off an object and received by the eye. (2) The relative brilliance of a color is considered by the degree of saturation, which is the relative purity of the color and ranges from full saturation of the hue to gray. (3) Last is luminance (brightness), which is measured on a scale that begins with black and progressively lightens to white. All hues do not have the same value. Each can be altered in value to be lighter or darker and can be reduced in brilliance until it reaches the lowest level of saturation (gray).

Color is one of the most value-laden means of human expression. Although the exact experience of what color is may differ from person to person, computer to computer, room to room, and light source to light source, the value of color as an expressive tool is obvious. The meaning with which we imbue color is as complicated as language itself, for color is its own language, loaded with information and with tremendous affinity to our emotions. It is one of the most pervasive and universal forms of visual and sensual experience.

Color affects many disciplines, and so there are many ways to approach it. Theories of color come from such areas as physics, optics, psychology, and even pathology. While this text primarily explores the visual components of color—for they are the most salient and cyberdesign is primarily visual—we should be mindful that all metafora are conditioned by an expression of color.

James Baldwin knew that a writer can use inflection in language in the same way that a designer uses hue: to add an element of expression and contrast to words. Musical composers use tone to complement rhythm in creating a mood.

To communicate effectively, the participants in the dialog must understand the changing connotations of each color. Because the

Color wheel

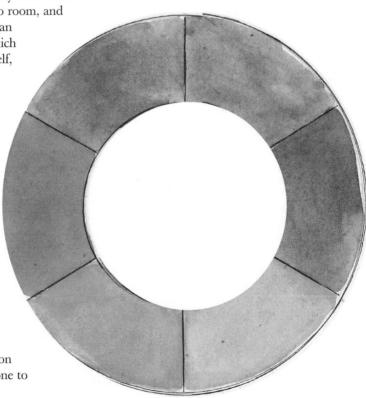

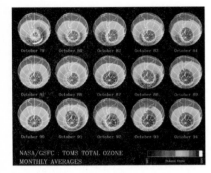

NASA/GSFC : TOMS TOTAL OZONE
MONTHLY AVERAGES

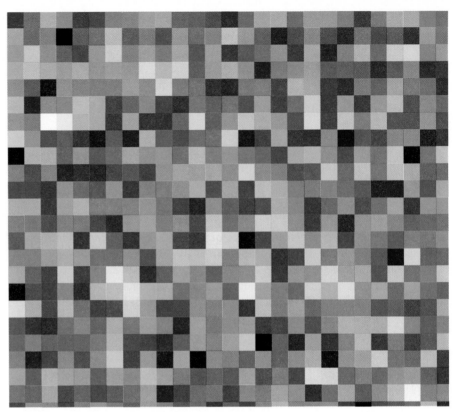

Harry Bowers developed a color management system in the 1990s, using test patterns like this to calibrate monitors to printers.

Digital-imaging techniques can now "see" portions of the electromagnetic spectrum that are beyond the range of normal human vision. Even data such as the amount of precipitation or ozone in the atmosphere can be recorded in digital images. Each pixel of a weather map, for instance, will contain a number that describes the amount of precipitation, and that number can be rendered as a color that can be used to visually evaluate data.

computer's schematics have been developed in the Western world, its programmers, designers, and editors must attempt to understand the varied connotations attached to each color. Are new color metaphors propagating like fast food? Each culture has associated meanings with color, which in the natural world is more or less fixed but in cyberspace can be easily changed. Thus, in the digital realm we have the opportunity to generate a unique set of cultural metaphors and values through the electronic palette. In digital operations, no color is permanent; colors can be shifted as logically and illogically as the creator's fantasies. The sky can be purple one minute and red the next, or vary for different users in the same space. Although these changes are all too often arbitrary, this random use of color may itself constitute a new aesthetic, the new norm.

Our understanding of color rests essentially with our reactions and our acculturation, and although color theories abound, there is no ultimate system. Aristotle noted that simple colors were created by blends of darkness and lightness. The ancients recognized that color and light were intrinsically connected. The color wheel that symbolizes our contemporary Western understanding of color was first described by Sir Isaac Newton in the seventeenth century. Newton observed that when a beam of sunlight passes through a prism, it not only is deflected but also spreads out into a band of brilliant colors—the process of dispersion. When the beam passes through a second prism, no further changes occur. From this he deduced that white daylight is composed of many elemental colors that are themselves indivisible. Entomologist and engraver Moses Harris (1731–1785), who published the first color chart, developed the notion of primary colors—those that can be combined to represent all others.

Newton proposed a seven-color notation—red, orange, yellow, green, blue, indigo, and violet—to correspond with the seven notes in a musical scale. He had, in his earlier lectures, discussed the chromatic scale in terms of only five colors, later adding orange and indigo in order to match the system of musical notation.

Extrapolating from the work of British scientist Thomas Young, who discovered that three light stimuli are sufficient to give all color sensation, German scientist Hermann von Helmholtz believed that red, green, and blue light were sufficient to produce the whole gamut of color sensation. This is the basis for our contemporary theory of color perception: the existence of concentric receptive fields whose centers would excite a ganglion cell if stimulated by the light of one wavelength, but would inhibit the cell if stimulated by light of a different wavelength, one that corresponded to the complementary color of the original stimulus. The normal human eye has receptors for red, green, and blue light, which is the basis of one working understanding of our common physiological experience of color, but does not preclude color theories based on other colors in the spectrum.

Study of color perception shows that most cultures have eleven basic color categories, although they may only have terms for as few as two colors. These basic color categories are white, black, red, yellow, blue, purple, orange, green, brown, pink, and gray. Knowing that we all perceive the same basic colors would indicate that our skulls are hard-wired in the same manner. The visible spectrum has no demarcations in it, though cultures create these boundaries and the various cultural connotations that go along with them. Although scientists do not know if these color terms change our actual perceptions of color—whether an African might see red differently from a European because of their different terminologies—it is unlikely.

In the West, red is blood, thus symbolizing danger and passion, whereas green reminds us of nature and of life itself. The tranquility of blue connotes placid skies and symbolizes a condition of peace and harmony. Yellow, mimicking the sun, is the symbol for energy and work. While the color of mourning is black in the United States, it is white in India, yellow in Burma, violet in Turkey, brown in

I know the colour rose and it is lovely,
But not when it ripens in a tumour;
And healing greens, leaves and grass,
so Springlike,
In limbs that fester are not springlike.

Dannie Abse, *Pathology of Colors*

Ethiopia, and red in China. Red was the ancient royal color of Rome, which gave rise to the red of the Roman Catholic cardinal's robes, and the color of Mao Tse-tung's revolution. These symbolic meanings are historically important and are now evolving in the global cyber village.

A new color palette has been infused into all aspects of contemporary design, from product to graphic to industrial. Colors once thought of as garish or in poor taste are now the standard-bearers of electronic chic. A new generation of designers, unfamiliar with the etiquette and meanings of previous generations and equipped with easy-to-use and inexpensive digital editing programs, are utilizing the electronic palette without conventional constraints. Bitmapped color is dynamic, fluid, and changing. We can previsualize our designs, attaching color to them in experimental ways unimagined by any exercise of the Bauhaus color theory class.

Because the computer takes color from the physical to the virtual and back again, it is necessary to understand the abstraction that has been created by the genius of software. Scanning a color, or capturing one with a digital camera, produces a number that is then used to control the action of a screen or printer to render it back and into human readable form. Artists, designers, and other users have been liberated now that colors can be literally pulled out of thin air without resorting to complicated mathematical formulas or the fumes and smells of a printmaking studio. As computer-generated color began to enter the designer's workflow in the mid-1990s, the world saw objects created in an entirely new palette, such as those of Apple's iMac computers, which quickly influenced everything from lamps to automobiles. The expressive value of color is perhaps nowhere better demonstrated than in automobile design, particularly the Volkswagen Beetles of the early twenty-first century, whose vibrant color palette is certainly influenced by electronic color design. The "hyper" colors of the electronic circuit have become ubiquitous in global culture. Electric-green baseball caps are as familiar in the streets of Japan as they are in the villages of Mexico.

The creativity of design lies in the management of color. It is a powerful signifier that is always loaded with meaning; its use cannot be arbitrary because these meanings inflect metafora. Like pitch or volume of sound, too much or too little color can make or break the effectiveness of the communication.

At bottom, to be colored means that one has been caught in some utterly unbelievable cosmic joke, a joke so hideous and in such bad taste that it defeats all categories and definitions. One's only hope of supporting, to say nothing of surviving, this joke is to flaunt in the teeth of it one's own particular and invincible style. It is at this turning, this level, that the word color, ravaged by experience and heavy with the weight of particular spoils, returns to its first meaning which is not Negro, the Spanish word for black, but vivid, many-hued, e.g. the rainbow, and warm and quick and vital, e.g. life.

James Baldwin, *Collected Essays*

Music and Color

Color composition is the pure interrelationship of colors and light values, similar to what we know in music as composition in acoustical relationships; that is, the composition of universal systems independent of climate, race, temperament, education, rooted in biological laws.

László Moholy-Nagy[16]

The Dadaists' graphic works demonstrate an interest in the relationship of letters and phonetic relations that struck "chords" outside the realm of the visual. Raoul Hausmann created graphic pieces that gave birth to phonetic poems. The variety of shapes and sizes of letters conveyed rhythmic implications for voice and even for gesture. In his performances, poetry was produced as sound, which he called "opto-phonetics." He wanted to reach beyond more sentimental arrangements of music and sound to explore the interactive modalities between audio and visual.

Tone can be thought of as the musical analog of color. Like color, different tones consist of differing frequencies, in this case sound waves rather than electromagnetic waves. Simple tones can be combined to make more complex ones. Tone can be changed without altering the overall composition, but it can alter the mood of a piece.

Kurt Schwitters worked on the correlation between the luminosity of whites and blacks and the scales of music. He also compared intervals between notes of the scale and those separating colors, as had Sir Isaac Newton before him. Once mixed and composed, colors take on a relationship of complex chords.

Since the birth of motion pictures, image and sound have been combined, first with a live musical accompanist, later by running a strip of audiotape along with the film. Filmmakers have long realized that the expressive power of film can be amplified not only by the use of color but also through the addition of sound. Although dialogue helps to further the plot and develop characters, it is the soundtrack that conveys emotion. We have yet to see a sophisticated integration of color and sound in the digital realm, but the tools are there, simply waiting for informed use. We cannot imagine the future of cyber interaction without the integration of sound and color.

The visual-effects generator—available with most computer programs—is capable of playing music that creates an abstract visual representation through shape, and particularly color, of the music it plays. While often slick and kitschy, it places the notion of the correlation between vision and motion (the title of another Moholy-Nagy book) in the minds of the young children who use it.

Kurt Schwitters, Untitled

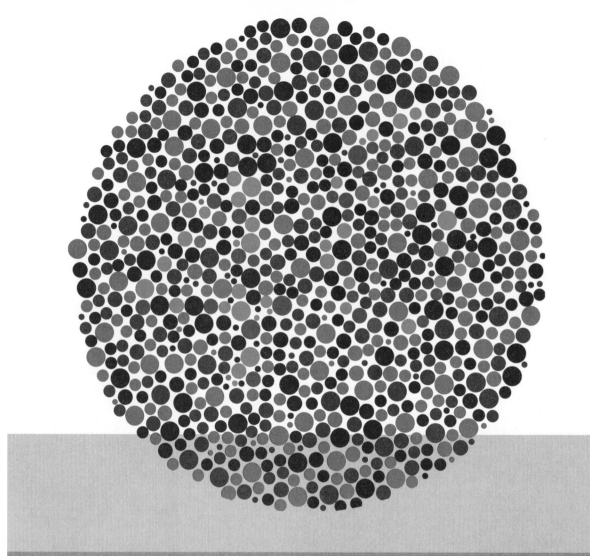

Color-blind

I know that colors carry importance for other people. . . . So I'll use color names when necessary to communicate with them. But colors as such carry no meaning for me. As a kid, I used to think that it would be nice to see colors, because then I would be able to have a driver's license and to do things that people with normal color vision can do. And if there were some way of acquiring color vision, I suppose it might open a new world . . . but it would also be very confusing. Color is something you have to grow up with, to mature with—your brain, the whole system, the way you react to the world. Bringing in color as a sort of add-on later in life would be overwhelming. . . . It would give new qualities to everything that might throw me off completely. Or maybe color would be disappointing, not what I expected—who knows?

Oliver Sachs, *The Man Who Mistook His Wife for a Hat*

This belt is used in dances by the Gelede society of

Meko, a Yoruba town in the west of Nigeria. The Yoruba

categorize colors into three main chromatic groupings,

each of which has a temperature: funfun (cool), which

includes white and silver; pupa (hot), which includes red,

pink, yellow, and other colors Westerners consider

warm; and dúdú (warm), which includes colors like black,

purple, and green. Colors also have spiritual connota-

tions, especially in beaded ceremonial garments, since

deities are associated with the colors that reveal their

temperament. So, the gbigbona gods who are hot and

temperamental are evoked with pupa, while the lo

wooro gods who are moderate are evoked with dúdú.

Color of Universe

cosmic lattè

In 2002, Karl Glazebrook and Ivan Baldry of Johns Hopkins University announced that the universe was beige. They arrived at this conclusion by averaging the color of all the light in the universe and analyzing it. When they put out a request to name the new color, their favorite response was "cosmic latte." The universe was not always this color: It started out blue and then grew redder as more stars became red giants.[17]

The eye may be said to owe its existence to light, which calls forth as it were a sense that is akin to itself; the eye, in short, is formed with reference to light to be fit for the action of light . . . like is only known by like . . . if the eye were not sunny how could we perceive light? If God's own strength live not in us, how could we delight in divine things?

Johannes Wolfgang von Goethe, *Theory of Colors*

In the classic *On a Philosophical Inquiry on Being Blue,* William Gass ruminated philosophically on color and its meaning. The authors of this book are particularly taken by its completeness in helping us to understand the realm of meaning applied to color. Blue may be reality itself, Gass points out. "It is the specific color of orgone energy within and without the organism. . . . It is a fact that the color blue is the color seen in all functions which are related to the cosmic or organismic energy . . . protoplasm of any kind, in any cell or bacterium is blue . . . thunderclouds are deeply blue . . . water in deep lakes and in the ocean is blue . . . the illumination in evacuated tubes charged with energy is blue."

And blue is the color of cyberspace as represented in popular culture. Hardly any symbolic representation of it exists without some spectrum of the color. As Gass points out, blue is a color we associate with sex, death, and control. Blue is the color of IBM. But does blue have to represent technology?

Might we infuse cyberspace with the joie de vivre colors of the baroque? Might we see cyberspace less forebodingly, less as a filament but as an experience, changing the mood and temperament of the colors of our lives? One of the first things people often do when they get a computer is to personalize the desktop with a colorful photograph.

The nature of blue in painting is such that when the pigment is applied to the canvas in a flat and even manner it seems to neither protrude forward nor recess backward, but floats in a kind of ethereal neutrality. For this reason, modern painters experimented radically with the color, particularly the abstract expressionists Robert Motherwell, Mark Rothko, and Ad Reinhardt. In these paintings, color becomes the subject matter. French painter Yves Klein was unconcerned with the representation of an object (in painting or sculpture), but with the blue itself, which he saw as the representation of the immaterial, the sovereign liberation of the spirit. His is a nonrepresentation that emphasizes the object as an end in itself—color. The paintings are extensions of a concept of nothingness—pure minimalism.

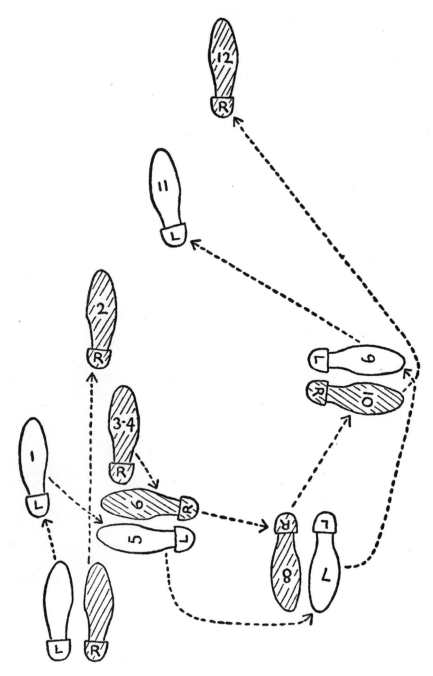

Foxtrot no. 7

I got rhythm, I got music, I got my girl,

With the rhythm, the rhythm, God bless the rhythm

It's the rhythm, rhythm; yes ya'll the rhythm

Shorty on the dance floor giving me rhythm

Hi Tek make ya'll nod ya'll neck to the rhythm

Talib Kweli, *Touch You*

Rhythm underlies every aspect of our existence, from the beating of our heart to the gait of our walk. Observation of the natural world offers our senses the paradigms of form, pattern, and energy that create rhythm. Nature is our cue. A simple act repeated gains new meaning as it becomes a rhythm. In the arts, rhythm gives pace to every form of creative expression, carrying with it structure and meaning. Edith Sitwell said, "Rhythm might be described as, to the world of sound, what light is to the world of sight." Today, the circuit provides a hub in the lives of those who have access to its technology, in which the multitasking of life's routines shapes the rhythm of our lives.

Because rhythm is inherent in all of our motions, from rapping a drum to making love, it can be a means of communicating on the most fundamental level. Through organizing sound, gesture, and dance, rhythm gave discipline to our earliest attempts to communicate as a society. Today, every form of representation strives to evoke rhythm, whether the sweep of Frank Gehry's Guggenheim Bilbao, or the repetitious scintillation of Philip Glass's music, or the unending syncopations of John F. Simon, Jr.'s digital grid. Bad design lacks good rhythm: "It don't mean a thing if it ain't got that swing."

An excellent example of the discipline of rhythm is the American Declaration of Independence. This great document of will lives in our consciousness primarily because of its carefully wrought cadence. We recognize it not only by its shape and contours as writing on parchment, but also as a resonating statement of stirring principles to be read aloud. Its Homeric line—"We hold these truths to be self-evident: that all men are created equal"—resounds because of its rhythm. The text uses rhetorical techniques that have their origin in the classical practice of oratory and is all the more remarkable for the fact that Thomas Jefferson wrote it, Benjamin Franklin embellished it, and many conceived it in an heroic collaborative effort. It demonstrates the syncopation of many creative minds, an interactivity established through its rhythm, which enabled one writer to continue the pace of another.

Who could ask for anything more?

Ira and George Gershwin

Navajo Two Grey Hills rug,
c. 1960

It is the harmonious correlation of parts that marks the arrangement of any inspired composition. Until the Renaissance, the Western visual world sought harmony in spatial compositions through a juxtaposition of parts to create symmetrical arrangements, which can be seen in a Byzantine icon or a Romanesque church, for example. It was a matter of keeping equilibrium while holding forces together, whether in painting, music, or architecture. These compositions achieved balance between fullness and emptiness, light and dark strokes, straight lines and curves, because everything could be broken down into measurable units or grids: patterns that were both graceful and stable, as can be witnessed in the elaborate grace of the Doge's palace of Venice, built between 1345 and 1438. The rhythm of the arches from the first story doubles in the second-story arcade.

Before the Renaissance, this same principle governed the work of scientists, engineers, and artisans alike, all of whose roles overlapped and who interchangeably served the state or church in the construction of their edifices. With the Renaissance and the rise of humanism, secular and erratic notions begin to intertwine with the once-static symmetry. Mathematics, and aesthetic organization based on geometric forms, enabled more complex uses of proportion, balance, and harmony. Movement, on the other hand, was of less concern to the management of space until the advent of the Industrial Revolution in the West and the ensuing mechanization of the nineteenth century. Speed and travel created displacement, and the elements of balance and symmetry had to be rethought. **Dynamism** echoed the rhythm of culture. It was seen in the blur of a photograph or the frenetic staging of an opera, and heard in new atonal music and the aerodynamic design of a car, even in the grind of the factory conveyor belt. The stable patterns of the past erupted into new rhythms brought forth from the communality of experience not just with the state and church, but with everyday things as well. Cézanne displaced an apple and Picasso fragmented a horse, while Joyce recorded a stream of thought.

Nothing expresses this explosion in the creative form better than the advent of the motion picture in the twentieth century. It is dynamic, successful because of its rhythmic structuring of music, sound, image, and illusion that are integrated with the narrative. The viewer suspends disbelief to be lost in the rhythm of gelatinous space, and is moved in effortless cadence anywhere in the imagination. When we are able to recognize the rhythm of our past patterns of experience, we learn from them while continuously repositioning ourselves in space. Looking down from a hot-air balloon in the eighteenth century created new perspective, and the speed of its flight anticipated momentous changes in the rhythm of daily life. From then on, equilibrium was no longer static.

Our experience in the realm of the circuit is one of hypermovement. Everything is in flux as we navigate though the filament of electronic signals, experiencing virtual structures. But this can be most frustrating and lack dynamism until we find a rhythm that gives form to the void and a pace to the form and, therefore, order to its never-ending choices. In cyberspace, the body seeks a tangible structure, and we are humanized by our creative management of algorithm into a rhythm of meaningful relationships. In a series of metaphoric signs and icons (the building blocks of cyber architecture), rhythm is the syntax and matrix that enables movement between ideas, programs, and computers.

Sophisticated automata are capable of looking at, and making a decision about, a task. The algorithms that do this are able to distinguish the differences between a lampshade and a hat. Although human beings are very good at this, teaching a machine to do so is not easy. We have made great strides in programming computers with this capability, not only in vision, but in haptic function as well. These developments, which lead to "intelligent" robotics that are capable of fulfilling menial tasks as well as more sophisticated ones, may ultimately relieve us of many burdensome activities.

Let us diverge briefly to discuss pattern. Rhythm makes and breaks pattern by helping us to group and regroup multiple elements of our metafora. In mathematics, the elementary representation is number and the simplest of nature's patterns are understood in numbers. Some ancient Greeks thought the entire universe was harmonious and based on mathematical laws. They developed a notion of the harmonious mean (Golden Mean) and applied it not only to music and other arts but also to the fields of science, including health and medicine. When the qualities of the body were in harmony, it was healthy. Everything was composed of a specific amount of the great indeterminate matter, and had a specific and unique algorithm or formula, which dictated how that matter was arranged. Those classic thinkers saw numbers as patterns within the world. No wonder the ancient Islamic culture that spurned figural images used geometry to stylize all things of natural origin. From script to tile to carpet, geometric pattern decoration was such that it multiplied itself with an unending continuity—only the borders disrupt the potentially infinite extensions.

Mosque interior, Morocco. The frieze decoration is ubiquitous to all cultures throughout the world. This is another example of the common use of rhythmic form. Even societies with no formal mathematical formulations understand, inherently, the order of nature as represented in their decorative arts.

We apply the patterns of form, the patterns of movement, and lastly those of randomness to equations and hypotheses in order to study the rhythms that structure our existence. Life forms of all sorts share a propensity to pattern, whether in their construction or in how they navigate, congregate, or reproduce their kind. Subatomic analysis reminds us, again, that these patterns are in a constant state of motion.

Deciphering the rhythms of the unseen is the business of our best endeavors. Computer technology extends the language of discovery, whether floating in an uninhabited space or probing the human chromosome. The computer enables us to magnify and reexamine the underlying patterns and rhythms of creativity and humanity, whether it is by looking for pattern within the data it holds or by enabling a musician to create new rhythms or weave existing ones together.

It is one of the prodigious privileges of art that the horrific, artistically expressed, becomes beauty, and that sorrow, given rhythm and cadence, fills the spirit with a calm joy.

Charles Baudelaire, *Théophile Gautier*

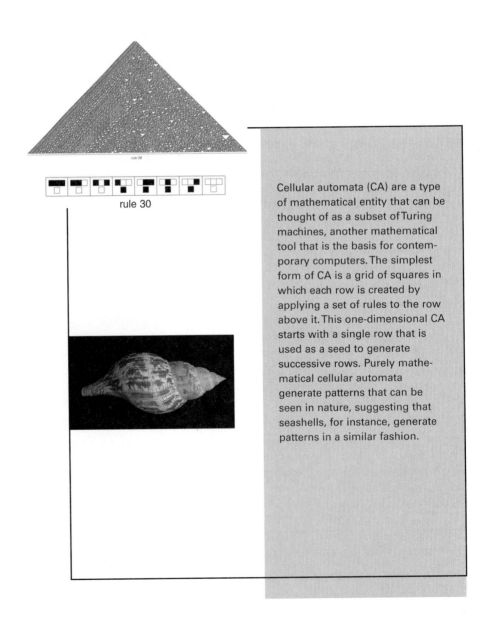

rule 30

Cellular automata (CA) are a type of mathematical entity that can be thought of as a subset of Turing machines, another mathematical tool that is the basis for contemporary computers. The simplest form of CA is a grid of squares in which each row is created by applying a set of rules to the row above it. This one-dimensional CA starts with a single row that is used as a seed to generate successive rows. Purely mathematical cellular automata generate patterns that can be seen in nature, suggesting that seashells, for instance, generate patterns in a similar fashion.

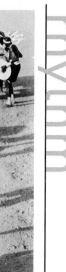

You wanna learn how to rhyme
You better learn how to add.
It's mathematics

mos def

African Music

In some African music, especially that from central and sub-Saharan Africa, rhythm is not only the foundation of musical composition, but music is an important part of many social rites. In northern Ghana the symbol of the Dagomba king's power is not the scepter but the drummer. Western music typically has one main rhythm, where as African music has at least two. Because there is no main beat, drummers in an ensemble find their entrance into a piece not by counting from the main beat, but in relation to the other musicians. The rhythm of the piece is further enhanced through interaction with members of the audience, expected to be active participants in creating its rhythmic structure.

Perhaps drumming is such an integral part of African culture because many African languages are tonal. Inflections of words carry different meanings, and these inflections can be imitated by varying the pitch of the drum. John Chernoff relates an incident that occurred as he sat in a bar in Ghana for a drumming lesson from master drummer Gideon Folie Alorwoyie. "During my first day practicing with Gideon, I was following him fairly well until he suddenly performed a rather complicated series of rhythms and then went back to the basic rhythm he was showing me. A few minutes later a man who had passed at that moment [when he played the complicated rhythms] returned with two bottles of beer." Gideon had deviated from the lesson for a moment to order drinks with his drumming.[18]

"I Have a Dream" August 28th, 1963

I have a dream that one day this nation will rise up and live out the true meaning of its creed: "We hold these truths to be self-evident: that all men are created equal." I have a dream that one day on the red hills of Georgia the sons of former slaves and the sons of former slave owners will be able to sit down together at the table of brotherhood.

I have a dream that one day even the state of Mississippi, a state sweltering with the heat of injustice, sweltering with the heat of oppression, will be transformed into an oasis of freedom and justice.

I have a dream that my four little children will one day live in a nation where they will not be judged by the color of their skin but by the content of their character.

I have a dream today.

I have a dream that one day, down in Alabama, with its vicious racists, with its governor having his lips dripping with the words of interposition and nullification; one day right there in Alabama, little black boys and black girls will be able to join hands with little white boys and white girls as sisters and brothers.

I have a dream today.

I have a dream that one day every valley shall be exalted, every hill and mountain shall be made low, the rough places will be made plain, and the crooked places will be made straight, and the glory of the Lord shall be revealed, and all flesh shall see it together. This is our hope. This is the faith that I go back to the South with. With this faith we will be able to hew out of the mountain of despair a stone of hope. With this faith we will be able to transform the jangling discords of our nation into a beautiful symphony of brotherhood. With this faith we will be able to work together, to pray together, to struggle together, to go to jail together, to stand up for freedom together, knowing that we will be free one day.

Reverend Dr. Martin Luther King, Jr., "I Have a Dream," August 28, 1963.

The remarkable power of oration to add inflection through rhythm can be seen in this excerpt from Dr. King's famous address to civil rights marchers in Washington, D.C., one of the greatest pieces of oration of modern times. Note the use of repetition: Rhythm relies on memory for its expressive power, and Dr. King uses the phrase "I have a dream" over and over to punctuate and drive the speech forward. The words seem lifeless on the printed page, without the stirring inflection of his voice.

rhythm

Harmony

Western music is based on the arrangement of tones: When they are played one after the other, they create rhythm, and when played simultaneously, they create harmony. While we can think of the opening of digital files or the succession of web pages linked by users' clicks as the rhythm of the computer, its operating system is what produces harmony. When any one thing is out of harmony—say an application makes a call to a nonexistent memory address—the computer crashes, the ultimate bad note.

Kyoto Zen garden, 1992

Writing is a question of finding a certain rhythm. I compare it to the rhythms of jazz. Much of the time life is a sort of rhythmic progression of three characters. If one tells oneself that life is like that, one feels it less arbitrary.

Françoise Sagan

Tao and Pattern

The way has never known boundaries; speech has no constancy. But because of [the recognition of] "this," there came to be boundaries. Let me tell you what the boundaries are. There is left, there is right, there are theories, there are debates, there are divisions, there are discriminations, there are emulations, and there are contentions. These are called the Eight Virtues. Beyond the Six Realms [Heaven, earth and the four directions, i.e. the universe], the sage exists but he does not theorize. Within the Six Realms he theorizes but does not debate. In the case of the Spring and Autumn, the record of the former kings of past ages, the sage debates but does not discriminate. So [I say,] those who divide fail to divide; those who discriminate fail to discriminate. What does this mean, you ask? The sage embraces things. Ordinary men discriminate among them and parade their discriminations before others. So I say, those who discriminate fail to see.

Chuang Tzu, *Basic Writings*

Ancient Islamic grave site, Morocco

The Chris I missed so badly was not an object but a pattern, and that, although the pattern included the flesh and blood of Chris, that was not all there was to it. The pattern was larger than Chris and myself, and related us in ways that neither of us understood completely and neither of us was in complete control of.

Now Chris's body, which was a part of that larger pattern, was gone. But the larger pattern remained. A huge hole had been torn out of the center of it, and that was what caused all the heartache. The pattern was looking for something to attach to and couldn't find anything. That's probably why grieving people feel such attachment to cemetery headstones and any material property or representation of the deceased. The pattern is trying to hang on to its own existence by finding some new material thing to center itself on.

Robert Pirsig
Zen and the Art of Motorcycle Maintenance

Li Chi and om

Chinese musicians plucked the strings of zithers as far back as 1000 B.C.E. For the ancient Chinese philosophers, music was spiritual; the harmony and rhythm of music would enable its practitioner and listener to become aligned with the harmony and rhythm of the universe. The *Li Chi,* which is one of the five classics of Chinese literature, believed to date from about 500 B.C.E., states: "Music is the harmony of heaven and earth while rites are the measurement of heaven and earth. Through harmony all things are made known, through measure all things are properly classified." The early Hindus saw music as a personification of the vibrations that underlay the universe—the om. All that exists derives from this fundamental tone. "The syllable OM, which is the imperishable Brahman, is the universe. Whatever has existed, whatever exists, whatever will exist, is OM. And whatever transcends past, present, and future is OM."

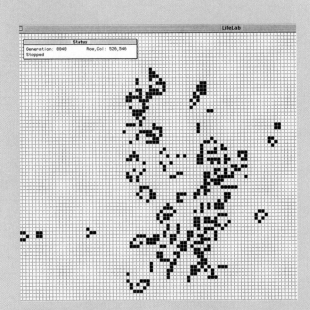

The game of Life

Cambridge mathematician John Conway developed the game of Life as a simplified model of John von Neumann's cellular automata (ca). He designed a CA that consisted of a grid, each square of which could be either on or off at any given time:

> Life occurs on a virtual checkerboard. The squares are called cells. They are in one of two states: alive or dead. Each cell has eight possible neighbors, the cells which touch its sides or its corners.

> If a cell in the checkerboard is alive, it will survive in the next time step (or generation) if there are either two or three neighbors also alive. It will die of overcrowding if there are more than three live neighbors, and it will die of exposure if there are fewer than two.

> If a cell on the checkerboard is dead, it will remain dead in the next generation unless exactly three of its eight neighbors are alive. In that case, the cell will be "born" in the next generation.[19]

The game was a purely mathematical model, simulated on checkerboards or on sheets of paper laid on the floor, covered with playing pieces. Soon, people realized that the game could be simulated on the computer, vastly speeding its pace. The image above is a screen shot from an implementation by R. Fronabarger. The black spheres represent cells that are alive. White space represents cells that are dead.

[A person] is a thinking intelligent being, that has reason and reflection, and can consider itself as itself, the same thinking thing in different times and places; which it does only by that consciousness which is inseparable from thinking, and, as it seems to me, essential to it: It being impossible for any one to perceive, without perceiving that he does perceive.

John Locke,
An Essay Concerning Human Understanding

William Hogarth meant to demonstrate the rules of perspective by breaking them.

Leon Alberti, Renaissance architect, writer, and sculptor described vision as a pyramid, with the viewer's eye at the apex. To paint in linear perspective, the canvas was imagined as a plane that intersected that pyramid and the imaginary lines that emanated from the viewer's eye.

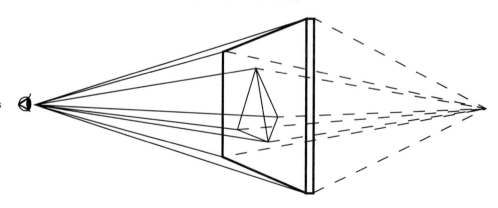

In the visual arts, perspective refers to the way in which the image (painted, drawn, or photographed) attempts to portray a three-dimensional scene on a two-dimensional surface. In writing we can think of perspective as the way in which the author constructs the work to convey a story, through first-person or second-person narrative, for example. In the composition of music, harmonies converge in the same way as lines in a drawing, and this arrangement of harmonies into melody is analogous to perspective.

Perspective may be the act of orienting oneself to the world. In the arts—from painting to photography to film to writing—it is the way in which the artist transforms observation into metafora, through either personal or systematic means. When we look at a work of art, we see a world filtered through the artist's perspective. In the dialog that emerges between the artist, the medium, and the audience, a transformation takes place, which enables the discovery of ourselves in the work of others.

The proliferation of photography has made us accustomed to a way of depicting a scene that we believe is "correct." Nevertheless, a photograph is a two-dimensional rendering of three-dimensional space and is no more correct in its observation than a realist painting that follows the same rules. The false assumption that photography is "correct" leads us to the equally false assumption that styles of painting that do not mimic photography (especially non-Western painting) are "incorrect." The human eye does not see as the camera does: Our sense of vision is generated from two eyes and complicated neural pathways that produce our experience of vision. Unlike a single lens that creates a two-dimensional picture, we see by creating a three-dimensional dynamic image that constantly changes as we move our eyes about to survey the scene in front of us. The photographic image is a flat, unmoving image that lacks the full range of tones we can normally perceive.

Linear perspective, the perspective we see when we look at a photograph, has its roots in Europe in the period between the Middle Ages and the Renaissance. It was in essence the application of a rigid set of mathematical rules, an algorithm, to the act of painting. Starting in the thirteenth century, concepts of an infinite, systematic, and therefore measurable world began to develop and continued through the Scientific Revolution. Viewing this world was the new individual, who stood outside a scene to observe it. In the early fourteenth century, Giotto di Bondoni began to paint with an intuitive perspective, placing figures in scenes that suggested a three-dimensional space. By 1420, Filippo Brunelleschi had demonstrated the rules of linear perspective, which were formalized in Leon Battista Alberti's *Della Pittura*. Western artists used a variety of devices, from mathematical calculations to mechanical devices such as the camera obscura or the camera lucida. So powerful was this idea of representing space (and by correlation time, because paintings in linear perspective portrayed a single instant) that it was by far the most common form used for nearly seven hundred years.

Draw The First Day!
No artistic talent? Don't worry!—with new Art Reproducer you don't need it. Draw, paint, sketch your family, friends, anything from real life—without lessons, as if by magic. Takes all objects, projects their images on paper, giving you a professional guide for expert results. Make figures, scenes, still life, Use to reduce or enlarge drawings, too. M 3294, Complete Kit **$1.98**

Learn to draw on the first day without learning the pesky rules of perspective!

There are a variety of methods for rendering a scene on a canvas, many of which do not depend on the emulation of the optical rules of photography. Several non-Western cultures developed alternate yet equally rigorous constructions of pictorial space. This is not to suggest an ignorance of the rules of geometry or optics; rather it represents a conscious disregard for them. The Chinese saw no need for an individual to be detached from the environment, though they had highly developed notions of mathematics that would have enabled them easily to construct a system of linear perspective if they so desired.

Western linear perspective presented the landscape as potential, a vista to be explored. The observer of a European painting stood outside the frame peering in, while the observer of a Chinese landscape floated in the scene. The painter Fan Kuan worked in the monochromatic landscape style around the turn of the second millennium (1000 C.E.). His painting exemplified the neo-Confucian notion that the self should not be detached from nature: "A reaching outward to imitate Creation/And a turning inward to master the mind."[20] Kuan's construction is one in which the work seems to have been painted from every point of view at once: A series of successive eye levels appear from top to bottom.

Centuries later, the Japanese master Hokusai's series *Thirty-Six Views of Mt. Fuji* began to abandon the prevailing Chinese perspectival constructions in favor of Western ones, although the principle of presenting a scene with many points of view is transformed into presenting it in many images, each with a single point of view. Hokusai's work was distributed throughout a nineteenth-century Japan that was captivated with printmaking. His thirty-six views were reproduced in massive quantities. In each print, the viewer is taken through the landscape, appearing in front of one feature in each print. The combined experience of viewing all the prints is related to the cubist work, which attempts to move the viewer around the portrayed object in one canvas.

By the turn of the twentieth century, the telephone enabled people to cast their voices across great distances. They spoke with loved ones and associates who traveled rapidly by train and steamship, and later by automobile, devouring space and expanding the individual's reach. Passengers on trains saw the landscape rush by them, their point of view changing second by second, while the hot-air balloon allowed a bird's-eye view of the world to be captured by the newly invented camera. Speed itself blurred the horizon. Linear perspective came into question as painting turned to more abstract modalities and toward an inward, more subjective point of view that complemented this new, modern experience of vision.

This mobility of body and voice was expressed in the new "isms" whereby the work of art became a thing to look at, rather than a window to gaze through. Paul Cézanne's canvases show a world that seems to shimmer and defies conventional representation of reality. Cubism—through the work of Pablo Picasso, Georges Braque, and Max Weber—created pictures that appear constructed from many perspectives at once, while Futurism—Giocommo Balla, Carlo Carrà, Filippo Marinetti—showed the viewer a landscape in dynamic motion, a vision transformed by the experience of railroad travel.

Concurrently, Hermann Minkowski, Albert Einstein, and other physicists laid waste to the Cartesian grid with theories such as the general theory of relativity, which postulated that the universe had no absolute system of measurement save the speed of light. Sigmund Freud debunked the view that we have control over our thoughts. He saw the mind as a dynamic system in constant conflict with

Landscape by Yang Jin, c. 1715

itself and the outside world. (Dadaism and surrealism were reflections of this psychological perspective.) The publication of *The Communist Manifesto* by Karl Marx and Friedrich Engels in 1848 analyzed the world in terms of conflict between the proletariat and the bourgeois classes. The early twentieth-century art movement of constructivism, epitomized in the work of Vladimir Tatlin, translated this economic theory by rejecting art for art's sake in the search for the utilitarian values of materials and ideas.

The birth of modern cinema reflected early twentieth-century notions of time and space. Filmmakers began to use editing techniques and radical shifts in orientation, whereby a scene was shot from several vantage points at once, then edited and spliced together, creating a sequential analog to cubism. One need only think of Orson Welles's *Citizen Kane* to experience the great agility of the medium in the compression and expansion of time, as well as incorporating a psychological perspective into the development of the characters. Today, filmmakers can instantly change perspective with techniques that include as many as a hundred different cameras arranged in the scene. These images are then collaged together and give the appearance that the camera itself is moving. This technique was used in films such as *The Matrix* and is employed by officials for televised football games, where replay is reviewed from whatever vantage point is needed. In the future, viewers might have control over which camera to monitor, situating themselves into the scene. These tools enable the audience to choose its own visual perspective.

Classical music also changed during the early twentieth century. In linear perspective, all lines converge to a single vanishing point, whereas in music, the tonic, the primary melody, is the lodestone to which all harmonies in a melody (and by extension the entire composition) converge. Secondary harmonies in the composition imply being pulled back to the tonic. Early twentieth-century composers tried to find a way out of the tonal system, as in Igor Stravinsky's 1913 symphonic ballet *The Rite of Spring*. Here Stravinsky started to play the primary and secondary chord at the same time, to lessen the distinction between them. Pantonalism, as this is called, is a deliberate attempt to destroy harmonic perspective and harmonic movement. After World War II, serial or twelve-tone techniques would completely discard any use of the tonal system.

Parallel to the visual and performing arts, literary perspective underwent enormous transformation toward the end of the millennium. Moving beyond the conventions of the eighteenth-century novel, which depicted a fixed and unchanging world, early twentieth-century advances made way for modernist authors such as James Joyce, who incorporated a "mixed" objective/subjective narrative strategy known as free indirect discourse, in which the tone and style of narration, although remaining essentially

Top: Hokusai, *Mt. Fuji at Dawn* from the series *Thirty-six Views of Fuji,* early 1830s

Bottom: Hokusai, not titled, c. 1815–1820

Development of new genres of music, such as punk, represents a new perspective on existing forms.

in the third person, is influenced by what is being described as well as by the perspective of the protagonist. Joyce uses this technique in *A Portrait of the Artist as a Young Man*, in which the narrative, though it remains in the authorial third person, is subjective and character-driven in approach. This style, which fuses external narration with interior monologue, was perhaps influenced by the emerging field of psychoanalysis and the increased attention to the role of the unconscious in conscious experience. Though the technique of shifting narration is as old as Petronius's *Satyricon*, Joyce and others' use of it mirrored modernist attitudes about the relation of the self to the increasingly unknowable and shifting exterior world.

Anna Deavere Smith wrote her groundbreaking play *Fires in the Mirror* in response to the events surrounding riots that engulfed the Crown Heights section of Brooklyn in New York City. The 1991 riots were sparked by racial and religious tensions that had been smoldering for years between Hasidic Jewish and Carribean residents. The innovative nature of Smith's play was that it refused to take sides or to moralize. Rather, she interviewed the inhabitants of Crown Heights, enabling them to tell the story in their own words. In many senses, this play embodies the "death of the author": It has no authoritative perspective, no single point of view. It is decentered and chaotic, like the world that produced the riots that shook New York City. Referring to Smith's play, Cornel West wrote: "Not to choose 'sides' is itself a choice—yet to view the crisis as simply and solely a matter of choosing sides is to reduce the history and complexity of the crisis in a vulgar Manichean manner."[21] This is a situation we are faced with every day in the contemporary media world, wherein news stories compete with "spin" and the multiple voices available on the World Wide Web.

> *The instance of there being more is an instance of more. The shadow is not shining in the way there is a black line. The truth has come. There is a disturbance. Trusting to a baker's boy meant that there would be very much exchanging and anyway what is the use of a covering to a door. There is a use, they are double.*
>
> Gertrude Stein

At the end of the twentieth century, we find a resurrection of fourteenth-century perspective in contemporary technological devices. Before the Renaissance's engagement with linear perspective, paintings in Europe were composed of many panels or frames within a canvas that told a story. Linear perspective transformed these frames into a single window. Beginning with Xerox's 1973 Alto system, and perfected by programmers at Apple computer in the 1980s, today's Windows-based operating system transforms the computer screen into a pre-Renaissance painting. No longer is the screen a window to look through; it contains objects to be looked at, allowing us to multitask, to split our attention among many things at once. It also offers the ability to show a scene from many points of view at once, as some 3-D design programs do, extending the multiple viewpoints of cubism over time. The computer program RasMol, for example, enables scientists to rotate models of molecules in real time.

The written word is also in transition. Chat rooms, text-based interactions among dozens of people at a time, have expanded perspective. No single voice dominates, and many conversations occur at once. Presenting answers to frequently-asked questions (**FAQs**) and the use in the programming world of requests for comment (**RFCs**) both involve the contribution of multiple voices in presenting a point of view.

Because the computer is able to synthesize media, Western linear perspective can be combined with other forms of perspective. The integration of media, itself so much an agile part of digitization, can broaden one's perspective of an experience. The ability of the user to manipulate any component of the experience to suit his or her "angle" of need may change not only the narrative itself but also the very stability of the conventions of authoritative perspective. Perspective is, after all, only a filter through which an author allows the reader to engage in the tale, or in the case of the news media, it is an editing of a complex situation (although this filtering is not without bias, overt or subtle). Today, practically any user has control over the filters that once belonged only to the so-called experts or authorities. What is creativity if not the constant changing of perspective?

perspective

So, with many other feminists, I want to argue for a doctrine and practice of subjectivity that privileges contestation, deconstruction, passionate construction, webbed connections, and hope for transformation of systems of knowledge and ways of seeing. But not just any partial perspective will do; we must be hostile to easy relativisms and holisms built out of summing and subsuming parts. "Passionate detachment" (Kuhn, 1982) requires more than acknowledged and self-critical partiality. We are also bound to seek perspective from those points of view, which can never be known in advance, which promise something quite extraordinary, that is, knowledge potent for constructing worlds less organized by axes of domination. In such a viewpoint, the unmarked category would really disappear—quite a difference from simply repeating a disappearing act . . . science has been utopian and visionary from the start; that is one reason "we" need it.

Donna Haraway
Simians, Cyborgs, and Women

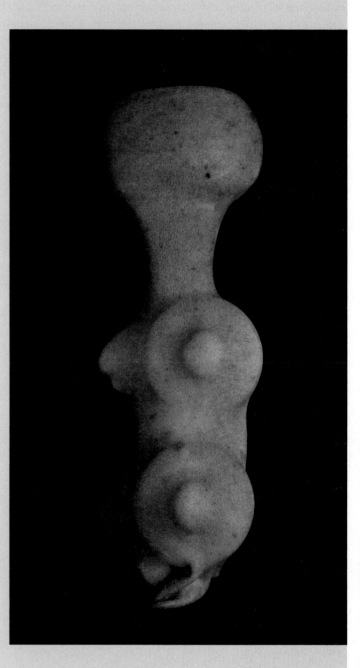

Aziz/Cucher, *Chimera*. This digitally manipulated photograph is a synthetic form with organic qualities, a new world of form.

Jon Haddock's images in the series *Screenshots* are painted in isometric perspective, like popular video games such as The Sims. These images portray fictional and historical events such as civil rights protesters being attacked with fire hoses in Birmingham, Alabama, in 1963.

Home Video

The lowered cost of producing moving pictures through home video equipment has made everyone an author. This phenomenon was noted as far back as 1979 in the Talking Heads song "Found a Job": "Judy's in the bedroom, inventing situations/Bob is on the street today, scouting up locations/. . . . If they ever watch T.V. again, it'd be too soon for them/Bob never yells about the picture now, he's having too much fun." The handheld camera aesthetic made popular by home videos resurfaces in television shows like *America's Funniest Home Videos*, in which viewers are shown other people's humorous video clips, which usually portray a physically or emotionally painful moment, or *Cops*, which is filmed from the point of view of a camera operator who is more often than not running at full speed behind police officers. This cinema-verité aesthetic has shown up in feature films as well, such as those inspired by the Danish Dogme 95 movement or *The Blair Witch Project*, which reconstructs the fictional disappearance of three young documentary filmmakers through the handheld video they shot while making their film. The voyeurism of "reality television" has some of its roots in the personal Web cam, which enables people to broadcast their personal lives on the Internet.

Akutagawa

In 1921, Japanese author Ryunosuke Akutagawa wrote his seminal short story "In a Grove," which would inspire Akira Kurosawa's 1951 film, *Rashomon*. The story revolves around the killing of a merchant by a bandit and the rape of a woman in medieval Japan. The story as we are told it is set at the trial after the events and narrated in turn by each of the characters: the bandit, the woman, and the ghost of the merchant. As each narrator tells the story, the events change, and the reader is left unsure of what the truth really is. Truth is a matter of from whose perspective the story is told.

Thomas Kuhn

Perspective can refer to more than just an individual point of view. Communities, including the scientific community, can have points of view as well. In his controversial 1962 book, *The Nature of Scientific Revolutions*, Thomas Kuhn defined the word *paradigm* to mean the scientific worldview. Scientific thought does not advance through the accumulation of more and more knowledge, but through paradigm shifts, ways of looking at the world in a different manner. The shift from Newtonian to quantum physics is one example. Furthermore, Kuhn argued, one paradigm is not necessarily more correct than another, merely more useful. Many contemporary philosophers take this notion to an extreme, saying, for example, that Western science is no more valid than astrology. The question becomes: Is there an absolute truth? Do we construct reality through science, or are different scientific notions simply alternate ways of looking at the world? What Kuhn seems to be saying is the latter: There is an objective, unchanging world out there; it is just a matter of how we look at it.

VR

Lev Manovich, in his book *The Language of New Media*, notes that with the advent of virtual reality (VR), the screen disappears and there is no need to render three dimensions into two: The viewer perceives three dimensions all at once. Ten years before Manovich's book, Wendy Kellogg, John Carroll, and John Richards noted that VR would eliminate the need for the graphical user interface as we know it. VR equipment could be used to "augment reality," to impose a user interface over the world as we know it.

Twentieth-century Chinese
advertisement for insect repellent

The elements of structure, with their rules and constituent parts, are merely a fanciful void without the imprinture of some creative authorship that connects both style and expression to them. Elusive at best, style and expression are symbiotic in their manifestation of a truly creative enterprise. Inherent in style is the repetition of forms and ideas and the ways in which the expressive ingredients can be presented or arranged. For the purposes of definition, we might use musicologist Leonard Myers' notion that style is a replication of patterning whether in human behavior or artifacts produced by human behavior, which results from a series of choices made with some set of constraints—and we would add, calculated risks.

The constraints are those rules or guidelines that are learned, adopted, broken, and reinvented through historical/cultural circumstances by individuals or groups. In the flux and flow of cultural exchange, the artist and the audience experience style as the ultimate synthesis of decisions regarding the limits of a given form of expression. Style is the balance between containing and pushing an idea. The meaning of a creative act—its resultant style—is the coming together of its elements of structure, techniques employed, and purpose to which it is put. Style is felt and is recognizable as it permeates the work. Both the audience and maker can understand it as something that gives an overall synthesis to the work and the œuvre. Style is communicated over the entire score or body of work, not in a single passage or a given image. It results from repeated performance, practice, and thinking, and is spurred by insight and talent.

Certain conditions, or an atmosphere, must exist within a culture that allows a style to be confirmed by an audience and to take hold. War and the technology of speed gace rise to Picasso's fractured world. Cultural fatigue with the sterile minimalist architecture of the modernist gave authority to Robert Venturi, Michael Graves, and others whose gestures and referential ornament enlivened late twentieth-century architecture. Some psychological or utilitarian need within an audience is served by the creative act, which allows it to gain its authority from the audience reaction. Style lies in an agreement between audience and creator.

Freud gives us further understanding of the psychological underpinnings of the expressive act as a turning away from reality in an active, creative play: "An artist . . . allows his erotic and ambitious wishes full play in the life of fantasy. He finds the way back to reality, however, from his world of fantasy by making use of special gifts to mould his fantasies into truths of a new kind, which are valued by men as precious reflections of reality."[22]

Critic Calvin Tomkins points out that "it takes considerable ingenuity to get beyond one's own self-expressed taste" to a new expressive language—style. In his discussion of the giants of twentieth-century art, he cites Duchamp, Cage, Tinguely, and Rauschenberg for their disrespect of traditional representations that

Above: Highboy chest, eighteenth century

Left: Glamour girl, circa 1950s

Left: Sophia Eliot Lipkin, *Untitled*, 2000

impose the artist's meaning and interpretation of reality on the audience. The maker of metafora can block the imaginative order of his creation by obscuring the view of the receiver with his own emotions. Tompkins quotes Robert Rauschenberg: "Art is not an end but simply a means to function thoroughly and passionately in a world that has a lot more to it than paint." John Cage substituted chance for personal control by allowing the randomness of "found sounds" to be themselves in his compositions. Tomkins sums up that Cage's desire was that music should not be concerned primarily with entertainment or communication, or the symbolic expression of the artist's ideas and taste, but should serve the function of helping the listeners achieve more awareness of their own lives.[23] A Zen idea indeed.

The modernist photographer Garry Winogrand, when asked why he depicted a certain subject, replied, "To see what it looks like as a photograph," knowing that expression and not reality was embedded in the photographic paper. All metafora gives freedom to the need for stylistic gesture that drives it into the consciousness of culture and pushes the possibilities of the medium or form that contains it to new life. Those who can manipulate the elements of structure in such a way are deemed to have great style. They have shifted our view of the world, changing patterns and thus shifting our perspective. In the end, style is style. We may not be able to define it, but we know it when we see it.

. . . we are not at all oblivious of the real distinction between what the ordinary person nowadays calls art, and the other things. Picture-painting, sculpture, music, are indeed art par excellence, but that they alone are now called art is not because they alone are or can be art, but because they alone to-day are the work of men not only skillful, and not tools in the hands of another, but workmen responsible for the things they make.

Eric Gill, *An Essay on Typography*

Information can be described as what we depend on for making statements or other representations. More precisely, we may define information in general as that which justifies representational activity.

Donald M. MacKay

The principles that obtain wholly and fundamentally in every kind of art are few but decisive; they determine what art is and what it is not. Expressiveness, in one definite and appropriate sense, is the same in all artworks of any kind.

Susanne K. Langer, *Feeling and Form*

Creativity is predicated on a system of rules and forms, in part determined by intrinsic human capacities. Without such constraints, we have arbitrary and random behavior, not creative acts. The construction of common sense and scientific inquiry derive from principles grounded in the structure of the human mind. Correspondingly, it would be an error to think of human freedom solely in terms of absence of constraint.

Noam Chomsky, *On Language*

New York, New York Casino, Las Vegas, Nevada

Postmodern Style

Postmodern thinking makes style obsolete. The concept of style presupposes the concept of working with real objects, yet Jean Baudrillard claims that today all is simulation, that the real is made real only after it is reproduced. Style becomes merely one more thing to copy, to appropriate. If nothing is real, then there are no objects to manipulate to create a style.

Order

Order may be the by-product of pattern, and it is inherently a part of any expressive communication. While the expression may come from the unique style, intonation, or gesture of the maker, order is implicit in the work no matter how abstract it may be. From fractals in art to pink noise in music, essential mathematical patterns are evident. *The Dot and the Line: A Romance in Lower Mathematics*, a classic book from the 1960s, best expresses this notion. A straight line, a vector, woos the dot, whose perfection entrances him. Yet she is hopelessly in love with a romantic, unkempt squiggle. The line finally wins her love by his discovery of his versatility and ability to embody mathematical patterns. "Freedom is not a license for chaos, but for order to achieve desired ends." When he discovers his versatility, he awes the perfect circle.

New York City, 2001

Frederic Jameson: Modernism is based on personal style or vision, private style, based on the notion of a unique and authentic self. Stylistic innovation is no longer possible, only pastiche.

We understand a work of art correctly, then, as soon as we perceive it correctly in the rhythmic-formal sense, and as soon as we feel its true emotional content through this correct formal perception.

Susanne K. Langer, *Reflections on Art*

While metafora comes from the Greek "to carry," perception comes from the Latin "to collect." It allows us to apprehend what others have made through metafora and to formulate a sense of who we are. We can understand the elements of structure because, as humans, we share the same common utilities for comprehending form, color, rhythm, perspective, and style in the medium of space-time. We collect information through our senses, and through our abilities of perception, we can manage this information, in order to position ourselves in our environment, whether real or virtual, and thus define a large part of who we are.

Brain function is more or less the same in all human beings. In visual perception, for example, the brain breaks down the stimuli it receives from the eye into different components, such as color, line, motion, and position, and reconstructs them into our sense of vision. This intrinsic hardwired trait enables us all to receive stimuli in essentially the same manner. It is because our perceptions function similarly at this fundamental level that the structures of metafora can be understood from one individual to another.

"The essence of perception is the selective attention to something important. And the recognition of what is important is trigger to creativity. The receptive system 'tunes itself' by adjusting the apparatus for clear reception. For example, the lens-retina–nerve–muscle system is not passive but active. It continually creates new stimuli for itself, searching out in an optical array the relations, ratios, grades and invariance of pattern that specify facts of the world. The amount of potential information in the light reaching the eye is unlimited."[24] What we do with that information is a matter of creativity.

The future holds great promise for further widening the doors of our perception. Computer interactivity and multimedia are intermodal sensory experiences. Arguably, the creative expression of cyberspace is unique as an experience in that it further allows us to differentiate ourselves from our physical surroundings, disconnecting us from them and enabling us to perceive things without the filters and impediments of our corporeal selves. We can fly through space in a metaphorical sense, unaffected by gravity, extending—with whatever prosthesis we can invent—the capabilities of gesture, sound, object, image, and word, through our ability to give them form, color, rhythm, perspective, and style.

Knowledge being to be had only of visible and certain truth, error is not a fault of knowledge, but a mistake of our judgment, giving assent to that which is not true.

John Locke, *An Essay Concerning Human Understanding*

Socrates Park, New York, 2001

Interlude: History of Perception

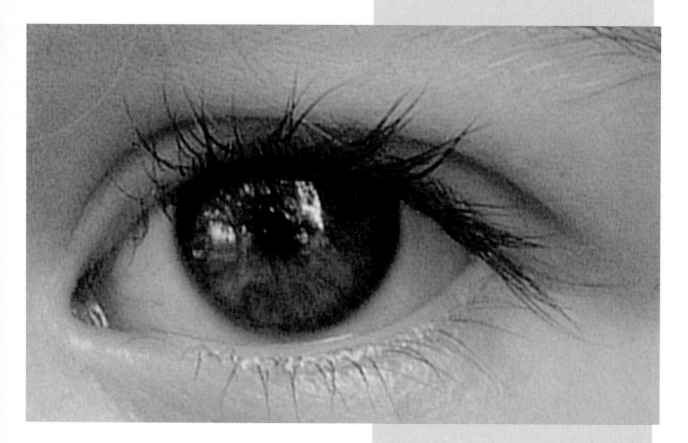

Light is elemental, and cannot be said to be composed of anything other than itself. Light has some properties of a wave–it travels through a medium at differing wavelengths; and of a particle–it can travel through a vacuum. It can also be thought of as energy, as expressed in Albert Einstein's famous formula, $E=mc^2$.

Newton analyzing light

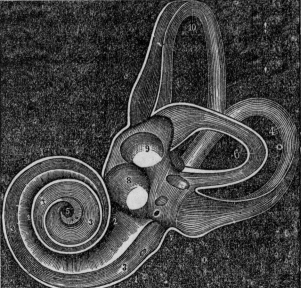

Diagram of the inner ear

Perception verifies our existence. Whether it is the eye that notes the color or shape of our surroundings, or the ear that informs us of the duration and intensity of a sound, or the body that measures the distance between action and consequence, our sense perceptions construct our coordinates in time and space. Our first creative act may be to establish our location in space. Once this has been achieved, we can then begin to travel through and mold space via the creation of metafora.

Thinking about perception and light were closely intertwined until the scientific revolution of the seventeenth century. In the early nineteenth century, Gustav Kirchoff postulated that light propagated as a wave, at right angles to the direction of travel, and that it traveled through the ether, a substance that pervaded all space, including the vacuums of space. In 1864, James Clerk Maxwell published his theory of electromagnetism, which described the shape of electromagnetic fields and how electricity and magnetism interacted. Light and electricity traveled at the same speed, and the only difference between them was the length of the wave. His theory obviated the need of an ether, the Greek notion of an absolute underlying substrate of the universe. Maxwell's paper would inspire Morse in his development of the telegraph. At the turn of the twentieth century, in 1905, Einstein published his special theory of relativity, which postulated that light and energy were related and that light could behave as though it were a particle or a wave.

Today, we think of light as the visible spectrum of electromagnetic radiation, which is the flow of energy through space in the form of electric and magnetic fields. At the lower end of the electromagnetic spectrum, we find ELF (extremely low frequency, used for submarine communication) and radio waves, whereas at the high end we find gamma rays, which are emitted by radioactive substances. The visible spectrum sits between ultraviolet (above violet) and infrared (below red) radiation at a frequency of approximately 1015 herz.

Light is received by receptors in the eye called rods and cones. As early as the 1840s, Hermann Helmholtz, a German physicist, noticed that the eye contained receptor cells—he called them fibers, whereas today they are referred to as cones. These cells, of which there are three types, are sensitive to particular wavelengths of light: red, green, and blue. Thus, color theory is entirely dependent on human sensitivities. Because the color spectrum is continuous, there is no physical reason—that is, a reason based on the properties of light or of electromagnetic radiation—to create a color theory based on red, green, and blue. It is done so only because of the sensitivity of the human eye.

Visual perception, the process through which we apprehend and understand the world through our eyes, is an active process that involves collaboration between the eye and the brain. The eye has receptor cells that translate light into neural activity, which is decoded by the brain. Speculations about the components and

If the doors of perception were cleansed every thing would appear to man as it is: infinite. For man has closed himself up, till he sees all things thro' narrow chinks of his cavern.

William Blake[25]

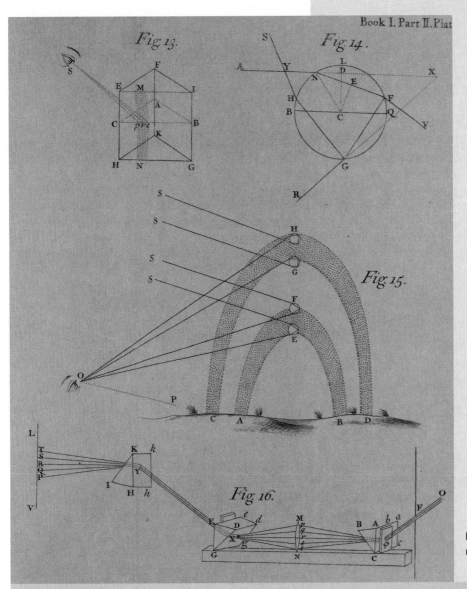

Fig. 13.

Fig. 14.

Fig. 15.

Fig. 16.

Pages from Newton's notebooks

For as found in a Bell or musical String, or other founding Body, is nothing but a trembling Motion, and in the Air nothing but that Motion propagated from the Object, and in the Sensorium 'tis a sense of that Motion under the form of sound; so Colours in the Object are nothing but a disposition to reflect this or that sort of rays more copiously than the rest; in the rays they are nothing but their dispositions to propagate this or that Motion into the Sensorium, and in the Sensorium they are Sensations of those Motions under the Forms of Colours.

Sir Isaac Newton, *Opticks*

mechanics of visual perception are as old as philosophy itself. Pythagoras posited a system in which the eye emitted rays that struck the perceived object, then bounced back to the eye. Much like the sense of touch, it supposed a direct contact with the object. Plato's famous cave analogy posits that what we perceive is not reality itself, but rather the mere semblance of objects, like shadows cast on a wall of a cave. It was not until the turn of the first millennium and experiments in the East some 1,500 years later that a true scientific exploration of optics would occur.

The great mathematician and scientist Alhazen (965–1040) wrote a groundbreaking treatise on optics in which he discussed the refraction of light rays through water and described how the eye functions. His work, translated into Latin as *Opticae Thesarus* in 1270, would influence Roger Bacon, Leonardo da Vinci, and many others. Alhazen also experimented with the camera obscura, some five hundred years before its widespread use in the West. He also heralded the use of the scientific method, which would spur the Renaissance and the Enlightenment.

The Enlightenment scientist Sir Isaac Newton, born in 1642, the same year that Galileo died, furthered our knowledge of vision in the seventeenth century. Described as a polymath colossus, he would push academic thinking away from the scholasticism of the Aristotelians, from learning based on the classic texts, toward the scientific reasoning of Bacon and Descartes. In his book *Opticks*, he explored the nature of light and our perceptions of color. Prior studies of light by Descartes had shown that it was governed by mathematical principles; by extrapolation, so was the universe. In contradicting thinkers that dated back to Aristotle, Newton demonstrated that colors do not arise from modifying light. Rather, through a series of experiments, he showed that white light contains all colors. His theory postulated that light was a particle, and for this reason his thinking on light fell out of favor when the scientific community adopted the wave theory of light in the nineteenth century. Only recently, with the discovery that light has properties of both a wave and a particle, has his thinking come to be respected once again. Depending on how the experiment is constructed, a scientist can come to either conclusion, as science too is subject to perspective and perception.

In the nineteenth century, scientists recognized that different areas of the brain control different cognitive processes. The biological mechanics of perception are essentially cognitive processes set in motion by an external stimulus. Speech, for instance, is controlled by the frontal lobe, while motor skills are controlled by the motor cortex. Visual information is carried from the eye to the brain via the optic nerve. There are different areas of the brain that process visual data, and the neurons, which process vision, account for nearly 50 percent of the brain. Currently, neurologists believe that the brain interprets visual data in terms of the "what and where" doctrine—that a perceived object is understood in terms of where it is (spatially) and what it is. The brain further breaks down the "what" portion into shape, color, and movement. It has also been shown that the brain has certain built-in sensitivities. Certain species of birds have a predisposition to see certain shapes in certain patterns of motion as predators, even with no direct experience of predators. Carl Jung and Joseph Campbell relate human predisposition to images in terms of a collective unconscious and "inherited images."

Ludwig Richter relates in his reminiscences how once, when he was in Tivoli as a young man, he and three friends set out to paint part of the landscape, all four firmly resolved not to deviate from nature by a hair's breadth; and although the subject was the same, and each quite credibly reproduced what his eyes had seen, the result was four totally different pictures, as different from each other as the personalities of the four painters. Whence the narrator drew the conclusion that there is no such thing as objective vision, and that form and colour are always apprehended differently according to temperament.

Heinrich Wölfflin, *Principles of Art History*

PLATE I.

Hearing

Sound waves cause a vibration of the eardrum in the middle ear, into the inner ear and the organ of Corti, which translates the vibration into nerve impulses. As with vision, hearing is not a passive process, but an active one in which aural stimuli are processed and understood by the brain in the temporal lobe. We understand musical sound in terms of pi.

Spatial Perception

Our sense of space is a perception in and of itself, the prime example of intermodal functions, which give us insight into all things that we create and encounter. Our survival and growth are dependent on this primary sense. Any animal knows that an object coming toward it grows in apparent size and must be paid attention to as threat or meal. Similarly, the sound that a car makes changes as it approaches us, giving us the ability to know where we are in relationship to it.

Circa 60,000 Notion of death—Neanderthals bury dead with flowers, indicating that perhaps they had a notion of an afterlife.

Circa 20,000 Early cave paintings at Lascaux and Altamira. Paintings seen as magical and used to remember a past event and influence the future.

Circa 20,000 The cycles of the moon and seasonal changes are probably used by early humans to note the passage of time.

Circa 8000 Change from nomadic to agricultural society gives rise to wider anxiety about nature. Rituals are used to overcome unpredictable factors as the seasons change.

Circa 6000 Elaborate burials suggest early ancestral worship in China and elsewhere. The cult of the ancestors becomes increasingly important in China and reinforces a broader notion of time within generational cycles.

4236 The beginning of the Egyptian calendar.

3760 The beginning of the Jewish calendar; also the traditional date of Creation.

3500 The gnomon is used in Mesopotamia and elsewhere. Essentially a pillar or stick in the ground, the gnomon is a large sundial that casts a shadow depending on the position of the sun to indicate the time of day.

3114 The Mayan calendar begins to use the "long count" to divide time into a series of cycles in which the world has been destroyed and re-created numerous times before the current age. The Dresden Codex, one of the few Mayan books to escape from being burned by Spanish clergy, not only contains accurate lunar and Venusian calculations but also describes the coming end of this age by a great flood.

3102 The beginning of the Kali Yuga within Hindu cosmology. Hindu cosomolgy divides time into four yugas, or cycles—Krta, Treta, Dvapara, and Kali. The Kali Yuga marks the final and lowest point of the ages. Like many cosmologies, Hindu cosmology begins with the age of perfection, the Krta yuga, and slowly declines to the present age, which is beset with numerous problems humans cannot overcome.

Circa 3000 Lunisolar calendar is used throughout much of Mesopotamia. In this system, the months are calculated based on the moon and the year by the sun. This system became widespread and is found in numerous calendar systems throughout the ancient world.

Circa 3000 The Mesopotamian calendar year is divided into two seasons: summer and winter.

Circa 3000 In ancient Egypt, the regular flooding and recession of the Nile River not only regulates agriculture and shapes daily life but also provides an environmental indicator of the passage of time and the season.

chronology: time

Circa 3000 In Egyptian civilization, the pharaoh symbolizes the triumph of an invincible divine order over chaos. The invincibility of the pharaoh is continued in death through the creation of elaborate tombs, the Pyramids, and intricate burial practices. According to the Egyptian Book of the Dead, bodies are embalmed, spells are cast, and elaborate rituals are performed to ensure the safe passage of the soul into the next world, and to guarantee that a soul is not trapped for eternity in purgatory.

Circa 3000 Egyptians divide day and night into twenty-four units, or hours.

Circa 3000 Egyptians use a Sothic cycle, based on the star Sirius, in addition to solar and lunar calculations, to help them calculate dates. Their complex system is highly accurate and calculates a 365-day year with little margin of error.

Circa 3000 In addition to the standard calendar, Egyptians measure years according to the reign of a particular king—counting each year during a reign and returning to "1" when a new king assumes the throne.

Circa 2700 Stonehenge is completed in England. Although its exact origins or function remains a mystery, it is believed that Stonehenge functioned as a lunar and solar calendar.

Circa 2500 In ancient Mesopotamia, time is divided into sixty units based on the Mesopotamian base-sixty counting system, which had not developed fractions and needed an easily divisible number.

Circa 2000 Early Chinese stone bell chimes are used to mark the hours in a day.

1500 As trade and cities develop, so does the need for greater accuracy in timekeeping; sundials evolve.

1400 Early water clocks, or clepsydras, are used in Egypt; dripping water is used to measure time.

6th century In India, notion of life as constant cycle of birth and rebirth is widespread. Although many Hindu philosophers grapple with this problem in India, the Buddha offers a new approach: the middle path, to escape the endless cycle of birth and rebirth (samsara).

6th century Zoroaster, Iranian prophet and founder of Zoroastrianism, predicts the coming of judgment day and the end of time. This belief is shared by the Egyptian civilization and was later incorporated into Christian, Muslim, and Jewish religious beliefs.

5th century Heracleitus (544–483), a Greek philospher, writes that nature is constantly in flux and change is the only permanent reality in the world.

300 Babylonian astronomer Berosus creates the hemispherical sundial (or hemicycle), which uses a stylus that casts an arc of varying lengths and degrees depending on the season and time. The hemicycle divides each arc into twelve sections, or twenty-four parts from night and day. Berosus's hemicycle continues in wide use in the Middle East up until the tenth century C.E.

Circa 100 Andronicus of Cyrrhus builds Tower of the Winds, or Horologium, in Athens. Andronicus's octagonal tower uses both a sundial and a clepsydra, or water clock, to keep time.

80 An early astrological machine, the Antikythera device, is built. This device calculates the phases of the moon and lunar months.

45 Julius Caesar introduces the Julian calendar with 365 1/4 days and a leap year every four years to correct for the extra day. The calendar had often been manipulated to prolong or shorten service of a ruler. By the time of Julius, the civil calendar was three months out of sync with the astronomical year.

C.E.

1st century The seven-day Jewish week is adopted throughout much of the Roman Empire.

95 The Gospel According to John and the Book of Revelations are written at this time. The concept of the Second Coming, or the return of Jesus Christ in glory to judge the living and dead, becomes widespread among Christian believers. The Book of Revelation also helps establish the belief in Christian millennialism, which evolved from the Jewish eschatological concept but sees Chrisitians triumphing over nonbelievers.

2nd century Astronomers measure day from noon to noon. Such distinct measurement did not apply to earlier civilizations, who often used the onset of dusk or dawn to indicate the passage of a day. For example, the day begins at dawn for Hindus, whereas Greeks measure a day from sunset to sunset.

200 The Mayans develop a highly sophisticated calendrical and astronomical system. The calendar accurately determines the solar year and contains a sacred year of 260 days. The Mayans are also able to accurately predict solar eclipses and correctly determine the positions of Venus and the moon.

3rd century In Imperial Rome, the day is divided into twelve hours, the lengths of which vary with the length of the day.

463 Victorius of Aquitaine is appointed by Pope Hilarius to reform the Christian calendar and improve the Julian calendar. Using the cycles of the moon and sun, Victorius establishes the Gregorian calendar. Often referred to as the New Style calendar, the Gregorian calendar begins on January 1, as opposed to December 25, for the Julian calendar, and provides an extraordinarily accurate measurement of the year. Although it took a long time for others to adopt this calendar, it has since become the standard on which our modern calendar is based.

525 Dionysius Exiguus, a Roman abbot, develops the Christian calendar. Exiguus' calendar not only includes a system of numbering consecutive years but also introduces the divisions B.C.E. and C.E.

chronology: time

7th century Astrolabes are in wide use in Europe in the Middle Ages. They are used both to observe and to calculate the position of the sun to determine the time of day.

622 Beginning of the Muslim era according to the Muslim calendar. The year Muhammad emigrates from Mecca to Medina, the date has enormous significance within Islam. Like most calendars at this time, the Muslim calendar is a lunisolar calendar that contains twelve months, each with twenty-nine or thirty days.

Late 7th century One of the Five Pillars of Islam is prayer (*salat*) five times a day—*salat al-fajr* (dawn), *az-zuhr* (midday), *al-'asr* (afternoon), *al-maghrib* (sunset), and *al-'ishà* (evening)—facing *ka'ba* of Mecca. The branch of astronomy termed *ilm al-miqat* determines the time of day for prayer. The times of prayer are determined by the *mwaqqit*, official timekeepers using a variety of methods, often astronomical.

8th century Canonical hours, used in monasteries, are widespread in churches throughout Europe. Divided into Matins, Lauds, Prime, Terce, Sext, None, Vespers, and Compline, the canonical hours regulate life in monasteries and dictate certain prayers and activities. Small bell chimes are often used to signal canonical hours.

725 Early clock built by Buddhist monk and mathematician, Yiking, in China.

10th century Differently scented incense is burned at different hours in Buddhist rituals in China.

10th century Indian ragas, or a musical framework on which improvisations are based, are tailored to specific times of the day. Incorporating instruments such as the sitar, tabla, santoor, and harmonium, ragas are designed to alter one's mood depending on the time of day.

1090 Advanced astronomical clock tower designed by Su Song, an engineer, astronomer, and expert at calculating calendars, at Kaifeng, China. Containing an observation booth, the clock is synchronized with movements of the stars. In operation for nearly thirty-five years, Su Song's clock is eventually moved and reconstructed when the Song Dynasty moves its capital from Kaifeng.

12th century Economic developments in Europe require more accurate time-keeping. Sundials become widespread in public places, and churches signal the passing hours.

1190 Maimonides, the foremost intellectual and philosopher of medieval Judaism, proposes that time consists of time-atoms (i.e, of many parts which on account of their short duration cannot be divided) in *Dalalat al-Ha'irin* (or "The Guide for the Perplexed").

13th century The Arab astronomer and scientist Abu al-Hassan introduces the idea of hours with equal length.

1283 One of the earliest mechanical clocks is built in Dunstable Priory, England.

14th century Mechanical clocks allow the accurate measurement of time in towns and cities. This period marks not only an effort to standardize time by dividing it into equal hours but also the shift from church to secular control of public clocks as commerce becomes increasingly important.

1315 Dante Alighieri (1265–1321) uses the clock as a symbol of divine harmony in "Paradiso," the third book in *The Divine Comedy*.

1330 Richard of Wallingford takes over St. Alban's Abbey and designs an elaborate astronomical clock that is able to predict lunar eclipses.

1335 One of the first public clocks to strike the hours is installed in Milan.

1370 Charles IV of France passes a decree that requires all public clocks to follow the clock of the Palais Royal. Charles IV's decree marks the increasing secular control over time and public clocks.

circa 1500 Peter Henlein, a German locksmith, creates the mainspring, which replaces the weights and pendulums used in clocks. This allows the invention of watches and the first portable clocks.

16th century Galileo uses a clepsydra in his experiments measuring falling bodies.

16th century Nocturnal, a nautical device used to tell time from the stars at night, comes into widespread usage. Nocturnals could be used only in the Northern Hemisphere because of the need to see the pole star. Much like a sundial and astrolabe, the nocturnal reads time off a scale that is aligned with the pole star.

17th century Sir Isaac Newton (1642–1727), an English scientist, philosopher, and key figure of the Enlightenment, introduces the notion of absolutist time. According to Newton, time is linear, without beginning or end and independent of the physical world. Newton's ideas have profound effect on subsequent scientists and philosphers until Einstein presents his special theory of relativity.

17th century Incense is burned to mark the time between the ringing of temple bells during the Tokugawa period (1600–1868) in Japan.

18th century The Industrial Revolution requires more clocks, exact timetables, and standardized time in order to coordinate trains, deliveries, and exact workdays.

1728 John Harrison, an English carpenter, constructs an accurate marine chronometer, a timekeeping device that allows sailors to calculate longitude at sea. It is known that the Earth rotates at a fixed rate, so that if one knows the time at a fixed point, say, the port of departure, and the time at the present location, one can calculate how far the Earth has rotated—one degree for each hour.

1761 Benjamin Banneker, a self-educated astronomer, mathematician, inventor, and important African-American intellectual, carves an elaborate wooden clock that keeps accurate time for years.

chronology: time

1780 The first self-winding pocket watch is invented in London.

1784 Benjamin Franklin suggests the practice of daylight saving in a satirical essay. The practice of turning the clocks ahead in the summer and back in the fall was later adopted in varying degrees in many countries. The United States, Great Britain, and Austria even adopt special summer daylight-saving practices during World War I and World War II, turning the clocks ahead as much as two hours to maximize the daylight and cut down on the need for artificial light.

1812 Dietrich Nikolaus Winkel (1776–1826) creates the modern metronome. Using a weighted pendulum, Winkel's metronome emits a ticking noise to keep tempo, or time, in music.

1840 Combining a pendulum and battery, the electric clock is invented.

1840 The German philosopher and theorist G. W. F. Hegel introduces his philosophy of history. Hegel believes that history is a dialectical process that evolves and moves forward through constant conflict of opposites, eventually leading to freedom and rationality. Hegel's notion of time and history enormously influence Karl Marx, who adopts Hegel's dialectical method.

1859 Commissioned by Sir Benjamin Hall and designed by Edmund Beckett and Baron Grimthorpe, Big Ben is installed in London, England.

1883 Standardized time zones are adopted by U.S. and Canadian railroads.

1884 Following an international conference, Greenwich Mean Time is established as the standard meridian. This leads to the establishment of various time zones (twenty-four total) around the Earth.

1904 Time signals are transmitted via radio waves to aid navigation.

1905 Albert Einstein introduces the special theory of relativity. Einstein's notion of the space–time continuum radically alters our notions of time and Newtonian physics.

1929 The quartz crystal is used in clocks. The accurate oscillations of the quartz crystal allow for much greater precision in timekeeping.

1946 U.S. physicist Willard F. Libby introduces the process of radiocarbon dating, or carbon-14 dating. Because carbon-14 decays at a constant rate, Libby's method allows scientists to date bones, fossils, and other archeological specimens with great accuracy.

1953 The first electronic wristwatch is created.

1955 Manipulating and drawing on the frequency of atoms, cesium in particular, the first atomic clock is created in Teddington, England.

1962 Artificial satellites are used to synchronize and transmit time signals.

CHAPTER FIVE

PAST, PRESENT, FUTURE

A creative interlocutor—a twenty-first-century artist—is the product and producer of an enlightened engagement within the realm of the circuit, fostered by an educational system that is transdisciplinary in nature and values the management of ideas as much as the teaching of them. We define the creative interlocutor as a person or group who facilitates the exchange of ideas between one need and another. This person is a navigator, helmsman, producer, director, and organizer of the infinite library of the dataset. More specifically, the creative interlocutor is an editor, collector, and curator who makes, weaves, welds, builds, and, finally, is a distributor of inspiration. Creative interlocutors are also programmers, inventors, and researchers who negotiate the revolutionary associations of the dataset with us and for us.

Creativity is a state of mind that never rests. It moves from place to place, from individual to individual, and from individual to community. It has always been more a process than a concern with the end product. It is constantly in motion, as we move from one site to the next, one application to another, one dataset to a grander pattern revealing previously unseen structures. The computer can be a tool that helps us to navigate, but new technology is meaningless without reassessing the metaphors for its use—unless these metaphors enable us to reinforce the patterns of working and living that weave us together as a culture. Where we are going and why we go there are issues of a quest for understanding. This quest can be undertaken only if one is guided by fundamental values that enforce and encourage the convergence of ideas, that amalgamate the elements of culture so we may create a dialog that furthers the story of culture.

The ever-expanding fields of knowledge require such competency that a high degree of specialization is necessary, one that precludes our ability to become more universally learned individuals. Yet such specialization need not limit the greater potential of crossing disciplines and interacting collectively with data and knowledge to find new relationships and meaning in our pursuits. We all hold the great creative charge of being learners and teachers, for today learning is not simply the process of finding the right answers, but of asking the right questions. History recounts the story of numerous people, places, and ideas that are models for negotiating the realm of the circuit—from Socrates' Academy to the modern Xerox PARC. We can't know everything, but we need to find the paths that allow us to associate between the great libraries and museums of the World Brain. Those who facilitate this—programmers, teachers, composers, and so on—are those to be celebrated in these times. There are many obvious models throughout history, such as Leonardo da Vinci, Francis Bacon, Thomas Jefferson, and others, and their genius needs to be understood, not only for what they gave us but also for how they were able to give it. Today, we can chronicle the record of our creative history in the digital archive to learn how to learn.

This chapter posits a new realm for individuals—what Ted Nelson calls "systems humanists"—to work together to create a universal repository of human endeavor: the World Brain. The following biographies and descriptions serve as examples and incitements. This is an eclectic list of people, places, ideas, and events that have stimulated the world of ideas and are exemplary paradigms for exploring our future. They are people, places, and ideas that, each in their own way, forever changed the world: Once you encounter any of them, it is impossible to go back to previous ways of seeing, thinking, or doing. Creative interlocutors are the champions of the circuit, utilizing multimedia interactivity that transforms data into knowledge which will then be redistributed and reworked by others.

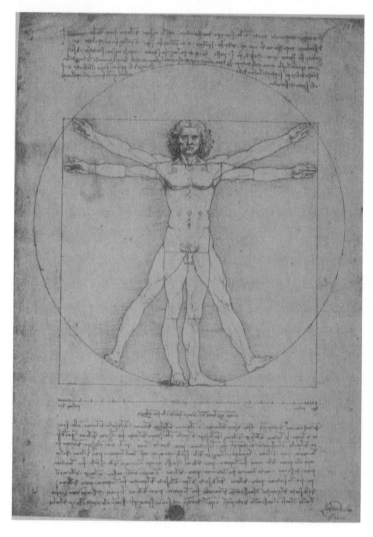

Leonardo da Vinci's work in the fields of art, science, and engineering exemplify the creative interlocutor. His illustration of the Roman Architect Vitruvius' description of human proportion is symbolic for us of the balance between the fields of human endeavor.

Boogie Down Productions is made up of teachers.
The lecture is conducted from the mic into the speaker.

Boogie Down Productions

How do you amalgamate in order to understand?

Richard Feynman

Akbar (1542–1605) The great Mughal emperor, who ruled India from 1556 to his death. An expert statesman, Akbar was able to unite the diverse population of India through his nonpartisan policies. Although illiterate, Akbar actively engaged in religious debate within his courts and hosted large religious conferences at which key religious scholars of Buddhism, Islam, Hinduism, Parsis (Zoroastrianism), and Christianity voiced their opinions openly. Akbar also commissioned the translation of numerous texts into Persian and often gave illustrated copies to members of his court. Fascinated by European illustrations that demonstrated linear perspective, Akbar commissioned his court painters to mimic this perspective in Mughal painting. Akbar used his position of power to generate a climate of cross-cultural debate and exchange.

Alchemy Commonly understood as the idea of transmuting lead into gold, alchemy stands somewhere between occultism, philosophy, and science as a discipline. Although its origins are unknown, alchemy has gone through continual bouts of popularity and revitalized interest through the centuries and has influenced various thinkers from Goethe to Jung. Alchemy can be seen as a spiritual quest: The transmutation of lead (the base metal) into gold is a metaphor for man's quest for spiritual enlightenment. Through the reinterpretation of existing knowledge and the discovery of greater truth, the alchemists' lifelong quest was to transform themselves into higher beings. In this sense, alchemy serves as a blueprint for humanity's continuous pursuit to attain an elevated understanding through science, technology, religion, and art.

Avicenna (Ali al-Husain ibn Abdullah ibn Sìnâ)

(980–1037) Born in Bukhara, Avicenna was one of the great intellectuals of his era and the most influential and famous of Islam's philosopher-scientists; a politician, mathematician, astronomer, and physician who wrote over 450 works. He contributed greatly to the field of Aristotelian philosophy and wrote the medical canon of the early Middle Ages (*The Quanun*). Encyclopedic in nature, it demonstrated that diseases could be diagnosed and treated accordingly. It listed over 750 drugs that had been tested on both animals and humans. *The Quanun* also described psychological illnesses. As a creative link between the East and the West, this book was released in fifteen editions in Latin and was the principal text for Western schools of medicine. In his writing, Avicenna linked the speculative philosophies of ethics with the practical philosophies of science. His genius lay in his collection of knowledge, assembled from his life of travel. It is said that *The Quanun* was fundamental to the beginnings of the Western Renaissance and to scientific method.

Muhammad Ali (b. 1942) Called "The Greatest," Ali is considered the world's most famous athlete. Three-time world heavyweight champion and an Olympic gold medal winner, Ali was an uncompromising advocate of civil rights. Born Cassius Clay, he converted to Islam in 1964 and given the name Muhammad Ali. His rise to fame was as much about his personal style as the popularity of the sport he loved: He was clever, witty, and eloquent both inside and outside the ring. Ali's boxing techniques were graceful and unorthodox, entertaining his fans while mocking his opponents through his impromptu rhymed witticisms ("float like a butterfly, sting like a bee").

Outraged at the racism in America, Ali threw his gold medal into a river. He later would refuse to be drafted, stating, "I ain't got no quarrel with the Viet Cong." Publicly ostracized for his antiwar stance, his boxing license revoked, Ali was sentenced to five years in prison for draft dodging. Eventually freed on appeal, he regained his heavyweight title in a fight against George Foreman.

Ali continued to be a political activist, working as a diplomat to help free American hostages in Lebanon, and founding the charity WORLD (World Organization for Right, Liberty and Dignity). In the face of incredible public persecution, Muhammad Ali used his celebrity to forward causes that were often contrary to the mores of the time. He had an amazing love of boxing and, more importantly, an unfailing sense of ethics and responsibility to his fellow citizens.

Laurie Anderson (b. 1947) Emerging in the early 1970s, Anderson was a key figure in New York City's downtown avant-garde art scene. After graduating from Barnard College, she went on to study sculpture at Columbia University in the late 1960s. Along with Nam June Paik and John Cage, Anderson rose to prominence through her early performance pieces that incorporated music, technology, and theater. She moved from smaller performances to large-scale productions at the Brooklyn Academy of Music, and producing *The Life and Times of Josef Stalin* in 1973. This twelve-hour multimedia epic incorporated music, theater, and song. In addition she staged such large-scale multimedia productions such as *Home of the Brave* and *Song and Stories from Moby Dick* (1999). Bridging the gap between modern and classical music, theater and opera, Anderson's multimedia work continues to challenge audiences and to address the complexities of our technological age.

Louis Armstrong (1901–1971) Satchmo Armstrong stands among the great creative geniuses of the twentieth century. Helped invent jazz as we know it and exerted a profound influence on the development of jazz and pop music in the twentieth century.

Born and raised in the slums of New Orleans, Armstrong played in several local jazz bands, including that of his idol, King Oliver, before forming his own groups. A trumpet virtuoso, Armstrong's beautiful tone, harmonic range, and innovative solos raised jazz to a new level and taught the world how to swing. His influential recordings with the Hot Five and Hot Seven in the 1920s freed jazz from a strictly group format. Armstrong was also an accomplished and influential vocalist—using his voice like an instrument, he sang popular and jazz songs to much acclaim and helped popularize scat singing. In 1929, his appearance in the Broadway musical *Ain't Misbehavin'* helped pave the way for the popular acceptance of jazz.

Louis Armstrong

Although criticized for his comedic roles and labeled an "Uncle Tom" by later generations of African Americans, Armstrong was outspoken critic of the United States' policies on race. While the jazz community remained largely silent, Armstrong vocally attacked Eisenhower for his failure to support black children during the early stages of integration in Little Rock, Arkansas. Through such influential recordings as "West End Blues," "Heebie Jeebies," "Potato Head Blues," and "Hello Dolly," Louis Armstrong changed the way we hear music.

ARPA/DARPA (Advanced Research Projects Agency/Defense Advanced Research Projects Agency) Founded in 1958 in response to the Soviet Union's launch of Sputnik, ARPA's mission has been to research and develop technology projects for the United States. Under the guidance of J. C. R. Licklinder, the head of DARPA's computer research team, DARPA helped lay the foundation for the Internet. In the Internetting Project, Linklinder and his colleagues created a system of protocols that became the TCP/IP Protocol Suite. The pioneering work of ARPA/DARPA virtually created the Internet and the network-based communication systems that lace our planet.

Afrika Bambaataa A musical innovator, Bambaataa is widely credited as a pioneer of hip-hop. In the 1970s, he was a Bronx disc jockey known for his eclectic musical tastes. While other DJs were spinning disco or R & B, he scoured record shops for everything from calypso to funk to whatever struck his interest, anticipating the practice of sampling. He collaborated on producing many of hip-hop's most important acts, including pioneers such as the Rock Steady Crew. In 1974, he founded the controversial Zulu Nation, which included people from what is now recognized as hip-hop culture: rappers, break dancers, and graffiti artists. The Zulu Nation emerged to fill the void left as the gangs of the Bronx began to disband, providing a creative outlet for the youth of the Bronx.

Benjamin Banneker (1731–1806) Born to freed slaves in Baltimore, Maryland, Banneker received little education beyond the eighth grade but nonetheless became an accomplished farmer, engineer, city planner, mathematician, astronomer, and social reformer. At the age of twenty-one, he was given a watch, which he took apart and used as the model for a wooden clock, which he carved using only hand tools. His clock, the first built in the United States, chimed on the hour for nearly forty years, and Banneker continued to design clocks throughout his life. His interest in timekeeping, gears, and mathematics led to research in astronomy and, in 1792, he began the publication of a farmer's almanac, which he published for ten years. Banneker was also appointed to the team that was to build the nation's capital in Washington, D.C. When the chief architect left in the middle of the project, Banneker redrew the plans from memory. A crusader for social change, Banneker challenged the widely held belief of that time that blacks were intellectually inferior to whites.

Benjamin Banneker's Almanac, 1795

Bauhaus (Staatliches Bauhaus) Established in 1919 by Walter Gropius in Germany, the Bauhaus was an enormously influential school of design, applied arts, and architecture that played a pivotal role in shaping twentieth-century art and culture. Combining technical craftsmanship with the fine arts, Gropius hoped to eradicate the boundaries between the applied and fine arts.

Rejecting the Arts and Crafts movement's emphasis on designer luxury items, the Bauhaus drew on the potentials of mass production and machine technology to create well-designed items for mass production. For Gropius and the faculty at the Bauhaus, the goal of the modern designer was to create objects that were at once functional and aesthetically pleasing. The Bauhaus' unique merger of arts and design revolutionized the role of artists in the twentieth century, offering new possibilities for creative and meaningful engagement with the world. The students and faculty of the Bauhaus saw themselves as artists and as architects for modern society. Bauhaus members are among the most influential artists of the twentieth century, and included László Moholy-Nagy, Paul Klee, Wassily Kandinsky, Oskar Schlemmer, Lyonel Feininger, Ludwig Mies van der Rohe, and Josef Albers.

Although Hitler closed the Bauhaus in 1933, its students and faculty carried the Bauhaus influences throughout Europe and the United States. Most prominently, László Moholy-Nagy founded the New Bauhaus (a.k.a. Institute of Design) in Chicago in 1937, where he educated a new generation of American artists.

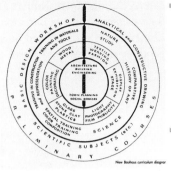

New Bauhaus
curriculum diagram, 1937–1938

Bayeux Tapestry
Approximately 20 inches high and 231 feet long, the ornately embroidered Bayeux tapestry illustrates the Norman invasion of England and the events surrounding the Battle of Hastings (October 14, 1066). Probably Anglo-Saxon in origin, it was surely the work of many hands. It is another epic tale, but one told in stitches, an essentially digital medium, a collaboratively formed dataset of the Middle Ages. It told a story to an illiterate public, who navigated the document by panning its length.

The Bayeux Tapestry,
c. 1066–1082

Tim Berners-Lee
(b. 1955) In the 1980s, while working at the European research lab CERN, he wanted to create a system to make documents widely available to scientists in the facility who were working on a variety of computer platforms. He proposed a client/server model that would evolve into the World Wide Web. This system had at its base a computer that would request documents (the client), a computer that would send documents (the server), and a system that would link documents through hypertext. He had many chances to commercialize and privatize his creation, but ultimately choose not to do so, realizing that for the Web to connect the world it could not be owned by a select few. Berners-Lee has a vision of the Web as a tool that would enable us to "make sense of what we are doing, where we individually fit in, and how we can better work together."

Currently the director of the World Wide Web Consortium, he works at the Massachusetts Institute of Technology.

Black Mountain College
Founded in 1933 by John Andrew Rice and Theodore Dreier, Black Mountain College played a pivotal role in shaping American culture and arts in the late twentieth century. A largely experimental college, Black Mountain drew on John Rice's educational theories that sought to combine the fine arts with the liberal arts.

Emphasizing cross-disciplinary arts education, communal living, and informal class structure, learning and living were intimately connected. Key to the college's success was its legendary faculty, which included John Cage, Walter Gropius, Josef and Hanna Albers, Charles Olson, R. Buckminster Fuller, Jacob Lawrence,

Merce Cunningham, Robert Motherwell, and Willem de Kooning. In addition to their classes, students participated in some of the earliest performance art in the United States and worked on revolutionary projects such as Buckminster Fuller's geodesic dome. Students also edited *The Black Mountain Review* (1954–1957).

Black Mountain's paradigm initiated similar cross-disciplinary work across the United States, and its faculty and students gradually left North Carolina for urban centers such as New York and San Francisco. Black Mountain College, which closed in 1956, has enormously influenced arts education and new generation of artists and creative thinkers.

Bletchley Park The Allies' success in World War II was, in part, a result of their ability to intercept and decode Axis communication. Due to the pioneering efforts of British cryptographers, the Allies were able to track German submarines, greatly reducing the impact of the so-called "Wolfpack." The center of the code-breaking effort against the Germans was Bletchley Park just outside of London. Housed in a converted mansion, Station X was home to a concentration of Britain's brightest mathematicians. Initially the codes were broken by teams of individuals working in huts. Mathematician Alan Turing and others at the park realized that their labor could be automated. The work of the code breakers was divided in much the same way that nineteenth-century factories separated production into smaller tasks. Turing created a machine to automate these tasks. Called the Bombe, it was an electromechanical contraption based on the work of Polish code breakers. Other mathematicians at Bletchley Park devised the Colossus, an electronic programmable calculator based on Turing's prewar papers. It was not a computer, but a device for comparing messages against known codes at a very high rate of speed. Turing's notion of an infinite-state machine would eventually lead to the development of the modern digital computer.

Vannevar Bush
(1890–1974) A distinguished scientist and engineer, Bush held several positions, including president of the Carnegie Institute, chair of the National Advisory Committee for Aeronautics, and director of the Office of Scientific Research and Development. It was in this last role, a presidential appointment during World War II, that Bush would coordinate some six thousand men in the effort to apply science to warfare, and he came to develop ideas that he published in 1945, in his influential article "As We May Think." This article advanced the idea that as the country moves away from war, science must then begin to concern itself with making the world's knowledge available to all. Based mostly on current trends in technology and science, Bush foresaw the needs and potentials of many future technologies. Most importantly, he introduced the idea of the memex, "a device in which an individual stores all of his books, records, and communications . . . an enlarged, intimate supplement to his memory." His ideas would later influence thinkers such as Douglas Engelbart and Ted Nelson. The memex stands as one of the earliest practical visions of the Internet.

Vannevar Bush

George Washington Carver
(1861–1943) Born the son of a slave in Missouri, Carver rose to prominence to become a scientist and inventor. Known primarily for his experiments with peanuts, sweet potatoes, and soybeans, Carver's inventions and products helped revolutionize the agricultural economy of the rural south. As the head of the agriculture department at the Tuskegee Normal and Industrial Institute, Carver dedicated himself to helping and restoring southern agriculture.

The South was a single-crop economy and faced both ecologic and economic failure after the U.S. Civil War. After a boll weevil infestation further depleted the cotton crop in 1914, Carver urged farmers to plant peanuts and soybeans in place of cotton. He worked to educate farmers on the dangers of soil depletion and the necessity of crop rotation. Although there was little demand for these crops at the time, Carver's nearly three-hundred products derived from peanuts and soybeans—everything from cosmetics to soaps and medicinal oils—helped to restore the South's depleted financial and natural resources.

Geroge Washington Carver

The importance of crop diversification and rotation helped to revive a crippled South, and Carver's initiative greatly advanced our knowledge of agriculture and agronomy. Over the next fifty years, peanuts and soybeans became two of the six major crops in the United States due largely to Carver's insights and experiments. Carver donated his life savings to help establish the Carver Research Foundation at Tuskegee for agricultural research, ensuring that his work would continue well beyond his death.

Dogme 95
Founded in 1995 by Lars Von Trier, Thomas Vinterberg, Søren Kragh-Jacobsen, and Kristian Levring, Dogme 95 is a group of filmmakers who have an "expressed goal of countering 'certain tendencies' in the cinema today." In short, they feel cinema has become overly preoccupied with spectacle and sensation, at the expense of truth and the human condition. With digital technology putting the potentials of film into everyone's hands, Dogme members believe that the avant-garde becomes all the more important. Therefore, they drew up a manifesto, comical at times, called "The Vows of Chastity," which lists

the rules that Dogme 95 filmmakers must follow, among them: Shooting must be done on location with no props or sets brought in; the camera must be handheld; the film must be in color; the scene must take place in the present; and genre films are prohibited. The filmmakers must "refrain from personal taste" and cannot think of themselves as artists.

Although seemingly extreme in its pronouncements, Dogme 95 has made a variety of innovative and compelling films, most notably *The Celebration, The Idiots,* and *Mifune*. In reaction to the decadence of current cinema, Dogme 95 members brought innovative perspectives to filmmaking, revitalizing creative possibilities and challenging others to question the potential and purpose of the art form.

John Dos Passos (1896–1970) One of the foremost American writers of the mid-twentieth century, Dos Passos was at that time, as popular as his contemporaries William Faulkner and Ernest Hemmingway at that time. Harvard educated, he served in World War I but was eventually sent back to the States because of his strong antimilitary views. Dos Passos was an extreme leftist during the first half of his life; his novels intermingled his personal politics amid tales of modern society. Although he later moved toward the conservative right, Dos Passos believed that his worldview remained consistent: He hated authority and felt that "organization was death."

Stylistically, Dos Passos was unique among American writers (and very influential to the French, particularly Sartre). Considered "montage novels," his epic narratives were laced with newspaper headlines, excerpts of articles, popular songs, and disjointed, impressionistic sections that he modeled after photography and the newsreel. His first novel, *Three Soldiers*, is still considered a vital account of World War I: graphic, compelling, and condemning. Author of over thirty books, his 1936 trilogy *U.S.A.* is his most famous work. Regardless of political agendas, Dos Passos attempted to reconfigure the possibilities of the novel in light of new technologies and an ever-transforming culture, and seeking to portray human experience and society amid the political, ideological, and scientific changes of the twentieth century.

Experiments in Art and Technology (EAT) Founded in the late 1960s by Billy Klüver, Fred Waldhauser, Robert Rauschenberg, and Robert Whitman, EAT was a nonprofit organization that attempted to foster cross-disciplinary collaborations between artists and engineers. In addition to gaining access to new materials and technology, artists worked closely with engineers and computer programmers. EAT began out of a nine-evening series of technologically enhanced theater performances and went on to have a renowned exhibit at New York's Museum of Modern Art in 1967. The show was a model to future shows that have blended technology and art. EAT has had more than forty collaborative projects worldwide and has worked with artists such as Jasper Johns and John Cage. Largely influenced by the writings of R. Buckminster Fuller and Marshall McLuhan, EAT worked to engage and explore the relationship between art and technology.

Farm Security Administration (1935–1942) Roy Stryker, drawing on the interdisciplinary work of his mentor Rexford Tugwell, an economic geographer and early New Dealer, was hired to head the newly-formed Division for Photographic Documentation under the Farm Security Administration. Stryker knew of the power of the photograph from the early works of social

documentarians Jacob Riis and Lewis Hine. He organized a remarkable group of photographers, including Ben Shahn, Dorothea Lange, Walker Evans, and Marion Post Wolcott, to create a visual record of life in rural America and to aid in the recognition of the plight of the rural poor and migrant agricultural workers. During its eight year existence, 77,000 images were created, comprising an archive that allowed Americans to see themselves in new and realistic ways. The endeavor was made possible by the network of roads linking the country, the portability of the 35-mm camera, and the dialog between Styker and the photographers in the field. By keeping in constant touch with the photographers by telephone and letter, they were able to understand and document issues such as the growth of uban blight and poor land management. That this record is intact and has been made available on the Internet would have made Stryker supremely happy.

Grandmaster Flash (b. 1952)
As a teenager in the Bronx in the 1970s, Flash dreamed of transforming the music that was played at the outdoor parties in his neighborhood. Many disc jockeys at that time were content simply to play hit records, but an intrepid few, among them Flash, Kool Herc, and Afrika Bambaataa, sought to change the way people heard music, often by physically manipulating the way the vinyl records spun on the turntable. Flash created a machine that allowed him to extend the bridge, a climatic interlude in musical composition. The bridge lasted only ten seconds, and there were few tools available in those predigital days to enable the bridge to be extended. Musicians such as Brian Eno had constructed elaborate devices that could play fifty-foot loops of tapes, which he strung around the studio like a conveyor belt, but Flash turned his attention to improving the turntables themselves. His quest brought him to junkyards, and he obsessively tinkered with radios and electronics. Eventually he enrolled in a vocational high school to learn about electronic circuits. Combining this technical knowledge with his musical obsession, Flash built a custom mixer. The mixer controlled the two turntables, allowing him to play music from one, while cuing up music on the other. He developed elaborate techniques, from the quick-mix theory to the clock theory, which enabled him precise control of the sound. Initial response to his musical innovation was not positive. It was not until he put a microphone next to the turntables and invited people to "verbalize" along with his mixing that it became popular. Flash developed the DJ/rapper model of hip-hop music still in practice today.

R. Buckminster Fuller (1895–1983)
A revolutionary thinker, a twentieth-century incarnation of the Renaissance man, Fuller was an inventor, engineer, mathematician, architect, cosmologist, choreographer, and poet. A former Navy officer, Fuller was concerned with maximizing the dwindling resources of what he called "Spaceship Earth," modeling his view of efficiency on the workings of a naval vessel. He coined the phrase "dymaxian living" and created the dymaxian house and the dymaxian car that were efficient, inexpensive, interactive, flexible, and people-oriented in their use. In his 1969 book, *Operating Manual for the Spaceship Earth*, Fuller declared, "We are all hurtling through the cosmos, united by our limited resources and common social problems. Needing to be mindful that we can no longer afford to be isolated and ignorant of our fundamental interdependence." He is perhaps best remembered for his invention of the geodesic dome, a tetrahedron-shaped dome that can support its own weight, which is now a common sight across the country. In 1985, scientists discovered highly stable clusters of carbon atoms arranged in the same shape as the geodesic dome and named them "fullerenes."

Bucky Fuller's geodesic dome

Gertrude Stein Repertory Theatre (GSRT) Based in New York, the GSRT was established in 1990 to bridge the gap between performance and current digital technology. Promoting cross-disciplinary intermedia productions and workshops, the GSRT seeks to educate people on the potentials of new technology in performance and theater.

Looking to innovative early twentieth-century artists for inspiration, GSRT members hope to rejuvenate American theater by creating new styles and forms. The company has employed the Internet and video-conferencing as means of teaching and also conducts research into computer-based multimedia and virtual reality. Global in scope, the GSRT is motivated to inform and shape theater with new technology and to use that technology as a means to foster new collaborative efforts.

Grameen Bank Founded in 1983 by Professor Muhammed Yunus of Bangladesh's Chittagong University, the Grameen Bank was created as an attempt to address the widespread poverty, famine, and debt that plagued Bangladesh. The bank pioneered the idea of microloans and offered banking facilities to the poor without the need for collateral. Fundamental to Yunus' vision was the belief that in order to eliminate the vicious cycle of poverty people must be given the opportunity to better themselves through fair credit and economic opportunities.

Dyeing thread, funded by the Grameen Bank

Primarily run by women, Grameen Bank and its lenders are composed of small groups who manage and control the bank's assets and loans. These small loans have proved enormously successful in giving women a head start in various entrepreneurial ventures. The success rate of loan repayment is an impressive 90 percent on average, and household incomes and savings from Grameen members are also greatly improved—averaging 50 percent higher than nonmembers. By giving the poor both the economic means for self-employment and control of a system they can manage, the Grameen Bank system has revolutionized banking and provided important economic tools for alleviating poverty. After its astounding success in Bangladesh, the Grameen Bank model has been replicated in other parts of Asia and in Latin America.

Guerrilla Girls The Guerrilla Girls were formed in the wake of protests that arose over the 1985 Museum of Modern Art show, "An International Survey of Painting and Sculpture." Containing no people of color and few women, the exhibit drew widespread protest. Frustrated by the prevalent sexism and racism of the art world, a coalition of female artists formed the Guerrilla Girls. Joining a long (and mostly male) tradition of masked avengers, the Guerrilla Girls' anonymity is maintained through the use of gorilla masks and subversive posters. Through the use of humor, incisive political commentary, posters, and demonstrations, the Guerrilla Girls have dedicated themselves to questioning and challenging the male-dominated art world.

Guerrilla Girls poster: Do Women Have to Be Naked to Get into the Met Museum?

Hacker Culture A community of programmers, known in the early days as hackers, arose first through the culture of the early computer labs in the 1950s and 1960s, and later through the Internet. The term as applied to computer programmers originated in the MIT Artificial Intelligence Lab to describe someone who was interested in programming or in exploring the ways in which a particular system worked. This meaning of the term was later applied to

teenagers who enjoyed breaking into, among other things, the networks of the New York City telephone system in the 1970s and 1980s, people also called "crackers." The two terms are often confused today, much to the chagrin of those who consider themselves hackers in the traditional sense. Hackers have maintained a fundamental political awareness of computer technologies and built communities that are based on free access to resources and the pursuit of progress. Perhaps more so than any other group, hackers have had a continuing relationship with computers and see them not merely as tools but as agents of social and cultural potential that create communities and new possibilities for human contact and interaction. This ethic led to the free software movement (see Richard Stallman, Linus Torvalds, and GNU/Linux in this chapter), founded on the notion that the community of computer users is best served when software is freely shared.

Harlem Renaissance
Following the U.S. Civil War, hundreds of thousands of African-Americans moved to northern cities in what is known as the Great Migration. Settling in cities such as Chicago and New York, a substantial middle class took advantage of the increasing educational opportunities available to African-Americans. New York City's Harlem neighborhood quickly became a locus for political, intellectual, and artistic output. Intellectuals and activists such as Marcus Garvey and W. E. B. DuBois created a new environment of political activism and racial equality during the turn of the century. Both DuBois's National Association for the Advancement of Colored People (NAACP) in 1909 and Garvey's back to Africa movement gained widespread support and bolstered a sense of racial pride among African-Americans. Magazines such as *The Crisis*, the NAACP's monthly magazine, and *Opportunity*, published by the National Urban League, employed writers such as Langston Hughes, giving venues to the political and literary thinkers of the time. Jazz music also flourished in the night-clubs and bars of Harlem. Duke Ellington, Louis Armstrong, Jelly Roll Morton, and Bessie Smith were all regulars playing before the racially mixed audiences of Harlem.

By the mid-1930s growing economic hardships brought on by the Depression, as well as increasing racial tensions and the departure from Harlem of many of its key writers and artists, caused a decline in this community. However, the Harlem Renaissance was an important cultural hub, which offered inspiration and ideas for generations to come. The literary and artistic output during this period not only changed the character of African American arts, but also greatly influenced a whole generation of artists. Books such as James Weldon Johnson's *The Autobiography of an Ex-Colored Man* (1912), Claude McKay's *Harlem Shadows* (1922), Langston Hughes's *The Negro Speaks Rivers* (1921), and Zora Neale Hurston's *Their Eyes Are Watching God* (1937) all helped define the literary achievements of the time.

Hiawatha and Iroquois Confederacy
The Iroquois Confederacy, probably formed sometime in the twelfth century, ranks as one of the oldest continuing democracies on earth and is a forerunner of the system of democracy fashioned by the founders of the United States. A federation of Native American tribes called the Six Nations by the early colonists included the Mohawks, the Oneida, the Onondaga, the Cayuga, the Seneca, and later the Tuscaroras. It serves today as a model of a covenant formed to maintin peace with a fifty-seat council chosen by clan mothers. Its ideas were passed on through

the centuries as an epic oral history still recited today at the confederacy campfires at Onondaga in New York State. Legend has it that all the tribes threw their weapons into a pit and planted a Tree of Peace.

The longhouse, a communal dwelling, became a metaphor for an invisible or virtual longhouse some three hundred miles in length that covered the territory of the confederacy. Each tribe was responsible for the maintenance of different aspects of the confederacy, with some gardening the so-called eastern doors and others the western, and still others maintaining the "central fire" or the administrative tasks. The whole became greater than its parts, a functioning synergy that was invincible until the onslaught of the Europeans.

Danny Hillis (b. 1956)

Scientist, toy designer, inventor, pioneer in the field of parallel computing, and the first Disney Fellow. Hillis, described by *Economist* magazine as a metatechnologist, is concerned with how machines might change the way people think and learn. Drawing analogies from one field and applying them to another is a means of solving problems. He uses the computers he designed to engage astrophysics, computer graphics, neurobiology, and financial analysis, among others. One computer, the Connection Machine, has sixteen thousand processors and is modeled after the human brain, with its lattice of neurons. His new company, Applied Minds, is an "idea factory" developing ideas about educational computing in an attempt to relieve us from limitations of the specialization of fields. He says, "We are educating people today in the same way as we were when there was one percent as much knowledge." We can't possibly process the vast amounts of knowledge of the twenty-first century without the computer's ability to store, process, and filter it.

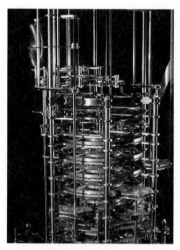

The Long Now Foundation's ten-thousand-year clock

Hua-yen Buddhism

("The Jeweled Net of Indra") A school of Buddhism within China, formalized and codified by the Buddhist scholar Fa-tsang (643–712), Hua-yen takes its name from the Flower Ornament Sutra. Although relatively short-lived, Hua-yen's teachings traveled to Japan, laying the basis for the Kegon school of Buddhism.

At the heart of Hua-yen's teachings lay the Buddhist principle of emptiness and conditional phenomena. Hua-yen taught that all substance and things lack a fundamental existence and exist in a web of a conditional relationship of all phenomena. One of the central metaphors that appears in Hua-yen texts is that of Indra's net. Stretching across our universe is a wondrous and infinite net with glistening jewels placed at each intersection of the web. The innumerable jewels all reflect on one another like an infinite hall of mirrors. By examining each of these jewels, we begin to see the interrelated nature of each part. As Francis Cook states in *Hua-yen Buddhism: The Jeweled Net of Indra,* "This relationship is said to be one of simultaneous mutual identity and mutual intercausality." Looking beyond the static nature of self and other, we can broaden our understanding of the world. Trapped in Indra's web, our existence is inescapably connected and dependent on one another.

IDEO

A design firm based in Palo Alto, IDEO has over three hundred employees and has produced more than three thousand projects since 1978, from grocery carts to toothpaste tubes the Palm Pilot. Product design begins with a brainstorming session, in which staff members assemble to interact and free associate in an attempt to develop unconventional solutions to design problems.

Staff is recruited from fields as diverse as psychology, engineering, and economics, with the belief that innovation in the outside world is the result of interaction between complicated desires and needs. At the heart of this approach is a methodology inspired by Maria Montessori, who believed that problems could be solved through playing with the elements that compose them. By fostering creative and collaborative engagement with technology, IDEO has become one of the most successful and forward-thinking design companies of the twenty-first century.

The Independent Media Center (www.indymedia.org)

Established in 1999, by a variety of organizations and activists, as a way to provide grassroots coverage of the WTO (World Trade Organization) protests in Seattle, Indymedia is an online resource for news and current events. Anyone can upload a story and anyone can post comments on that story. IMCs have been set up on every continent and in most major cities across the globe. They have democratized news and made people more aware of the subjective nature of media. They encourage people to seek understanding of news issues, rather than simply being passive receptors. Indymedia is a key example of newer generations using technology and the ideals of a global community to transform the world through innovative methods of political activism.

Athanasius Kircher (1602–1680) A man of prodigious talents, Kircher

was one of the preeminent intellectuals and inventors of his era. A Jesuit priest, Kircher studied astronomy, musicology, magnetism, archaeology, and linguistics, cutting across disciplines. In addition to collecting the artifacts that filled the Museo Kircheriano, one of the first *wunderkammern* (cabinet of curiosities) in Rome, Kircher invented the first slide projector, talking statues, and catoptric cameras (a series of mirrors and lenses that produce a convincing apparition). Kircher's unusual inventions and writings crossed disciplinary boundaries and probed the limitations of our knowledge in inventive and whimsical ways.

Knowbotic Research (KR+cF) Formed in 1991, Knowbotic Research

is a loosely structured group of media artists, academics, and scientists who attempt to bridge the gap between art and science to foster a new dialog of creative interaction. Its work draws the public into a discussion on the very nature of networked communications such as the Internet and the new reality that technology proposes. Focusing on issues of legality and artistic freedom, Knowbotic Research creates interactive online environments that highlight issues of control and power. It is at the forefront of experimental information interface and network-based communication arts.

Timothy Leary (1920–1996) A psychologist and author, Leary played a

key role in the counterculture movement of the 1960s in the United States. He was a vocal supporter of the use of LSD (lysergic acid diethylamide) and other psychoactive drugs. After leaving an academic position at Harvard University, Leary traveled and lectured to countless young people in America–urging them to "turn on, tune in, drop out." In the 1980s, Leary became an early and vocal advocate for the potentials of virtual reality and the Internet, giving lectures throughout the country. Seeing the computer as the new mind-altering medium of the future, he designed computer software and web sites, and attempted to put his whole house and archives online.

Ts'ai Lun (50–121 C.E.) The chief eunuch and court officer under Emperor Ho-ti (88–105/106) of the Eastern Han Dynasty, Ts'ai Lun is credited with the invention of paper. Before Ts'ai Lun created paper, books and manuscripts were often written on bamboo tablets and silk in China. Using sesame fibers, tree bark, and hemp fibers, Ts'ai Lun created primitive paper far superior and much more readily abundant than the traditional silk or bamboo. Papermaking remained a secret in China until the mid-eighth century when the information traveled to the Middle East, eventually reaching Europe.

Pattie Maes (b. 1962) An MIT scientist who has described herself as a mother, a wife, a career woman, an academic, an entrepreneur, an inventor, an artist, an intellectual, and a traveler. In other words, a creative interlocutor. She founded Agents, Inc. in the mid-1990s, a software company that pioneered the use of small semi-intelligent programs referred to as agents. They perform the tasks that humans typically do themselves such as buying airline tickets. These programs are able to learn by watching the behavior of their users, while searching for patterns and attempting to replicate them. Maes also pioneered the field of collaborative filtering in which software tracks a user's behavior (in buying books, for example) and attempts to anticipate future behavior by comparing it with that of others. Like many other computer pioneers (such as John von Neumann and Paul Baran), she was fascinated by biological systems. She closely watched the ways in which the cuttlefish was able to react quickly to changing environmental conditions and applied what she learned to problem solving with intelligent agents.

Maria Sibylla Merian (1647–1717) Author, natural scientist, and artist, Merian not only wrote popular and influential scientific texts on insects but also was a skilled illustrator and engraver providing elaborate paintings and drawings for her own texts. At a time when scientific illustrations often lacked accuracy, Merian created detailed and beautiful engravings that are also scientifically accurate. Merian's books include the two-volume *Wonderful Transformation and Singular Flower-Food of Caterpillars* (1679) and *Metamorphosis of the Insects of Surinam* (1705). At a time when there were few options for women, Merian traveled alone, conducted detailed scientific research, and wrote and illustrated numerous books. Infusing the natural world with beauty, Merian's combination of scholarship and artistic skill not only has enriched our understanding of the natural world but also has offered new ways of visually communicating scientific information.

Maria Montessori (1870–1952) A pioneering education activist, Maria Montessori helped shape modern education and child care in the twentieth century. Born and raised in Italy, Montessori graduated from technical school in 1886. The Montessori Method challenged traditional approaches to childhood education by addressing the child as an equal and giving each one an unparalleled freedom to explore an environment designed for learning. Its three principles—observation, individual liberty, and preparation of the environment—allow each child to learn at his or her own pace. This system reversed the nineteenth-century notion of an active teacher leading a passive class.

Samuel F. B. Morse (1791–1872) An inventor, painter, student of the liberal arts at Yale University, and founder of the National Academy of Design. Morse was a communicator at heart and chronicled the founding of American democracy in his paintings. Fascinated by Benjamin Franklin's experiments with electricity, and on hearing a fellow passenger on a steamboat remark that electricity could pass instantaneously through a length of wire, Morse excitedly replied: "If this be so, and the presence of electricity can be made visible in any part of the circuit . . . intelligence may be instantaneously transmitted by electricity to any distance." The rest is history: Morse, with almost no knowledge of engineering or electromagnetism, connected himself with those who did to pursue his great invention. His work demonstrates how one discourse, the visual, can affect another: communications technology.

NASA (National Aeronautics and Space Administration) Formed in 1958 as a reaction to Russia's success with the Sputnik satellite, NASA is an independent U.S. governmental agency designed to research, develop, and promote the exploration of space. Its early goals culminated with the moon landing of 1969, a project then so grand in scope the U.S. government had invested in only two things of equal expense: the building of the Panama Canal and the Manhattan Project. Since then, NASA has moved past its cold war origins, cooperating with Russia's space program and developing such projects as the Hubble telescope, countless innovations in aerodynamic research, and a continued process of stellar exploration via probes and satellites. Far from a mere space exploration program, the works and research of NASA have helped shape the information age by touching everything from weather reports to cellular phone communications. Perhaps most important though, NASA has fundamentally transformed our relationship to the world. By stimulating public interest in outer space, NASA has opened up an exciting new world to the public imagination: No longer is the Earth the sum total of human experience, but rather just a vantage point from which we can experience an entire universe of possibilities.

Ted Nelson (b. 1937) Sociologist and philosopher, Nelson wrote some of the earliest influential works on digital media and hacker culture (*Computer Lib*), and is responsible for developing the term *hypertext* in 1965. Plagued by memory loss and attention deficit disorder (ADD), Nelson envisioned a computer-enabled library that would contain and preserve all of human knowledge. He called this system "Xanadu" after the Samuel Coleridge poem that describes the palace of Kubla Khan, and felt it would ultimately bring into place the utopia that unbounded and egalitarian access to information implies. A long and often protracted history of near success and constant failure, Xanadu has not been realized (Nelson argues that the current World Wide Web is a poor and inadequate example of his dream). Whether this is the fault of Nelson's initial vision or just the limits of current technology remains to be determined. Regardless, Xanadu and Nelson's work are important in the history of ideas and in the ways people conceptualize the potentials of technology and the Internet— Nelson did not just try to find an application for existing tools; he proposed a vast undertaking that would transform society and has searched ever since for the ways to make it a reality.

John Oswald If anybody can really be given credit for "smash-ups" (dowloading pop songs, remixing them, and then redistributing them), it is John Oswald. In the late 1960s, Oswald started "plunderphonics," the process of taking existing audio works and reprocessing them to better suit individual listening preferences, and he has been doing it ever since, despite running afoul of copyright law and countless lawyers.

Samuel F. B. Morse

Oswald believes that because we are constantly bombarded by media, we have the right to do with it as we will. Because there is no escaping from pop songs and similar commercial culture, we can at least take it and make it our own. For Oswald, this has entailed pitch-shifting Dolly Parton's voice so that she duets with herself as a man, turning the theme from Mayberry into an ambient whale song, and trimming down an entire Metallica album to the two minutes he liked. He released these recordings privately, only making them available to libraries, radio stations, and interested parties, but not offering them for sale; however, he suffered litigation from the Canadian music industry (whose copyright laws are not quite as lenient as those in the United States). The end result was that all the copies of the album were recalled and destroyed. Many survived, of course, and still circulate via the Internet and various bootlegged reissues.

Not everybody had a problem with Oswald's work though. Indeed, Elektra Records, Metallica (ironic, given their opposition to file-trading technologies such as Napster), and the Grateful Dead all commissioned Oswald to perform similar reconstructions of their music. He created remixes, music for dance performances, and classical compositions, and continues to lecture on copyright and the arts. At the heart of Oswald's work is a love for music, a belief that it is an interactive process in which the listener is as important as the musician, as well as an attempt to reconfigure the world rather than accept what it offers.

Oulipo (*Ouvroir de Littérature Potentielle*) The Oulipo (Workshop for Potential Literature) is a French experimental writing group that attempts to discover new forms in literature. Founded in 1960 by writer and former surrealist Raymond Queneau and mathematician François Le Lionnais, the Oulipo began as a subcommittee of the Collège de Pataphysique (another French group concerned with the works of Alfred Jarry), but it soon distanced and distinguished itself as a separate organization. The Oulipo's work is based on the idea of constraint: By using mathematical structures and often seemingly arbitrary rules, the Oulipo seeks to reveal significant forms for creating new literary works and thus enable individual creativity.

The Oulipo sees most classical forms of literature and poetry as being made up of the same sorts of rules. The sonnet, for example, has a set number of lines, a particular syllabic pattern, and a specific rhyming scheme. The Oulipo members have invented hundreds of possible forms, such as N+7, by which a text is chosen and each noun is replaced by the seventh following noun from a dictionary; or structuring novels based on the layout of a deck of cards. Some of the well-known Oulipo works include Italo Calvino's *If on a Winter's Night a Traveler*, Harry Mathews's *Cigarettes*, Georges Perec's *A Void*, Jacques Roubaud's *The Great Fire of London*, and Queneau's *Cent Mille Milliads de Pòemes (One Hundred Thousand Billion Poems)*.

Palindrome Inter-media Performance Group Formed in 1995 by choreographer Robert Wechsler and computer engineer Frieder Weiß, the German-based Palindrome incorporates computer technology into dance and movement performances. Interactive and multimedial, Palindrome creates unique and inventive dance pieces that cross and fuse disciplinary boundaries. It has developed interactive computer systems, such as sound sampling and motion detectors that create musical soundscapes based on movement, and it regularly tours internationally to critical acclaim. Palindrome believes that new technologies are automated and not interactive, and it seeks to reverse this—creating interactivity between artists, audience, and the world, ultimately hoping to bring humans into contact with each other.

Palo Alto Research Center (PARC)

Created in 1970 by the Xerox Corporation, PARC is an exemplar of the modern lab. Initially started out of fear that the computer would make Xerox's own products obsolete, it became one of the premier research and development groups for new technology throughout the 1970s and 1980s. Without PARC, it is hard to imagine computers existing as we know them today. Besides being the birthplace of inventions such as laser printing, ethernet, the mouse, object-oriented programming, and the local-area network, PARC developed what is considered the first personal computer, the Alto, along with many of the tools and innovations that were key to Apple's early success.

Guided more by the innovative philosophies of men like Bob Taylor and Mark Weiser than by Xerox business plans, PARC has been at the forefront of developing and expanding human-to-computer interaction, realizing the potential of technology in everyday life, facilitating networks, applying technologies, and creating interfaces. It has reached across disciplines, involving social scientists, philosophers, anthropologists, and artists in its work; hosted a variety of research groups; and always looked toward the future potential of technology and its place within society. Emphasizing interdisciplinary research and innovation, PARC has helped to create some of the most inspired technology to date, transforming the way people interact, work, and live.

Robin Hood

(mythic) Robin Hood is an example of an enlightened character who has captured our imagination for almost eight hundred years. Whether based on an actual person or not, his tale is carried forth in ballads and songs that have given inspiration to the illiterate and oppressed for generations. Like all such stories, it changed and grew with the audience.

From the first printed record in *Piers Plowman* by William Langland in 1378 to Mel Brooks's 1993 film *Men in Tights*, Robin Hood and his Merry Men were an experiment in communal living, innovative use of technology, and ecology in their quest for freedom from tyranny. Robin Hood was an early superhero.

The Rosetta Stone

A black basalt slab dating from 196 B.C.E., the Rosetta stone was the key element that allowed the eventual deciphering of the Egyptian hieroglyphs. Found in 1799 by Napoléon's troops in the town of Rosetta (located in lower Egypt near the western delta of the Nile), the stone bore the same inscription in three different scripts: hieroglyphic, demotic, and Greek—a decree by the priests of Memphis in honor of Ptolemy V Epiphanes, king of all Egypt. Knowledge of hieroglyphs had been lost since the fourth century C.E., and by using the Greek script to translate the other two, British physicist Thomas Young and French Egyptologist Jean Francois Champollion were able to prove that hieroglyphs represented a spoken language and eventually enabled future generations to translate almost all of Egypt's hieroglyphs. The discovery of the Rosetta stone bridged time and cultures, opening up the history of Egypt for successive generations, and it remains a vital metaphor for any idea or tool that allows disparate ideas to be connected or mysteries to be unlocked.

Saladin (1138–1193) One of history's most compelling and renowned figures, Saladin was a Kurdish warrior who consolidated power in the Middle East and secured Jerusalem against the Crusaders. After serving in various military campaigns and various political positions, Saladin first ignored and then eventually conquered his fatamid rulers, becoming sultan of Egypt and thus beginning the Ayyubid Dynasty. By all reports, he was a caring and compassionate ruler who revitalized Egypt's economy and military forces. When Saladin took over Cairo, he did not seek revenge on its dispossessed rulers, nor did he seize their wealth; however, he did exile these rulers from their palaces and allowed the Egyptian citizenry to live in these massive dwellings. He had mosques, hospitals, and palaces built (though not for himself), along with a fortress known as the Citadel, considered one of Cairo's great landmarks.

Saladin extended his empire, conquering Yemen and Damascus, and attempted to overtake all of Syria and Palestine. This brought him into conflict with the Crusaders and Richard I. Eventually he would negotiate an armistice with Richard I, which, while relinquishing much of Palestine, kept Jerusalem in Muslim hands. Saladin had a reputation among the Christians as generous and chivalrous, and he is one of the few historical figures of the age who is respected equally by both Christian and Muslim historians. Saladin always looked toward the greater good of his people and is considered a paragon of princely virtue.

Sarvodaya Shramadana Movement (SSM) Founded by A. T. Ariyaratne in the late 1950s, the Sarvodaya Shramadana Movement began as a community-based rural development program in Sri Lanka. Loosely translated as "communal awakening," SSM has spread through grassroots initiatives working in thousands of different villages in Sri Lanka. Fusing Buddhist principles, economic theory, and social activism, SSM tries to achieve communal and individual reawakening: Students work with the rural poor and socially disenfranchised on rural and village development projects that fight against class and caste taboos. By working with the villagers in closely knit communal groups, SSM attempts to foster economic self-reliance and community development. By engaging at a grassroots level, Ariyaratne hoped individuals and communities would not only enact meaningful local change but also broaden their perspectives of their community and the world.

Raymond Scott (1908–1994) Anybody who grew up watching *Bugs Bunny* cartoons, or even *Ren & Stimpy*, is intimately familiar with the work of Raymond Scott. His manic big band-esque compositions, filled with humorous juxtapositions of melody and sudden changes of style, have been in countless cartoons. But Scott never actually composed a single note for cartoons: jingles, films, television shows, Broadway plays, ballets, yes; but cartoons, no.

Astoundingly popular in the 1930s, Raymond Scott and his quintette were something of an oddity, playing intricately composed pieces that owed as much to Scott's classical training as to jazz. While critics did not care for Scott and his "un-jazz" jazz works, nor his seemingly frivolous attitude (characterized by titles such as "Dinner Music for a Pack of Hungry Cannibals"), the public loved it, as did people like Igor Stravinsky. Eventually Warner Brothers would license his music for Looney Tunes, and Scott would go on to take the command of the CBS orchestra. Scott never abandoned his love of engineering, and has come to be regarded as an important figure in the history of electronic music. He invented countless electronic instruments, including one of the earliest synthesizers and possibly the first sequencer. He composed music for infants that was stylistically similar to later works by Philip Glass and Terry Riley. He worked for Motown, heading its electronic music research and development for a time, and collaborated with Jim Henson on several short films.

Kenneth Snelson

(b. 1927) Computer artist, sculptor, and photographer who developed the concept of tensegrity. Snelson demonstrates the crossing the boundaries between disciplines. The story of tensegrity connects engineering, biology, and the fine arts. In 1948 Snelson attended a summer session at Black Mountain College, the experimental school in North Carolina. There, he studied art with the Bauhaus master Josef Albers and architecture with R. Buckminster Fuller. By the end of the summer, Snelson had begun to develop his ideas on tensegrity, a system of creating structures composed of two types of elements—those that have compression strength and those that have tensile strength: struts and cables. By combining them in sophisticated ways, Snelson can create objects whose structural integrity comes from the fact that they are prestressed and so can flex and move as load is continuously transmitted across the structural members. As it turns out, principles of tensegrity applied to nearly every structure in the human body, from the individual cells (which behave precisely as tensegrity structures do) to the body itself, composed of muscles (cables) and bones (struts). Donald Ingber, a biologist who had once studied sculpture, says, "The question of how living things form has less to do with chemical composition than with architecture." Snelson also realized that cell behavior could be accurately described by models of tensegrity, and this notion has been confirmed by the work of other biologists.

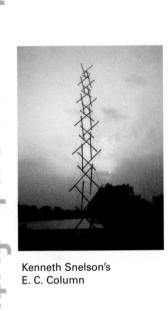

Kenneth Snelson's
E. C. Column

Richard Stallman, Linus Torvalds, and GNU/Linux

At the end of the twentieth century, there were three major computer operating systems: Microsoft's Windows, Apple's Macintosh, and UNIX, originally developed by AT&T. All three were developed through the traditional corporate model, one which saw software as a commodity to be sold. In the 1980s, a free version of UNIX developed. Called Linux or GNU/Linux, it was a remarkable collaboration by thousands of programmers who radically rethought the way in which software, the quintessential commercial product of the computer age, was developed, owned, and distributed.

Linux started with the work of Richard Stallman, a programmer at the Massachusetts Institute of Technology (MIT) Artificial Intelligence Lab in the 1970s. Largely influenced by the hacker community of the time, Stallman developed his concept of free software, embodied in the GPL or GNU public license. GNU (a recursive acronym that stands for "GNU's not UNIX") was a free software project whose terms of use for any program covered by its license stated that users could modify and redistribute the program's source code, provided that they made these modifications available to others. Biographer Sam Williams writes, "As hacks go, GPL stands as one of Stallman's best. It created a system of communal ownership within the normally proprietary confines of copyright law. More importantly, it demonstrated the intellectual similarity between legal code and software code. Implicit within the GPL's preamble was a profound message: Instead of viewing copyright law with suspicion, hackers should view it as yet another system begging to be hacked." Perhaps the most brilliant aspect to this was the conceptualization of software not as property to be hoarded, but as information, something always in process, which demands the participation of those using it to share with others and to contribute to its implementation.

Stallman began the GNU project in the early 1980s by posting a message to a Usenet newsgroup stating he was going to write a UNIX clone from the ground up, then give it away for free. He resigned from MIT so it could make no claim to the software, and in 1983, began to write code. While GNU itself is a masterwork of programming, the GNU manifesto and the GPL are also tremendously important. The GNU manifesto outlines the reasons for writing GNU, and Stallman's philosophy about software and programming. For Stallman, programmers have an obligation to share their work with other programmers and with society at large. "If anything deserves a reward, it is social contribution. Creativity can be a social contribution insofar as society is free to use the results." To further the goal of free software, Stallman started the Free Software Foundation, through which he could attract funding and fellow programmers.

Hacker Linus Torvalds was inspired by Stallman's concept that because no hacker writes perfect code, a distributed method of creating software had great advantages. Torvalds began to create his own version of UNIX, which he dubbed Linux. It began with a few programs—a terminal emulator and a disk driver—that Torvalds posted on the Internet, inviting anyone to take a look and contribute their thoughts or improvements. By 2002, Linux was a full operating system, incorporating the Linux kernel along with many components from GNU (especially the GNU C compiler), and had an established base of more than ten million users in one hundred twenty countries. Linux and Stallman's Free Software Foundation continue to evolve today.

Rabindranath Tagore
(1861–1941) Poet, dramatist, educator, musician, and 1913 Nobel laureate. Tagore is best known for his poetry, plays, and stories. Born in Bengal was also active in the Indian nationalist movement and close friends with Mahatma Gandhi. Knighted by the British Crown in 1915, Tagore resigned the honor a few years later in protest of British policies in India. Tagore was also the founder of Shantiniketan (Visva Bharati University) in 1921—an experimental college located in modern Bangladesh. The university not only integrated Upanishadic ideals of education, but also attempted to bridge cultural boundaries between the East and West.

Rabindranath Tagore

Timbuktu
Built in the twelfth century, the ancient city grew into one of the great destinations for trade, as well as for the riches of its salt mines, its cloth, and its linking together the Islamic world of Africa and beyond. Its wealth, and the inevitable cultural exchange that accompanied trading, made it in the Middle Ages one of the great seats of learning and information storage in the world, a prototype for the World Brain. Its mosques held vast libraries: It is said that by the sixteenth century as many as twenty-five thousand students studied in one hundred and fifty schools a course of learning that could last ten years and whose subjects included astronomy, medicine, law, and the arts. The journey to Timbuktu often induced foreigners to spend great lengths of time in the city pursuing its cultural riches. Anyone who had endured the long journey there could have an education at the Fankor Mosque, the principal site of Islamic scholarship of the region underwritten by the community. Through the support

of trade guilds, poorer apprentices were also guaranteed an education by their mentors. The scholars in turn provided legislation, planning and development of the city's resources, and the copying of manuscripts, which were brought into the city by caravan from other places that expanded the great wealth of the city.

Booker T. Washington (1856–1915)
In addition to being a scholar, author, and reformer, Washington is best know as the founder of Tuskegee Normal and Industrial Institute in 1881. At a time when educational opportunities were virtually nonexistent for African Americans, Washington helped pioneer a school that taught industrial and craft skills to disenfranchised African-Americans. Although Washington received criticism for his emphasis of economically viable skills over civil rights, his tireless efforts helped provide countless African-Americans new avenues of economic self-sufficiency.

Edward O. Wilson (b. 1929)
Harvard professor Edward O. Wilson is primarily known as the foremost expert on ants and the father of sociobiology, the controversial field that looks at behavior through the lenses of biology and sociology. In his book *Concilience*, Wilson draws on the teachings of the Enlightenment, attempting to weave together disparate fields of knowledge into a unified theory of human existence: "The greatest enterprise of the mind has always been and always will be the attempted linkage of the sciences and the humanities. The ongoing fragmentation of knowledge and resulting chaos in philosophy are not reflections of the real world but artifacts of scholarship." Wilson argues that it is only by bridging the gaps that exist between disparate fields of knowledge that we will begin to give our understanding and knowledge of the world a deeper and richer meaning.

World's Fair (1850)
The great London exhibition of 1850 was conceived by Prince Albert as a showcase of the wonders of the Industrial Revolution, inspired by smaller exhibitions that had been held since the turn of the century in France. It was housed in the newly completed Crystal Palace, remarkable for its construction of iron beams and plate glass, embodying the spirit of technology and exhibition. One large display case, the Palace was itself a macrocosm of the nearly seventeen thousand exhibitions it held (self-similar like a fractal) from countries around the world. True to the capitalist spirit that it exhibited, the Palace was financially self-sufficient, and proceeds were directed to build other museums in London including the Science Museum, the National History Museum, and Albert Hall. It was the inspiration for a century of World's Fairs to follow, sites for anyone and everyone to peer into the future and wonder at the great potential of the human imagination and spirit, an optimistic vision of the future. There were destinations in the fairs for recreation, learning, and commerce as they acted as global repositories of the exchange of information. They were precursors of the Internet and the realm of the circuit, a method for sharing ideas, a place for people to explore and become inspired by the creative endeavors of others.

World Wide Web Consortium
Created in 1994, the World Wide Web Consortium, or W3C, is a consortium of companies, universities, and organizations that works to promote and develop the potential of the Web. With around five hundred member organizations and seventy members, the W3C has the goals of universal access to the Web, creating software that allows the best use

of the Web's resources, and to "guide development with careful consideration for the novel legal, commercial, and social issues raised by technology." In a sense, it is the governing body of the Web, setting the technical specifications for its infrastructure and trying to help realize its full potential. Importantly, the W3C exists as a de facto ruling body that seeks to balance the common good of a technology with its commercial potential in the development of a new and vital frontier in society and culture.

Lily Yeh (b. 1944) Painter, urban designer, and social activist. Yeh's Village of Arts and Humanities in Philadelphia allows a community to redevelop itself from the ground up, block by block, using the arts as the "bone structure." In the abandoned lots of North Philadelphia, Yeh organized an inner-city community in a mural-painting project, which led to the renovation of buildings, development of parks, and community education and arts programs. This initiative has formed a model for other similar community projects from Africa to Asia. Yeh conceives of a village as a living piece of sculpture that is a communal event, with residents participating in all aspects of planning, development, and design. Her approach is organic and evolutionary, utilizing available resources that evolve from older, existing structures. Yeh says, "We want to create meaningful jobs, not just McDonald's jobs, but jobs built on community enterprises."

Tree of Life Mural, Village of the Arts and Humanities

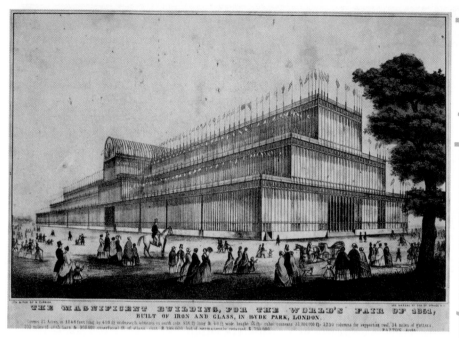

THE MAGNIFICENT BUILDING, FOR THE WORLD'S FAIR OF 1851,
BUILT OF IRON AND GLASS, IN HYDE PARK, LONDON.

The Crystal Palace, 1850

Media content is no longer about aspirations or the quest for understanding. Rather, it is a displacement in the celebretising and sensationalizing of individuals and events.

Throughout this book, we have chronicled how the digital revolution has created the possibilities of revitalizing thought, interaction, and creativity. The digital computer, with its accompanying methodologies, gives unprecedented opportunities for working that emphasize relationships between bodies of knowledge and human minds. It allows inquirers to share a commonality of human expression that reunites communities of thought. A new state of mind exists in the quest to expose the unseen, and the computer's value lies in its ability to allow creative interlocutors to forge new pathways.

How do we adapt to the quantum developments that technology demands of us? Will we become all the more regulated because we are forced to adapt to the machine's logic and move at its pace? Or will we be able to allow it to manage the tasks to which it is best suited—number crunching of the more banal transactions of investigation—leaving us to even greater whimsy. Creative artists, scientists, and technologists once had to work with only a limited fund of knowledge stored on paper or in memory. The creative hand is likewise hobbled, limited by the constraints of its own dexterity. Yet the computer can navigate the new virtual spaces almost instantaneously, unfettered by either physical awkwardness or failing memory, aiding our recognition of the empirical patterns in the vast fields of information, both inside and outside of our personal realm.

We argue for an engagement in learning that has at its core the development of curiosity and heightened associative powers. This curiosity is fed by the integration of discourse of both the arts and sciences. It is informed not so much by practice as by an understanding that constitutes meaning and the possibility for the enrichment of the human psyche. The learning process should allow the student the ability to search and find content in a readily acceptable manner to further the quest for understanding. This engagement does not need to be merely an external search. We can build a three-dimensional jigsaw puzzle in virtual reality from the core of our personal histories, cultivation, and experience. The new possibilities for the recognition of pattern within one's own biosocial psychological condition might be revealing. Marvin Minsky has portrayed the mind as a society of tiny components that form a magnificent tapestry of evolving inspiration. He draws on Seymour Papert, who theorized that intellectual progress is based not simply on the acquisition of new skills, but also on the acquisition of new administrative ways to use what one already knows. Our conception of the computer as an creative tool and communication device is just that of an instrument that fosters and encourages the creative readministration of information.

The human mind is an associative, analog machine. When Gary Kasparov played chess with IBM's Deep Blue in 1997, he was severely challenged by a machine that surpassed his logical abilities. And he sought to win by playing its game, and so lost the first two games to its superior ability to crunch numbers. He was only able to win games after realizing that his own pattern of thinking was fallible. He could employ illogical, whimsical moves and in these instances the inventive strategy of the human mind could prevail. It is curious that we have come to see this chess match as a watershed event in computer intelligence, the point where computers surpassed the human mind, for chess is in essence a game of algorithms played on a logical Cartesian grid, with a definite start and end—all things at which the computer excels.

We can calculate data through algorithm with great accuracy, but we cannot predict what the human mind will do. It defies logic: It is neither deliberate nor exact, and it often works miraculously, without apparent motive or intent. We have the propensity for thought that stretches beyond any formal system. Mental processes are a long way from being computerized, and may never be. They work on intuition and aesthetics. Ideas happen not to come in sequences but are often formed in what one might call explosions of thought. It is random, whimsical interactions that often produce the light. Truly great technological innovations (and often great artistic ones as well) spring from the juxtaposition of seemingly unrelated things, as a chess master might notice patterns on a chess board. This flashlike act can be the transgression of previously uncrossed boundaries, or the creation of new collaborations enabled by the digital. Today, new thinking comes for the most part from collaborations between individuals, places, and ideas themselves, networked by a circuiteer in a constant stream of exchange and association.

Vannevar Bush foresaw a future where individuals would organize knowledge by creating associative trails through knowledge, using the memex. These trails were not only for individual use, as Bush imagined that they would be linked together, allowing one person's creativity to infect others. Such contagion stimulates curiosity, which is fed by the integration of all of our experiences, whether in the arts or the sciences. This curiosity is not so much informed by practice or rote learning, but by understanding how things interlace to constitute meaning and the great patterns of life. Computer-enhanced learning can today allow us the ability to search and find content in a readily available manner to further the quest for understanding. Today, Bush's vision is embedded in the World Brain.

Human life is evolutionary and adaptive. But who is adapting to what? Good programmers must become intimately acquainted with the logical inner workings of the computer. But all too often they fail to create their programs or interfaces with a sympathy for the workings of the human mind. As a result, the applications, digital cameras, or even programming languages they create do not use the computer to support the mind's shortcomings or to bolster the strengths of the way it thinks. This is in essence a failure of design: Good design results in successful interaction. Successful interfaces are easy to use but hard to create. Unfortunately, most people's experience with the computer is often tainted by poorly designed interfaces. This situation is a fault not only of the engineer, but equally that of artists and humanists, who must be held accountable for not understanding the necessity of working with and further developing this great tool of the millennium.

Have we labored under the illusion that technology's promise owes us something? We expect the digital world to deliver itself packaged with ease of access, adapted to our every whim, and sympathetic to our psychological complexity. Shouldn't we reeducate ourselves to its realities and to engage its development from all disciplines of our human discourse? Ask not what the computer can do, but what you can do for the computer. Humanists have in the past approached the technology tentatively because they have failed to see their role in its development. Science, too, is limited by its proliferating specialties, which do not allow the scientist or technologists to grasp the larger sphere of human endeavor (this happens in the humanities as well).

John Dewey realized that no individual could hold the vast amounts of accumulated modern knowledge. Similarly, no single institution can be expected to be the repository of the treasures of our ever-evolving culture. Models for the creative interlocutor such as Vannevar Bush, Buckminster Fuller, Lazslo MoholyNagy, and Maria Montessori, understood education as a tool that enables the individual to find information and form new relations within it. Their genius lies in their imaginative administration, which sought to penetrate the walls of existing schools of thought. We must continue to learn all throughout our lives, and learning requires that we also become teachers. If the artist understands intuitively that there are no ultimate truths but merely an ever-evolving refinement of expression, the scientist strives to formulate answers to immediate problems that allow us to renegotiate the unsolvable riddles inevitably raised as knowledge expands. The conundrum is that each looks for truth that can never be found.

In the future, it is unimaginable that any individual will be able to command knowledge as diverse and as complete for the age as did Bacon, or al Hazen before him, or Jefferson or Goethe, noted as the last man to know everything. We are all aware that no individual is capable of knowing the entirety of even a single specialty today. Our culture mandates that we become creative interlocutors—systems humanists in the words of Ted Nelson—who can navigate and ameliorate our libraries and museums to interact with the knowledge held in the World Brain, as our needs evolve.

The future of community rests now more than ever on recognizing Buckminster Fuller's 1960s proposition that the earth is a ship hurtling through space and that we are more than ever interdependant, not only on our limited resources but also upon each other to navigate. Paradoxically, the technology that allows such individuality and personal freedom is the technology that requires the refinement of and investment in collaborative effort. Are we unable to stop wars and the divisiveness that destroys precious life? Can we lessen the gap between the haves and the have-nots? Technology of all sorts allows for many different forms of intermingling, interrelationships, new associations, and new paths that are unexpected. But—and this is a big but—such dreams are possible only when the great majority are truly in the realm of the circuit that holds together our spaceship earth, or our World Brain. Shouldn't we all take the responsibility for enabling others to have similar access?

Technology is more than just a tool, although we must initially approach it as one in order to learn it, and to feel comfortable and even unthreatened by it. It should be seen as what allows us to fulfill certain creative tasks with simplicity and efficiency. It will extend existing tools and make others obsolete. As with any apparatus, grace and technique must be learned. However, once several generations have grown up with what is now the ubiquitous computer, clearly its utility will change. It is likely that life in the virtual worlds of tomorrow will be such that what was once regarded as a tool or a skill will be taken for granted as a simple extension of our own humanness. In the past, virtual worlds were described as places to practice for life in the real world. At present, it seems that we are practicing in the real world to exist in the virtual world. In the future, there may be no demarcations at all. In other words, how we think about our life with technology will define our life.

The language of the computer—including the Internet, interactive multimedia, and other new forms and spaces—is a shared language for all of those who choose to partake in the discussion. Collectives are replacing the lone artist in a web of connection being woven that continually redefines a kind of collective creative genius. Talent, innovation, the avant garde, and the bleeding edge no longer define an elite. A new vision is defined by the simple notion that all communication from previously defined components of cultural interchange—sound, music, word, text, drawing, photograph, file, folder, icon, image, or metaphor—are reduced to the same common denominator—the digit—and shared through the circuit.

starting point

Notes

⬚ ⬚ ⬚

Chapter One
FOUNDATIONS

1. Schwartz, John, "In the tech meccas, masses of people, or 'smart mobs,' are keeping in touch through wireless devices," *New York Times,* July 22, 2002.
2. Freidman, Thomas L., "Iran's Third Wave," *New York Times* Op Ed, June 16, 2002.
3. Peirce, Charles S., *Selected Writings.*
4. Wagner, Richard, in Packer, Randall, and Ken Jordan, *Multimedia: From Wagner to Virtual Reality.*
5. Dewey, John, *Art as Experience.*
6. Wells, H. G., *World Brain.*
7. Levy, Steven, *Artificial Life: A Report from the Frontier Where Computers Meet Biology.*
8. Fong, Wen C., and James C. Y. Watt. *Possessing the Past.* New York: Metropolitan Museum of Art, 1996, p. 553.

Chapter Two
METAFORA

1. Masters, Edgar Lee, "Petit the Poet," *Spoon River Anthology.* Dover: New York, 1992.
2. http://www.kaiserworks.com/duoframe/duoartworks.htm.
3. Ibid.
4. Pinker, Stephen. *How the Mind Works.*
5. Machlis, Joseph, *The Enjoyment of Music.*
6. Christoph, Henning, Klaus E. Muller, and Ute Ritz-Muller. *Soul of Africa: Magical Rites and Traditions.*
7. Quoted in "Worlds Within Worlds," pamphlet from the Asia Society exhibition, March–August 1996.
8. Mitchell, W. J. T., *Iconology: Image, Text. Ideology.*
9. Barthes, Roland, *Camera Lucida.*
10. Peirce, Charles S., selected writings.
11. Baudrilliard, Jean, "Procession of the Simulacra." in Wallis, Brian, ed., *Art After Modernism,* New York: New Museum of Contemporary Art, 1984, p. 253.
12. Pinker, Stephen, *How the Mind Works.*
13. Gates, Jr., Henry Louis, *The Signifying Monkey: A Theory of African American Literary Criticism.*
14. Nietzsche, Friedrich, "On Truth and Lie," in *The Portable Nietzsche,* translated by Walter Kaufmann, New York: Penguin Books, 1982, pp. 46–47.
15. Langer, Susanne K., ed., *Problems in Art.*
16. *McClure's* Magazine, February 1902, pp. 291–299.
17. Thoreau, Henry David, *Walden.*
18. http://www.uic.edu/sph/cade/kidsmco/meeting2001/cade_handouts/internet_vs_www.htm
19. Rayward, W. Boyd, "Visions of Xanadu: Paul Otlet and Hypertext." *JAIS* 45 (1994): 235–250.
20. Bush, Vannevar, "As We May Think," *Atlantic Monthly,* July 1945.
21. See Stewart Brand's web site: http://www.well.com/user/sbb/

Chapter Three
DIALOG

1. Campbell, Joseph, *Primitive Mythology,* vol. 1 of *The Masks of God.*
2. Erikson, Erik, *Childhood and Society.*
3. Turkle, Sherry, *Life on the Screen: Identity in the Age of the Internet.*

4. Solovitch, Sara, "The Citizen Scientists," *Wired Magazine*, September 2001.

5. Levy, Steven, *Artificial Life: A Report from the Frontier Where Computers Meet Biology*.

6. Jung, Carl G., *Man and His Symbols*.

7. Minsky, Marvin, *The Society of the Mind*.

8. McLuhan, Marshall, *Understanding Media: The Extensions of Man*.

9. Baudrilliard, Jean, "Procession of the Simulacra," in Wallis, Brian, ed., *Art after Modernism*, New York: New Museum of Contemporary Art, 1984, p. 253.

10. Samuel Johnson (1709–1784), British author, lexicographer, in *Works of Samuel Johnson*, Yale Edition, vol. 2, eds. W. J. Bate et al., eds. (1963). The Idler, no. 40, *Universal Chronicle* (London, Jan. 20, 1759).

11. Jung, Carl, *Archetypes of the Collective Unconscious*.

12. http://ourworld.compuserve.com/homepages/ken_crossman/Gore.htm

13. Herz, J. C., *Joystick Nation: How Videogames Ate Our Quarters, Won Our Hearts, and Rewired Our Minds*.

14. Kemeny, John G., *Man and the Computer*.

15. Levy, Steven, *Artificial Life: A Report from the Frontier Where Computers Meet Biology*, p. 141.

16. Vonnegut, Kurt, *Wampeters, Foma & Granfaloons*.

17. See Stewart Brand's website: http://www.well.com/user/sbb/

18. Laing, R. D., *The Politics of Experience*.

Chapter Four

ELEMENTS OF STRUCTURE

1. Jakobson, Roman, "Linguistics and Poetics: Closing Statement" in *Style in Language,* edited by Thomas Sebeok.

2. Gates, Jr., Henry Louis, "Thirteen Ways of Looking at the Black Man," in *Narrative Reader,* edited by Martin McQuillan, p. 290.

3. Barthes, Roland, *Image-Music-Text*.

4. Forster, E. M. "The Story and The Plot," from *Aspects of the Novel*.

5. Ricoeur, Paul, *Narrative Time*.

6. Minkowski, H. "Space and Time," address delivered at the 80th Assembly of German Natural Scientists and Physicians, 1908, trans. W. Perrett and G. B. Jeffrey, in H. A. Lorentz, et al., *The Principle of Relativity,* London, 1923, p. 75.

7. Friedman, William J., *About Time: Inventing the Fourth Dimension*. Publisher: MIT Press - 1990

8. Virilio, Paul, *The Vision Machine*, 1994, p. 61.

9. Bolter, Jay David, *Turing's Man: Western Culture in the Computer Age*.

10. Gibson, William, *Neuromancer*.

11. Packer, Randall, and Ken Jordan, *Multimedia: From Wagner to Virtual Reality*.

12. Mitchell, W. J. T., *Iconology: Image, Text, Ideology*.

13. Leary, Timothy, *Storming the Reality Studio?*

14. Adorno, Theodore, *Essays on Music*. Berkeley: University of California Press, 2002.

15. Derrda, Jacques, *Of Grammatology*.

16. Moholy-Nagy, László, *Painting, Photography, Film*.

17. http://www.pha.jhu.edu/~kgb/cosspec/

18. Chernoff, John Miller, *African Rhythm and African Sensibility*.

19. Levy, Steven, *Artificial Life: A Report from the Frontier Where Computers Meet Biology*.

20. Yuan, Kuo Li Ku Po Wu, et al., *Possessing the Past: Treasures from the National Palace Museum Taipei*.

21. West, Cornel. Introduction to Anna Deavere Smith, *Fires in the Mirror*.

22. Freud, Sigmund, *Formations on Two Principles in Mental Functioning*.

23. Tomkins, Calvin, *Off the Wall: The Art World of Our Time*.

24. Gibson, James J, *Pictures, Perceptive, and Perception in Visual Arts Today*.

25. Blake, William, *The Marriage of Heaven and Hell*.

Chronology of World Events

□ □ □

B.C.E.

40,000 Early cave paintings in Europe.

20,000–10,000 The last ice age.

Circa 20,000 Man crosses the Bering Strait into North America.

Circa 20,000 Use of eyed needles, thought to be for sewing.

8000 Agriculture develops in Middle East. The development of agriculture marks the transition from hunter-gatherer based societies and allows the development of permanent settlements and cities.

7000 Pottery develops in Mesopotamia.

5000 Early settlements in Sumer.

3100 First Egyptian dynasty.

Circa 3000 Bricks are developed and used in Egyptian and Assyrian civilization.

Circa 3000 Candles used in Egypt and Greece.

Circa 3000 Use of rings in wedding rituals in ancient Egypt. They symbolize not only the marriage agreement but the woman's possession of her husband's wealth. This ritual continued in ancient Rome and was eventually adopted by the Christian church.

2900 Indus valley civilization develops.

2800 First stage of Stonehenge is completed in England (the final stages are completed between 1100 and 1000 B.C.E.). Although its exact origins or function remains a mystery, it is believed that Stonehenge functioned as a lunar and solar calendar.

2780 Commissioned by Zoser, the ruler of Egypt, and designed by his physician, Imhotep, the first pyramid is constructed in Egypt.

2700 One of the earliest known uses of papyrus.

Circa 2500 The Great Pyramids of Giza are constructed on the bank of the Nile River during the 4th Dynasty of the Egyptian Empire.

2500 Bronze Age in Europe. The second phase in the Stone-Bronze-Iron Age sequence, the Bronze Age signals the development of metallurgy and the use of metal tools.

2300 Bow and arrow used in Egypt.

1500 Hindu religion begins in India.

1400–800 Iron Age in western Asia and India. As in the Bronze age before it, the iron metallurgy allowed the production of sturdier tools and weapons.

1250 Moses leads the Israelites out of Egypt.

1200 Moses receives the Ten Commandments.

Circa 1000 Mayan civilization develops in Central America.

Circa 1000 Early kites appear in China, constructed from bamboo and silk.

Circa 800 Homer composes *The Iliad* and *Odyssey*.

753 Rome is founded.

776 First Olympic games.

Circa 600 Graffiti is written in Nubia by Roman soldiers.

563 Birth of the Buddha (563–483 B.C.E.).

Circa 560 Water clock used in Assyria.

551 Confucius is born (551–497 B.C.E.).

546 Romans build plumbing system with pipes.

509 Roman Republic is established.

447 Hollowed gourds made into stringed instruments in India.

Circa 400 Advent of the yoke used with horse-drawn plow and wagon, allowing the use of the horse in agriculture and transportation.

285 Papus of Alexandria describes five machines: cogwheel, lever, pulley, screw, and wedge.

271 Early compass used in China to determine magnetic north.

218 The Second Punic War (218–201) between Rome and Carthage. Hannibal, a Carthaginian general, leads an army of over 50,000 troops with elephants over the Pyrenees into Italy, defeating the Roman army and Publius Cornelius Scipio at the river Ticinus.

215–214 Construction of the Great Wall of China, the only human-made object visible from space.

Circa 5 Jesus (5 B.C.E.–30 C.E.) is born in Bethlehem.

C.E.

30 Jesus is crucified.

77 Romans conquer England.

275 German monks bowl as part of religious practice.

306 Constantine I becomes Emperor of the Roman Empire (306–337).

313 Constantine converts to Christianity and makes Christian worship legal in the Roman Empire with the Edict of Toleration.

370 Huns invade Europe.

410 Goths capture Rome.

570 Muhammad (570–633) is born in Mecca.

595 First decimal reckoning, India.

633 Abu Bekr, Muhammad's father-in-law, becomes the First Caliph after Muhammad's death.

850 Coffee discovered by Arabs.

Circa 850 Chinese Taoist scholars invent gunpowder. Some scholars believe that Muslims had invented gunpowder several centuries earlier.

1002 Leif Ericsson, a Norse Viking, explores North American coast.

1066 William I, the Conqueror, the first Norman king (1066–1087), captures England in the Battle of Hastings.

1096 The First Crusade begins. Initiated by Pope Urban II, the First Crusade was an attempt to free Jerusalem and the Christian shrine of the Holy Sepulchre from Islamic control. Subsequent Crusades followed up on this mission, but also included other goals. In total, there were seven crusades during the twelfth and thirteenth centuries.

12th century Under the leadership of Temujin (Genghis Khan) and his grandson, Kublai Khan, the Mongols dominate Central Asia.

1150 Angkor Wat, perhaps the greatest of the shrines built atop artificial mountains, is completed by the Khmer Empire in Cambodia.

1161 Explosives are used in China.

1187 Saladin, founder of the Ayyubid dynasty, captures Jerusalem from Christian control.

1215 The Magna Carta is written. One of the key building blocks for modern democracy, the Magna Carta helped barons gain rights from the King of England—such as no imprisonment without a trial, legal tax collection, and equal justice for all men regardless of rank or social status.

1325 Aztecs found Tenochtitlán, which later becomes Mexico City.

1338 The Hundred Years' War begins (1338–1453). Essentially a series of wars between France and England, the Hundred Years' War was caused by English claims to the French throne.

1348 An estimated twenty-five million people die as the bubonic plague sweeps through Europe.

15th Century The Renaissance. Literally meaning "rebirth," the Renaissance was a period of cultural and intellectual growth following the Middle Ages. Marked by a return to classical learning and values, the Renaissance brought profound changes in the arts, architecture, science, and politics.

1438 Incan Empire (1438–1532) is established in Peru. The Incans eventually construct Machu Picchu, an enormous city complex on the top of the Andes.

1455 The War of the Roses (1455–1485) occurs in England between the royal houses of York and Lancaster.

1455 Johannes Gutenberg prints the first Gutenberg Bible—the first book printed using movable type and a printing press.

1473 The Sistine Chapel is built in Italy by the architect Giovanni dei Dolci for Pope Sixtus IV.

1478 The Spanish Inquisition. Under the authorization of Sixtus IV, Ferdinand and Isabella punish Jews who fail to fully convert to Christianity and still practice Judaism in secret.

1492 Christopher Columbus sails across the Atlantic and explores the West Indies, beginning the European "Age of Exploration."

16th century The Protestant Reformation. A period of religious upheaval and widespread questioning of the Catholic Church. The Reformation began in 1517 when Martin Luthur posted his Ninety-Five Theses on the door of the Castle Church, Wittenberg.

16th century Sikh religion founded by Nanak (1469–1539), taking elements from Hindu and Islamic religions.

1518–19th century African slave trade. Slaves are brought from Africa to the New World through the Middle Passage.

17th and 18th centuries Age of Enlightenment, also known as the Age of Reason. The Enlightenment was an intellectual movement in Europe that began to question ideas concerning God, nature, and humanity. Championing the powers of reason, the Enlightenment led to radical changes in notions of religion, science, politics, and philosophy.

1603 The Tokugawa family seizes power in Japan. Weary of Western missionaries and foreign influence, the Tokugawa family keeps Japan in isolation until U.S. naval officer Matthew Perry opens Japan to trade in 1854.

1607 The English found Jamestown colony in Virginia, the first European colony in North America.

1618 Thirty Years' War (1618–1648). A period of general conflict in Europe between various nations and for various reasons.

1620 Pilgrims reach Cape Cod in the Mayflower and found New Plymouth.

1633 Galileo Galilei is tried in Rome by the Inquisition and convicted of heresy for his teachings on astronomy.

1653 Commissioned by the Mughal Emperor Shah Kahan, the Taj Mahal is completed in Agra, India.

1692 Salem Witch Trials take place in Salem, Massachusetts. Over twenty people are convicted of practicing witchcraft.

18th century The beginning of the Industrial Revolution. The Industrial Revolution marked the shift from an agrarian-based economy to one run by machines and industry. Key features included the uses of steel, iron, coal, and other fossil fuels, the invention of new industrial tools such as the power loom, and the development of travel and communication technology (i.e., the steam engine, radio, telegraph etc.).

1757 Following a long period of trade controlled by the East India Company, the British establish colonial rule in India.

1775 American War of Independence (1775–1783). Following the Treaty of Paris, the United States successfully gains its independence from Great Britain.

1776 The U.S. Declaration of Independence is signed.

1787 The U.S. Constitution is signed.

1789 The French Revolution begins.

1791 The U.S. Bill of Rights is passed.

1791 Toussaint l'Ouverture successfully leads a slave rebellion against the French in Haiti. Although France later regains power, Haiti regains its independence in 1804.

1792 Mary Wollstonecraft publishes *A Vindication of the Rights of Woman*. Stressing the need for women's education, Wollstonecraft's text profoundly influenced later feminists.

1796 Edward Jenner develops the process of inoculation. His process is used to inoculate livestock against anthrax and cholera. Jenner's discoveries are later used to inoculate humans against numerous diseases.

1799 The Rosetta stone is discovered and successfully translated by French scholars, unlocking the mystery of Egyptian hieroglyphics.

1804 Napolean Bonaparte crowns himself Emperor of France.

1805 Oliver Evans invents the first refrigeration machine. By 1834, the first practical machines were introduced by Jacob Perkins.

1810 An early method for canning food is invented by Nicolas Appert of France.

1830 The first steam powered passenger railroad is in operation in England.

1833 Slavery abolished in British colonies.

1837 Queen Victoria (1837–1901) assumes the throne of England, thereby beginning the Victorian Age in England.

1839 The First Opium War (1839–1842) occurs between China and England. After England began illegally importing opium into China, large-scale social unrest lead to an armed conflict over trading privileges. Following the Second Opium War (1856–1860), England is able to secure extensive trading rights in China.

1839 Louis Daguerre and Henry Fox Talbot present the first photographic processes–the daguerreotype and the calotype.

1845 The Potato Famine devastates Ireland. Thousands starve when a potato blight wipes out almost an entire crop of potatoes.

1846 Elias Howe invents the sewing machine.

1848 The Gold Rush begins in the United States, sending people west to California in search of riches.

1848 Karl Marx and Friedrich Engels publish the *Communist Manifesto*.

1848 The "Year of Revolutions" in Europe. A combination of food shortages, rising nationalism, and social unrest causes rebellions in France, Austria, Hungary, Germany, Italy, and Turkey.

1848 Elizabeth Cady Stanton and Lucretia Mott lead the first women's rights convention in the United States, at Seneca Falls, New York. The efforts of Stanton, Mott, Susan B. Anthony, and others lead to the passage of the nineteenth amendment, which gave women the right to vote in 1920.

1851 The first World's Fair is held in London, England.

1851 James King invents the drum washing machine. In 1908, the Hurley Machine Company introduces the first electric washing machine.

1854 Crimean War (1854–1856). England, France, and Turkey fight Russia. The Crimean War is the first to be documented using photography.

1857 Indian Mutiny (1857–1858). A failed rebellion led by sepoys, or Indian troops in the Bengal Army, employed by the British East India Company, the Indian Mutiny was an attempt to drive the English out of India.

1859 Charles Darwin publishes *On the Origin of Species*, introducing the concept of evolution through natural selection.

1861 The U.S. Civil War (1861–1865).

1863 Abraham Lincoln issues the Emancipation Proclamation, freeing all slaves in the Southern Confederacy.

1865 The Thirteenth Amendment abolishes slavery in the United States.

1869 Ives McGaffey patents the first vacuum cleaner as a "sweeping machine."

1874 The first impressionist exhibition in Paris includes Pierre Renoir, Claude Monet, Paul Cézanne, and Edgar Degas.

1886 Coca-Cola invented by Dr. John Stith Pemberton. The Coca-Cola Company was incorporated in 1893.

1899 Sigmund Freud (1856–1939) publishes *The Interpretation of Dreams*, which describes the role of dreams in the psyche. Freud is considered the founder of psychoanalysis.

1900 The Boxer Rebellion in China. Led by a Chinese sect called I-ho ch'üan (or "Righteous and Harmonious Fists"), known as Boxers by foreigners, the general uprising was an attempt to drive all foreigners out of China following a period of economic hardship and natural disasters.

1902 Kellog's introduces cornflakes.

1902 Willis Haviland invents air conditioning. Initially limited to commercial use, it eventually is used in residential buildings.

1903 Orville Wright and Wilbur Wright successfully fly a plane in Kitty Hawk, North Carolina.

1905 Albert Einstein introduces the special theory of relativity. In 1916, he elaborates upon this theory with his general theory of relativity.

1908 The Model-T is manufactured by Henry Ford.

1911 Igor Stravinsky's *Le Sacre du printemps* (*Rite of Spring*) debuts in Paris' Théâtre des Champs-Élysées. Full of dissonant noise and chaotic dancing, the performance by he Ballet Russes and Stravinsky causes a riot in Paris.

1912 The republican government of Sun Yat-sen replaces the Ch'ing Dynasty in China.

1912 The *Titanic* sinks in the Atlantic Ocean–1513 people perish.

1912 The Balkan Wars (1912–1913).

1913 The modern brassiere is invented by Mary Phelps Jacob, a New York socialite.

1913 The Armory Show, officially known as the International Exhibition of Modern Art, in New York City helps introduce modern art to the American public.

1914 Archduke Francis Ferdinand of Austria is assassinated by a Serbian nationalist, triggering World War I (1914–1918). The Allied Powers consisted of the United States, France, England, Russia, and Italy; the Central Powers were Germany, Turkey, and Austria-Hungary.

1917 The United States enters World War I.

1917 Lev Sergeivitch Termen invents the Thermin, the first electronic organ. It was played not by actuating keys or levers, but by the movement of the player's body. It later inspires Bob Moog to invent the synthesizer and was used in the Beach Boys' song "Good Vibrations."

1917 The Russian Revolution. Under the leadership of Vladimir Lenin, the Imperial government was overthrown and the Bolsheviks seized power, establishing a socialist government.

1919 The League of Nations is formed. Established by the Allied powers at the end of World War I, the League of Nations' goal was to preserve the peace, foster international cooperation and prevent further aggression.

1919 Mohandas Gandhi begins campaign of passive resistance (*satyagraha*) against the British in India.

1919 The Bauhaus is founded in Germany by the architect Walter Gropius.

1920s The Harlem Renaissance occurs in New York City.

1922 The first modern shopping mall is built in Kansas City, Missouri. Called Country Club Plaza, it was the first commercial development designed to be accessible by automobile. The first enclosed mall was built in 1956. It was called Southdale and opened in Edina, Minnesota.

1924 Vladimir Lenin dies and Joseph Stalin becomes the leader of the Soviet Union.

1929 The beginning of the Great Depression in the United States. Triggered by a massive stock market crash on October 4, millions lost their jobs and life savings and were left destitute.

1933 Black Mountain College is founded by John Andrew Rice and Theodore Dreier in North Carolina.

1934 Adolf Hitler is elected Fürher of Germany (1934–1945).,

1939 Hitler invades Poland starting World War II (1939–1945). Allied Powers consisted of the United States, England, France, and the Soviet Union; the Axis Powers were Japan, Germany, and Italy

1939 Blectchley Park, a mansion north of London, becomes the base for Ultra, a secret team of mathematicians and code breakers who successfully crack the German ENIGMA code machine.

1941 Japan bombs Pearl Harbor and the United States joins the Allies in World War II.

1941 Penicillin is introduced. Discovered by Alexander Flemming, penicillin revolutionized the treatment of bacterial infections, forever changing the field of medicine.

1942 Enrico Fermi demonstrates nuclear fission in a squash court in Chicago. A coded message told of his success: "Italian navigator has just landed in the new world."

1945 Atomic bombs are dropped on Hiroshima and Nagasaki, Japan by the United States.

1945 The United Nations is formed. Founded in the wake of World War II, the UN's aim was to maintain peace and stability in the world. Although containing representatives from all over the world, the core of the UN was the Security Council, which consisted of the United States, the United Kingdom, France, China, and the Soviet Union.

1945 Nuremberg Trials are conducted in Germany. During these trials, twenty-two Nazi officials were tried for their involvement and crimes committed during the Holocaust.

1946 In a speech delivered at Westminster College in Missouri, Winston Churchill declares an "Iron Curtain" has descended between the West and the countries controlled by the Soviet Union and Communism. Churchill's speech marks the beginning of the Cold War between the Western powers and the Soviet bloc.

1947 India gains independence from England. India and Pakistan are formed.

1948 The state of Israel is established.

1948 Gandhi is assassinated by Hindu extremists.

1948 The Berlin blockade begins. The Soviets, in opposition to economic reforms and the attempted reunification of West Germany, impose a blockade on the city of Berlin. The United States responds by airlifting supplies into Berlin.

1948 North Atlantic Treaty Organization (NATO) is formed. It includes the United States, Italy, Belgium, Denmark, Norway, France, Great Britain, Iceland, Canada, Luxembourg, the Netherlands, and Portugal. It is established to deter the Soviet Union from further aggression following the Berlin blockade.

1949 Apartheid, a policy of extreme racial segregation, is adopted by the white government in South Africa.

1949 Communist rule is established in China after a long war between Chinese Nationalists, led by Chiang Kai Shek (1887–1975), and the new Communist Party, led by Mao Tse-tung (1893–1976). Following the Communist victory, China is renamed the People's Republic of China.

1950 The Korean War (1950–53) begins when North Korea crosses the 38th parallel and invades South Korea. Fearing the invasion would start another world war and the expansion of Communism in Asia, the United States sent troops to stop North Korea. When the armistice is finally reached, the border between North and South Korea is reestablished along the 38th parallel.

1950 U.S. Senator Joseph McCarthy leads the Un-American Activities Committee to root out Americans with radical and Communist ties.

1951 The People's Republic of China invades Tibet.

1955 Warsaw Pact established in opposition to NATO. The countries include the Rumanian People's Republic, the Hungarian People's Republic, the People's Republic of Bulgaria, the German Democratic Republic, the People's Republic of Albania, the Union of Soviet Socialist Republics, the Polish People's Republic, and the Czechoslovak Republic.

1955 Ray Kroc opens the first McDonald's restaurant franchise in Des Plaines, Illinois.

1958 English-speaking nations meet and agree to adopt the metric system of measurement.

1957 *Sputnik*, the first space satellite, is launched by the Soviet Union.

1958 The Great Leap Forward begins in the People's Republic of China. At the cost of many lives, the Chinese government attempted to rally the rural population and conduct large-scale rural improvement projects in an attempt at rapid industrialization.

1959 Tibetan revolt against the Chinese occupation. During the confusion, the Dalai Lama escapes to India.

1959 Ruth and Elliot Handler, founders of Mattel Toys, introduce the Barbie Doll at the American Toy Fair

1959 The Cuban Revolution. Fidel Castro assumes power and establishes a Communist government.

1960 Nokia, a rubber manufacturing company, establishes its Cable Works Electronics department, laying the foundation for the company's expansion into telecommunications.

1961 Berlin Wall built, dividing Berlin into East and West Berlin.

1963 U.S. President John F. Kennedy is assassinated.

1963 The Nuclear Test Ban Treaty is signed by the United States, the Soviet Union, and Great Britain.

1964 The Tonkin Gulf Resolution is passed by the U.S. Congress, marking the official U.S. involvement in the Vietnam War.

1966 The Cultural Revolution takes place in the People's Republic of China. Largely carried out by Chinese youths, or Red Guard, the Cultural Revolution was Mao Tse-tung's attempt to revitalize the Communist Party and purge the country of corrupt influences. The Cultural Revolution, like the Great Leap Forward, led to the death of countless people and destruction of much of China's cultural heritage.

1968 Martin Luther King and Robert Kennedy are assassinated.

1969 Neil Armstrong is the first human to walk on the moon.

1972 Watergate Scandal. Several men are caught burglarizing the Democratic headquarters under authorization of President Richard Nixon. The scandal led to the eventual resignation of Nixon in 1974.

1975 Pol Pot and the Khmer Rouge, a radical guerrilla group, take control of Cambodia. During Pol Pot's rule, it is estimated that over one million Cambodians were killed or died.

1975 Salesman Gary Dahl starts the pet rock movement.

1975 The Metric Conversion Act of 1975 (Public Law 94-168) passes Congress. The act created the U.S. Metric Board to encourage and coordinate usage of the metric system. The U.S. Metric Board is disbanded by Ronald Reagan in 1982.

1977 Elvis Presley is rumored to have died.

1979 The Iranian Revolution. The Ayatollah Khomeini returns from exile and expels the Shah of Iran, forming a new Islamic republic.

1979 Sony introduces the Sony Walkman TPS-L2, the first personal tape player.

1979 Pope John Paul II commissions the Pontifical Academy of Sciences to conduct a study into the heresy case of Galileo. Finally, in 1992, the charge of heresy against Galileo revoked by Catholic Church.

Late 1970s Early cases of HIV and AIDS develop in San Francisco, California. In the years following the early infections, HIV/AIDS spreads rapidly throughout the world.

1981 The United States launches the first reusable spacecraft, the space shuttle, into space.

1987 Mikhail Gorbachev, the leader of the Soviet Union, initiates democratic reform under the policies Glasnost and Perestroika. Glasnost stressed openness and eased many of the restrictions on speech and movement, whereas Perosroika was the name for sweeping reforms.

1988 The first democratic elections are held in the Soviet Union.

1989 The Berlin Wall comes down after Erich Honecker and the Communist leader of East Germany lose power. Divided for twenty-seven years, Berlin is reunited. East and West Germany are formally reunited in 1990.

1989 The World Wide Web debuts.

1989 Students conduct pro-democracy rallies in Tiananmen Square, China. The Chinese government cracks down on the students who were occupying Tiananmen Square, killing numerous demonstrators.

1990 Nelson Mandela, leader of the African National Congress (ANC) and political prisoner in South Africa, is freed. Following his release, Mandela works with President F. W. DeKlerk on democratic reform and takes steps toward the creation of a multiracial democracy—the first steps toward effectively abolishing apartheid in South Africa.

1990 The Gulf War begins. Following the Iraqi invasion of Kuwait, the United States, backed by an international coalition, sent troops to drive Iraqi forces out of Kuwait. After sustained air attacks, the United States successfully drove out the Iraqi troops and liberated Kuwait.

1994 Nelson Mandela is elected the first black President of South Africa.

1994 Genocide in Rwanda. The Tutsi minority, the political rulers of Rwanda, are slaughtered en masse by majority Hutus. In an estimated 100 days, almost 800,000 Tutsis were killed by Hutu The United Nations and the West do little to stop the slaughter.

1995 The Murrah Federal Building in Oklahoma is bombed by Terry Nichols and Timothy McVeigh.

1996 After numerous years of fighting and the Dayton Peace Accords, democratic elections are held in Bosnia.

1996 The Taliban captures Kabul and gains control of Afghanistan.

1998 U.S. Embassies in Nairobi, Kenya, and Dar el Islam, Tanzania are bombed by members of Osama bin Laden's terrorist network, Al Qaeda,

1999 Fighting erupts in Kosovo as Muslim Albanians rebel against ruling Serbian minority.

1999 Following massive student demonstrations, democratic parliamentary elections are held in Indonesia.

2001 Al Qaeda terrorists attack World Trade Center and Pentagon.

2001 Euro currency begins circulation. By March 1, 2002 Euros completely replace national currencies within most countries in the E.U.

Glossary

□ □ □

algorithm A mathematical formula that produces an answer to a question. For example, long division answers the question how many times does one number go into another. As a key element of computer programs, algorithms also sort and organize information and data structures.

ambient music Coined by producer and musician Brian Eno in the late 1970s, ambient music abandons traditional song structure and focuses on creating sonic environments that blend with the environment. Played at low volumes, ambient music colors and adds new dimension to the atmosphere of a room.

analog A method of encoding data or signals. Analog devices represent data by physical qualities such as voltage, frequency, rotation of a gear, pressure or length. A signal (such as a sound wave) can be represented by an analog (a thing that is analogous). Sound waves are represented on vinyl LP albums by a groove that has been cut into the surface of the record which resembles the sound wave.

atonal A musical style, pioneered by Arnold Schoenberg in the early twentieth century, characterized by the rejection or absence of any traditional tonal or musical scale.

aura A tangible field or emanation that surrounds a person, place or thing. Critic Walter Benjamin used the term in his classic essay, "Work of Art in the Age of Mechanical Reproduction," to refer to some special quality of a work of art, one that is diminished as it becomes reproduced by photo-mechanical means, such as printing or photography.

avatar An incarnation in human form (in Hinduism and other religions) or the embodiment of a specific concept, philosophical ideal in a person. The term has been applied to a user's icon (the thing which represents the user) in virtual reality, especially video games, first appearing to refer to characters in MUDs.

balance A stability produced by the even distribution of weight, balance can also refer to wide range of medium including art, film, music, literature and more.

binary A numerical system consisting of the digits zero and one. Computers use a binary numbering system because it is easy to represent zeros and ones as the presence or absence of current in a circuit. Furthermore, the functions of the Boolean system of logic can be represented in binary notation.

bit A single digit of binary information; a zero or a one. The word is a contraction of binary and digit.

bitmap A graphic image which is composed of a grid of squares. The color of each of the squares (called pixels) is represented by one or more bits: The greater the number of bits representing each pixel, the more colors the image can represent. The larger the grid, the more information it holds, and so it can be used to create a larger print.

Boolean logic Based on English mathematician George Boole's algebraic systems, Boolean logic is a symbolic logic system often used in computers and computer science.

CAD An abbreviation for computer-aided design, most commonly used in architecture and industrial design. Current 3D animation tools used in film are based on the principles pioneered in CAD.

Cartesian grid A grid which is uniform and infinite. Any point on the grid can be represented with numbers describing its coordinates. Based on the work on René Descartes.

cellular automata A mathematical game in which a grid evolves over time based on a set of rules. The squares of the grid exists at time *a* in a particular state. As the game progresses to time *b,* each square consults a set of rules to determine how to change.

chatrooms Virtual spaces which allow users to anonymously exchange information, talk, share stories, create friendship and communicate. Generally organized by themes, subjects usually range from community activism to teen chat rooms.

Client-server model A model in which the server computer responds to requests by the client, according to a commonly accepted protocol. An example is the World Wide Web, where a client (the web browser) sends a request to the server (which hosts the website) to send a particular page.

combinatorial Concerning the combinations of things, numbers, objects etc. In mathematics, combinatorial refers to the arrangement mathematical elements into finite sets.

Communist Manifesto In German, *Manifest der Kommunistischen Partei*, the Manifesto was written by Karl Marx and Friedrich Engles in 1848 as the platform for the newly formed Communist League. The Communist Manifesto argued that all history is the history of class struggle. Looking back since feudalism to nineteenth-century capitalism, Marx and Engles' argued that the current capitalist system was destined to be overthrown and would be replaced by a worker's society.

compact disc A plastic disk containing computer data or recorded music in digital format. The CD format was developed by Sony and Philips corporations, and is a standard format for encoding and decoding information.

Constructivism An artistic movement started in Russia around 1913. The term "constructivism" was coined in a manifesto published by Antoine Pevsner and Naum Gabo, two Russian sculptures. Both artists had great admiration for machines and modern technology and saw the potentials for art and design to merge and address the conditional of our modern age. Using glass, metal, wood and plastic, the artist was re-envisioned as the artist-engineer engaged in the process of social construction and engagement. Perhaps the most influential members of the Constructivism movement were El Lissitzky and Alexander Rodchenko. The lessons and goals of Constructivism not only played a key role in shaping the philosophy and pedagogy of the Bauhaus, but also radically altered the art, aesthetics and design of the twentieth-century.

cookies Data sent from a web server to a users web browser. The browser then saves this information and sends updates to the server. "Cookies" are most often found on websites that require logins, registration or have preset user profiles (i.e., online shopping cart settings). They can also record the user's browsing habits.

CPU An abbreviation for central processing unit, the "brain" of the computer, which performs the instructions given to it.

creative interlocutor An individual who embodies the new digital creativity, that person or collaborative of persons who, through their own imaginative programming, directorial expertise, or editorial overview, manages to facilitate the needs for creativity through other people's uses of the dataset.

cyberpunks A term that has its roots in William Gibson's influential science fiction novel *Neuromancer* (1982). Cyberpunk is both a genre of science fiction and a term for a computer hacker.

cyberspace Defined by William Gibson in *Neuromancer* as a navigable information space, jockeyed by cyberspace cowboys. Today, the term has expanded to include virtual reality spaces, and even the internet.

cyborg A human being whose abilities have been supplemented by mechanics, especially machines implanted in the body. The term features heavily in Donna Haraway's essay, "A Cyborg Manifesto," in which she posits that the boundaries between machine and human (and between living and nonliving) are becoming increasingly unclear. For her, the cyborg presents the opportunity for a new origin myth, and a new feminist political system.

Dadaist An artist associated with the Dada movement. An antiart movement that flourished in Europe in the early twentieth century, Dada grew out of disgust with bourgeois values and a general dismay over the horrors of World War I. Dadaists explored the nonsensical spontaneous potentials of art to give voice to their feelings of dismay and disenfranchisement.

database A collection of data, ideally arranged for ease of retrieval. The computer allows the ability for fast retrieval of information, and the creation of complex relations within it. Networked databases allow access from any wired user.

dataset Originally used by IBM programmers to refer to a digital file. We use it to refer to digital files which are structured and structurable—digitized sounds, video, text or photographs that reside in the computer or in other digital media. Datasets can be stored, transmitted and transmitted. Digital files can hold programs, but datasets are the digital artifacts of creative endeavor.

Death of the Author Roland Barthes' idea that any literary work contains a variety of voices, not all of which can be reconciled with those of the author: is a particular passage in a book meant to be an editorial comment from the author, a character within the novel, an accepted moment of universal truth? From this view, the reader becomes more important than the author, and interpretation becomes the only guiding principle of reading a text. For Barthes, this is "truly revolutionary since to refuse to fix meaning is . . . to refuse God and his hypostates—reason, science, law."

Deconstructionism The work of Post-Structuralist Jacques Derrida, Deconstructionism is a process of examining texts which seeks to undermine their own inherent logic and claims to truth. The theory posits that all texts are composed of binary pairs (good/evil or masculine/feminine for instance), the first of which is always given positive connotations, the second negative. By isolating a specific section of a text (often a mere footnote or similar small fragment), Deconstructionism attempts to show how these pairs are actually equivalent and of equal moral value. Through this system, it follows that all text is based on ambiguity and that any final truth or interpretation is impossible.

Deism A religious belief beginning in the seventeenth century in Europe which held that some religious knowledge is inborn, and can be developed through reason. For the Deists, God created a rational universe whose workings can be understood through scientific observation. Natural sciences are a way of knowing God. The supernatural world was of little importance to the Deists because it is irrational.

digital A means of representing data or signals. Digital data is represented by discrete integral numbers from a finite set. Signals can encoded into digital form by sampling different qualities (in sound, for instance, pitch, amplitude and so forth) and representing those qualities with numbers. Computers today use binary numbers. Circuits can be designed as digital circuits; those whose inputs and outputs are represented by discrete variables instead of continuously varying ones.

DSL An abbreviation for Digital Subscriber Line, DSL is a radical improvement over traditional modem lines. Although DSL uses traditional phone lines, it greatly increases the speed of internet access and information downloads to as much as 1.544 megabits per second.

dynamism Futurist artist Umberto Boccioni was fascinated with the ways in which he could break down form and mass dynamically through his sculpture. Philosophers Arthur Schopenhauer and Friedrich Nietzsche proposed that music could be understood through dynamism; music has little relation to space, as do other art forms, but great relation to the process of inner expression. For Schopenhauer, music is the translation of will into dynamic form.

ENIAC An abbreviation for Electronic Numerical, Integrator and Computer. Developed during WWII and completed in the 1940s by John Mauchly and J. Presper Eckert, the ENIAC was the first general-purpose digital computer. Occupying a whole floor at the University of Pennsylvania, the ENIAC was enormous by today's standards. Initially used to automate wartime production and calculations, ENIAC was later put to more civic and scientific uses such as weather prediction, optics design and wavelength studies.

encryption The transformation of data into a secret code or cipher, thereby rendering it indecipherable by unauthorized parties. Various schemes, including encryption, have been developed to protect intellectual property.

Enlightenment A broad movement in European intellectual history (during the seventeenth and eighteenth centuries) that questioned ideas of nature, reason, man and God. Often called the Age of Reason, enlightenment thinkers such as Francis Bacon, René Descartes, and Sir Isaac Newton, challenged the orthodoxy of the Roman Catholic Church and offered radical new ways of looking at world and man based on reason and logical analysis. It was also during this time that political theoreticians such as John Locke and Jean-Jacques Rousseau offered modern secularized theories of politics and ethics. The powerful ideas of the Enlightenment played a fundamental role in the shaping of modern history, political theory, philosophy, ethics and religion,

ethernet A network connection that links computers in a local network or LAN.

FAQ (frequently asked questions) Often found on websites or informational texts, the FAQ list addresses typically asked user questions.

firewall A security system that uses both hardware and software programs to protect network systems from security breaches.

Foucault's Genealogies Named after Nietzsche's *On the Genealogy of Morals*, Foucault's theories owe an equal debt to the work of Wilhelm Reich. By examining marginalized ideas and peoples throughout history, in pioneering books covering madness and sexuality, Foucault demonstrated that the literary canon and the hierarchy of knowledge was simply one of power and social control. A recurrent theme throughout Post-Structuralism, Foucault's work re-defines the process of history as the struggle between competing ideologies.

fractals A repeating geometric pattern that produces irregular shapes, patterns and angles not normally found in classical geometry. Often used in computer models to duplicate irregular patterns in nature, Fractals are unique in that they can be subdivided into smaller parts that mirror the whole.

frequently asked questions *See* FAQ

front-end Software that interfaces between the user and a more complicated piece of software. A good front-end is user-friendly, it presents the user options in a naturalistic or intuitive fashion.

FTP (File Transfer Protocol) A common internet protocol for transferring files in a client-server model, implemented in any one of a number of computer programs. It is widely installed on servers, fast and easy to use, though not as secure as other methods.

general theory of relativity Completed by Albert Einstein in 1916 to expand the special theory of relativity proposed in 1905. It attempted to expand the theory of relativity beyond the realm of electrical and magnetic phenomena and integrate the effects of gravity on the time and space continuum.

GIF (graphical interchange format) A standard graphic file format, GIFs are generally used to store simple graphics such as logos or line art. The GIF format is a codec, or coder/decoder, standard. One program, such as Photoshop, will use the GIF compression scheme to encode an image, and another program, such as Internet Explorer, will use the GIF decoder to expand it.

griot An oral historian, musician, performer and entertainer originating in Western African. The griot was the creative interlocutor of the oral tradition. Traditional performances include tribal histories and genealogies. The griot tradition has continued most visibly in hip-hop and rap music.

GUI *See* graphical user interface.

harmonic progression The movement from one chord to another within a musical composition. Dependent upon function, individual chords imply and suggest movement from one to another laying the groundwork for a larger musical structure.

harmony The agreement and congruity of various parts in a connected whole. Harmony also refers to the simultaneous combination of musical notes in a chord.

HTML *See* hypertext markup language.

http (hypertext transfer protocol) Http is a standard for transmitting web pages between a web server and client so that it can be viewed in a web browser.

hypertext A system consisting of documents (nodes) cross-referenced in a particular fashion with links. The term was coined by Theodor Holm Nelson in 1965. The web is a (limited) implementation of his idea; web pages are the documents, and hyperlinked text creates the links; when a user clicks on a link on a web page the client (or web browser) sends a request to the server (or web site) for another page. Hypertext systems allow the user to interactively associate between concepts. (see client-server and http)

hypertext markup language (HTML) HTML is used create web pages. It was designed to be easy to use, so HTML can be written in a simple text editor or word processing program by nearly anyone. HTML is a standard, and so is interpreted in commonly agreed on ways by any web browser such as Internet Explorer or Netscape Navigator.

industrial music Originally a term coined to describe the musical output of the band Throbbing Gristle and similar artists on the late 1970s label Industrial Records. Influenced by Burroughs, Dada, and punk, Throbbing Gristle's music incorporated tape manipulations, early synthesizers, noise, and at times outrageous performance art. Since then, the term industrial has transformed over the years: at first indicating bands such as Einstürzende Neubauten (who use power drills, metal pipes, and other raw materials as instruments) and now generally used to describe any loud or aggressive music that incorporates more mechanical sounds, be it distorted techno or heavy metal bands with drum machines.

infomercial Significantly longer than the average commercial, informercials are a unique fusion of commercial and talk show formats. Designed to entertain, informercials generally focus on new products or services not readily available in traditional stores (i.e., skin care and health products, kitchen appliances, financial information, etc.) Through personal testimonials and demonstrations, infomercials attempt to familiarize and entice potential customers with a product.

infotainment Much like infomercials, infotainment is a blend of content and news presented in a lively or entertaining fashion. As the avenues and outlets for information and news proliferate in the digital age, networks and news suppliers have faced increased competition. In efforts to gain a larger audience share, media providers have often adapted entertainment techniques in the presentation of their content resulting in a new form of news and media information.

integers Aany one of the sets of positive whole numbers (1, 2, 3 . . .), negative whole numbers (–1, –2, –3 . . .) and zero. Integers can be used to count (there are five sheep) or to order (that is sheep number five).

interface The point or system of interaction between two unrelated systems. In computers, the interface between the programs and user often takes the form of GUI (graphical user interface) (i.e., the use of icons and mouse to manipulate data), as well as actual programming language such as DOS, lingo or HTML.

Java A programming language used to develop software for use on the internet. It was meant to be easy to use, and programs written in Java can be implemented across many computer platforms.

JPEG (Joint Photographic Experts Group) A standard graphic file format, JPEGs are generally used to store photographic images. It was developed by a consortium of photographers and computer programmers. Like GIF, it is a codec.

Koran The holy book of Islam, the Koran (Qu'ran) is believed to be the true word of God (Allah) as revealed to the Prophet Muhammad. Written in Arabic and composed of 114 chapters, or *surahs*, the Koran is the paramount text for Islamic society. Recitation of the Koran is central to Islam. Central to the Koran are the Five Pillars of Islam—the profession of faith, five daily prayers, tithing, fasting and the pilgrimage to Mecca.

LAN (local area network) A small local network, often limited to a building, school or business.

mainframe Originally, the cabinet that housed the central processing unit (CPU) of a computer from the 1950s or -60s. The term now denotes the refrigerator-size computers of the 1970s, also called big iron.

mandala A geometric design symbolic of the universe and its powers, frequently seen in Hindu or Muslim art, but also seen in the designs of many cultures.

matrix From the Latin for womb, a matrix is an enclosure, grid or substance from which something originates or develops. In computer science, a matrix is a set of numbers arranged in a rectangular array on which mathematical operations can be performed. It has also been used to describe complex computer networks such as the internet.

meatspace A term used by hackers to describe the physical world we inhabit. Meatspace is the physical corollary to virtual reality or cyberspace in the digital world.

memex Short for "memory extender," memex was Vannevar Bush's original name for a hypertext precursor, which he invented in the 1930s. Through the use for "enhanced microfilm" or other devices, the user could navigate their way through a virtual library of different information.

metafora The basic formulation of creativity on the computer.

monad According to Gottfried Wilhelm von Leibnitz, monads are indivisible: the most elemental units of physical reality.

Morse code Created by Samuel Morse in 1867 to solve the particular limitations of communicating by telegraph: it is a codec which is well suited to transmission over telegraph wires. Morse code is a communication code composed of either short or long sounds, or short and long dashes.

Mosaic Developed by programmers at the National Center for Supercomputing Applications in 1993, Mosiac was the first web browser to have a multimedia graphical user interface (or front end) for the world wide web.

MP3 A digitally compressed audio file in an MPEG (Moving Pictures Experts Group) standard. Most often found on the Internet, MP3s can be downloaded via many different internet sites (e.g., Napster) and played on a variety of different devices from the personal computer to MP3 players.

MUD An abbreviation for Multi-User Dungeon, Multi-User Domain or Multi-User Dimension, MUDs are computer programs that allow a number of users to interact over the Internet in virtual-reality role-playing games.

multimedial Creative works utilizing more than one media.

Napster A file sharing program developed in the late 1990s that allowed users to freely share and download MP3 files via the internet. Enormously popular, Napster was eventually shut down by lawsuits from the music industry in an effort to curb what they saw as illegal copyright infringement protection.

network A system of interconnected computers or information channels that share information and data.

nucleotides The basic building blocks of nucleic acids, the key elements of DNA (deoxyribonucleic acid) and RNA (ribonucleic acid).

open source software A program in which the basic code is open and available to users. The ability to read the underlying programming code allows users to change, alter or customize the software to their needs. Linux is open source.

Open Text A concept of the Italian novelist and theoretician Umberto Eco, Open Text is the idea that any literary work is reliant upon the reader to form many of the necessary details. Eco's example is that of Moby Dick, wherein it is never stated that the sailors have two legs, yet this assumption is implicit in a reading of the text. In this sense, Eco sees literature as "parasitic," dependant on a greater body of work to give it meaning.

packet switching A technique of sending information where the message is broken into smaller packets, each of which pass through a store and forward network. The packets are re-assembled at their destination. This method of sending messages is slower than sending them as whole messages, though vastly more reliable: If one packet is lost, the sender can simply re-send that individual packet.

pagoda A multistoried building prominent in the Far East. Pagodas are memorials or shrines, and sometimes libraries.

pantonal Arnold Schoenberg's preferred term for atonal

phonemes The smallest phonetic unit within a language that can convey meaning

protocol The rules of standard procedure for regulating data transmission and operations between computers.

Renaissance Literally meaning "rebirth," the Renaissance was a period of intellectual and cultural growth in European history following the Middle Ages. It was the rebirth of culture spurred by an investigation of classical values. Characterized by a enormous flourishing of artistic production, scholarship and learning, the Renaissance saw the exploration and discovery of new continents, the revolutionary ideas of Copernican astronomy, the growth of commerce, and the invention of paper and printing. Central to the intellectual growth of the Renaissance was an intellectual movement known as Humanism. Initiated by men of letters, such as Dante and Petrarch, Humanism looked for the unity of truth in various philosophical schools and movements, stressed the struggle of creation and the efforts to master nature, and optimistically looked to the renewal of human dignity and wisdom. It was also during this time that artists, such as Giotto, Fra Angelico, Raphael, Leonardo da Vinci, Michelangelo and Titian and Masaccio, pushed forward traditional notions of visual representation to embrace linear perspective.

rhizome Many types of plants have rhizomes instead of roots. Rhizomes extend underground, then shoot out new rhizomes and form new plants when the root-like structure emerges from the ground. A group of ferns, for example, are connected through this network-like structure: They are in some ways the plant. French theorists Gilles Deleuze and Felix Guattari use the term to describe decentralized networks: one point in a rhizomatic network connects to many other points simultaneously.

satori Sudden enlightenment, from the Buddhist tradition.

Satyricon Written by Gaius Petronius (27–66 C.E.), Emperor Nero's advisor, in 61 C.E., Satyricon describes the encounters and journeys of two scholars in the Mediterranean. A comedic and satirical exploration of an Empire in decline, Petronius' work has often been described as the first European novel.

scientific method The empirical process of scientific investigation. The scientific method typically involves the observation of a phenomenon, the creation of a hypothesis regarding that observation, experimentation to prove or disprove that hypothesis and a final determination that supports or alters the original hypothesis.

spam Also known as UCE (unsolicited commercial email), a slang term used to describe unsolicited email sent via mass mailing lists from companies, newsgroups or individuals.

standardized time A key development in the Industrial Revolution, standardized time was introduced as railroads developed, to synchronize rail schedules. Time was distributed by wires laid alongside the rail lines. Standardized time became essential to synchronizing the vast network of commerce and transportation that came about in the Industrial revolution.

store and forward A technique of sending information from node to node in an information network. Each node stores the information until the next node is ready for it.

string theory A broad theory with variations within quantum mechanics, string theory proposes that elementary particles align in string line formations rather than discrete points. Whereas Einstein's theories have explained the physics of planetary motion and quantum mechanics have explained the physics of subatomic particles, we still lack a unified theory that would account for all phenomena. While still unrealized, string theory was developed as a means of creating such a unified theory.

syntax An agreed-upon way of arranging elements. In language, it is an aspect of grammar that deals with the ways in which words are arranged and grouped to form clauses and phrases. In programming it is the rules that govern how programmers must write their code.

talking head A term coined by theorist Marshal McLuhan, the "talking heads" are the newscasters who sit behind desks and read the news. McLuhan wrote that the "talking head" of modern evening news foretold the resurgence of the oral in what had been a predominantly visual Western tradition.

taxonomy The science of classification that indicates that there is an ordered system based on natural relationships between things.

telepresence The means by which a user can project their presence over a distance.

telnet An internet program that allows users to log onto remote computer systems.

The Matrix This 1999 film was greatly influenced by the science-fiction writings of Philip K. Dick and William Gibson, *The Matrix*'s bleak cyberpunk vision of the future grapples with the increasing role of technology in our lives and blurred lines between reality and virtual-reality.

tonic The key note of a musical composition.

Turing machine Created by English mathematician and logician, Alan M. Turing in 1936, the Turing Machine was created as a hypothetical computing device. His remarkable 1936 paper, "On Computable Numbers," laid the groundwork for modern computing.

UNIX An operating system developed at the Bell Telephone Laboratories, UNIX is an interactive time-sharing operating system invented in the late 1960s and became widespread in the early 1990s. It is used on most of the web servers and runs much of the animation software used in motion pictures.

Upanishads A Sanskrit term for "session." The Upanishads are one of the key holy books in Hinduism. Comprised of approximately 108 books, they comprise the key elements of later Indian philosophy (1000-60 B.C.E.). Largely concerned with the nature of reality, the Upanishads also deal with the nature of morality, eternal life and the transmigration of souls.

URL An abbreviation for Uniform Resource Locator, URL is the term for online address of a document. As a part of the world wide web, Tim Berners-Lee envisioned that any document on the web should have a unique address: a URL.

Universo theatro A concept introduced by Renaissance writer Samuel Quicheberg in 1565, a universo theatro was an all-embracing museum that would be a reflection of encyclopedic knowledge. The collection would be arranged to reflect the four cardinal points, those of the compass, the seasons, the elements and the ages of man.

virtual reality *See* VR.

virus A program which has similarities to a biological virus: it is composed of code (as a biological virus is composed of DNA), subverts the hosts' processes to create copies of itself, and then spreads to other hosts through a vector.

VR The use of computer simulation to creation a artificial, three-dimensional environment or other sensory experience. Through devices such as goggles, headsets, body suits or gloves, the viewer can immerse themselves in this environment. Beginning in the 1960s, virtual reality programs began as flight simulators and quickly were adopted by various branches of the United States government before they became more widely available in displays, games, biotechnology and architectural applications.

WWW A protocol for sharing hypertext files over a network (most often the internet) based on client and server software. A user uses client software (also called a browser) to access files stored on a server. The web, along with graphical browsers such as Mosiac, provided a new way to post and retrieve information.

Bibliography

Abse, Dannie. *Collected Poems:1948–1976*. London: Hutchinson, 1977.

Aicher, Otl. *Analogous and Digital*. Berlin: Ernst & Sohn, 1994.

Aiello, Rita, and John A. Sloboda. *Musical Perceptions*. New York: Oxford University Press, 1994.

Akutagawa, Ryunosuke. *In a Grove and Other Stories*. New York: Liverlight, 1999.

Alberti, Leon Battista. *On the Art of Building*. Cambridge: MIT Press, 1988.

Alexie, Sherman. "Crazy Horse Speaks." In Sherman Alexie and Elizabeth Woody, *Old Shirts and New Skins* (Native American, No. 9). American Indian Study Center, 1993.

Anderson, Laurie. *United States*. Warner Brothers, 1984.

Arnheim, Rudolf. *Art and Visual Perception*. Berkeley: University of California Press, 1983.

Attridge, Derek. *Poetic Rhythm: An Introduction*. Cambridge: Cambridge University Press, 1995.

Bachelard, Gaston. *The Poetics of Space*. Boston: Beacon Press, 1969.

Bailey, James. *After Thought: The Computer Challenge to Human Intelligence*. New York: Basic Books, 1996.

Baldwin, J. *Bucky Works: Buckminster Fuller's Ideas for Today*. New York: John Wiley, 1996.

Baldwin, James. *Collected Essays*. New York: Library of America, 1983.

Banks, Russell. *Hamilton Stark*. New York: Ballantine Books, 1986.

Baraka, Amiri. *Eulogies*. New York: Marsilio Publishers, 1996.

Barnett, Jo Ellen. *Time's Pendulum: From Sundials to Atomic Clocks—The Fascinating History of Timekeeping and How Our Discoveries Changed the World*. San Diego: Harvest, 1999.

Barrow, John D. *The Artful Universe*. New York: Oxford University Press, 1995.

Barthes, Roland. *Camera Lucida*. New York: Hill and Wang, 1981.

——. *Image-Music-Text*. New York: Hill and Wang, 1977

Barzan, Jacques. *The Culture We Deserve*. Hanover: Wesleyan University Press, 1989.

Bate, W. J., John M. Bullitt, and L. F. Powell, eds. *Works of Samuel Johnson*. New Haven: Yale, 1963.

Baudelaire, Charles. *Théophile Gautier*. Pantin: Le Castor Astral, 1923.

Baudrillard, Jean. *America*. London: Verso, 1988.

Benedikt, Michael. *Cyberspace: First Steps*. Cambridge: MIT Press, 1991.

Blake, William. *The Marriage of Heaven and Hell*. New York: Dover, 1994.

Bolter, Jay David. *Turing's Man: Western Culture in the Computer Age*. Chapel Hill: University of North Carolina Press, 1984.

——. *Writing Space: The Computer, Hypertext, and the History of Writing*. Hillsdale, NJ: Lawrence Erlbaum, 1991.

Borges, Jorge Luis. *Labyrinths: Selected Stories and Other Writings*. New York: New Directions, 1964.

——. *The Library of Babel*. Boston: David R. Godine, 2000.

Burroughs, William S. *The Electronic Revolution*. Munich: Bresche Publikationen, 1970.

Bush, Vannevar. *Endless Horizons: History, Philosophy, and Sociology of Science*. New York: Arno Press, 1975.

Butler, Octavia E. *Pattern-Master*. New York: Warner Books, 1976.

Calvino, Italo. *Six Memos for the Next Millennium*. New York: Vintage Books, 1988.

Campbell, Joseph. *Primitive Mythology: The Masks of God*. New York: Penguin, 1972.

——. *The Inner Reaches of Outer Space: Metaphor as Myth and as Religion*. New York: Harper Perennial, 1986.

Campbell-Kelly, Martin, and William Aspray. *Computer: A History of the Information Machine*. New York: Basic Books, 1996.

Carter, Rita. *Mapping the Mind*. Berkeley: University of California Press, 1998.

Chambers, Ephraim. *Cyclopedia*. London, 1728.

Chernoff, John Miller. *African Rhythm and African Sensibility: Aesthetics and Social Action in African Musical Idioms*. Chicago: University of Chicago Press, 1979.

Chomsky, Noam. *On Language*. New York: New Press, 1990.

Christoph, Henning, Klaus E. Muller, and Ute Ritz-Muller. *Soul of Africa: Magical Rites and Traditions*. Cologne, Germany: Konemann, 1999.

Chu-i, Po. "A Lute of Jade." In L. Cranmer-Byny, *Lute of Jude: Selections from the Classical Poets of China*. E-text at Project Gutenberg, http://promo.net/pg.

Cicero, Marcus Tullius. *Cicero: De re publica: Selections*. Cambridge: Cambridge University Press, 1995.

Conckelton, Sheryl. *Frederick Sommer: Selected Texts and Bibliographies*. New York: G.K. Hall and Company, 1995.

Confucius. *Analects*. New York: Penguin, 1998.

Cook, Francis. *Hua-yen Buddhism: The Jeweled Net of Indra*. University Park, PA: Penn State University Press, 1977.

Cowley, Malcolm, ed. *Writers at Work: The Paris Review Interviews: First Series*. New York: Viking Press, 1958.

Daston, Lorraine, and Katherine Park. *Wonders and the Order of Nature 1150–1750*. New York: Zone Books, 1998.

Davies, Char. Osmose. http://www.immersence.com.

De Bary, W. M. Theodore, ed. *Chuang Tzu: Basic Writings*. New York: Columbia University Press, 1964.

Derrida, Jacques. *Of Grammatology*. Johns Hopkins University Press, 1998.

Dewey, John. *Art as Experience*. New York: Perigree, 1980.

Diderot. *L'Encyclopedie*. Paris: Booking International, 1996.

Dondis, Donis A. *A Primer of Visual Literacy*. Cambridge: MIT Press, 1974.

Drewal, Henry John, and John Mason. *Beads Body and Soul: Art and Light in the Yoruba Universe*. Los Angeles: UCLA Fowler Museum of Natural History, 1998.

Drucker, Johanna. *The Alphabetic Labyrinth: The Letters in History and Imagination*. New York: Thames and Hudson, 1995.

DuBois, W. E. B. *The Souls of Black Folk*. New York: Viking, 1990.

Duncan, Carol. *Civilizing Rituals: Inside Public Art Museums*. London: Routledge, 1995.

Eco, Umberto. *The Nature of the Rose*. New York: Harvest Books, 1994.

Edgerton, Samuel Y. *The Heritage of Giotto's Geometry: Art and Science on the Eve of the Scientific Revolution*. Ithaca: Cornell University Press, 1991.

Eglash, Ron. *African Fractuals: Modern Computing and Indigenous Design*. New Brunswick: Rutgers University Press, 1999.

Eisenstadt, S. N. *Japanese Civilization: A Comparative View*. Chicago: University of Chicago Press, 1996.

Elkins, James. *The Domain of Images*. Ithaca: Cornell University Press, 1999.

Elliot, T. S. "Tradition and the Individual Talent." In T. S. Elliot, *The Sacred Wood: Essays on Poetry and Criticism*. London: Methune, 1920.

Ellison, Ralph. *Invisible Man*. New York: Vintage, 1995.

Embree, Ainslie T. *Sources of Indian Tradition*. New York: Columbia University Press, 1988.

Erikson, Erik. *Childhood and Society*. New York: W. W. Norton, 1950.

Euclid. *The Elements*. New York: Dover, 1956.

Fernando, Jr., S. H. *The New Beats: Exploring the Music, Culture, and Attitudes of Hip Hop*. New York: Anchor Books, 1994.

Feynman, Richard P. *Six Easy Pieces*. Cambridge: Perseus Books, 1995.

Focillon, Henri. *The Life of Forms in Art*. New York: Zone Books, 1989.

Fong, Wen C. *Beyond Representation: Chinese Painting and Calligraphy 8th–14th Century*. New York: Metropolitan Museum of Art, 1992.

Fong, Wen C., and James C. Y. Watt. *Possessing the Past*. New York: Metropolitan Museum of Art, 1996.

Forster, E. M. "The Story and the Plot," in *Aspects of the Novel*. London: Penguin, 1963.

Francastel, Pierre. *Art and Technology in the Nineteenth and Twentieth Centuries*. New York: Zone Books, 2000.

Freud, Sigmund. *The Interpretation of Dreams*. New York: Basic Books, 1965.

Friedman, William J. *About Time: Inventing the Fourth Dimension*. Publisher: MIT Press, 1990.

Fuller, R. Buckminster. *Nine Chains to the Moon*. Garden City, NY: Anchor Books, 1971.

——. *Operating Manual for Spaceship Earth*. Chicago: Southern Illinois University Press, 1978.

Fuller, R. Buckminster, Jerome Agel, and Quentin Fiore. *I Seem to Be a Verb*. New York: Bantam Books, 1970.

Gass, William. *A Philosophical Inquiry on Being Blue*. Jaffrey: Nonpareil Books, 1991.

Gates, Jr., Henry Louis. *The Signifying Monkey: A Theory of African-American Literary Criticism*. Oxford: Oxford University Press, 1989.

Gershenfeld, Neil. *When Things Start to Think*. New York: Henry Holt, 1999.

Gibson, William. *Neuromancer*. New York: Ace Books, 1984.

Giedion, Siegfried. *Mechanization Takes Command: A Contribution to Anonymous History*. New York: Oxford University Press, 1948.

——. *Space, Time and Architecture: The Growth of a New Tradition*. Cambridge: Harvard University Press, 1982.

Gifford, Don. *The Farther Shore: A Natural History of Perception, 1798–1984.* New York: Vintage Books, 1991.

Gill, Eric. *An Essay on Typography.* Boston: David R. Godine, 1930.

Goethe, Johann Wolfgang Von. *Theory of Colours.* Cambridge: MIT Press, 1970.

Goldberg, Rose Lee. *Performance Art: From Futurism to the Present.* New York: Harry N. Abrams, 1988.

Grandin, Temple. *Thinking in Pictures and Other Reports from My Life with Autism.* New York: Vintage Books, 1995.

Greene, Brian. *The Elegant Universe: Superstrings, Hidden Dimensions, and the Quest for the Ultimate Theory.* New York: W. W. Norton, 1999.

Grimm, Brothers. *Kinder und Hausmarchen.* 1812.

Guedj, Denis. *Numbers: The Universal Language.* New York: Harry N. Abrams, 1996.

Hafner, Katie, and Matthew Lyon. *Where Wizards Stay Up Late: The Origins of the Internet.* New York: Touchstone, 1996.

Hall, Edward T. *The Hidden Dimension.* Garden City, NY: Anchor Books, 1969.

Haraway, Donna J. *Simians, Cyborgs, and Women: The Reinvention of Nature.* New York: Routledge, 1991.

Harrison, John. *Synaesthesia—The Strangest Thing.* Oxford: Oxford University Press, 2001.

Havelock, Eric A. *Preface to Plato.* Cambridge: Harvard University Press, 1963.

——. *The Literate Revolution in Greece.*

Hayakawa, S. I. *Symbol, Status, and Personality.* New York: Harcourt, Brace & World, 1953.

Heidegger, Martin. *The Question Concerning Technology and Other Essays.* New York: Harper Torchbooks, 1977.

Heims, Steve Joshua. *The Cybernetics Group.* Cambridge: MIT Press, 1991.

Heller, Steven. *The Education of an E-Designer.* New York: Allworth Press/School of Visual Arts, 2001.

Herz, J. C. *Joystick Nation: How Videogames Ate Our Quarters, Won Our Hearts, and Rewired Our Minds.* Boston: Little, Brown, 1997.

Hitler, Adolf. *Mein Kampf.*

Hoffman, Donald D. *Visual Intelligence: How We Create What We See.* New York: W. W. Norton, 1998.

Hooks, Bel. *Outlaw Culture.* New York: Routledge, 1994.

Houis, Jacques, Paola Mieli, and Mark Stafford. *Being Human: The Technological Extensions of the Body.* New York: Agincourt/Marsilio, 1999.

Huggins, Nathan Irvin. *Voices from the Harlem Renaissance.* New York: Oxford University Press, 1995.

Hugo, Victor. *Les Misérables.*

Hurston, Zora Neale. *Every Tongue Got to Confess: Negro Folk Tales from the Gulf States.* New York: HarperCollins, 2001.

——. *Moses, Man of the Mountain.* New York: Harper Collins, 1993.

Illingworth, Valerie. *Dictionary of Computing.* Oxford: Oxford University Press, 1990.

Innis, Harold A. *The Bias of Communication.* Toronto: University of Toronto Press, 1951.

Itten, Johannes. *The Elements of Color.* New York: John Wiley, 1970.

Jean, Georges. *Writing: The Story of Alphabets and Scripts.* New York: Harry N. Abrams, 1987.

Signs, Symbols, and Ciphers. New York: Harry N. Abrams, 1998.

Johnson, Steven. *Interface Culture: How New Technology Transforms the Way We Create and Communicate.* New York: Basic Books, 1997.

Jones, Caroline A., and Peter Galison. *Picturing Science, Producing Art.* New York: Routledge, 1998.

Joyce, James. *Ulysses.* New York: Modern Library, 1961.

——. *The Portrait of the Artist as a Young Man.* New York: Penguin, 1993.

Jung, Carl. *Archetypes of the Collective Unconscious.* Collected Works ed., vol. 9. New York: William McGuire, 1959.

——. *Man and His Symbols.* New York: Dell, 1964.

Juster, Norton. *The Dot and the Line: A Romance in Lower Mathematics.* New York: Random House, 1963.

Kalidasa. *Shakuntala Recognized: A Sanskrit Play.* Universe.com, 2000.

Keats, John. *Complete Poems and Selected Letters of John Keats.* New York: Random House, 2001.

Kelly, Kevin. *Out of Control: The New Biology of Machines, Social Systems, and the Economic World.* Reading, MA: Addison-Wesley, 1994.

Kemeny, John G. *Man and the Computer.* New York: Charles Scribner's Sons, 1972.

Kenseth, Joy. *The Age of the Marvelous.* Hanover, NH: Hood Museum of Art, Dartmouth College, 1991.

Kern, Stephen. *The Culture of Time and Space, 1880–1918.* Cambridge: Harvard University Press, 1983.

Kerouac, Jack. *On the Road.*

Kesey, Ken. *One Flew Over the Cuckoo's Nest.*

Kittler, Friedrich A. *Gramophone, Film, Typewriter.* Stanford: Stanford University Press, 1999.

Knobler, Nathan. *The Visual Dialogue: An Introduction to the Appreciation of Art.* New York: Holt, Rinehart and Winston, 1969.

Kuhn, Thomas S. *The Structure of Scientific Revolutions.* Chicago: University of Chicago Press, 1962.

Kurzwell, Ray. *The Age of Spiritual Machines*. New York: Viking, 1999.

Laing, R. D. *The Politics of Experience*. New York: Pantheon Books, 1967.

Landow, George P. *Hyper/Text/Theory*. Baltimore: Johns Hopkins University Press, 1994.

Langer, Susanne K., ed. *Reflections on Art*. Baltimore: Johns Hopkins Press, 1959.

——. *Feeling and Form*. New York: MacMillan Publishing Co, 1977.

——. *Problems in Art*. New York: MacMillan College Division, 1977.

——. *Philosophy in a New Key: A Study in the Symbolism of Reason, Rite and Art*. Cambridge: Harvard University Press, 1957.

Lapman, Lewis H. *Understanding Media: The Extension of Man*. Cambridge: MIT Press, 1994.

Laramee, Eve Andree. *A Permutational Unfolding*. Cambridge: MIT List Visual Arts Center, 1999.

Laurel, Brenda. *The Art of Human–Computer Interface Design*. New York: Addison- Wesley, 1990.

Leary, Timothy. "The Cyberpunk: The Individual as Reality Pilot." Essay in Larry M. McCaffrey, *Storming the Reality Studio*.

Leonard, Andrew. *Bots: The Origin of New Species*. New York: Penguin, 1997.

Levy, Steven. *Hackers: Heroes of the Computer Revolution*. New York: Delta Books, 1984.

——. *Artificial Life: A Report from the Frontier Where Computers Meet Biology*. New York: Vintage Books, 1993.

——. *Insanely Great: The Life and Times of Macintosh, the Computer That Changed Everything*. New York: Penguin Books, 1994.

Lewis, Bernard. *The World of Islam: Faith, People, Culture*. London: Thames and Hudson, 1976.

Locke, John. *An Essay Concerning Human Understanding*. London: Clarendon Press, 1975.

Lovejoy, Margot. *Postmodern Currents: Art and Artists in the Age of Electronic Media*. Upper Saddle River, NJ: Prentice Hall, 1992.

Ludlow, Peter. *High Noon on the Electric Frontier: Conceptual Issues in Cyberspace*. Cambridge: MIT Press, 1996.

Ludwig, Mark. *The Giant Black Book of Computer Viruses*. Show Low, AZ: American Eagle Publications, 1998.

Machlis, Joseph. *The Enjoyment of Music*. New York: W. W. Norton, 1970.

Maleuvre, Didier. *Museum Memories: History, Technology, Art*. Stanford, CA: Stanford University Press, 1999.

Manovich, Lev. *The Language of New Media*. Cambridge: MIT Press, 2001.

Manuel, Peter. *Caribbean Currents; Caribbean Music from Rumba to Reggae*. Philadelphia: Temple University Press, 1995.

Marinetti, F. T. "The Futurist Manifesto." In Kristine Stiles and Peter Howard Selz, eds., *Theories and Documents of Contemporary Art: A Sourcebook of Artists' Writings*. Berkeley: University of California Press, 1996.

Martinich, A. P. *The Philosophy of Language*. New York: Oxford University Press, 1990.

May, Rollo. *The Courage to Create*. New York: W.W. Norton, 1975.

McCafferey, Larry, ed. *Storming the Reality Studio: A Casebook of Cyberpunk Fiction*. Durham, NC: Duke University Press, 1991.

McCloud, Scott. *Understanding Comics: The Invisible Art*. New York: HarperCollins, 1993.

McCullough, David. *The Great Bridge: The Epic Story of the Building of the Brooklyn Bridge*. New York: Touchstone, 1982.

McLuhan, Marshall. *The Gutenberg Galaxy: The Making of Typographic Man*. Toronto: University of Toronto Press, 1962.

McLuhan, Marshall. *Understanding Media: The Extensions of Man*. Cambridge: MIT Press, 1994.

—— and Quentin Fiore. *The Medium Is the Massage*. New York: Bantam Books, 1967.

McQuillan, Martin. *The Narrative Reader*. London: Routledge, 2000.

Miller, Arthur I. *Insights of Genius: Imagery and Creativity in Science and Art*. Cambridge: MIT Press, 2000.

Minsky, Marvin. *The Society of the Mind*. New York: Touchstone, 1985.

Mirzoeff, Nicholas, ed. *The Visual Culture Reader*. London: Routledge, 1998.

Mitchell, W. J. T. *On Narrative*. Chicago: University of Chicago Press, 1981.

——. *Iconology: Image, Text, Ideology*. Chicago: University of Chicago Press, 1986.

——. *Picture Theory*. Chicago: University of Chicago Press, 1994.

Moholy-Nagy, Laszlo. *Painting, Photography, Film*. Boston: MIT Press, 1987.

Mook, Delo E., and Thomas Vargish. *Inside Relativity*. Princeton, NJ: Princeton University Press, 1987.

Morris, Desmond. *Manwatching: A Field Guide to Human Behavior*. New York: Harry N. Abrams, 1977.

Morrison, Toni editor. James Baldwin, *Collected Essays*. NY: Library of America, 1998.

Mumford, Lewis. *Technics and Civilization*. San Diego: Harvest, 1963.

——. *Art and Technics*. New York: Columbia University Press, 2000.

Murray, Janet H. *Hamlet on the Holodeck: The Future of Narrative in Cyberspace*. Cambridge: MIT Press, 1997.

Nabokov, Vladimir. *Speak Memory*. New York: Everyman's Library, 1999.

Narazaki, Muneshige. *Masterworks of Hiroshige: The 53 Stations of the Tokaido*. Tokyo: Kodansha International, 1969.

Newton, Sir Isaac. *Opticks*. New York: Dover, 1952.

Norman, Donald A. *Things That Make Us Smart: Defending Human Attributes in the Age of the Machine*. Reading, MA: Addison-Wesley, 1993.

Olmert, Michael. *Milton's Teeth and Ovid's Umbrella*. New York: Touchstone, 1996.

Orvell, Miles. *After the Machine: Visual Arts and the Erasing of Cultural Boundaries*. Jackson: University Press of Mississippi, 1995.

Packer, Randall, and Ken Jordan. *Multimedia: From Wagner to Virtual Reality*. New York: W. W. Norton, 2001.

Panofsky, Erwin. *Perspective as Symbolic Form*. New York: Zone Books, 1997.

Peirce, Charles S., and Philip P. Weiner. *Charles S. Peirce: Selected Writings*. New York: Dover, 1990.

Petronius. *Satyricon*. Oxford: Oxford University Press, 1999.

Pinker, Steven. *How the Mind Works*. London: W. W. Norton, 1999.

Pirsig, Robert. *Zen and the Art of Motorcycle Maintenance: An Inquiry into Values*. New York: William Morrow & Co, 1974.

Plant, Sadie. *Zeros + Ones: Digital Women + The New Technology*. New York: Doubleday, 1997.

Plato. *Phaedrus*. In John M. Cooper, ed. *Plato, Complete Works*. Indianapolis: Hackett Publishing, 1997.

Poole, Steven. *Trigger Happy: Videogames and the Entertainment Revolution*. New York: Arcade Publishing, 2000.

Popper, Frank. *Art of the Electronic Age*. London: Thames and Hudson, 1993.

Provenzo, Eugene F. *Video Kids: Making Sense of Nintendo*. Cambridge: Harvard University Press, 1991.

Rasmussen, Steen Eiler. *Experiencing Architecture*. Cambridge: MIT Press, 1959.

Raymond, Eric S. *The New Hacker's Dictionary*. Cambridge: MIT Press, 1999.

Rhodes, Rochard. *Visions of Technology*. New York: Simon & Schuster, 1999.

Riemschneider, Burkhard, and Uta Grosnick. *Art at the Turn of the Millennium*. Koln: Taschen, 1999.

Robinson, Andrew. *The Story of Writing: Alphabets, Hieroglyphs and Pictograms*. London: Thames and Hudson, 1995.

Ronell, Avital. *The Telephone Book*. Lincoln: University of Nebraska Press, 1991.

Rose, Tricia. *Black Noise: Rap Music and Black Culture in Contemporary America*. Hanover, NH: Wesleyan University Press, 1994.

Rosen, Jonathan. *The Talmud and the Internet: A Journey between Worlds*. New York: Farrar, Straus and Giroux, 2000.

Rothstein, Edward. *Emblems of Mind: The Inner Life of Music and Mathematics*. New York: Avon Books, 1995.

Rower, Alexander S. C. *Calder Sculpture*. New York: Universe, 1998.

Rowland, Wade. *Spirit of the Web: The Age of Information from Telegraph to Internet*. Toronto: Somerville House, 1997.

Sachs, Oliver W. *The Man Who Mistook His Wife for a Hat and Other Clinical Tales*. New York: Touchstone Books, 1998.

Sagan, Carl. *Cosmos*. New York: Random House, 1980.

Salinger, J. D. *The Catcher in the Rye*. Boston: Little, Brown, 1951.

Sarup, Madan. *An Introductory Guide to Post-Structuralism and Postmodernism*. Athens: University of Georgia Press, 1989.

Schall, Jan. *Tempus Fugit: Time Flies*. Kansas City: The Nelson–Atkins Museum of Art, 2000.

Schoenberg, Arnold, and E. Stein. *Arnold Schoenberg:Letters*. New York: St Martin's, 1965.

Schopenhauer, Arthur. *The World as Will and Idea(1819)*. New York: AMS Press, 1977.

Scott, Geoffrey. *The Architecture of Humanism: A Study in the History of Taste*. New York: W. W. Norton, 1974.

Sebeok, Thomas, ed. *Style in Language.*. Cambridge: MIT Press, 1960.

Sexton, Anne. "The Wonderful Musician." In Anne Sexton, *The Complete Poems*. New York: Mariner Books, 1999.

Shakespeare, William. *All's Well That Ends Well*. In David Bevington, ed. *The Complete Works of William Shakespeare*. Boston: Addison-Wesley, 1997.

Shelley, Percy Bysshe. "Ozymandias." In *The Complete Works of Keats and Shelley*. New York: Random House, 1978.

Shlain, Leonard. *Art and Physics: Parallel Visions in Space, Time and Light*. New York: Quill William Morrow, 1991.

Silverman, Hugh J. *Postmodernism–Philosophy and the Arts*. New York: Routledge, 1990.

Slusser, George, and Tom Shippey. *Fiction 2000: Cyberpunk and the Future of Narrative*. Athens, GA: University of Georgia Press, 1992.

Small, Christopher. *Musicking: The Meaning of Performing and Listening*. Hanover, NH: Wesleyan University Press, 1998.

Smith, Anna Deavere. Fires in the Mirror. Crown Heights, Brooklyn and Other Identities. New York: Anchor Books, 1993.

Smith, Henry D., and Amy G. Poster. *One Hundred Famous Views of Edo*. New York: George Braziller, 1986.

Sommer, Frederick. *Selected Texts*. New York: McMillan Library Reference, 1995.

Stafford, Barbara Maria. *Good Looking: Essays on the Virtue of Images*. Cambridge: MIT Press, 1996.

Stephenson, Neal. *In the Beginning Was the Command Line*. New York: Avon Books, 1999.

Stokstad, Marilyn. *Art History*. 2 vols. New York: Prentice Hall and Harry N. Abrams, 1995.

Stolzenberg, Daniel. *The Great Art of Knowing: The Baroque Encyclopedia of Athanasius Kircher*. Stanford: Stanford University Press, 2001.

Strunk, William, and E. B. White. *The Elements of Style*. New York: Macmillan, 1979.

Taylor, Joshua C. *Learning to Look: A Handbook for the Visual Arts*. Chicago: Univerity of Chicago Press, 1981.

Thompson, D'arcy. *On Growth and Form*. London: Cambridge University Press, 1961.

Thoreau, Henry David. *Walden*. Boston: Beacon Press, 1998.

Tolstoy, Leo. *What Is Art?* New York: Penguin, 1996.

Tomkins, Calvin. *Off the Wall: Robert Rauschenberg and the Art World of Our Time*. New York: Viking, 1981.

Toole, Betty Alexandra. *Ada: The Enchantress of Numbers, Prophet of the Computer Age*. Mill Valley, CA: Strawberry Press, 1992.

Toop, David. *Rap Attack 2: African Rap to Global Hip Hop*. London: Serpent's Tail, 1991.

Tse, Lao. *Tao Té Ching*. New York: Knopf, 1994.

Traub, Charles H., and Jonathan Lipkin. "If We Are Digital." *Leonardo 31* (1998).

Tufte, Edward R. *Envisioning Information*. Cheshire: Graphics Press, 1990.

Turkle, Sherry. *Life on the Screen: Identity in the Age of the Internet*. New York: Simon & Schuster, 1995.

Turner, A. Richard. *Inventing Leonardo*. Berkeley: University of California Press, 1992.

Turner, Howard R. *Science in Medieval Islam: An Illustrated Introduction*. Austin: University of Texas Press, 1997.

Tzu, Chaung. *Collected Works*.

——. *Basic Writings*. New York: Columbia University Press, 1974.

van der Rol, Ruud, and Rian Verhoeven. *Anne Frank: Beyond the Diary*. New York: Penguin, 1993.

Vasari, Giorgio. *Lives of the Painters, Sculptors, and Architects*, Everyman's Library. New York: Alfred A Knopf, 1996.

Venturri, Robert. *Iconography and Electronics upon a Generic Architecture*. Cambridge: MIT, 1996.

Venturri, Robert, Denise Scott Brown, and Steven Izenour. *Learning from Las Vegas*. Cambridge: MIT Press, 1977.

Virilio, Paul: *The Vision Machine*. London: British Film Institute, 1994.

Vonnegut, Kurt. *Wampeters, Foma, & Ganfalloons*. New York: Delta, 1999.

Wallis, Brian, ed. *Art after Modernism*. New York: New Museum of Contemporary Art, 1984.

Watson, Burton, ed. *Complete Works of Chuang Tzu*. New York: Columbia University Press, 1968.

Watt, Ian. *The Rise of the Novel: Studies in Defoe, Richardson and Fielding*. Berkeley: University of California Press, 1957.

Wells, H. G. *World Brain*. New York: Doubleday, 1938.

Weschler, Lawrence. *Mr. Wilson's Cabinet of Wonder*. New York: Vintage Books, 1995.

Whitkin, Robert. *Adorno on Music*. New York: Routledge, 1998.

Whitman, Walt. *Leaves of Grass*.

Whitrow, G. J. *Time in History: Views of Time from Prehistory to the Present Day*. Oxford: Oxford University Press, 1988.

Wideman, John Edgar. *Brothers and Keepers*. Houston: Texas Bookman, 1996.

Wiener, Norbert. *The Human Use of Human Beings*. New York: Da Capo Press, 1954.

Wilson, Edward O. *Consilience: The Unity of Knowledge*. New York: Vintage Books, 1999.

Wolfflin, Heinrich. *From Principles of Art History*. New York: Dover Publications, 1950.

Yuan, Kuo Li Ku Po Wu, Wen C. Fong, and James C. Watt, comps. *Possessing the Past: Treasures from the National Palace Museum, Taipei*. New York: Abrams, 1999.

Zettl, Herbert. *Sight, Sound, Motion: Applied Media Aesthetics*. Belmont, CA: Wadsworth, 1990.

Image Credits

Chapter One: Foundations

1 Courtesy of Stelarc. *2* Library of Congress. *3* Courtesy of Intel Corporation. *4 (top)* Courtesy of Intel Corporation. *4 (middle)* Private Collection. *4 (bottom)* NASA/GSFC/METI/ERSDAC/JAROS, and U.S./Japan ASTER Science Team. *5* Collection of the authors. *6* Collection of the authors. *7* Paul Baran, "On Distributed Communications: Summary Overview," RAND/RM-3767-PR, Santa Monica, CA: RAND, 1964. © RAND 1964. Reprinted by permission. *8* Courtesy of Intel Corporation. *9* Powerbook X-ray by Jason Diefenbacher. *10* Charles Traub. *11* Library of Congress. *12* Photo © 2001 Mary Ann Carter, courtesy of James Irsay. *13* Library of Congress. *14-15* NASA/GSFC/METI/ERSDAC/JAROS, and U.S./Japan ASTER Science Team. *16* The Academy of Natural Sciences of Philadelphia, Ewell Sale Stewart Library. *17* Private Collection. *18* NCSA Media Technology Resources. *19* Collection of the authors. *20 (left)* Collection of the authors. *20 (right)* Collection of the authors. *21 (top)* Jonathan Lipkin. *21 (bottom)* Collection of the authors. *22* Jonathan Lipkin. *23* Reprinted from Samuel Y. Edgerton, Jr., *The Heritage of Giotto's Geometry: Art and Science on the Eve of the Scientific Revolution.* © 1991 Cornell University. Used by permission of the publisher, Cornell University Press. *24* Garden of L, © Premyslaw Prusinkiewicz. *25* Courtesy of Infogrames Interactive, Inc. *26 (left)* Thierry Hubin, Museum of Natural Sciences, Brussels. (right) Library of Congress. *27* Courtesy of IBM Corporation. *28* Collection of the authors. *29* (left) Suellen Parker. (right) Suellen Parker. *30* New Hacker's Dictionary. *31 (left and right)* Collection of the authors. *32 (top)* Courtesy of Greg Meluson. *32 (bottom)* Library of Congress. *33* Suellen Parker. *34* Courtesy of Keith Winstein and Marc Horowitz. *35 (top)* IBM Corporation. *35 (middle)* IBM Corporate Archives. *35 (bottom)* Collection of the authors. *36 (top)* Collection of the authors. *36 (middle)* IBM Corporation. *36 (bottom)* IBM Corporation. *37 (top)* Getty Images Inc., Hulton Archive Photos. *37 (bottom)* Library of Congress. *38 (all)* Jonathan Lipkin. *39 (from top)* Courtesy of the Musical Museum, London; CA; Paul Klee Stiftung, Kunstmuseum, Bern; Institute of Radio Engineers and Russell Kirsch, © 1958 IEEE; NASA. *40-41* Jonathan Lipkin. *42 (left)* NASA Goddard Laboratory for Atmospheres. *42 (right)* Image generated by the molecular graphics program RasMol. *44* Collection of the authors. *45* Registered trademarks of the Jelly Belly Candy Company. Used with permission of the Jelly Belly Candy Company. *46-47* From "Panspermia," animation by Karl Sims. *48* PhotoBank, Inc. *49 (left)* Courtesy of Stelarc. *49 (right)* Library of Congress. *50 (top)* Ministere de la Culture et des Communications. (bottom) Library of Congress. *51* Library of Congress. *52 (top)* Library of Congress. *52 (bottom)* Government of India. *53* Private Collection. *54* Charles Traub. *56* Charles Traub. *57* Charles Traub. *58* MRI. Courtesy of David A. Silbersweig, Cornell University. *59* Jonathan Lipkin. *60-61* Jonathan Lipkin. *62* Collection of the authors. *64* Library of Congress. *65* Jonathan Lipkin. *66* Fitch-Febvrel Gallery, New York. *67 (left)* Library of Congress. *67 (right, top)* Jonathan Lipkin. (right, bottom) Monticello/Thomas Jefferson Foundation, Inc. *68* Fitch-Febvrel Gallery, New York. *70* Art Resource, New York. *71* Reproduced by permission of The Huntington Library, San Marino, California. *72* Jonathan Lipkin. *73 (top)* Jonathan Lipkin. *73 (middle)* Jonathan Lipkin. *73 (bottom)* National Palace Museum, Taipei, Taiwan. *74* Charles Traub. *75* Pennsylvania Academy of the Fine Arts. *76 (left)* Jonathan Lipkin. *76 (right)* Courtesy of eBay.com. *77* Charles Traub. *78* Austrian National Tourist Office. *79* Library of Congress. *80-81* Garden of L, ©

Premyslaw Prusinkiewicz *83 (both)* Collection of the authors. *87 (top)* Library of Congress. *87 (bottom)* Collection of the authors. *102* Collection of the authors.

Chapter Two: Metafora

107 Library of Congress. *108 (all)* Jonathan Lipkin. *109* Charles Traub. *111* Jonathan Lipkin. *112* Collection of the authors. *113 (top)* Jonathan Lipkin. *113 (bottom)* Courtesy of Apple Computer, Inc. *114 (top)* United Media/United Feature Syndicate, Inc. *114 (bottom)* James Seawright. *115 (top)* Costune, Kazushi Nishimoto. *115 (bottom)* © Tomas Egger. *116-117* Charles Traub. *118-119* Library of Congress. *120-121* Shelly Eshkar and Paul Kaiser. *122* Library of Congress. *123 (top)* Jonathan Lipkin. *123 (bottom)* Getty Images Inc., Hulton Archive Photos. *124 (top)* David Soldier and Richard Lair. *(bottom)* Suellen Parker. *125 (top)* Collection of the authors. *125 (bottom)* Elizabeth Police Department. *126* Jonathan Lipkin. *127-128* Charles Traub. *129 (both)* Suellen Parker. *130* Library of Congress. *131 (left)* J. Stieler, 1819. *131 (right)* Jonathan Lipkin. *134* Philadelphia Museum of Art. *135* Microsoft Corporation. *136* Jonathan Lipkin. *137* Jonathan Lipkin. *138 (top)* Ananova.com. *138 (bottom)* United Nations. *140 (left)* Collection of the authors. *140 (right)* Jonathan Lipkin. *141* Netscape, Inc. *142* Corel Gallery 2. *146* Reproduced by permission of The Huntington Library, San Marino, California. *148* Art Resource/Museum of Modern Art. *149* Charles Traub. *150* "Life," by Decio Pignatari, adapted by Eugene Wildman. *152 (top)* Jonathan Lipkin. *152 (bottom)* Jonathan Lipkin. *153* Charles Traub. *155 (all)* Courtesy of Apple Computer, Inc. *156* Private collection. *157 (top)* Private Collection. *157 (bottom)* Collection of the authors. *160* Library of Congress. *162* Library of Congress. *163* Library of Congress. *164* Collection of the authors. *165 (all)* Collection of the authors. *167 (top)* Private Collection. *167 (bottom)* Jonathan Lipkin. *168* © Mundaneum, © Vincent Algain. *169* Ted Nelson, *Computer Lib/Dream Machines.* *170* Dan Bricklin and Bon Frankston. *171* From Jeffrey Shaw's work, Legible City. *173 (both)* Jonathan Lipkin. *174 (top)* Jonathan Lipkin. *174 (bottom)* The British Museum Great Court Ltd. *175* Library of Congress. *176-177 (top left to right):* 1. Library of Congress, 2. Library of Congress, 3. Collection of the authors, 4. Library of Congress; *(bottom left to right):* 1. Library of Congress, 2. Collection of the authors, 3. Courtesy of Intel Corp., 4. Collection of the authors.

Chapter Three: Dialog

179 Private Collection. *180* Charles Traub. *182* Charles Traub. *184* Jonathan Lipkin. *185 (top)* Suellen Parker. *185 (bottom)* Kindly provided by Dr, Amarjit Chahal, Vita-Tech Canada Inc., www.vita-tech.com. *186* Collection of the authors. *187 (left)* Jonathan Lipkin. *187 (right, top)* Library of Congress. *187 (right, bottom)* Collection of the authors. *188 (left, top)* Jonathan Lipkin. *188 (left, middle)* Courtesy of Peter Whitney. *188 (left, bottom)* Jonathan Lipkin. *188 (right)* Courtesy of Alex Kasprzyk. *189* Collection of the authors. *190* Charles Traub. *191 (left)* Library of Congress. *191 (right)* Charles Traub. *192* Jonathan Lipkin. *193 (both)* Library of Congress. *194-195* Charles Traub. *196* Charles Traub. *197* Computer History Museum. *198 (top)* Jonathan Lipkin. *198 (bottom)* Courtesy of Stelarc. *200 (top)* Collection of the authors. *200 (bottom)* Apple Computer. *201* Jonathan Lipkin. *202* Collection of the authors. *203* Collection of the authors. *204* Suellen Parker. *205 (top)* Courtesy of Ben Hammersley. *205 (bottom)* Courtesy of Matt Jones, http://www.black-beltjones.com. *206-207* Library of Congress. *208 (both)* Library of Congress. *209 (left)* Charles Traub. *209 (right)* Library of Congress. *210 (left)* Larry E. McKinney *210 (right)* Library of Congress. *211* Collection of the authors. *212* Library of Congress. *213* Private Collection. *214 (top)* Library of Congress. *214 (bottom)* Library of Congress. *216* Library of Congress. *217 (top)* Charles Traub. *217 (bottom)* Collection of the authors. *219* Courtesy of Hormel Foods Corporation. *220 (top)* Collection of the authors. *220 (bottom, left)* Rare Book, Manuscript, and Special Collections Library, Duke University. *220 (bottom, right)* Jonathan Lipkin. *221* Courtesy of Peter Chelkowski and Hamid Dabashi. *223 (both)* Charles Traub. *224 (top)* Charles Traub. *224 (bottom)* Jonathan Lipkin. *225* Jonathan Lipkin. *227* Charles Traub. *230* Library of Congress. *231* Jonathan Lipkin. *233 (left, top)*

Charles Traub. *233 (left, bottom)* Collection of the authors. *233 (right)* Library of Congress. *234* Jonathan Lipkin. *235* Courtesy of Briana Hussey. *236 (all)* Ellen Whitney. *237* Aaron Siskind Foundation. *238* Collection of the authors. *240* Courtesy of Ubi Soft Entertainment. *243* Collection of the authors. *244* Private Collection. *245 (top)* Library of Congress. *245 (bottom)* Charles Traub. *247* Collection of the authors. *248-249* Images courtesy of the New York Stock Exchange/SIAC/Asymptote. *251* Collection of the authors. *253* Jonathan Lipkin.

Chapter Four: Elements of Structure

257 Jonathan Lipkin. *258* Jonathan Lipkin. *261 (top)* Collection of the authors. *261 (bottom)* Library of Congress. *265* John F. Simon Jr., courtesy of Sandra Gering Gallery. *266* Library of Congress. *267* Collection of the authors. *268* Library of Congress. *269* NASA. *270* Courtesy of Char Davies. *271* "Tree Pond" digital frame captured in real-time through HMD (head-mounted display) during live performance of immersive virtual environment Osmose (1995). Courtesy of Char Davies. *272* Jonathan Lipkin. *273* Courtesy of Asymptote. *274* Jeff Weiss/Laurence Miller Gallery. *278* Collection of the authors. *280* Hansjorg Meyer. *281 (top)* Charles Traub. *281 (bottom)* Jeff Mermelstein. *282* Collection of the authors. *284* Charles Traub. *285* Screen shot reprinted by permission from Apple Computer, Inc. *286* Steinway & Sons. *288* Ellen Whitney. *289 (all)* Private Collection. *290 (left)* Charles Traub. *290 (right)* Jonathan Lipkin. *291 (left)* Charles Traub. *291 (right)* Jonathan Lipkin. *292 (top)* Collection of the authors. *292 (bottom)* Charles Traub. *293* Jonathan Lipkin. *294* Library of Congress. *295* Private Collection. *296 (top)* Bodleian Library. *296 (bottom)* Suellen Parker. *297 (top)* Suellen Parker. *297 (bottom)* Jonathan Lipkin. *298 (both)* Andy Keane, Evolved Beam. *299* Charles Traub. *300* Gehry Partners, LLP. *301* Jonathan Lipkin. *303* Apple Computer. *304* Jonathan Lipkin. *305* Collection of the authors. *306* John F. Simon Jr., courtesy of Sandra Gering Gallery. *307* Jonathan Lipkin. *308* Collection of the authors. *311* Jonathan Lipkin. *312* Suellen Parker. *313* Jonathan Lipkin. *318* Collection of the authors. *319* John F. Simon Jr., courtesy of Sandra Gering Gallery. *320 (top)* Private Collection. *320 (bottom)* Jonathan Lipkin. *321* Charles Traub. *322 (top and middle)* © Stephen Wolfram, LLC *322 (bottom)* Jonathan Lipkin. *323* British Information Services. *325* Library of Congress. *326* **[??]** *328* Charles Traub. *329* John Conway, The Game of Life. *330 (top)* Jonathan Lipkin. *330 (bottom)* Suellen Parker. *331* Collection of the authors. *332* Jonathan Lipkin. *333 (both)* Jonathan Lipkin. *334* Jonathan Lipkin. *336* Henry Urbach Architecture. *337* © Jon Haddock, courtesy of Howard House, Seattle. *338* Suellen Parker. *340* Jonathan Lipkin. *341 (left, top)* Jonathan Lipkin. *341 (left, bottom)* Collection of the authors. *341 (right)* Jonathan Lipkin. *344* Jonathan Lipkin. *345* Charles Traub. *347* Jonathan Lipkin. *348* Private Collection. *349 (both)* Jonathan Lipkin. *351* Library of Congress. *353* Collection of the authors. *358* Collection of the authors. *359* Collection of the authors.

Chapter Five: Past, Present, Future

363 Library of Congress. *365* Library of Congress. *366 (top)* Charles Traub. *366 (middle)* Reading Museum Service (Reading Borough Council). All rights reserved. *366 (bottom)* The Maryland Historical Society, Baltimore, MD. *368 (top)* Courtesy of the North Carolina Office of Archives and Records, Division of Historical Resources, Raleigh, NC. (bottom) Library of Congress. *369 (top)* Library of Congress. (bottom) Collection of the authors. *371* Library of Congress. *372 (top)* © Grameen Bank and Grameen Foundation USA. (bottom) © 1989, 2002 by the Guerrilla Girls. *374* Rolfe Horn, courtesy of The Long Now Foundation. *376* Private Collection. *381* Kenneth Snelson. *382* Library of Congress. *383* Tree of Life Mosaic Mural, Meditation Park, designed by Lily Yeh; mosaic by James Maxton. *385* Library of Congress.

Index

Friedman, William 265
Frieze, 321
Fronabarger, R., 329
Fuller, R. Buckminster, 103, 104, 368, 371, 381, 388
Furby, 256
Futurism, 82, 332

G

Gagarin, Yuri, 90
Galileo, 282, 352, 358
Games, 112, 237. *See also* Video games
Gass, William, 314
Gates, Bill, 104
Gates, Henry Louis, Jr., 147, 260
Gehry, Frank, 110, 300, 319
Genetic algorithm (GA), 298
Geodesic dome, 371
Germany
    early advertising, 227
    libraries, 94
    video-television sculpture display, 104
    zoos, 102
Gertrude Stein Repertory Theatre (GSRT), 372
Gesner, Conrad, 95
Gesture, 112-124
Ghana, 252, 323
Gibson, William, 125, 269
Giddens, Gary, 130
Gideon, Sigfried, 279
Gilbreth, Frank, 279
Gilbreth, Lillian, 279
Gill, Eric, 158, 342
Giotto, 134
Glass, Philip, 319, 381
Glazebrook, Karl, 313
Glider, 88
Globe Theatre, 101
GNU/Linux, 382
Gnutella, 65
Goddard, Robert, 89
Goebbels, Joseph, 222
Goethe, 388
Goldberg, Rube, 114
Golden Mean, 31, 321
Goldmark, Peter, 103
Graffiti, 239
Grameen Bank, 372
Grandmaster Flash, 127
Graphical User Interface (GUI), 103, 155, 157, 169, 254, 255
Graves, Michael, 340
Gray, Eliot, 162
Great Zimbabwe civilization, 93
Greece
    democracy, 252
    drama, 100
    Horologium, 356
    mythology, 226
    Olympic games, 84

Parthenon, 100
    time, 356
Green, William Edward, 102
Greenwich Mean Time, 359
Grimm, Jacob and Wilhelm, 97
Grimthorpe, Baron, 359
Griot, 261
Gropius, Walter, 367, 368
Guerilla Girls, 372
GUI. *See* Graphical User Interface
Guinness Book of World Records, 98
Gutenberg, Johann, 94, 101, 174, 227
Gutenberg Press, 94

H

Hackers, 372-373
Haddock, Jon, 337
Hagenback, Carl, 102
Half-tones, 102
Hall, Edward T., 277
Hall, Sir Benjamin, 359
Hammurabi, 210
Handbills, early use of, 228
Haraway, Donna, 199
Harlem Renaissance, 373
Harmony, 326
Harris, Moses, 308
Harrison, John, 86, 358
Hart, Michael, 175
Hausmann, Raoul, 311
Havelock, Eric, 156, 161
Hearing, 353
Heart, Michael, 99
Hegel, G. W. F., 359
Heidegger, Martin, 276
Heiroglyphics, 92, 100, 156, 167, 380
Heisenberg, Werner, 82
Helicopter, 88
Helig, Morton, 103
Helmholtz, Hermann, 350
Henlein, Peter, 358
Henson, Jim, 381
Heraclitus, 355
Herc, Kool, 371
Hiawatha, 372-373
High culture, 165
Highway system, 5, 20, 89, 90
Higinbotham, William, 240
Hill, Rowland, 5
Hillis, Danny, 5, 46, 374
Hinduism, 231, 295, 297, 356
Hine, Lewis, 370
Hip-hop, 126, 147, 255, 285
Hitchcock, Alfred, 262
Hitler, Adolf, 112, 222
Hogarth, William, 227, 330
Hokusai, 332
Holbein, Hans, 252
Holland, Frank, 98
Hollerith, Herman, 88
Home video, 338

Homing pigeons, 84, 85, 87
Hood, Robin, 379
hooks, bel, 219
Horologium, 356
Horses, 84, 85
Hsün, Ou-yang, 93
Hua-yen Bhuddism, 374
Hue, 307
Hughes, Langston, 373
Human Genome Project (HGP), 99
Hurst, Sam, 254
Hurston, Zora Neale, 373
HyperCard, 105
Hypermedia, 104
Hypertext
    history of, 166-170, 377
    HTML, 367
    HTTP, 367
Hypertext Hotel, 255

I

IBM, 88, 89, 256
I Ching, 29
Icon, 143
Identity, dialog and, 185-198
IDEO, 375
Idrisi, Al, 85
Image, 143-145
IMAX, 104
Independent Media Center, 375
Index cards, 168
Indexical signs, 112
India
    Bhuddism, 226
    cycle of birth and rebirth, 355
    electric telegraph wires, 87
    myths, 202
    ragas, 357
Indra's net, 374
Industrial music, 125
Industrial Revolution, time and, 358
Infomercial, 239
Information overload, 125
Infotainment, 239
Ingber, Donald, 381
Instant replay, 333
Intellectual property rights, 7
Intelstat, 90
Interactivity, 2
    architecture and, 265
    of books, 166
    chronology of, 252-256
    closure and, 260
    dialog and, 250-256
    performance and, 237
    real-time, 147
    storytelling and, 237
International Institute of Bibliography, 98, 168
Internet. *See also* World Wide Web
    Advance Projects Research Agency
        (ARPA), 90